The Last American Newspaper

Stan,

Always remember
newspapers are the window
through which people see th
world.

3-22-23

The Last American Newspaper

An Institution in Peril, Through the Eyes of a Small-Town Editor

KEN TINGLEY

Foreword by Gary Kebbel

McFarland & Company, Inc., Publishers

Jefferson, North Carolina

ISBN (print) 978-1-4766-8826-8
ISBN (ebook) 978-1-4766-4626-8

LIBRARY OF CONGRESS AND BRITISH LIBRARY
CATALOGUING DATA ARE AVAILABLE

Library of Congress Control Number 2022033218

Front cover image: Long-time *Post-Star* Editor Ken Tingley
sits in an almost empty *Post-Star* newsroom on a quiet
Sunday in June 2021 (photograph by Jenn March)

Printed in the United States of America

*McFarland & Company, Inc., Publishers
Box 611, Jefferson, North Carolina 28640
www.mcfarlandpub.com*

To the men and women who gave their all in *The Post-Star* newsroom
to make our community a better place to live and work, none more so
than Will Doolittle as an editor, reporter, columnist, writing coach
and leader. Most editors just change copy; Will changed lives.

Table of Contents

Acknowledgments

It did not take long after I arrived in 1988 to fall in love with the community of Glens Falls. It will always be Hometown, USA, for me.

What made life so rewarding at the newspaper were the dozens of editors, reporters and support staff I worked with over the years. Reviewing their work over the past two decades for this book was inspiring.

Working with editors Greg Brownell, Bob Condon and Will Doolittle from start to finish over the 21 years I was editor was a privilege and an experience few have in the workplace anymore. Whenever they were in the newsroom, I knew things were in good hands.

When Mark Mahoney left as editorial page editor, it left a terrible hole in our newsroom and in my social life. The best decision I ever made was making Mark editorial page editor. He not only won the Pulitzer Prize; he regularly changed lives and viewpoints in our community. It is so rewarding to see he has found his way back to newspapers as the editorial page editor of the Schenectady *Gazette*.

I am still in debt to Jim Marshall, my first publisher, who took a chance on a guy with absolutely no news experience and made me managing editor. More importantly, he was the standard for a publisher in balancing the editorial and business demands of the newspaper. He was always hands off, even when it cost the newspaper money. Our time working together was too short. I regularly tell people that my greatest accomplishment in the news business was surviving six different publishers after Jim left.

I could see from the beginning that Will Doolittle was as talented a writer and editor as I had ever met. In the early days as sports editor, whenever I had a strong feature or column, I turned to Will for one final look.

Over the years, his eyes were the last to see my columns before they were published, so when I took on this project, it was natural for me to gravitate back to Will. At first, I just wanted some feedback on the initial chapters, but soon he was offering me advice about developing the journalists as characters. He went on to read the entire book. And then he offered to edit it as well—all on his own time. Just as he did with my columns, he made this book better.

Thank you to current *Post-Star* journalists Bob Condon, Kathleen Moore and Doolittle for their thoughts and insights. They continue to do demanding and important work that serves the community well.

Thank you to all my former colleagues for taking the time to recall their memories of specific events in their reporting career. Many of the interviews involved their reporting on tragedies, and it was clear each of them carried a little bit of trauma from those events as well. They included David Blow, Lydia Davenport, Betsy DeMars, Patrick Dowd, Nancy Gautier, Meg Hagerty, T.J. Hooker, Don Lehman, Michael Lewis, Jim Marshall, Konrad Marshall, Martha Petteys, John Purcell, Thom Randall, Nick Reisman, Will Springstead, Matthew Sturdevant, Maury Thompson and Darrin Youker.

Also thanks to those civilians who gave me their perspectives on stories they were involved in: Inge Kimmerly, Roy McDonald, David Moats, Judy Chittenden Moffitt, Jack Sherwin and Dan Miner.

From our earliest days covering Adirondack Red Wing playoff games, Greg Brownell and I have worked well together. It was Greg who helped me locate so many of the file photos to illustrate this work. Greg continues to hold down the fort as one of just two in *The Post-Star* sports department.

Thanks to Lee Enterprises for granting permission to use *The Post-Star* images to illustrate so much of the great work in this book. Those images are used as they were originally intended in *The Post-Star*. And also a nod to their hands-off policy. I never once had to deal with the corporate folks interfering in any aspect of news content.

Thanks to my former interim publisher, David Stoeffler, for his insights and feedback on several chapters of the book. I hope to repay him with a "Moose Drool" in the near future.

I wore many hats as editor of *The Post-Star*. I was responsible for all content, for setting the bar high for journalism, hiring and firing and often choosing the projects the newsroom tackled. There was editing, some page design, lots of personnel issues and a continual stream of feedback from the readers in the community who demanded that we be better every day. When I got done with all that, I did what I loved the most—writing.

I estimate I produced close to 3,000 columns over my 31 years at the newspaper. I owe a debt of gratitude to every person who agreed to sit down with me for an interview and tell me their story. And thanks to all the readers who read me faithfully. I miss that daily conversation.

In March 2008, I got a call from a young pastor at the Gospel Lighthouse Church in Kingsbury. I was looking for a way to make a bigger difference with my column writing, and Paul Mead provided me one of the first opportunities. His story of redemption still resonates. I consider that the beginning of my writing career. Paul would say it was divine providence. Whatever it was, I consider us linked forever by that first column. When I announced my retirement in 2020 and reprinted a series of columns in a "Flashback" series, there was no question in my mind that the column about Paul had to be first. And when I published a book of my columns in 2021, the column on Paul was first as well.

There were so many readers who reached out with words of kindness and encouragement over the years, including one from a letter writer named Al Scoonzarielli urging me to strike back with my words after an especially critical letter had been printed about one of my columns. Instead, I wrote about Al's email. He stayed in touch after I retired as well. So did many others.

There were so many others who helped me, tutored me and made me a better journalist and man over the course of my career. The newspaper business is made up of dedicated, passionate professionals who want to make a difference. Anything else you might have heard is not true.

I hope the stories chronicled here show that, but maybe more importantly, they show a community engaged with being the best it can be.

I hope that never changes.

Foreword: *The Last American Newspaper*

BY GARY KEBBEL

Most of us wouldn't live in a community where people didn't think it mattered if the water company or the power company closed. Most of us don't see the decimation of our newspapers as that kind of problem. But it is. Healthy newspapers tell their communities about the water company's problems long before the water runs dry. Or they tell us that our local hospital can't afford to stay open or the youth in our community have a serious drinking and driving problem. Newspapers give us information we can use to improve our quality of life. They also provide the information that makes our democratic form of government work.

In his book *The Last American Newspaper,* Ken Tingley shows the quality of life that a community loses when its newspaper shrinks to a shell of its former self. He was editor for 21 years of *The Post-Star* in Glens Falls, New York, a Pulitzer-Prize winning newspaper near Lake George in the foothills of the Adirondacks. At its peak, *The Post-Star* had a newsroom of 50 people, a good size for its approximate 36,000 circulation. But when he retired in 2020, general economic conditions and the economic needs of its corporate owners had reduced the size of the newsroom to eight people, a cut of 84 percent. What industry, what business can survive that? And we're not talking about companies that produce widgets. We're talking about the only industry protected in the U.S. Constitution, in the First Amendment. It's also the only industry that provides the foundations of a healthy democracy and a thriving community. When authoritarians subvert democracy, the first thing they do is kill the messenger of free-flowing information.

In the best of times, a community newspaper is a "super citizen," serving as a watchdog on powerful people and established institutions. It pushes citizens to engage with one another so that together they can discover, consider and solve problems that affect the quality of life for everyone. No other person or institution takes on this role. If the newspaper doesn't have a strong publisher and editor with a good and sufficient staff, then problems fester unattended until they become the giant pothole that breaks your car's axle.

Tingley asks the question that clearly drives him to write this book: "Who is going to do the journalism of the future?" Left unsaid is a fear that also propels the passion in this book: Perhaps no one. And a greater fear: Will the community notice, will it care?

Each chapter is an example of what a community loses when undiscovered, unattended, and unreported problems harm the quality of life for all. Most chapters are a poignant story, often terribly sad, of a problem that can be lessened, if not solved, once people know about it and resolve to act with courage and conviction. Most chapters are stories of lives that could be improved or saved. This is the essence of the interrelationship of journalism, community life and democracy. We all need accurate, truthful, verified information to act on so that we can improve our lives. Communities can't come together to fix problems that they don't know about. Democracy doesn't last without accurate information.

The Last American Newspaper challenges us to envision what happens when the last American newspaper stops serving its audience. Tingley shows us the human devastation from cruel problems the Adirondack region would not have known about without the dedicated and careful work of *The Post-Star* staff. Stories were paired with editorials and columns to do more than just report on a problem. The staff actively engaged and enraged the community to help it make changes that literally could save lives. The editor applied this winning formula to problems that included a heroin epidemic, teenage drinking and driving deaths, spousal abuse, difficulties of growing up gay, the financial problems of the region's most important hospital and the abuse of power by elected officials as well as political party leaders. *The Post-Star*'s efforts were rewarded with a Pulitzer Prize for editorial writing, as well as numerous journalism industry awards for best reporting, best opinion columns and best overall newspaper.

Journalism used to be taught as the dispassionate, objective means to help a community learn about its problems. The idea was to give the community accurate information so it can act in its own best interest to improve its quality of life. But that's only half of the story and is simply inadequate. *The Last American Newspaper* shows that newspapers at their best are passionate "super citizens" tasked with doing what no one else does or even wants to do: Find information about good and bad, right and wrong to *engage with the community* to improve everyone's life. Don't just give the community information and hope people act on it. That's not the end of the story. A good newspaper is also a good citizen that provides leadership to help solve the problems it writes about. In this book, we see lives improve when the process works, and we are foretold the harm ahead when newspapers don't have the resources to do their jobs.

From 1986 to 1990, Gary Kebbel was assistant managing editor, then managing editor of The Post-Star *in Glens Falls, N.Y. He then became managing editor of the* Troy (N.Y.) Record, *graphics editor at* USA TODAY, *a founding editor of* USATODAY.com, *a home page editor of* washingtonpost.com, *a member of the team that created* Newsweek.com, *news director at AOL, and then news director at the John S. and James L. Knight Foundation. He later became dean of the College of Journalism and Mass Communications at the University of Nebraska–Lincoln.*

Preface

"The Last American Newspaper" is not a concept to be taken literally. It is a metaphor for the hundreds of community newspapers all across the country now struggling to survive.

I have used my experiences at my own newspaper—*The Post-Star* in Glens Falls, New York—as a way to tell the story of how community newspapers made their cities and towns better by sparking debate and discussion as a way to address community problems and concerns while also celebrating their successes.

Using my 21 years as editor as a time frame (1999–2020), I have chronicled the events and issues my community faced as they happened. The story of *The Post-Star* is not unique among community newspapers. There are hundreds of publications like it that made the same kind of impact. Sadly, there has been less and less in-depth journalism over the past ten years as newsrooms staffs were gutted after advertising revenue declines.

Who is going to do the journalism in the future? It's a question every citizen should be asking.

Ultimately, this is a celebration of the work done by the men and women at newspapers all across the country. This is an opportunity to meet some of these dedicated individuals and hear their inspiring stories. Many are still doing the work while others have moved on to other professions and careers. Some, like me, have retired.

I benefited from a long-term conversation with readers in my "From the Managing Editor" column. It addressed why the newspaper did what it did twice a month for two decades. The content of those columns provided insights into what I was thinking at the time and what readers were concerned about. Those columns provided a roadmap for this book.

The book is organized chronologically as a series of vignettes about the news stories the Glens Falls newspaper covered, the issues it addressed and the work its journalists did. While researching the book, I was able to provide context for many stories that unfolded over years. Newspapers do their work in the moment, but this book provided an up-close-and-personal view readers rarely see as I connected the dots.

I painstakingly reviewed all the significant stories from the past 20 years, then interviewed approximately 25 of my former colleagues to get their perspectives and memories. The source material was almost entirely from the newspaper articles. I have cited hundreds of *Post-Star* newspaper stories and the impact they had on the community.

The stories published here also provide a significant history of the Glens Falls region while giving context to the role newspapers played in communities, especially in regard to the impact of commentary and editorials. In recent years, some readers have insisted newspapers should not be weighing in with opinions. I have tried to show the importance of editorials and columns during the past two decades.

Introduction:
Mary Joseph

What I remember nearly two decades later is standing alone in front of the elevators at Glens Falls Hospital and knowing I had found an excuse.

There was no volunteer at the information desk, no one to guide me to Mary Joseph's room upstairs.

It was a Sunday morning in November 2001, and the hospital lobby was deserted. I convinced myself this was a roadblock I could not overcome. My visit would have to wait for another time.

It wasn't like Mary and I were close friends. We were colleagues for over a decade, both working in the newsroom of our small newspaper late at night. Occasionally, we exchanged small talk about music or movies as we labored with our words, stories and deadlines.

I was the sports editor and Mary a copy editor in features who looked the part with thick glasses, black curly hair and a bookish demeanor of a librarian.

Producing a daily newspaper is intense, tedious and stressful. There is always another story and another edition to put out. It is a relentless series of deadlines, but I never saw Mary angry, never heard her curse or cave to the pressure.

I turned and took a few steps toward the hospital exit, then stopped and considered my decision again. After all, I was only here out of a sense of obligation as the editor of the newspaper, and this was my day off.

Mary had worked at the Glens Falls newspaper for 16 years. It was the city where she had grown up, and the "Joseph" name was synonymous with a successful family restaurant on Broad Street. Glens Falls was known as "Hometown, USA." For Mary, that was literally the case.

Mary's job was hardly glamorous. Like most positions on the copy desk, she worked nights that often turned into mornings. I think she liked it that way so she could work with the words she loved at a pace she enjoyed. There was no one looking over her shoulder. Outside of her family, few people in the community would recognize her name.

When I was promoted to editor in 1999, I became her boss. I told her I was concerned about her late nights. I suggested it was not necessary for her to read every wire service story in such painstaking detail.

I was suggesting a shortcut to lighten her workload.

I was trying to make her job easier.

She stared back at me defiantly and said, "I am not going to put anything in my section I have not read."

Mary was old school and continued to turn out the newsroom lights night after night.

It's what stays with me all these years later, not only about Mary but about so many of my colleagues over the past three decades. It was something our readers, our community in general, rarely understood about the dedication, the commitment, the effort it took to bring the miracle of a daily newspaper to their doorsteps every single day for pennies. We all cared so much.

I wonder now if that heart-and-soul effort was ever fully appreciated by the community as the staff sacrificed family time, relationships, and in some cases their health toward what they believed was a greater good. Maybe only they appreciated it.

The past decade has been a time of worry about the future of community newspapers and concern about the gaping hole left behind when they are gone.

I worry now about who stands up for the community and sounds the alarm when things are not right.

Who will explain the complexity of mental illness and suicide, warn us of the growing heroin problem and the shortcomings with health care and senior living deficiencies?

Who will celebrate community triumphs, report the births of our children, the marriages of our loved ones and lament the loss of another life lived well? Community newspapers, like ours, were the town squares of modern times, their reporters and editors the beating hearts and moral compass at its center.

"The *Post-Star* was my father's favorite and mine, too," a reader wrote me in February 2016. "We put one in the casket so he would have something to read when he got to heaven."[1]

That's the status community newspapers once had.

Maury Thompson, a reporter who served our newspaper and the community faithfully for two decades, sent me this quotation he found in an old weekly newspaper in the midst of the pandemic in 2020: "A newspaper is a window through which men look out upon all that is going on in the world. Without a newspaper, a man is shut up in a room and knows little of what is happening outside of himself."[2]

That quote was over 100 years old, but as far as I was concerned, it had stood the test of time.

By the end of 2019, it was clear the type of community journalism that so many in Glens Falls had taken for granted for over a century was in jeopardy as retail advertising faded and newsroom positions evaporated.

The window for viewing the world was closing.

The Last American Newspaper is not just about our small community newspaper in upstate New York; it is a metaphor for institutions all across the country that revered a free press and its role in keeping their communities informed. It was an integral part of doing good in the community, a partner, a friend who was always willing to tell you the truth.

It was perhaps something simpler than that as well. It was a vehicle to tell the human stories of all those who had lived and died there. It was one of hundreds of like-minded community newspapers all across the country that are sadly disappearing. Our newspaper's story was not unique but representative of hundreds of others.

My career and the careers of so many others were about telling the personal stories of people who not only suffered hardships and tragedies but persevered to be an inspiration for friends and neighbors. Sometimes, it was just chronicling simple acts of kindness.

"Newspapers need to validate people's lives and connect with their communities," I wrote in a column to readers in April 2000. "Honesty and integrity have to be the cornerstones of the organization, and we will never fool the readers on that point. Our credibility and standards are what people depend on."[3]

We did that aggressively and diligently until it was taken for granted by the communities we served and betrayed by the corporations who reaped the financial benefits and, finally, attacked by a new type of politician waging war on the facts we reported each day. What may have been most disappointing of all was that many of our readers believed them.

It was another world as we approached our centennial year in 2004. We were a community institution and one of the rare businesses to survive a century of progress.

"Many of our readers who have traveled have told us that after reading different newspapers across the country, they were glad to get back to their *Post-Star*," *Post-Star* publisher Jim Marshall wrote in our "A Century of Progress" special edition. "At the core of our philosophy is a sense of community. We know this is your newspaper and we have always made it a priority to be part of that community."[4]

We stood for something.

The New York State Legislature passed a resolution marking our 100 years of service, saying in part, "this legislative body is to pay tribute to those illustrious journalistic organizations which have diligently and consistently, year after year, recorded the history of their communities and brought local news and news of the larger world to their readers."[5]

It was a reminder of our role as the first draft of history.

Senator Elizabeth Little, a native from neighboring Queensbury who would serve another 16 years in the state senate, also congratulated the newspaper for its 100 years of community service on the senate floor. "I look forward to another 100 or 200 years," she said.[6]

At the time, so did I.

The newspaper had evolved from an eight-page newspaper hand-delivered to your door at a cost of two cents per copy to a hand-delivered 38-page (60 pages on Sunday) newspaper at 50 cents per copy ($1.75 on Sunday). We had evolved from horse-drawn carriages to cars and trucks.[7]

Our product had appeared on the doorsteps of residents every morning for 100 years, or about 33,000 editions.[8]

Just a month earlier, in 2004, I wrote glowingly about my hopes for the newspaper's future.

"For those who were thinking newspapers and dinosaurs would soon have something in common, think again; we're just getting started," I wrote.[9]

I believed it, too.

Our daily sales fluctuated between 35,000 and 40,000—depending on the season—and we had reason to be optimistic. Originally, just a Glens Falls newspaper, we now served parts of three upstate counties—Warren, Washington and Saratoga—and teamed with an Albany television station to open a bureau in Saratoga Springs, a thriving neighbor to the south.

And we were ridiculously profitable.

Over the next couple of years, we bucked the national trend and increased print circulation. At our peak, we had nearly 50 in our newsroom. It allowed us to undertake ambitious journalistic projects many newspapers did not have the resources to pursue.[10]

Of course, the iPhone had not been invented yet, and our understanding of digital media was in its infancy.

More often than not, members of the community trusted us to tell their stories, too. They met us halfway in issue-oriented focus groups because these were problems all our readers faced at one time or another. We all seemed to understand we were in this together. I can't help but wonder now who will do those stories in the future.

After four decades working at newspapers, I believe the personal connections readers have with small newspapers like *The Post-Star* are stronger and more intimate than any other institution in the community.

When big, terrible events happened in our community—railway tanker spills, an E. coli outbreak, tragic fires and murders—we were there, not to sensationalize the news, but to help our community make sense of it, identify the problems, expose malfeasance, and sometimes to help it grieve.

When the community started burying teenagers after alcohol-related accidents in 2002, it was the newspaper that connected the dots, identified the carnage and brought the community together to find solutions.

The work was important.

Classified advertising disappeared first, followed by declines in retail advertising and circulation. Readers told us they didn't have the time to read anymore. Each year, we had fewer people in the newsroom and fewer people reading us.

What didn't change was the dedication and passion by the reporters and editors. We are a group like no other.

That dedication to this ideal of making a difference in our little corner of the world is the foundation that drives so many of us. It certainly is not the money or prestige—neither are in abundance at small-town newspapers.

Newspaper people like Mary Joseph were part of that unique group trying to tell a great story. Sometimes we caught the bad guys, other times just a misspelled word.

Mary created features pages that made regular readers "want to read" important stories that were often detailed, complex and long. She was part of a team that worked together to provide a new and unique product each day. Few businesses do that.

Mary's job was a subtle, nuanced part of the profession that is hard to explain to people with regular jobs, but I suspect many often found themselves late to work because they were drawn into a riveting story by Mary's compelling page presentations, a clever headline and her commitment to the beauty of the printed word.

I'm sure Mary could have done other things with her life. She was an intelligent woman, but she always wanted to go into journalism, and she did it in her hometown.

Maybe that's what finally stopped me in the lobby of Glens Falls Hospital that day in 2001. Mary was a kindred spirit, one of us.

I turned around.

Mary had a noticeable large mole on her neck. But as it began to change shape and color, Mary convinced herself it was nothing. The mole grew so large and ugly that Mary covered it with a Band-Aid so no one would see it. When she finally had it looked at, she was diagnosed with advanced melanoma, a form of skin cancer.

She later told me she was angry with herself because she knew better. She had let it go too long. She was smarter than that. For the duration of her illness while undergoing treatment, Mary kept working.

As I rode the elevator that Sunday morning in the hospital, I remembered she had put out the Sunday Arts/Life section just two weeks earlier without any help.

I found Mary in her room with her mom. Mary was sitting up in bed and gasping for breath when I got there. We talked just briefly as nurses hurried in and out of the room. Her mother told me they were about to take her to intensive care.

We made some small talk, but it was clear I was just getting in the way. I didn't stay long.

As I prepared to leave, Mary looked intensely at me and between breaths choked out a few words.

"I really ... miss ... working ... at ... the paper," she said.[11]

At the time, the words seemed out of place considering her condition, but over the years they stayed with me like no others. Perhaps it was the context as she struggled to get out each word between breaths. Or maybe there was something in the way she said it, in the intensity of her gaze that caught me off guard, as if she needed me to understand what I had and she soon would not. Or maybe she felt I was one of the few people who would understand what made us put our heart and soul into it every day.

That was November 18, 2001.

Mary died a few hours later at the obscenely young age of 39.

I wrote this a few days later in a column: "Newspapers are too often seen as the faceless institutions taken for granted by their communities, a daily visitor with their readers' cups of coffee who can spin a good yarn one morning and leave you cut-off-in-traffic-angry the next."[12]

I asked our readers to take a moment to think about the faces behind the newspaper, the men and women who live and breathe their professions. People like Mary Joseph.

I guess I'm asking you to do that now, too.

To consider all those people who toiled in relative obscurity at your hometown newspaper to make your community just a little bit better.

More than once over the subsequent years, I thought about how I stood in front of the elevators at Glens Falls Hospital trying to figure out a way to blow off my visit with Mary, what would be my final visit with Mary.

I wondered if that visit and Mary's words made me appreciate the journey just a little bit more and hopefully work just a little bit harder. I also wonder now, if she had lived, would she eventually have been one of those dedicated souls I had to let go during the hard economic times, despite her loyalty and devotion.

What was such a shame about losing Mary then was the best days were still ahead for our newspaper. The work we would do—that she would have been an integral part of—was something I'm sure she would have relished, work that would make a difference in our community and work she would have found a way to make better.

Six weeks before Mary died, there was no talk in our country of "fake news" on 9/11. The work we did that day—like so many newspapers across the country—was journalism at its best. In small towns like ours, it showed we were all in this together. We were one as Americans and a community. That is how it worked in those simpler times.

It is hard to fathom why it did not last.

By 2017, I lamented a dark time for newspapers as five of my colleagues at another newspaper, people I had never met but who reminded me of people in my own newsroom, were killed in the *Capital Gazette* shootings in suburban Maryland. By then, many in the political universe were labeling us "enemies of the people."

On the day five members of its staff were shot to death, the newspaper published. Its editorial page was blank except for these solemn words:

> Today we are speechless.
> This page is intentionally left blank today to commemorate
> victims of Thursday's shootings at our office:
>
> Gerald Fischman
> Bob Hiassen
> John McNamara
> Rebecca Smith
> Wendi Winters
>
> Tomorrow this page will return to its steady purpose of offering
> our readers informed opinion about the world around them,
> that they might be better citizens.[13]

That was written from the back of a pickup truck. The *Capital Gazette* newsroom was a crime scene at the time.

The losses over the next three years were far more subtle but momentous just the same as readers turned to the convenience of their phones and social media for news.

In January 2020, a local leadership group visited our newsroom in Glens Falls, and I talked to them about the value of the journalism we do.

I explained how recent studies had found that in communities where a newspaper had closed, civic engagement dropped and fewer people voted because they could not identify the candidates in local elections.[14]

Another study found that borrowing costs for municipal building projects were more expensive because there was not a newspaper to hold politicians accountable. That meant taxes went up.[15]

A University of North Carolina study found that news organizations often set the agenda for public debate by bringing particular issues to the public's attention. Without newspapers like ours, those issues will not be addressed.[16]

The group in our conference room that day was a good audience.

They nodded and shook their heads at all the right times and genuinely showed concern about what a community like Glens Falls might look like without a robust daily newspaper.

At the end of the meeting, our circulation manager, Tom Salvo, asked how many of the 25 people in the room had a subscription to the newspaper.

One person raised his hand.[17]

We were the last American newspaper.

We were making our last stand.

At that moment, I was absolutely sure of that fact. I thought back to Mary Joseph and her final words, and I wondered how many others would miss the newspaper and its place as the community town crier.

The last American newspaper is a tragedy of epic proportions that I fear will not be realized for many years to come.

Like Mary, I now have a chance to put my own newspaper's place in context by telling the stories behind the stories, by revealing the work and commitment of the journalists who have been, more often than not, taken for granted or lost to time.

1

"My high school is on TV"

If you want to understand this story, if you want to appreciate the work that was done and the men and women who did it, you have to understand the people and perhaps the community of Glens Falls itself.

The city sits 180 miles due north of New York City and about 50 miles north of the state capital in Albany. It is actually a little closer to Montreal than New York City.

Glens Falls is a small working-class city of about 15,000 wedged hard by the Hudson River and an ugly paper mill. It was founded by Abraham Wing as Wing's Falls, but colorful community lore suggests Wing lost the name of the town in a poker game to Col. Johannesburg Glen.

The region was a hub of activity during both the French and Indian War and the American Revolution. But Glens Falls' enduring legacy is a 1946 *Look* magazine feature story that gave the city its nickname of "Hometown, USA."[1] That portrayal as a model of small-town American life and patriotic values is still revered by residents today.

For the newspaper, Glens Falls is just the hub, with similar like-minded communities sprouting up in all directions in the form of rural towns and villages across three counties. Just ten miles to the north, Lake George—the queen of American lakes—drives a tourist economy seen as an economic savior since the manufacturing jobs faded away. It is one of the few tourist destinations where arcades and miniature golf are the draw and a reminder of simpler times. The great Adirondacks lie to the north just beyond the lake.

Saratoga Springs, 15 miles to the south, is the center of the thoroughbred horse racing universe each summer, but its history is long and rich with people coming for the "waters" as far back as the 1700s. The Battle of Saratoga is still considered the turning point in the Revolutionary War. Just a few miles north of the city, President Ulysses S. Grant spent the final days of his life finishing his memoirs at a small cottage on Mount McGregor.

You can find whatever type of lifestyle you are looking for within a short drive of Glens Falls—suburban, city, rural, agricultural, mountain. It has it all.

Washington County, with its rolling farmland, is home to dairy farms, medical device manufacturing plants and stone quarries, as it bumps up against Vermont to the east. Fort Edward is the site of an early frontier fort where Robert Rogers and his rangers trained but eventually became home to a General Electric plant that polluted the Hudson River with PCBs and precipitated one of the largest environmental cleanups in history.

Besides the paper mills, Glens Falls has a vibrant downtown, a hospital in the center of the city and a small college—SUNY Adirondack—next door in Queensbury.

Local politics—almost everywhere—is historically conservative.

That I managed to spend most of my life there is one of those lucky flukes for which I will be forever grateful.

By 1987, I was a sports editor on my fourth newspaper in eight years since graduating from college. Reporters and editors clawed their way up the ladder in those days, moving from one community newspaper to the next for a few dollars more and some added responsibilities.

But my latest move had not worked out.

There was almost immediate friction with my boss at the Kingsport, Tennessee, newspaper where I was second in command of the sports department at a newspaper three times the size of my previous publication in upstate New York. I was trying to make my mark on the newspaper and its staff, and it wasn't long before I was in trouble.

Just weeks after my wife and I moved into our new house, the managing editor told me he was taking away my management responsibilities and putting me on probation. I had 30 days to prove I could do the job as a copy editor with the new paginated computer layout system, or I would be fired.

I had a new career goal: Don't get fired.

Failure is a great motivator.

My wife and I stopped unpacking boxes at home, and I started looking for a new job. I became a model employee at work, making deadline each evening and offering guidance to the writers who wanted help, while ignoring the less motivated staff members.

This was survival.

I didn't get fired.

In the summer of 1988, I went on two promising job interviews. The first was for a sports copy editor position in Greenville, South Carolina, where they were making the transition to the same computer layout system I was using in Kingsport. The carrot was I "might" be named assistant sports editor if I did well. The second job was as sports editor in Glens Falls where I would be in charge.

The Glens Falls newspaper had a lot going for it. It had a good-sized sports staff for a paper its size, plenty of news space in its daily section, a professional hockey team and downtown arena that hosted the state high school basketball tournament each year. It also covered the storied Saratoga horse racing meet each summer. It was also closer to our families. It was a place where being a "Yankee" was acceptable to everyone but the folks in Boston.

For the first time ever, I had two job offers. The Greenville newspaper was three times the size of the Glens Falls newspaper and covered Clemson University sports. Moving to South Carolina was the smart career choice, but I wondered if the sports editor wanted me only because of my expertise with the computer layout system. I accepted the Greenville job.

We called the moving company for an estimate. After the man went through the house counting the unopened boxes, he sat down at the dining room table to complete the moving estimate and asked, "OK, where are you moving to?"

I sat quietly, thinking.

I guess he thought I didn't hear him, so he asked again.

"Is it possible to get an estimate for two places?" I said.

My wife, Gillian, peeked her head around the corner and said sternly, "What are you doing?"

After the moving man left, I called the managing editor in Glens Falls and told him about my second thoughts. Our hearts were up north closer to our families in Connecticut and Long Island, but we were unsure if we could find a house we could afford in Glens Falls. I told him I would send my wife to Glens Falls, and if she could find an acceptable house, I would take the job.

She found a house.

The Greenville sports editor was rightfully angry. He told me, "You will never be anything more than a big fish in a small pond."

But I thrived in that small pond.

Over the next 11 years, with Greg Brownell as my assistant sports editor, we created a sports product that was among the best in the country for our size newspaper, and I started writing a regular sports column I loved.

But by my 41st birthday, I wanted more.

In the spring of 1998, the Albany *Times Union*, the dominant newspaper in the state capital just south of us, had an opening for an executive sports editor. After a decade leading the staff in Glens Falls, I was looking for a bigger challenge.

Times Union executive editor Jeff Cohen invited me to Albany for an interview. It was the start of several discussions about the job, but it gradually became clear to me, and I believe to him, that I would not be the best fit in Albany.

While still in discussions with Albany, I met with *Post-Star* publisher Jim Marshall. With my two-year-old son sitting on my lap—I worked nights and took care of my son during the day—I informed Jim I was in discussions with the *Times Union* about their executive sports editor opening. I wanted him to know about it before I made a decision. I was hoping he might offer me a little more money to stay in Glens Falls.

Instead, Marshall said he was thinking about making a change at managing editor and was going to offer me the job.

When I called my father to tell him his sportswriter-son was getting the keys to the newsroom, he responded, "Do you know what you are doing?"

On New Year's Eve 1998, Marshall fired managing editor Stephen Bennett. On Monday, January 4, Marshall introduced me to the staff as the new managing editor. I became a little bit bigger fish in my little pond.

Mark Mahoney was a big teddy bear of a man with a quick wit and easy demeanor until something really ticked him off; then he could be volcanically explosive, and he didn't care where he was or who was watching.

He had been a meat-and-potatoes reporter who had been hired at *The Post-Star* without ever writing a newspaper article. That was unusual.

He was an Ithaca (NY) College graduate who worked in radio before coming to the Glens Falls newspaper nine months before me in 1988. Mahoney was promoted to regional editor just two years after being hired as a reporter and then city editor—the No. 2 job in the newsroom—two years after that in May 1992. He worked hard and cared.

The city editor position was the lynchpin of the newsroom's success. It was the city editor who crafted a daily menu of stories for the news fronts. He was in charge of all the reporters and photographers' assignments. He set the tone and called the shots.

As the new editor, I wanted in-depth stories that went beyond the basic news every day of the week, but I questioned whether Mahoney had the organizational skills and insights to deliver anything more than the basic government meeting coverage and breaking news.

Each day, Mahoney seemed to be flying by the seat of his pants, his desk buried in a sea of papers, and, as he was pulled in different directions, there were often emotional outbursts.

Privately, I questioned his vision and considered firing him.

Instead, I chose a different course. I told Mahoney I wanted him to become our editorial writer while also editing copy at night and returning to his former role as regional editor. It was part of a larger newsroom shake-up involving all the top editors. Mahoney was not happy.

"This sounds like a demotion," he said to me sternly at the time.

I argued it wasn't, but I knew he was right. I told him this was an opportunity for him to give the newspaper a larger voice in the community with his writing. What I knew for sure was Mahoney was not the city editor I needed. I thought it was 50–50 he would come back the next day.

Bob Condon, our regional editor, was promoted to provide the foundation for our daily news coverage because of his organization and planning skill set. What I didn't realize at the time was the calming influence Condon would have in the newsroom. Where Mahoney often responded angrily to reader and reporter complaints alike, Condon was always on an even keel. He was the calm voice of reason despite the high-stress level of the job. He would remain that way for the next 20 years.

Condon, a Syracuse University graduate, had been hired from a small weekly newspaper in Newport, New Hampshire, six years earlier. His credentials were initially overlooked by the last managing editor when his resume literally slipped through the cracks.

"I remember getting a call that my resume had slipped behind his desk and had been lost for months," Condon remembered. "Finally, he had found it and wanted to talk to me."[2]

As regional editor, Condon's job was to coordinate and edit the often rough copy of freelancers into a readable form. It required meticulous organizational skills and an enormous amount of patience for writers who were not professional journalists. It was great training for an editor.

Will Doolittle was our night editor who had a deft touch editing deadline copy and was a creative wordsmith who wrote an excellent column, mostly about his family. When I previously needed an editor for one of my sports columns or features, I sought out Doolittle.

Fred Daley was our quiet and meticulous Sunday editor. I saw the Sunday section as our premier product of the week and the place a new editor like myself could make a difference immediately with in-depth front-page journalism and eye-catching displays.

After switching the responsibilities of Mahoney and Condon, I asked Doolittle and Daley to change jobs as well. In a decision resembling musical chairs more than sound management, it sent a message that I was in charge and things would be different.

"I looked at it as a power play," Doolittle said in 2020. "I thought you made the right move with Mark. I didn't think Mark fit that job that well. The big impact of that was that was really a wake-up call for [us] editors. We better do what he says, because he means business."[3]

Looking back 20 years later, the idea of switching the jobs of all four key editors simultaneously could have been a train wreck. Their ability to check their egos and give me a chance was something I did not appreciate until years later.

These editors were talented and dedicated and exist in some form in every community newspaper. Each took different paths before landing in Glens Falls. I just needed them doing the right jobs.

As I looked around the newsroom, it was clear we had the talent to be a much better newspaper.

At the time, we had approximately ten news reporters. Don Lehman and David Blow, two Castleton (VT) University grads who cut their teeth on the same nearby weekly newspaper, were the heart and soul of the reporting staff. They were scanner guys who would rush out of the office to cover a fire or accident without ever being told. They took pride in turning out lots of stories.

Lehman was the cops and courts reporter who produced more copy than any other reporter. He was the absolute standard for public safety reporting. He was a fighter, a scrapper, someone who hustled from one story to the next and refused to accept being stonewalled by the sheriff, a beat cop or the district attorney. God help the person who tried to hide something from him. He didn't have a chip on his shoulder; he had a boulder.

Lehman was a writing machine who constantly kept us a football field ahead of any of the other publications in the Capital District while often berating all of us—reporters and editors alike—for our failures. He could be a tough guy to work with.

Blow was the optimist and energy source in the newsroom, always finding a feature or profile he thought had great potential and then selling it for page one. He was a people person who was liked by his sources and colleagues alike.

Neither was bashful about talking truth to power, especially Lehman, who always seemed to be complaining about something.

There was also the quirky Thom Randall, who frustrated the editors one minute by showing up for work late or missing a deadline on a simple story, then dazzling them with the type of in-depth journalism that would later prove to be our staple. He was our Hunter Thompson.

In June 1999, I took notice of a prolific correspondent named Maury Thompson who had been covering Ticonderoga and Essex County in the northern reaches of our circulation area. Thompson worked closely with Condon when he was regional editor and produced more copy than most of our full-time writers. I suggested to Condon we bring Thompson to Glens Falls as our new business writer.

I didn't know Thompson's story—we had never met—but after Condon told me he was legally blind and unable to drive, I believed he would be unable to do the business writer job. Condon convinced me otherwise.

The staff was top heavy with government meeting coverage. It was important but dry. I wanted stories that explained to readers what impact those government decisions had on their lives. I wanted stories that helped them to understand the world in which they lived and celebrated the people who lived there. I wanted stories that made our readers laugh and cry.

"There was some resistance to that at first," Doolittle remembered. "Like most small papers, we got the news covered and got it in the paper as soon as possible. Yeah, we could have done more reporting, but no, it was best to just get it in the newspaper. This was true of the whole newspaper. We were reactive. We react to news, cover the news, but not actively shaping what the paper is going to be next week, next month. We are not setting an agenda. The agenda is set by events. I think there was a lot of inertia to overcome there at first."[4]

Condon became the organizational center of everything we did. He kept the press running on time by hitting all our deadlines, he married photographic excellence with more in-depth assignments, but most of all, he oozed calm.

Doolittle became part writing coach and part project aficionado who took complex issues and built teams to report and explain their findings in bite-sized chunks all our readers could understand. I don't think he ever made a bad hire.

Greg Brownell, promoted to sports editor after I became editor, continued our excellence in sports, led a mission to diversity to our newsroom and brought a parade of talented sportswriters through our doors.

The basic day-to-day stories got better, with each depth and enterprise story building on the last until we were undertaking staff-wide projects that grabbed the community by the throat and forced it to pay attention and then act.

Our goal was to be one of the best small newspapers in the country. The first step was to set the bar high.

We got that chance in April 1999.

By the time we settled into our daily "Page 1" meeting, we knew something bad was happening in Colorado. This was the beginning of a horror that would become regular news over the next two decades.

That's when Patrick Ridgell, one of our young sportswriters, walked into the meeting looking shaken.

Sportswriters don't come to the "Page 1" meeting very often, so it got our attention.

He spoke haltingly about his old high school being on television, and there might be lots of casualties. Ridgell, then 24, spent his sophomore year at Columbine High School. It was April 20, 1999. This was the first school shooting.

There was no playbook for this, no formula for reporting a mass shooting at a suburban high school similar to many in our communities.

I was 41 years old and in my fourth month as editor of *The Post-Star*.

As reporters and editors gathered around the newsroom television set in stunned silence, we watched fleeing students wiggling through school windows and armed police officers marching them away with their arms over their heads, not knowing for sure if one of them might be the attacker.

It would become a familiar sight.

My strength as a newspaper editor in those early days was big-event coverage. From my sports experience, I knew how to mobilize resources on deadline to cover an event from a variety of angles and perspectives. I asked Ridgell to write something for the front page about his time at Columbine, about what the community, people and school were like.

"I sat down to write and I didn't know what to put down on paper," Ridgell wrote that day. "I didn't know what I should say. Sportswriters can't really know how to describe a situation of such weight. To give it some—any—perspective. I wonder who can?"[5]

It was a pronouncement that holds up two decades later for the hundreds of mass shootings across the United States. It was also a sentiment that would permeate our newsroom, and to a greater extent our community, over the next two decades as there was increasingly less horror and shock, replaced by a more pedestrian reaction, "Not again."

"I heard the Jefferson County sheriff describe the school library as 'a gruesome sight,'" Ridgell wrote, followed by his recollection that, in that very same library where police would find ten murdered students, he had mustered the courage to ask a girl he liked out on a date for the very first time.[6]

We asked our education writer, Tucker Cordani, to get the reaction from local school officials. But Cordani discovered something more insidious, the seeds of recent student behavior that, in the hours after Columbine, had new meaning.[7]

A week earlier, a high school student from Fort Ann, New York, was suspended for five days after school officials learned he had brought a rifle on the school bus.

A 12-year-old Cambridge, New York, student was facing charges in Washington County Family Court for allegedly bringing a pellet gun to school.[8]

And 39 students were evacuated from a school bus in Hudson Falls after a resident spotted what turned out to be an active pipe bomb on the lawn of a residence near the school.[9] These were all recent events, and they all happened nearby, but standing alone none seemed significant at the time. They did now. They pointed to the possibility there could be a more serious problem in our own communities.

"It grips my heart with fear ... of what children can do to each other," said Michael P. Klein, president of the Fort Ann School Board.[10]

"I'm glad it's on the other side of the country," Klein said. "But it's too close."[11]

It would always be just around the corner. The murder of children was now a local story and how we kept them safe a local issue. "Yes, it could happen here." We would repeat that over and over during the next 20 years.

"We here at the newspaper are often taken to task when we report these stories about the youth in our communities," I wrote that next Sunday about the local incidents. "Administrators, teachers, parents and students sometimes don't like it when negative things are said about their schools, when their kids and their communities are portrayed in a bad light. But after seeing the events of this past week unfold at Columbine High School, I wonder if we did enough with some of those articles. I wondered if we should have been shouting it from the front page."[12]

It showed that our community newspaper could make a difference. We made Columbine "our" story, too, and showed readers they should be concerned.

I'd like to say Columbine was the impetus for a robust discussion about school security, gun control and identifying mental illness in our communities. I'd like to brag that this was our opportunity to call out long-held beliefs about Second Amendment rights and that we led a dramatic community debate in a rural region of upstate New York where gun ownership was sacrosanct.

But we did not do that.

It is a reminder that editors, like other professionals, evolve and are shaped by their experiences. In newspapers, that means one news story at a time with the production of each new edition building on the next as you push your staff and yourself to better serve your readers and the greater community good.

Four months into my tenure as editor, I did not see Columbine as the beginning of something, or a threat to our community, and I was not sure what to do next. I did not realize the power a newspaper's voice could have in leading an uncomfortable community discussion.

We had not written any editorials favoring gun control, and we would not after Columbine either. We knew instinctually that taking any position limiting guns was going to be trouble for us, maybe too much trouble.

Even then, it was not unusual to be called "the liberal media."

It was a recurring theme in those early years as editor. Newspapers, like government and communities in general, are slow to respond to significant problems. It would take multiple deaths repeated in incidents around the country before we finally launched a team of reporters into in-depth reporting supported by editorials calling for change.

What I didn't know at the time was how important it was going to be to have a strong, independent voice to responsibly address the issues at hand. In 1999, I had never written a local editorial.

I was going to need help with that, a partner who knew the issues, was familiar with the politicians, and had that intangible ingredient at the heart of any great journalist—a moral compass—who could translate outrage and indignation into words capable of moving others to action.

I would need someone to stand shoulder to shoulder with me when the shit hit the fan. I later realized that person might have a really messy desk.

When Mahoney left my office that day early in 1999, he was no longer the city editor of the newspaper. He was angry and hurt at being demoted, and I didn't know if he would come back the next day.

"You have to realize, I had been the city editor for seven years," Mahoney said in 2020. "I was pissed for three days and then I was over it."[13]

The editorial page was now his baby. He would have to figure it out editorial by editorial. As I embarked on my new job, I depended on Mahoney to be our voice. I don't think either of us understood the power we had.

"I think I could have taken the editorship change in a negative way," Mahoney wrote me a year later. "But instead, I approached it enthusiastically as a new opportunity to best use my talents to contribute to the paper."

We began a decade-long journey as Mahoney became my closest colleague and an integral part of the newsroom while we all tried to change our little corner of the world.

We pissed people off.

Twisted their arms.

Demanded change.

Screwed up in full public view.

And had heated arguments in the middle of the newsroom.

It was wonderful.

A few years later at one of those nonprofit community cocktail parties where all the movers and shakers are obligated to appear, I looked around the room and asked Mahoney, "How many people in this room do you think we have pissed off?"

He slowly scanned the room and said, "All of them."

"I guess that's why we're over here alone," I said.

Mark Mahoney's love of professional hockey made sense when you considered his psychological makeup. If he had been a professional player, I saw him as an enforcer, the guy who had Wayne Gretzky's back, rarely scored a goal but was always ready for a fight. In some ways, that was what I was asking Mahoney to do when I took away the city editor job. I wanted him to be our enforcer, to watch the community's back and give us a louder voice in the discussion without getting any of the credit.

When Mahoney was city editor, I saw a harried editor pulled in a multitude of directions with a desk buried in paper as he tried to stay one step ahead of the chaos. Mayhem was the norm then. Now, I saw a person with a clear understanding of his mission and also a path forward personally. His job had been brutally simplified, and he seemed happier.

The best moves are sometimes the ones you don't make. I was thankful I had not fired him. The kid who had started out in radio quickly built a national reputation as an editorial writer who would put our newspaper on the journalism map.

"The thing that people always said about *The Post-Star* was that it was a paper that punched above its weight," former reporter Nick Reisman said in 2020. "Even though it was a local daily, it would give the larger regional papers a run for their money. It was the favorite thing on my resume."[14]

Mahoney quickly became a heavyweight.

So many of us had a unique story of how we got to Glens Falls. Looking back, it's as if it was preordained by some ink-stained deity that this group of editors should work together.

Six years before I became editor, Will Doolittle found himself in Bennett's office, where the interview wasn't going well.

After nearly three years as the managing editor of a small newspaper with just 7,000 readers in Malone, New York, Doolittle desperately sought a move to *The Post-Star*, a newspaper five times the size of his current publication in a community with a quality of life far superior and a climate more bearable than the one he was living in 154 miles to the north and just a stone's throw from Canada.

Glens Falls was putting its best foot forward as it always does late in September with hot-air balloons filling the skies during the annual Adirondack Balloon Festival.

It was a dramatic departure from what Doolittle and his wife, Bella, were used to in Malone, a small prison and farming community of about 15,000 at the rooftop of upstate New York. Its painful, howling winds made the winters long and brutal.

Plugging in your car at night to keep the engine block from freezing was mandatory. Doolittle remembered one winter the car door would not close, so he tied a rope to the other door to keep it from flying open while the cold air whistled through the cracks.[15]

"We were always struggling with the cars," Doolittle remembered. "We couldn't afford to buy a new one."[16]

This was a typical story for the young people who fell in love with newspapers and journalism.

The couple was in their early 30s, and Bella had two young children from a previous marriage. Malone was the type of stop many journalists made early in their careers as they hopscotched from one newspaper to another in hopes of moving up and making a modest living. By 2010, as everyone in print downsized, moving up became almost impossible.

"Malone had all of the bad characteristics of small North Country towns, and none of the good ones," Doolittle explained. "There was no arts community, no alternative progressive thinking. It was all kind of conservative country people who were not very cheerful."[17]

For a time, Bella went back to bartending at the "340 Club," a biker/trucker bar that was one of Malone's more notorious hangouts.

"Out of fear for my safety, she insisted I never go there," Doolittle said. "But those guys cowered if she got mad."[18]

As a young, aggressive editor of the local newspaper, Doolittle felt the pressure daily from doing real journalism and holding local officials accountable. Everyone knew who he was, and he often ran into people in the grocery store who had found their way into the police blotter.

"There could be a lot of tension," Doolittle remembered.[19]

Inside the newspaper office at Lawrence and Cooper streets that day in 1993, there was also some tension.

Bennett, who had been managing editor for just a couple of years, was old school. In his 50s, his resume included reporting stops at *The Boston Globe* and *The Baltimore Sun* as a reporter before landing in New Hampshire as the publisher of his own weekly newspaper. When that didn't work out, he moved to Glens Falls to be city editor before eventually becoming managing editor.

In his Oklahoma twang, Bennett regaled Doolittle with stories of his earlier years of reporting, and then through a series of unfortunate digressions, Doolittle learned how the perfect candidate for the job he wanted so desperately had just moved on to another newspaper.

"It didn't go well," Doolittle remembered. "For an hour and a half he talked about [former reporter] Ed Fitzpatrick. It was weird."[20]

Doolittle wondered why he was even there, and, as he exited, he doubted he would take the job. When he got home and broke the bad news to Bella, she acted decisively.

"I remember that she literally grabbed me by the shirt, pushed me up against the wall and told me, 'You are taking that job,'" Doolittle said. "And that was it."[21]

If Mark Mahoney was our conscience, Will Doolittle became our intellectual cornerstone who had a mastery of local, state and national issues that he cared about deeply.

While Mahoney was able to perfect the art of the 700-word arm-twist, Doolittle bounced masterfully from artful columns to hard news briefs, meticulous line editing that made sloppy copy come to life, while being a constant source of inspiration for the young, ambitious writers on our staff.

After I became the editor, he was the one person I could count on to deliver a journalistic home run.

In his 1993 cover letter to managing editor Bennett, Doolittle wrote what should have been enough to get him the job of night editor: "I grew up in the newspaper business and have spent my career working at community newspapers."[22]

I find it ironic all these years later that, at the age of 32, Doolittle thought he had already had a "career." He was just getting started.

We all were just getting started.

Doolittle's years as Sunday editor, feature editor and projects editor—beginning in 1999—were much different than those as night editor. Each night for his first six years at *The Post-Star*, he changed words. Over the next 22, he changed lives.

I'd like to think we all did.

When I was a small boy, my dad took me to work to pick up his paycheck. As we walked through the factory offices, he pointed out the men wearing ties and told me, "That's what you want to do. You want to wear a tie to work."

My father did not wear a tie to work. Like most of the men in his family, he took a shower after work, not before.

In those first days, my parents weren't sure what their oldest son had gotten himself into. Being sports editor made sense to them for their sports-crazed oldest son, but being editor was the real world.

Not long after I moved into the big office, they came to visit me at the newspaper. I told our receptionist, Lucy Dunbar, I wanted to have some fun with them. When they arrived, I instructed Lucy to tell them to have a seat in the lobby, and she would see if I could see them. I also told her to return after they were in the office and give me an important message.

Sitting behind the big, antique desk in my office, I asked them what they thought. My 70-year-old mom immigrated from Ireland after meeting Dad in the Navy, while my 67-year-old father had worked in the factory for the past 40 years. Neither had ever been in the office of a newspaper editor. They both seemed uncomfortable as if they expected someone to kick them out.

My father looked a little worried and for the first time a little small.

After a few minutes, Lucy returned and politely knocked on the door. "Excuse me, Ken, the congressman is on the phone for you."

"Tell him I will have to call him back because I'm with my parents right now," I said.

When Lucy left, my father waited a minute, then gave me that worried look and said, "Are you sure you know what you are doing?"

Dad never visited the office again. He died just after Christmas two years later.

I was just getting started as editor, but I take consolation that during my dad's only visit to my office, I was wearing a tie.

2

"Get up, get out"

Pam Brooks was rousted from her slumber in the early morning hours of August 30, 2000.

"My arm was being pulled, yanking me upward into the dawn," Brooks later recounted in *The Post-Star*. "The house was dark and an insistent familiar voice seemed to be shouting at me."[1]

Brooks, then 52, had been a freelancer for the Glens Falls newspaper for a number of years and was paid by the story. She was not the traditional newspaper reporter with formal journalism training. That is often the case at small community newspapers.

She grew up in Connecticut, attended prep school in Maine, business school in Connecticut and university in Kansas. After college, she worked in Boston for a time before eventually relocating to a commune in West Virginia. After all, it was the 1960s.

She later moved to Washington, D.C., and worked as a legislative assistant for a congressman which, of course, prepared her for her next career, caring for thoroughbred show jumpers in Florida and New Jersey.

These life experience credentials are often far more important than a journalism degree.

Brooks covered meetings and events for the newspaper, but like so many of our correspondents over the years, her work was something more. She provided the type of community connection that many of our young, full-time reporters never could. She lived here. She was one of the people.

"If you read one of her stories, you were bound to find a gold nugget along the way," city editor Bob Condon wrote on Facebook in 2019.[2]

But none of it prepared her for being at the center of the biggest local news story of the year in 2000.

"Get up! Get up! We have to get out!" screamed her companion. "It's an ammonia spill. The whole town has to get out."[3]

Fort Edward is a sleepy, blue-collar community about five miles southeast of Glens Falls. It is sandwiched between the Hudson River on the west and the Champlain Canal on the east with a D&H railway line and an old-fashioned train station halfway down East Street that still picks up Amtrak passengers twice a day.

At 11:06 p.m. on Tuesday, August 29, employees at Environmental Soil Management, just north of the Fort Edward train station, detected an ammonia odor and called Canadian Pacific rail officials. Fort Edward Fire Department officials arrived on the scene at 11:15 p.m.[4]

24

When the small village of Fort Edward, New York, was evacuated early on the morning of August 30, 2000, city editor Bob Condon responded with the type of "flood the zone" coverage that the newspaper would become expert in over the next two decades. But one story that stood out more than the others was a first-person account from correspondent Pam Brooks (front page courtesy of *The Post-Star*, Glens Falls, NY).

Brooks lived in Fort Edward.

By 1 a.m., evacuations of 800 village and town residents began with residents first being evacuated to the downtown firehouse, then farther north up Route 4 to Fort Edward High School. Police officials began closing roads as they searched for the source of the smell.

When Condon first heard about Brooks's ordeal the next day, he asked her to give a first-person account of the evacuation.

Brooks responded with a second-by-second narrative from the time she was awakened until the key turned in the ignition of the pickup truck.

This was a reporter using all her senses.

"I began to sniff rather than breathe, understanding immediately what a lungful of acrid air might do," she wrote as she described a "vague diaper smell in the bedroom."[5]

Her companion, an all-night convenience store worker, related what he knew about the spill as she dressed, describing what he had seen around the community. He said those who were evacuated began milling around the store at 3 a.m. with people sitting on the curbs wondering what to do.[6]

"A grandmother bundled kids in her car and rode around the streets trying to make a plan," Brooks wrote.[7]

"Moving from room to room, I sought out shoes, spit out toothpaste and located a comb. Within a minute I was dressed and we were exchanging terse phrases about what to do next. The smell was everywhere, inescapable, heavy—and scary. I wanted what I couldn't have—one breath of clean air."[8]

At the end of her piece, Brooks wrote: "Time elapsed between being awakened and turning the key in the ignition: 6 minutes."[9]

It was the work of a true professional and one of hundreds of pieces of community journalism Brooks wrote for the newspaper over the years.

Condon later did a search of *Post-Star* archives that brought up more than 2,200 articles under her byline.[10] She was another unique example of what every day small-town reporters look like and what they do.

When something terrible happens in the middle of the night, it is the newspaper that communities count on to keep them informed. That was true in 2000, and I believe it is still true today. And when it is a crisis, the newspaper must respond in force. It must be at its best and in many cases fearless.

Don Lehman was always the reporter heading out the door first when there was breaking news. Sometimes that meant leaving his bed in the middle of the night to get important information to the community.

In many ways, news reporters are like first responders, running toward the danger instead of away from it, not in pursuit of some ghoulish thrill but because getting information to the public during a crisis is important. It is their job.

Lehman was perfectly suited to be the newspaper's police reporter. He had a vast array of sources, got people to tell him things confidentially first, then on the record later, and he was so competitive, he didn't want any other news outlet to beat him on a story. He was a throwback to another era.

You can make a case that the great reporters like Lehman are rarely created in a college classroom. Most are born with a gift that is two-parts street smarts and three-parts hustle. Some of it may have been the life they had growing up.

Lehman was a kid from north Jersey who was a bit of a wild child in his younger days. He also had that early connection to newspapers.[11]

His father, a social studies teacher, was a part-time sportswriter for the *Bergen Record* when Lehman was growing up. When his father covered high school games, he would take one of his three boys with him.[12]

"I enjoyed it," Lehman told me in 2020. "I would take my own notes during games and get to hang out in the *Bergen Record* newsroom."[13]

Lehman was an average student in high school but played varsity baseball and was recruited by the baseball coach at Castleton University in Vermont. He visited the college, liked the place, but more importantly it accepted him as a student. But by the end of his freshman year, Lehman was already academically ineligible and his baseball career over.[14]

"I was initially thinking I'd be a teacher, but it didn't resonate with me," he said.[15]

Terry Dalton, the adviser for the Castleton student newspaper, told Lehman he was a good writer and he should get on the school newspaper.[16]

That did resonate.

At Castleton, he met David Blow and was part of a group that hung out together. Once he discovered the newspaper, Lehman's GPA rose from 1.6 to 2.8 by the time he graduated.[17]

The standard for many of us at most small newspapers is there is no one road to employment. The path is filled with odd turns, strange twists and the occasional lucky break on the way to a lifetime career.

Not a job, a career. There is a big difference.

Blow was a year ahead of Lehman at Castleton and worked with him on the school newspaper. He says Lehman hasn't changed much over the years.

"Honestly, he was very similar throughout," Blow said. "I think he was in trouble some as a kid. Him and his brothers raised a lot of hell. There is a reason he had a roommate nicknamed Satan."[18]

"I've always been that way going back to elementary school," Lehman said. "If you tell me I can't do something, I'll figure out a way to do it."[19]

Eventually, Lehman found a career where that was an attribute.

With Blow going first, the pair followed the same path. Blow was hired by the *Granville Sentinel*, a small weekly newspaper in northern Washington County, hard by the Vermont state line and not far from Castleton. When Blow was hired by *The Post-Star* a year later, Lehman replaced him in Granville. A year after that, Lehman was also hired by *The Post-Star*. He had hoped to be a sportswriter but settled for any reporting job he could get.[20]

It's traditional for each succeeding rookie reporter to happily pass on the police beat to the next reporter in the door. Most find there is too much stress, too many bad hours and a surplus of contentious relations with police officers who can be secretive and difficult under the best of circumstances.

But the police beat is where the action is every day. There are crimes, arrests, court cases, accidents and investigations. It is the very definition of news. There is no end to the mayhem, and that suited Lehman perfectly.

The police beat was often a crash course in civics, as reporters learned the ins and outs of the court system, how the district attorney's office worked and how to deal delicately with crime victims.

Or, in some cases, how not to deal with victims.

Not long after Lehman started in Glens Falls, Paul Gugina, the city editor in the early 1990s, assigned him to go to a wake in nearby Hudson Falls and get a story about a young victim who had died in a car accident.[21]

These are the types of stories that need to be handled delicately. Reporters often ask the funeral director to act as an intermediary so the family is not taken off guard and understands the type of story the reporter is doing. The reporting has to be done discreetly at a time when emotions are running high.

"I just showed up at the funeral home in Hudson Falls and started interviewing family members," Lehman said. "Pulled out my notebook right there. I just didn't know any better."[22]

He was soon confronted.

"I was literally chased out of there by family members," Lehman said. "I was running up Main Street with them yelling at me."[23]

But here is the lesson: Lehman told his editor he had enough for a story for the next day's newspaper.

"I got a call from a family member the next day thanking me for saying such nice things in the article," said Lehman.[24]

On the morning of the tanker spill, Lehman was slow to react. When Condon learned of the spill that morning, his first call was to Lehman. But instead of his usual "go get 'em" attitude, Condon got the impression Don didn't think it was a big deal.[25]

"God bless him, he is everywhere, but one of my recollections was I kind of had to push him to get over there," Condon said in 2020.[26]

By the time Lehman made it to Fort Edward early the next morning, all the roads into the village of Fort Edward had been blocked by emergency responders.

Lehman drove around a few back roads, parked his car over to the side and headed into the woods.

"The thing I remember the most was going through the woods and going through the backyard of a house and popped up right in the rail yard," Lehman said in 2020. "I remember one of the DEC guys wanted to arrest me for going around the roadblock."[27]

It would not be the last time someone wanted Lehman arrested.

From his reporting, the newspaper was able to produce a graphic that showed what the tanker car and the valve gasket looked like, because he had seen it for himself.

"You could see the mist coming out of the top of the tanker," Lehman remembered. "It was really eerie. They had cobbled together some type of duct tape to slow it down. It was amazing they had slowed it down as much as they had."[28]

Over the next two days, the newspaper's team of reporters provided a clear and concise understanding of what had happened, what the dangers were to the people in Fort Edward and when the 800 evacuated residents could return home.

Condon had been city editor long enough—just over a year—to know our "flood the zone" philosophy on big stories was what was called for here.

With Lehman acting as the lead reporter, we printed that the Department of Environmental Conservation believed the leak began when a gasket on a gas release valve came loose on a 30,000-gallon tanker of anhydrous ammonia. Lehman knew it was accurate because he had seen it for himself.[29]

While Lehman and Brooks were at the center of the breaking news at the beginning, our coverage eventually involved the entire staff.

The leaking tanker car in Fort Edward was on its way to Finch, Pruyn & Co.—the Glens Falls paper mill—where the anhydrous ammonia is used to soften wood for papermaking. Lehman reported the gas could be deadly when inhaled in heavy quantities.[30]

Before dawn the next morning, residents of Fort Edward began arriving at Glens Falls Hospital complaining of breathing problems and chest pains.[31]

The hospital reported that exposure to the ammonia affected people with asthma, aggravating their symptoms and making breathing difficult.[32]

Sixty-one people were eventually treated, including ten emergency rescue personnel and four children.[33]

With all the roads to Fort Edward closed, the newspaper's veteran chief photographer, Monty Calvert, rented a small airplane to get aerial shots of the tanker car and the railroad yard.

Evacuees were not allowed to return to their homes the next day, and an overnight shelter was established a few miles north at Hudson Falls High School.

Lehman produced four stories for the next day's coverage, including one about local officials renewing a call for establishing a regional team to respond to hazardous materials spills. Thank goodness he wasn't arrested.

The coverage reflected an emergency response that went smoothly, with only a few people getting seriously ill. It also summed up the plans to contain the spill so residents could go home.

The August 31 newspaper included Lehman's main news story, Brooks's first-person account, Calvert's aerial photograph and a time line of events that included an early evening update that the SPCA of Upstate New York had organized two caravans of volunteers to go into the village to rescue more than 50 pets. It was probably the most read story of the day.[34]

Also on the front page of our local section was this brief item:

> *Post-Star* subscribers who've been evacuated from their homes because of Wednesday's ammonia gas leak will be able to pick up today's newspaper at the high school in Fort Edward.
> About 450 subscribers live within the area police evacuated early Wednesday. But today, stacks of papers will be dropped off at the Fort Edward High School and subscribers from the affected area can simply go there and pick them up at no charge.[35]

This was one of our communities in crisis, and we were their prime source of information. It wasn't just our job, it was our responsibility.

A year later, the Press Club of Atlantic City honored the newspaper with a National Headliner Award for spot news coverage.[36] It was our first national award.

The most memorable story was Pam Brooks's account of those initial harrowing moments.

Her obituary in February 2019 said, "Pamela Anne [French] Brooks-Gibbs had left for an unknown adventure."[37]

I suspect she may have written that herself.

Six months later, Condon posted a tribute on Facebook and recounted some of her more memorable stories.

It showed the connections our regional editor had made with the correspondents and contributing writers working for a few dollars on the side. Condon pointed out that Pam also had insisted her byline read, "Special to *The Post-Star*." That seems obvious now since she was part of our newspaper's special community.

"Sometimes we get lost in the years, it is difficult to remember the specifics of day-to-day interactions and phone calls," Condon wrote at the end of that Facebook tribute. "My memories of Pam are fond but foggy. To be sure, she was an integral part of *The Post-Star*, and as reporters came and went she delivered consistency, local know-how and fluid writing to our pages. I wished I had told her that when we worked together."[38]

3

9/11

The phone rang five minutes before 9 a.m. It was Stacey Seymour, our advertising director's assistant, calling from the advertising building across the parking lot.

"Nick [advertising director Caimano] said I should tell you that the Trade Center is under attack," Stacey said.

I was confused.

The village of Lake George, a big upstate tourist destination just north of Glens Falls, had been debating building a "trade center" in recent months to attract meetings and conventions, and that was obviously on my mind.

"They haven't even built it yet," I replied.

"No, the one in New York," Stacey said without any alarm in her voice. "Turn on the television."

Newsrooms are quiet places in the morning, and this Tuesday morning was no exception as reporters and editors trickled in for the morning meeting. Many were working a later shift because of the primary election scheduled in New York that day. The newsroom television was dark.

I left my office and yelled for Sunday editor Will Doolittle to turn on the television.

There were about ten of us in the newsroom looking at the image of smoke billowing from one of the Twin Towers in New York City. We all have seen the image. We wondered aloud how a plane could accidentally hit one of the towers.

Then, the second tower exploded.

After watching the replay again and again, it was clear this was not a small plane, and this was not an accident.

Gradually, the stunned silence turned to conversation about doing a reaction story. My first instinct was that this was not a local story but something left to the wire services. I did not see the big picture yet.

Just a three-hour drive from New York City, Glens Falls rests along the same Hudson River that empties into New York harbor. The city is an easy train ride from the Rensselaer train station that sits across the river from the state capital in Albany.

Television then reported there was an explosion at the Pentagon in Washington, D.C., and there were four or more hijacked planes still in the air.

We looked at each other and asked aloud: "What the heck is going on?"

David Blow, the Castleton (VT) University grad who was now our assistant city editor, made the most important decision of the day with an email to everyone in the newsroom to contact anyone they knew who might work in Manhattan or Washington who could add a local angle to the events unfolding nationally.[1]

31

On a day when newspapers all across the country were at their best, *The Post-Star* turned out an award-winning effort that produced 27 local stories and was honored the next year with a National Headliners Award. But right up until the last minute, the editors debated the choice of the headline "My God!" (front page courtesy of *The Post-Star*, Glens Falls, NY).

I turned to Martha Petteys, one of our feature writers for our Arts/Life section, and told her to make the 45-mile drive to Albany International Airport.

"What do you want me to do when I get there?" Martha asked.

"I'm not sure," I answered.

Within the hour, Blow was on the phone with Kevin Tenant, a field technician for Verizon who was a frequent visitor to nearby Lake Luzerne. Tenant worked on the ninth floor of the World Trade Center and told Blow he was talking to him from a nearby building after the planes hit.[2]

"Don't let him off the phone, no matter what," I told Blow.

Tenant had stopped to buy an egg sandwich about a block from the Twin Towers when he heard a piercing whine overhead, followed by a monstrous explosion. He first thought it was an automobile accident.[3]

"I had no idea it was a plane," Tenant told Blow.[4]

"But the second one I saw clear as a bell. I was standing right outside. I had paperwork and business cards from people's desks falling on top of me," Tenant said.[5]

Tenant abruptly ended the phone call, saying, "Oh man, we're getting smoke in here. I've gotta go."

While Blow was reporting to me what Tenant had said, our publisher, Jim Marshall, called for a department head meeting.

I briefed the other department heads about what I knew, and we decided to put out a 12-page special section on the events of the day. We were told we could have as much space as we needed.

Pat Dowd, our news editor who usually works a night shift, came into the room and told us one of the towers had collapsed and that 2,000 to 3,000 people could be dead.[6]

There was silence for a few seconds, then we resumed talking about the logistics of an 8 p.m. deadline for an "Extra" section that would be inserted into the regular newspaper.

Then the second tower came down.

"We were all there in the newsroom at 9 a.m. and we all knew we were going to do a big front page, but then you came out of the meeting and said we are going to do a whole pull-out section," Mark Mahoney remembered. "We were like, 'Wow, this guy is thinking big.'"[7]

By the time the meeting was over, Tenant had called Blow back from a less smoky computer room in the basement of the Chase Plaza.[8]

Blow said Tenant sounded distraught as he recounted seeing people covered in blood, running into a bathroom. Tenant talked about the policemen and firefighters who undoubtedly had died when the first tower collapsed.[9]

"They're all dead," he told Blow.[10]

He said he saw a person jump from one of the upper floors in the towers.[11]

"I can handle a lot of things, but this is sick," Tenant said before Blow lost contact with him again.[12]

By 10:30 it was clear this was going to be a big local story, too. Our community had many connections in New York City.

Reporter Matthew Sturdevant, with just a year's experience under his belt, hit the streets in downtown Glens Falls hoping to do a general reaction story, when he ran into a man in a business suit outside the Queensbury Hotel.[13]

With his tie whipping wildly in the breeze, the man said he had just arrived from Manhattan for a business meeting and that his office in the city was just five blocks from the Trade Center.[14]

"I can't imagine this," he said. "The total disregard for human life."[15]

He refused to give Sturdevant his name and walked into the hotel lobby where another 30 people were gathered around a television set.[16]

Down at Albany International Airport, Petteys began talking to random travelers. All planes had just been grounded, and many of them were stranded, unsure of what to do next.

Petteys interviewed a rattled businesswoman, Jeanne Servin, from Worcester, Massachusetts, who said she had caught an 8:50 a.m. flight out of Logan Airport in Boston, the origination point for two of the hijacked planes. She was on her way to a meeting in Syracuse.[17]

"Servin shook when she thought about how close she must have come to crossing paths with the planes that were hijacked," Petteys wrote.[18]

At first, I expected we would have two or three reaction stories, but what you need to know about reporters—at least the good ones—is how they gravitate toward big news stories. They demand to be part of the coverage. They raise their game to another level when the story is most important.

It was soon clear this was a news event of unparalleled significance.

At one point in the late morning, I noticed Terry Pluto, the Cleveland *Plain Dealer* sports columnist, in our newsroom. Pluto had flown in from Cleveland that morning to give a seminar for our sports department. I had already forgotten it was scheduled.

He instead asked for a place to write.

That was the case on 9/11. Everyone needed to be part of the coverage, no matter what department you worked in.

By noon, I expected we would have four or five stories, but our reporters kept finding new and significant angles. By that afternoon, reporter Thom Randall found Glens Falls native Gary French, who was a multimedia graphics branch chief at the Pentagon. French worked in Corridor No. 2. The plane hit Corridor No. 3.[19]

"We were at our computers trying to gather information about the attack on the World Trade Center, when there was this enormous shaking of the building and debris fell from the ceiling," French told Randall from his Maryland home. "Then there were people running through our building, ordering us to get out immediately. We believed we were under attack.[20]

"Some employees fleeing the building were crying, screaming and sobbing—people were making a mad dash to get outside," French continued. "After thousands of people were evacuated, we looked up and saw debris falling from above and smelled the fumes of burning jet fuel."[21]

This was original reporting by one of our reporters.

Then Tenant called Blow back a second time. He had survived the collapse of the second tower as well. He described to Blow walking away from the carnage through four to five inches of dust and debris. He described the fighter planes buzzing the city.[22]

Later that evening, sportswriter Jim Tracy tracked down Mike and Caitlin Hickin, both former athletes from neighboring Queensbury who were in Manhattan when the planes hit. The brother and sister were at opposite ends of the island, with Caitlin attending classes at Columbia University uptown while her brother Mike was just arriving to work at Goldman Sachs downtown, two blocks from the World Trade Center.[23]

"I saw all the debris, paper was flying, and opaque smoke engulfed the whole area," said Mike Hickin, a former track athlete. He started running with the crowd and the dust.[24]

"The smoke was so thick you could not see anything," he said. "Everyone was running for their lives."[25]

His destination was Columbia University to check on his sister.[26]

The stories kept coming and mounted one on top of another. When it became clear we could fill two facing pages with local copy inside, I asked Doolittle and reporter Mike Mender to write columns to give the events context and perspective.

Both focused on the reaction of their own children.

Mahoney, who was just starting to build a reputation as a top-notch editorial writer, told me he was already working on an editorial. He also got a reaction from local Rep. John Sweeney, who was desperately trying to get back to Washington.

I took a few moments to call my wife, and we both agreed we would not tell our five-year-old about the events in New York—at least not today—and we would not let him watch any of the news coverage.

By late afternoon, we needed to start our special "Extra" section on the day's events.

David Lemery, a young news copy editor who had also gotten his start in sports, was put in charge of the design. He had the overwhelming task of summing up the historic events of the day. I suggested he organize the section by devoting one page of coverage to each of the most significant events as they happened: the first plane crash, the second plane crash, the Pentagon attack, the first tower falling, the second tower falling and the plane crash in Pennsylvania.

About a half-hour later, Lemery came back into my office and said, "I don't know what to do. I don't know where to start."

I remembered a book I had read as a young man, *The Day Kennedy Was Shot*, by Jim Bishop where he reprinted the wire service bulletins from United Press International verbatim from November 22, 1963.[27]

I started sketching out a design.

At the top of each inside page below the logo, "Terror Comes to America," I put the brief ten- to 20-word bulletins the Associated Press had moved on the morning of September 11:

8:53 a.m.—APNEWSALERT—NEW YORK—Plane crashes into World Trade Center, according to television reports.

9:04 a.m.—APNEWSALERT—NEW YORK—Explosion rocks second World Trade Center tower.

9:09 a.m.—APNEWSALERT—NEW YORK—Plane crashes into second World Trade Center tower.

9:45 a.m.—APNEWSALERT—WASHINGTON—An aircraft has crashed into the Pentagon, witnesses say.

9:50 a.m.—APNEWSALERT—NEW YORK—One World Trade Center tower collapses.

10:30 a.m.—APNEWSALERT—NEW YORK—Second World Trade Center tower collapses.

11:33 a.m.—APNEWSALERT—PITTSBURGH, Pa.—United Airlines confirms flight from Newark, N.J. To San Francisco crashed near Pittsburgh.

12:23 a.m.—APNEWSALERT—NEW YORK—High-ranking city police official says the number of people killed or injured could be in the thousands.[28]

"I think that was the spark that got a lot of that organized," Dowd remembered in 2020. "That evening was probably the biggest organizational challenge for a small newspaper trying to figure out how to take this enormous event that was earth-shattering and figure out how you were to do your job in a way that made sense and helped the readers to understand what happened."[29]

Lemery had the roadmap he needed and went to work. His front page of the special section consisted of a full-page photograph of a collapsing tower, with the headline "Attacked."

Our newsroom produced 25 stories from 14 reporters on that tragic day, including stories from Pam Brooks, Don Lehman, Thom Randall and Blow.

It was getting late, and I still had not seen Mahoney's editorial.

"It was a struggle. It took me all day," Mahoney remembered in 2020. "Up until 10 p.m., I didn't know what I was going to write. I knew I had to say something profound and you don't want to screw it up."[30]

Then Mark talked to his mother on the phone.

"Keep safe and pray," Mark remembered her telling him. "That was my lead."[31]

All that was left as we approached deadline was writing the main headline on the front page.

This was for history, and we all knew it.

Dowd, who oversaw the copy desk and the production of the news pages, had strong opinions about national and international news coverage that sometimes led to heated exchanges during our page one meetings. He had a strong sense of history and morality.

Both Dowd and city editor Bob Condon remembered reading an early version of an Associated Press story where an anonymous observer in Manhattan was quoted as screaming, "My God!"

Early in the evening, Dowd insisted this should be the lead headline.

When I talked to him in 2020, Dowd remembered how we argued about the headline.

"My argument was this, this is ... unprecedented...." Dowd told me in 2020, but then there was silence.[32]

Nineteen years later, Pat Dowd was back there again and choking up just remembering 9/11.

"This has got to be what we say tomorrow," Dowd said after regaining his composure. "This was for history. Even at that point, we were thinking about 10 years and 20 years from then. This would be a newspaper edition that would be referenced."[33]

I objected because there was no attribution to the quote, and it just seemed too emotional.

"I remember having an argument with you in your office," Dowd said. "I said I would put it in as a placeholder until later."[34]

During the course of the evening, we looked at other headline possibilities, but none captured the enormity of the event and its emotional shock.

As we neared deadline, Pat brought a printed copy of the front page into my office with "My God" as the lead headline. The subhead read: "Thousands feared dead as terrorist attacks destroy World Trade Center, damage Pentagon."

I thought for few seconds, then I told Pat to go ahead.

No other newspaper duplicated that headline. I thought it captured the reaction of all Americans.

Still does.

Years later, Condon, perhaps our most conservative editor, admitted he still second-guessed the choice.[35]

When he had filed his story, Randall said he wanted to go to Manhattan the next day. I was at first opposed to the idea.

"I just knew there would be these just incredibly powerful stories that people would have to talk about," Randall told me in 2020. "This would be an experience I would never have [again] to hear about the destruction and loss and just really compelling experiences."[36]

I told Randall he could go.

Later that night, before Pluto, the Cleveland sports columnist, left for the evening, he talked to me about what he saw in our newsroom.

"The atmosphere in the newsroom today was one of people with a purpose. There was no panic," he said.[37]

"What really stands out in my mind was the mobilization that you initiated in the newsroom," Randall, now 72, said in 2020. "How serious everyone was. How uncertain we were about our future. You had sports people writing stories and we were all so serious. Everyone had these stone-faced, resolute expressions. I was so proud to be part of that newspaper that day. When that came off the press, it blew me away."[38]

I didn't leave until well after midnight, and even then I could not sleep. I wasn't alone.

"When I got home that night after we put the paper to bed," Dowd remembered. "I just couldn't get to sleep. It was too much to process."[39]

Reading the coverage two decades later, I'm struck by its serious, matter-of-fact quality and its utter lack of hysteria. Our reporters told our readers the story with levelheaded intensity.

I wrote this in my "From the Managing Editor" column the Sunday after 9/11:

> When our reporters and editors heard about the unfolding tragedy Tuesday, they headed to work immediately and most didn't leave until late in the night. They were not allowed to show their emotions, to let the enormity of the situation, or their anger, affect what they were writing. They had information to report, stories to write and pages to construct. That's what we do in the newspaper business. It is the curse and it is the blessing.[40]

Our sports editor Greg Brownell approached me during the evening and said, "This is the worst part of being in sports. I feel so helpless."[41]

It was a day when we were called on to do our very best, and that day, I think we did.

On September 12, Randall boarded New York City-bound Amtrak train 291 at

6:55 a.m. at the Rensselaer train station along with seven other passengers. Normally, there were approximately 200. It was the last train allowed into New York City.

"Yesterday, a train full of people went down to New York City, and very few came back last night," train mechanic Keith Collesides told Randall. "We're wondering if some people who went down yesterday will ever make it back. I hope a lot of our regular commuters are just stuck in New York. We've seen enough already."[42]

This was the type of reporting that Randall had been wanting to do for some time. He was 53 at the time, had spent two years at Bard College studying English literature and did not have a journalism degree. But he knew how to talk to people, and he knew how to get them to talk to him.

Another passenger was frantically trying to reach her sister. When she finally did, she let Randall interview her sister on the phone.[43] Randall always found a way to get the interview.

"I was at Battery Plaza headed for a job counseling, and I was in a crowd looking at the one tower burn," the sister told Randall. "Then I heard a deafening noise, and a jet flew right above us, took a sharp turn, and then went right through the other tower. There was a big fireball and a puff of black smoke and then for a few seconds you could see the sky right through the gaping hole in the building. It was so overpowering, I couldn't stop screaming. Then debris fell on us everywhere and people were running and screaming."[44]

The puzzling part about Randall was that while his news instincts were unparalleled, and he was utterly fearless when it came to reporting a story, he often lacked basic common sense.

After arriving in the city, Randall spent the rest of the day trying to make his way to Ground Zero while doing interviews all along the way. He had worn dress shoes and socks, believing he would be able to get transportation downtown. His feet soon blistered.

"It was stupid of me," Randall said. "I should have been better prepared."[45]

Randall believes he walked as far as 10th or 11th Street before being prevented from going any farther and began interviewing residents there.[46] Manhattan resident Mikki Willis had been at Ground Zero helping emergency workers search through the rubble.

"It's a scene beyond any description," Willis said, as he broke down sobbing while talking to Randall. "There's twisted, mangled wreckage and any building that is not dust is gutted by fire. We've seen bodies excavated and we've walked through body parts, but we couldn't immediately recognize them because everything is buried in ash."[47]

"It was a ghost town," Randall remembered in 2020. "The air was dusty and putrid from the stench of the burning rubble from Ground Zero. People were walking north past those barricades, some of them covered with that grey dust from the collapse of the buildings. I was concerned about whether there was asbestos in the World Trade Center's construction materials and my fears turned out to be justified. I felt so bad for all those who lived in lower Manhattan. The plume of smoke from the World Trade Center area dominated the southern sky.[48]

"There was no traffic," Randall continued. "It was incredible. The streets were empty. People walked dazed right down the middle of the streets."[49]

Mahoney responded with another editorial about the outpouring from Glens Falls residents who donated nearly 400 pints of blood and organized fund drives while rescue workers prepared to lend aid. It's these type of words years later that are forgotten in the age of "fake news."

"There seems to be no end to the generosity," Mahoney wrote about the community efforts. "There's one more way residents can demonstrate their generosity: by being generous toward each other. In the wake of such incomprehensible violence, it's natural for victims—in this case, we as Americans—to rush to judgment and seek out targets for our rage. Let's never lose sight of the fact that these acts were not perpetrated by a particular ethnic or religious group, or by anyone living among us. They were carried out by hateful people with no regard for the sanctity of human life. The scope of our generosity will be defined not only by our actions, but by the actions we chose not to take."[50]

Mahoney was showing the value of editorial writing to our readers like never before while bringing timeliness and urgency to the editorial page.

It's the grander, loftier goal that newspapers often provide in times of crisis and the crater that will be left behind in the future, perhaps something we have already seen during the pandemic. In this case, the newspaper made a call for calm and reason and humanity. People who say newspapers should not write editorials have not read Mahoney's work.

On the Saturday after 9/11, we reported on the front page how the region came together on a day of mourning. President George W. Bush visited Ground Zero on Friday.

The coverage, and Mahoney's editorial, captured the spirit of a community, and it was clear I had made the right decision changing Mahoney's job:

> The young and old among us traveled to churches, encircled flagpoles that held flags at half-staff, placed flowers at makeshift memorials and donned every red, white and blue piece of clothing they could find.
> At every turn, new American flags were popping up. The Stars and Stripes adorned car antennas, hung in doorways, and were draped from the sides of businesses illustrating a stronger than ever commitment to freedom and democracy.
> More than 4,000 patriotic ribbons and pins were handed out at the Glens Falls Armory alone, and money poured into area relief funds.
> God Bless America and America the Beautiful resonated from impromptu gatherings, leaving many with tears in their eyes.[51]

In my September 21 column, I wrote about a game my five-year-old and I had invented on the way to school.

"Let's count all the American flags we see along the road," I said to my son. The number was over 20 in the first mile before he tired of the game. What was the challenge? The flags were everywhere.[52]

There was more heartwarming than heart-wrenching news to report in the succeeding days.

Queensbury resident Jackie Albino, whose sister worked on the 42nd floor of the North Tower, reported she was safe.[53]

"When I saw what had happened, my heart broke to pieces," Albino told reporter John Gereau. "I was literally on my knees sobbing. The wait was the most devastating thing. We had actually begun to give up hope."[54]

Then Albino got the call from her sister.

"I felt numb," Albino said. "In my heart, she had died and come back."[55]

On Sunday, September 23, Randall delivered another heart-wrenching feature story about a local couple's three children who all survived 9/11 in New York City.

One of the siblings was a New York City firefighter, the second a vice president of American Express who worked near the Twin Towers and the third a New York City fire company battalion chief in the Bronx who performed search and rescue afterward.[56]

The final local piece of 9/11 reporting was not published until December 23 when sportswriter Ryan O'Halloran reported the story of local Olympic hockey player, Kathleen Kauth, and the death of her father, Don Kauth.[57]

Kauth, a bank analyst for Keene, Bruyette & Wood, was on the 85th floor of the South Tower—the second tower hit in the attack. On the day they announced the final roster for the women's Olympic hockey team, Don Kauth had driven the five hours to Lake Placid to surprise his daughter.[58]

"Wow! Wow!" he half-yelled after hearing the news she had made the team, then picking up Kathleen in a joyous hug for the ages.[59]

"After everyone was sort of clearing out to go home, and there were like 20 of us together that night, Don came over to me," said Anne Kauth, Kathleen's mother and Don's ex-wife. "I had never seen a human being so happy. He just hugged me and said, 'We did this. This is what we did.' I'll never forget that look on his face."[60]

The date was August 22.

The story showed readers the personal trauma in their own community. It also showed the power of newspapers when they are at their best.

Everyone remembers where they were when they heard the news about 9/11, but I prefer to think about the stories we wrote in the newspaper during those difficult days and the effect they had on our community.

The newspaper's role in small communities like Glens Falls during a national tragedy is to not only report the news but capture the community's heart and soul.

After President Bush called for a day of prayer, the newspaper published two facing inside pages of dispatches from five different events attended by our reporters around the region. The page was titled "WE MOURN."

"Many choked back tears as the group ended the memorial service by reciting the Pledge of Allegiance," reporter Mender wrote of a ceremony outside Glens Falls' tallest building downtown.[61]

In 2002, The Press Club of Atlantic City honored *The Post-Star* with a prestigious National Headliner Award for its spot news coverage of the September 11 attacks for newspapers with a circulation under 75,000 readers.

The judges did not award a second- or third-place prize.

"Within minutes of the attack on the World Trade Center this past Sept. 11, *The Post-Star* news staff was in action to cover a story that was three hours away, but still a local story. By the end of the day, the staff of 14 reporters had turned out 25 local stories on how the attacks had affected the community and region including eyewitness accounts from local people at the World Trade Center and Pentagon. The copy desk responded with a 12-page special section giving an hour-by-hour account of the day's tragic events that had to be printed by 8 p.m. for insert in the next day's paper."[62]

"It is in times of crisis like this that people depend on their local newspaper, and on this terrible day, I think we responded to our readers with all the information that they needed and demanded," *Post-Star* publisher James G. Marshall said at the time.[63]

Most importantly, our young staff learned we could make a difference.

4

Maury

Maury Thompson was one of those guys who couldn't seem to find his niche in the world.

He admitted he was an "oddball" growing up in Pennsylvania and eventually relocated to Ticonderoga in upstate New York after working summers at a YMCA summer camp on Lake George. A year out of high school, he married a local girl and had three children in five years. The marriage ended in divorce.[1]

Along the way, Thompson sold encyclopedias door to door, wrote radio commercials for an auto dealer and hustled as a short-order cook at multiple diners and restaurants while raising a family.[2]

The days after the divorce were difficult. While getting counseling, he was asked what he wanted to do with his life. He talked about his dream of going to college and being a writer.[3]

"Why can't you go off to college?" the counselor asked.[4]

Thompson ticked off one reason after another. He was too old, didn't have enough money and wasn't smart enough.[5]

The counselor told him that people went to college in their 20s and 30s all the time.[6]

It was a fork in the road.

"I walked two blocks down the street to the community college campus in Ticonderoga and asked, 'How do I apply for financial aid,'" Thompson said in 2020.[7]

It is another example of the odd paths and quirky backgrounds so many of our best reporters took on their way to finding a career in Glens Falls. Many never studied journalism. Others did not have a college degree.

Thompson became one of those people. He attended North Country Community College in Ticonderoga for two years, then applied to prestigious Middlebury College in Vermont when he heard they had financial aid for nontraditional students.[8]

That was Thompson—nontraditional.

The day of his interview at Middlebury College, his car broke down in the middle of the old Crown Point bridge, and he missed his meeting. He told the people at Middlebury of his dilemma. They told him if he could make it there the next day, they would see him. Thompson convinced a friend to make the hour's drive north, and Maury got his financial aid.[9]

It took him six years to complete his four-year degree, working multiple jobs to afford his education and a new life.[10]

"One time, I was on the schedule at one restaurant for breakfast, another for

Maury Thompson was a quirky misfit who didn't seem to fit in anywhere. After a difficult divorce, Thompson went back to college to get his degree while working a variety of jobs to make ends meet. When he graduated, he began freelancing for the Glens Falls newspaper. When he was hired full-time in 1999, he began an 18-year run as one of the most beloved newspaper reporters in the region. Maury Thompson finally fit in (*Post-Star* photograph by Bill Toscano).

lunch and another for supper," Thompson told *Post-Star* reporter Kathleen Phalen-Tomaselli in 2017.[11]

Along the way, he met and married his second wife, Nancy, and in 1992, he graduated from Middlebury College with a degree in English.[12]

He was 34.

Thompson taught part-time at North Country Community College and did some freelance work for the local Ticonderoga weekly newspaper. He eventually reached out to *Post-Star* regional editor Bob Condon about doing freelance work.

"I called Bob and sent him some clips," Thompson said. "I called Bob quite frequently, and he finally said, 'If you are this persistent as a reporter, you will do a good job.'"[13]

He started by covering meetings and events in Essex County and Ticonderoga where *The Post-Star* had a few hundred readers. By 1999, his output had become prolific.

Thompson was producing more stories as a freelancer than most of the full-time reporters in Glens Falls. In 1998, he made $23,000 at the newspaper in $25 and $35 increments. He was often working 14- to 18-hour days.

"There were times I would get up at 4 in the morning and write the story I reported the night before," he said. "Then, I would cover a daytime event, write it and file it, then go to a night meeting and file again.[14]

"I worked seven days a week," he said, before correcting himself, "Actually, it was six and a half days. I took a half day off on Sunday."[15]

But being a newspaper reporter was never Thompson's goal.

"I was trying to write enough to have a portfolio and write a book," Maury said. "I did not plan to stay in newspapers that long."[16]

It was not the plan, but it was his destiny.

Thompson was an odd presence with thick glasses. He was one of those people always at the edge of the conversation, shuffling up to the group, listening, eaves-dropping, even, waiting for an opportunity to join in. He often seemed to be hovering nearby in the newsroom, waiting to add his perspective but never bold enough to interrupt. When he told a story, it often ended with a thunderclap of a laugh even though the story was not that funny.

"Journalism has been a vehicle for me to finally fit into society," Thompson told Phalen-Tomaselli. "I've been the oddball. Journalism and writing provided a way for people to overlook my quirks and see the real me."[17]

By the spring of 1999, shortly after I became editor, I noticed Maury's coverage of outlying Essex County and Ticonderoga was better than anything we had in our core market.

I asked city editor Bob Condon if we should bring Thompson to Glens Falls as a full-time business writer. Condon endorsed the move but told me I needed to know something.[18]

Thompson had a degenerative eye disease. Before cornea transplant surgery in 1994, he was virtually blind in one eye, and the vision in the other eye was getting worse. The cornea transplant saved his sight, but his poor vision prevented him from driving.[19]

While a journalism degree was not mandatory, having a driver's license was essential in our rural region. Even more importantly for me, being unable to see would be a significant handicap for a reporter.

But Condon disagreed. He told me Thompson's condition never prevented him from going where he needed to go to get the news. He always found a way.[20]

Thompson was 42 when he was hired full-time as *The Post-Star*'s business reporter in 1999. He turned his handicap into his signature characteristic.

Thompson's version of the shoe-leather express was a throwback to another time when reporters, like cops, walked their beats and found stories along the way. He believed it made him a better reporter.

"I tell reporters, 'Leave your car at *The Post-Star*.' When you are driving, you can wave at someone. When you are walking, you can talk to them," Thompson told Phalen-Tomaselli.[21]

When needed, his wife, Nancy, or a co-worker would give him a ride to an outlying town. He sometimes took a taxi or bus.

Thompson always looked older than he was. When he was 42 and starting at *The Post-Star*, he looked 52. It probably gave him some needed credibility because he looked more like Perry White than Jimmy Olsen.

He became a regular sight walking the streets of Glens Falls with his graying hair, a slow, steady gait and a determined straight-ahead gaze through thick Mr. Magoo glasses.

More than once I pulled off to the side of the road on my drive to work and asked Thompson if he wanted a ride. As he settled into the seat beside me, it was only then he realized who was giving him a lift.

Thompson said he went through three pairs of shoes a year.[22] He simply wore them out. Through sleet and snow and rain, Maury made his rounds in a way that would make the postman envious. Not even a foot of snow could stop him.

More importantly, Thompson delivered an upbeat, breath-of-fresh-air demeanor to those he met along the way. It was clear he loved meeting and interacting with people, and it allowed him to find stories other reporters drove by.

By 2001, Thompson had been thrown into the middle of a contentious strike at the local Finch, Pruyn paper mill, the community's largest commercial employer at the time. The strike would last 159 days and was often boisterous and ugly.

At one union event, workers marched from the plant down by the Hudson River, up Glens Falls' Main Street through downtown. When they spotted Thompson, they hurled expletive after expletive at him. He smiled back, waved and said he would talk to them later.[23]

He never flinched.

It was one of the few times I ever heard anyone say anything bad about Thompson.

"Calling names was actually part of the theater," Thompson told me years later. "The difficult part was not getting personally swayed by either side."[24]

Thompson's good work on the business beat led to a promotion to the city of Glens Falls beat. He was evolving as a reporter who could charm you with a folksy column or drive home a point with no-holds-barred political coverage. His sources didn't see him as someone to be feared. When Senator Charles Schumer came to town, he often greeted Thompson by his first name.

"Tell the readers something they don't know, make them think, make them laugh or cry," Thompson told Phalen-Tomaselli.[25]

It's a credo all reporters should remember.

But opening your own life up for inspection is a special gift few reporters possess.

Nancy Thompson had been battling cancer for some time when Maury first wrote about it in 2002.

By late June, Maury acknowledged that Nancy had stopped treatment, and it was only a matter of time. I expected he would ask for some time off to be with her. Instead, he asked if he could write a series of columns about her final days.

Over a two-week period, Maury took readers through an emotional journey that offered a rare glimpse into the raw emotions of losing a loved one as it was happening. They were columns from the heart.[26] If you had ever lost a loved one, you could relate.

Even now, I don't know how to characterize this extraordinary gift of sharing. Maybe it was just how reporters deal with the most important stories in their lives— they write about them.

On June 27, 2002, Maury explained to his readers that Nancy's cancer had spread to her liver, and she had decided she was too weak to endure any more chemotherapy.[27]

"Accepting the reality that she was dying wasn't as hard as one might think, perhaps because we had months to prepare," Maury wrote. "In some respects, waiting to die is easier than struggling to stay alive."[28]

It was a reminder of the life and death that goes on all around us every day and how community newspapers are at the heart of reporting births, deaths, marriages and graduations. They are central to the lives of the readers they serve.

In some ways, the death of Nancy Thompson was just another daily occurrence in the community. But in this case, it was totally public.

"For my own part, I struggled night after night once everyone left to come up with some grand parting speech," Maury wrote on July 4. "But all I could manage to say is that we've had 18 great years together, and I was sure going to miss her."[29]

The honesty of that moment is still so powerful all these years later. Who could not relate?

"Death is a lot like romance," Maury wrote. "Trite sayings are cute Valentine's Day cards, but when you hold someone in your arms, 'I love you' is about the only phrase that seems fitting."[30]

Maury Thompson had reached his ultimate goal. He was now a professional writer.

In those final weeks, I noticed Maury spending more and more time at the office. More than once, I took him aside and told him to go home and not worry about work. I told him to go be with his wife.

A few days later, I received a letter from Nancy in strong handwriting. She told me that Maury had told her about my insistence he spend more time at home. She told me that she wanted Maury to do the thing that made him most happy—working at the newspaper.

I think Maury and Mary Joseph would have gotten along quite well.

I stopped bugging Maury.

A few days later, Nancy died.

On July 11, Maury closed his series on Nancy with these words:

On June 23, nine days before she died, Nancy was sitting up on the side of her hospital bed when I awoke.

I sat down beside her and put my arm around her waist.

She said to me, "A philosopher once said, 'Sometimes I sit and think, and other times I just sit.'"

"Which one are you doing today?" I asked, to which she replied, "A little bit of thinking, but mostly just sitting."

She had been listening to the birds, she went on to tell me.

Years of intimacy with nature had enabled Nancy to identify each species by its sound.

The thrushes are the first ones to begin chirping, she said. They appear at about 4 a.m. just before the rosy finger of dawn.

What value could one possibly place on hearing the birds sing one last time?[31]

It's the type of journalism you don't hear much about, more poetry than breaking news. It's the type of story that touches your soul, that brings a tear to your eye and gives a beating heart to the ink and paper.

How do you replace that when your newspaper is gone?

It is what Maury Thompson brought to the newspaper.

It is what newspapers bring to the community.

Not too long after Nancy died, a group of the men from the local paper mill visited Maury at the paper. They were some of same men who hurled expletives at Maury during the strike.[32]

"After the strike was over, when my wife died," Maury remembered, "a group of union men came to *The Post-Star* and presented me with a Bible that they give out to union members when a loved one died. The fact that I could come out of that [the strike] and be respected by both sides says a lot."[33]

And life goes on.

Not too long after Nancy died, Maury remarried. Debbie and Maury had been together 14 years in 2020.

In 2006, Thompson got permission from a man named Ken Ball to tell his story of his final days in hospice. It was not only the type of story few reporters want to tackle, but few are capable of doing justice.

"When I wrote about the House of Grace [and their hospice care] opening, I mentioned to their director, Irv West, that if they had a patient who wanted to tell their story, to let me know," Thompson said. "He called me a couple months later."[34]

Patients are only admitted to hospice when they have less than three months to live. That was the case with Ball. Thompson visited Ball three or four times a week and let him tell the stories of his life, his hopes and his fears about death.

But newspapers also run on schedules and have deadlines.

The Sunday editor scheduled Thompson's story on hospice five months after Thompson started visiting Ball. But a month before the story was due, Ball was still alive.

The story was postponed again, and again, and again.

We joked at the newspaper that the hospice man had found the fountain of youth. Finally, Thompson told the Sunday editor not to schedule the story again until after Ball passed.

Ken Ball lived ten months in hospice, and his family members later told Thompson they believed his visits lengthened Ball's life.

It was a difficult story for Thompson.

"You have to remember I went there three or four times a week," Thompson said. "You have to remember your role is as a storyteller. You can't let yourself get too emotionally involved."[35]

During one part of the series, Thompson shared Ball's observation about the geese he saw flying overhead, correcting Maury that they are "Canada geese" and not "Canadian geese."[36]

"It's a technical thing," Ball said.[37]

Thompson wrote this at the conclusion of the series:

Ken Ball taught me death doesn't have to be an ugly thing.

I began this writing project expecting to chronicle the musings of a man grappling with fate. But Ken dealt with the uncertainty of death the way a parent deals with a child who is afraid of the dark.

He turned a night light on, so to speak. Once the shadows were gone, the room wasn't such a scary place at all.[38]

I wondered after all that time how Maury had maintained his objectivity.

"The week the story was set to run, Debbie and I were at the Schuyler House mansion," Maury remembered. "We were waiting in line for the next tour when a flock of geese flew overhead, heading south. That's when it really hit me."[39]

Maury later became our political reporter and soon was on a first-name basis with U.S. Senator Charles Schumer.

His blog "All Politics Are Local" was one of our most popular digital features for years.

Another time while doing a story on a local rap artist, Thompson went into the studio and made a rap video for our website. This little man with the thick glasses was fearless.

He played the piano at nursing homes and coffee shops around town. He played at Nancy's memorial service, too.

In 2007, Thompson was honored by our parent company with Lee Enterprises "Spirit Award" for his "outstanding personal commitment" to the newspaper. But that wasn't quite right. This was about his commitment to the community.[40]

Thompson continued to gravitate toward historical projects. That led to "The 55" project in 2010.

Thompson chronicled the stories of the 55 local young men who lost their lives in the Vietnam War. He not only told their stories, but the bigger story of how the war affected the community.[41]

Health issues took their toll on Thompson in later years, and he counted down the number of days until his retirement in 2017 so he could pursue his real passion—writing books with a historical theme.

In 2011, Thompson published "The Biggest Kid at the Balloon Festival." It was a story about Adirondack Balloon Festival's Founder Walt Grishkot.[42] This was the work Thompson had always dreamed of doing.

In the spring of 2021, I read in the newspaper that Thompson had just completed production of a documentary on the life of Glens Falls native and Supreme Court Justice Charles Evans Hughes that would be shown on the regional PBS channel.[43]

For 18 years, Thompson let Glens Falls readers see the world around them with precision, detail and clarity while opening up his heart to everyone he met. Not bad for a guy who was legally blind.

What was so rare was that Thompson did his work quietly, without controversy or animosity from his sources or any of our readers.

During his final Common Council meeting in 2017, Glens Falls Mayor Jack Diamond issued a proclamation for "Maury Thompson Day" in Glens Falls, and Thompson received a rousing ovation from the mayor, Common Council and all those in attendance.[44]

Newspaper reporters rarely get their own day.

Heck, they rarely get a pat on the back.

Thompson loved to tell the tales of his daily exploits in the newsroom, punctuated by that booming laugh.

When conducting phone interviews in the newsroom, he could drown out conversations around him. Once, when reconfiguring the newsroom desks, our publisher at the time took me aside and suggested Thompson's desk be as far from his office door as possible. He was too loud.

After Maury Thompson retired in 2017, the newsroom was far too quiet.

But Maury could not stay away for long. By 2022, Maury's byline was regularly appearing in *The Post-Star* again.

5

Growing Up Gay

Sometimes, it is what happens after the story is published that is more important and sometimes more disturbing.

It was the conversation that took place in our Glens Falls community and around the region in coffee shops, at dinner tables and on the pages of the newspaper over the rest of that hot summer that reveals the heart of what newspapers do.

Those words, those arguments were in many ways some of the first steps in working through and accepting those who might be different. Newspapers have the power to do that in small communities.

"During his high school years, John Cozzens III said he spent a lot of nights crying into a pillow and thinking he was a freak."[1]

That's how *Post-Star* reporter Matt Sturdevant started his story on Sunday, July 14, 2002.

But I know that's not what grabbed the readers by the throat.

The headline read: "Growing up Gay" with the first two words "GROWING UP" stretching across one column of the front page and "GAY" blown up boldly to stretch across the second line in much bigger type. It was designed to catch the eye of the reader.

The subhead explained further, even if it was understated: "North Country homosexuals say isolation was difficult."

But it wasn't the headline that was the body blow to readers that morning; it was the photograph over three columns of newsprint that ran next to it.[2]

Our editors deemed the photo controversial enough that I took the rare step of running it by publisher Jim Marshall several days before it ran.

I explained to him the context of the Sunday front-page story, the depth of the journalism and my own belief that many of our readers would be shocked by the image. I told him we would take some heat.

He looked at the photograph for a long while.

The full-color photo showed a young couple about to kiss in a wedding photo-type setting next to a fountain in Congress Park in Saratoga Springs. It is a place where wedding photos are still taken.

Marshall told me to go ahead and print it.

In a 300-word explanation of the couple-kissing photo that ran on the front page that day, I asked our readers: "So what's wrong with that?"[3]

Both were members of the same sex, I revealed in the next paragraph.

"I knew there would be quite a reaction," Marshall remembered 18 years later. "But I didn't have any problems with that stuff. I didn't think it was a big deal in our community, so why not bring it up."[4]

My managing editor column that Sunday addressed and acknowledged that we believed this would be a controversial photograph for some readers.

"On the front page of today's *Post-Star* there is a photograph that some of our readers might not like," I wrote. "But when we saw the photograph that goes with the story, we paused and we paused again. We did not want to appear that we were trying to sensationalize the story with the photo. We did not want the photo to overshadow the story to the extent that people would not want to read the story. It's not that we felt our readers are homophobic—although I'm sure some are—but homosexuality can be a controversial topic and the last thing we wanted was for people not to read the story."[5]

I explained how we made the decision and how at our weekly Sunday meeting, several editors expressed concern about running the photo. One suggested we run the photo on an inside page instead of on the front page. Another suggested we run the story on another day of the week instead of Sunday.[6]

Finally, a third editor said that one of the reasons we were doing the story was for disenfranchised young people. She said there were young people growing up in our community right now trying to come to grips with their sexuality.[7] Interviews from the story confirmed how difficult it was to grow up without gay role models. Several of those interviewed confirmed how scared and miserable they were because they thought they were all alone.

"Maybe the photo will get just such young people to read this story so that they will see that they are not alone as they come to grips with who they are," I wrote in my column. "This is an important message to deliver."[8]

Two weeks later, Ruby A. Hayner of Johnstown confirmed the importance of that goal with a letter to the editor, thanking us for the "Growing up Gay" story.

"It really seems wonderful for a close-by newspaper to finally have the courage enough to write about gays and lesbians. After all we are people," Hayner wrote in a letter to the editor published July 31. "For a long time, the closed-mindedness of individuals who think that homosexuality is nasty and homosexuals should be treated differently and with disgust and total disregard at times for our lifestyle really makes my blood boil. I think I may speak on behalf of all the gays and lesbians out there when I say that all we want is to live our lives in harmony with others. We want to raise our families, work our jobs, pay our taxes, and live just like anyone else would."[9]

Sturdevant had been working on the story for several months, I explained to our readers. He had talked to many gay men and women, young and old, about growing up gay in a mostly rural and conservative area—our region in eastern upstate New York.

"We felt it was an important story to tell about a segment of our community that we often do not report on," I wrote that day. "In the past 10 years, gay men and women have become more open about their lifestyles than ever before and we thought it would be important to tell their stories."[10]

Talking to Sturdevant 18 years later, he said it was important to understand the context of the times.

"Above all, the legislative and pop culture context is key in understanding what I was thinking in 2002," Sturdevant said. "In 2002, it was just two years after Vermont had allowed civil unions and the backlash was swift. Nebraska had the 'one man, one woman [legislation].' There was Proposition 22 in California. And if you think about pop culture, there was the musical *Rent*, you had Ellen DeGeneres telling *Time* she was gay, followed by the popular entertainer Rosie O'Donnell and the *Will and Grace* television show was a hit."[11]

At that time, I think we were like many newspapers in conservative communities who avoided delving too deeply into social issues because of the blowback.

Just acknowledging there was such a thing as a gay lifestyle was at least a step forward as states and communities around the country grappled with the issue of allowing same-sex couples to be legal partners.

It was during this national discussion that Vermont—which bordered several small communities our newspaper served to the east—became the first state to introduce civil unions in July 2000. It was a debate that was deeply polarizing and carried over into Vermont's fall election.

David Moats, the editorial page editor at the *Rutland Herald* at the time, remembered the debate in Vermont going back even further. Rutland was a community newspaper similar to ours.[12]

"The whole issue of gay rights had been brewing for the previous decade," Moats said in 2020. "Something like 1996, there was a big furor about a book in the library, *Heather has Two Mommies*, where there was a big public hearing. I remember engaging with the issue on the editorial page, so I had a sense of how sensitive it was."[13]

When the Vermont Supreme Court ruled in 1999 that the civil union issue was the responsibility of the legislature, Moats said, "all hell broke lose."[14]

Moats described a four-month period in 2001 when the Vermont State Legislature debated the issue. It dominated the news throughout Vermont, and Moats made the decision to weigh in repeatedly on the newspaper's editorial page.[15]

"There was not unanimity within the newspaper on whether to take a strong stand being pro on civil unions," Moats remembered. "People [at the newspaper] were selling ads and would encounter resistance. They had to face merchants and shopkeepers who had their own ideas that were not pro civil unions. The newspaper was right in the middle of it."[16]

When the civil unions legislation finally passed, Vermont governor Howard Dean made tempered remarks and signed the bill privately with just a few aides present.

"There is much to celebrate about this bill," Dean said in 2000. "Those celebrations, as the subject of this bill, will be private. They will be celebrated by couples and their families, by people making commitments to each other.... I believe this bill enriches all of us as we look with new eyes at a group of people who have been outcasts for many, many generations."[17]

Sturdevant was a 25-year-old features reporter who had joined the newspaper a year and a half earlier after graduating from SUNY Oswego. To his credit, he was looking to do something significant when it was his turn to do a Sunday project.

"Civil unions were roiling things in Vermont, and obviously the Adirondacks are right next door," Sturdevant said.[18]

Sturdevant remembered conversations with Sunday editor Will Doolittle about the issue. They wondered who was calling for civil unions in the Adirondacks. There had to be advocates.[19]

"Surely these people in the Adirondacks don't feel comfortable telling their stories," Sturdevant said. "What are the stories of those people in Fort Ann and Ticonderoga. This is before social media, before people had an opportunity to see other gay teenagers growing up."[20]

Sturdevant said it was Doolittle who was instrumental in urging him to tell the story in a broader context that crossed generations with a variety of voices.

"I think Will showed me that taking a bold and brave stand in reporting and writing is always a good idea," Sturdevant said. "Being bold in your writing leads to having those difficult conversations."[21]

Perhaps that bold approach is what resonated most with our readers and maybe what they objected to with the story.

Sturdevant provided heart-wrenching experiences of local people, young and old, male and female, who had grown up in our communities and been ostracized and ridiculed.

If there is one thing our communities take great pride in, it is this reputation as "Hometown, USA," where the quality of life is unparalleled, a little slower, a little less complex and old-fashioned values are a way of life. Sturdevant's reporting showed a darker side to those old-fashioned values for those who were different.

"These were pretty powerful interviews," Sturdevant said. "Look, one guy said he had contemplated suicide. That was jarring for me … and sad. I wanted to tell the stories of people who felt marginalized."[22]

From an editor's viewpoint, what was especially impressive was that Sturdevant was able to get everyone on the record. Perhaps that was the pop culture influence of Ellen DeGeneres and Rosie O'Donnell that allowed others—even in the smallest of our rural communities—to be brave and tell their stories, too. These people wanted to make a difference.

Sturdevant wrote this in the article:

> But life can be isolating in the North County, where young gays and lesbians have few, if any, local role models. It's hard for local homosexual teens to feel accepted when they keenly feel their differences with their peers. And some say they will face taunting from family members and other students.[23]

Sturdevant had to find the people, coax them to tell about the difficulties they had in their lives and convince them to be identified in the story.

"They have to live here," Sturdevant said in 2020. "They are coming out, not just to their close friends, but to the entire tri-county area."[24]

What was so strong about Sturdevant's reporting was the diversity of the subjects who talked with him and went on the record. He talked to high school and college students as well as those who were older and had grown up in the 1970s and 1980s. This wasn't just a recent development; it had been going on for generations.

Walter Lape, a 59-year-old retired English teacher from Queensbury High, stood out for providing context on the experience and the survival.

"Queers" were perceived to be "the worst possible thing," Lape told Sturdevant about his time growing up in Albany, New York, in the 1970s.[25]

"I never even considered dating or dancing with a man—that just wasn't done," said Lape. "When I was growing up, being homosexual was considered a mental illness. Some people still think it is, and some people think it's a choice, but it's neither."[26]

It's a jarring reminder now of how far we've come, but in 2002 there were many who still felt that way.

Sarah Brunetto, a 17-year-old from Warrensburg, told Sturdevant about being accosted by three boys while walking to her father's house in the small town.

"They told me I should leave," Brunetto said in the article, "that I was a disgrace to my town and my family, and that I'll never amount to anything."[27]

The article dug deeply into the psychological challenges that so many individuals grappled with in accepting their sexuality.

"I was 8 years old when my dad asked my mother if I was gay," Chris Sherman said in the article. "Coming out was not an issue because of my homophobic father and homophobic school. I was perceived to be gay. People made phony advances toward me.... It was completely humiliating."[28]

After graduating, Sherman was asked to speak at other schools about his experience growing up gay. At one high school, he told a story about a time in the gym locker room when two students poked at his backside with a broom handle. They said, "You probably like that, don't you?"[29]

Mike Wilming, a 19-year-old student at Adirondack Community College (now SUNY Adirondack), told Sturdevant, "I would always hide myself from people, so I wouldn't have to face abuse. I put on a different face when I was home. I was made fun of by my family and my father. I guess you could say I lived a lonely life."[30]

Another 16-year-old said he decided to come out after seeking therapy. Others admitted they sought therapy as well because of their sexuality.

"Being gay is hard because it's such a closeted thing," said Marvin Day, who was a physician's assistant in 2002. "There are no norms in place, you didn't see any positive role models in the community when I was growing up."[31]

The stories, piled one on top of another, were heartbreaking because of the bullying and ignorance. Some readers criticized us for promoting a gay lifestyle.

Caity Creitz, a 17-year-old from Cambridge who was instrumental in organizing the first school board-approved Gay/Straight Alliance in her small school in Washington County, pulled a poster from her diary of a Gay/Straight Alliance meeting. Written on the poster were the words "Hate Fags."[32]

"No matter what you do, there is going to be hate," she said.

Lape, the 59-year-old former teacher, told Sturdevant it was important for people not to believe stereotypes.

"Gay men and women are not only artists, and they're not the best chefs," he said. "That perception of gay people is as skewed as the other extreme that all gays are running around with chains and whips. They're both stereotypes."[33]

The reporting was enlightening to the uninitiated in 2002.

When Lape's partner died in 1995, the Queensbury Parent Teacher Student Association noticed the obituary in the newspaper.

"To show you how beautiful the community of Queensbury is, the PTSA sent a sympathy card," Lape said.[34]

In 1995, such a small acknowledgment was unprecedented and obviously something Lape saw as a monumental step forward.

Lape recounted a story about reading an excerpt from his book *Alaska Waters* to one of his classes.

"The mission of 'Alaska Waters' was to have some gay characters in the book where that's not the issue, although it's part of the story," he explained in the article.

"Little by little, people change their point of view and their perspective on things and the more they know someone who is different, the more they realize that they are not different," Lape said. "Sexual orientation should be a non-issue. It isn't, but gradually it's becoming less and less important."[35]

That's how Sturdevant ended the story with hope for change and understanding in our communities.

Hope and understanding were not what we saw initially in the community response.

"I think that without a doubt I expected a [negative] reaction," Sturdevant said 18 years later. "At least 20 or 30 emails came in that either wished me dead, or worse, I was going to go to hell. Many invoked religion, calling me amoral for giving voice and highlighting the experience growing up gay. There was a lot of vitriol. Over 16 years as a journalist, you grow a tough skin."[36]

But Sturdevant did not have that protective layer at the age of 25. "These had some sting to it," he admitted.[37]

The day after the story ran, a woman called to complain. She told me she now had to explain to her eight-year-old son what homosexuality was after he asked about the photo on the front page of the newspaper.

"Is that a bad thing?" I asked.[38]

The letters to the editor were brutal in their bigotry.

Consider some of the headlines for the letters over the succeeding three weeks:

July 22, 2002
Paper should avoid
Offensive subjects[39]

Politically correct is
Not morally correct[40]

July 23, 2002
Homosexuality just
A human weakness[41]

Picture offensive,
Story misleading[42]

July 25, 2002
Story on homosexuals
Inappropriate, trashy[43]

July 28, 2002
Lonely men, women
Should turn to God[44]

Story did not address
Needs of readers[45]

July 29, 2002
Gays should stay
In the closet[46]

Photo choice
Was disgusting[47]

August 3, 2002
Media promotes
Liberal agenda[48]

August 4, 2002
"Tender moment,"
Subject are sickening[49]

August 10, 2002
Front-page photo
Was in poor taste[50]

"Disgusting, inappropriate and disappointing are some of the words which come to mind to describe the front page of *The Post-Star* on Sunday, July 14," wrote Jamie and Barbara Thew of Granville on July 22, 2002. "Disgusting because our family doesn't need to be exposed to the gay lifestyle/agenda in our own home. The gay lifestyle is a perversion of God's plan for mankind. Inappropriate because we would venture to guess that the vast majority of people are not gay; so we don't want to see or hear about it. Seeing the front page picture was unavoidable because of its layout [which I'm sure was the intention]. Our young son brought in the newspaper that day as he usually does; you can bet he saw that picture."[51]

On the same day, Carl Thomas of Stony Creek wrote this: "This was the last straw for me. *The Post-Star* has reached the bottom of the cesspool. Today I was greeted by a repulsive picture along with an article on homosexuality and the gay lifestyle."[52]

Eighteen years later, Thomas was still writing letters to the editor to be published in the newspaper. I think that says something, too.

"Imagine opening my Sunday, July 14 *Post-Star* to a photograph of two homosexuals smooching in Congress Park! And it only got worse as I read Matthew Sturdevant's article," wrote Robert Lockrow in his July 23 letter. "Biased and distorted, it depicted those who oppose the homosexual lifestyle as cruel and vulgar louts."[53]

He concluded his letter by saying, "Everyone is born with weaknesses, which if indulged lead eventually to destruction. Homosexuality is simply another human weakness."

For the next three weeks, the criticism of the article—and some who defended it—continued on our letters to the editor page.

The conversation was in full throat.

On July 28, two weeks after I had explained to readers the reason for our photo and story, I followed up with readers on the response.

"So I expected people to be uncomfortable. And I expected it to cause a community debate. But it is a compelling story about the trials and tribulations of growing up gay in our communities," I wrote in my managing editor column. "What I did not expect was the amount of pure venom and hate that spewed from so many of our readers. Many took issue with the decision to run the photo, some because it ran on a Sunday, others because they felt it promoted a gay lifestyle and some because they felt we were pursuing some gay agenda. Unfortunately, most of the reaction was pure and unadulterated hatred toward homosexuals. I was shocked to hear such hate from people—men and women alike—who could be my neighbors."[54]

Over the years, I learned that an initial negative reaction from the community is often followed by a second wave with a different viewpoint.

Eighty to 90 percent of the readers who initially responded had a negative reaction to the article. But then we started to hear more encouraging words.

"Let's not leave out that there was a lot of positive," Sturdevant remembered. "There was some people who said, 'You know, it is an affirmation for me to see gay culture in the newspaper written about and talked about because it was very isolating growing up here. So if a paper isn't leading courageous conversation, what other forum in the community will do it?'"[55]

It is a point even more valid today.

The Rev. Anthony W. Green of Schuylerville wrote this in a letter to the editor published on July 28:

> Thank God for *The Post-Star* and reporters like Matthew Sturdevant. And thank God for the young people who stepped out in the face of hate and oppression. I have deep respect for your act of courage. You have helped to break through the wall of silence and fear so that life may be a little easier for all of us who are gay and want to claim our dignity. This is especially true for the generations to follow.[56]

Mary Hewitt heard about the article on the other side of the state in Buffalo, New York, and wrote this in a July 27 letter:

> I am very proud of your courage in writing and publishing an article on homosexuality in your area. I know it was a brave, difficult decision to make. If more people were educated about this subject, there would not be so much homophobia in the world.[57]

And Al Laubinger of South Glens Falls wrote this in a letter published on August 7:

> I salute *The Post-Star* for publishing, and compliment Matt Sturdevant for writing, your recent exceptional article on gays and lesbians in the Glens Falls area. The persecution by those who have set themselves up as the sole arbiters of personal behavior is unfair, unjust and intolerant, and if I may say so bigoted.[58]

But no letter was as heartening as the one from Jennifer Leitch in the small town of Fort Ann in Washington County:

> I am appalled by the reaction of so many *Post-Star* readers. I have seen the words "nauseating, unnatural and sickening" used to describe the article, homosexuals and their basic human right to happiness. One gentleman [if you could call him that] was so bold as to blatantly lump homosexuality in with acts such as "incest, bestiality and cannibalism." Don't true respondents realize that by their words they are only fueling a fire of ignorance and malice that is spreading to our youth?[59]

Marshall, *The Post-Star* publisher, remembered getting a phone call from one of the newspaper's owners—Howard Publications at the time—reminding him that this type of subject matter was best to be avoided. Marshall never shared the thought with anyone in the newsroom.[60]

It had been just a year since our neighbor to the east—the *Rutland Herald*—was honored with the Pulitzer Prize for editorial writing for David Moats's editorials on the civil union debate in Vermont. The citation read: "For his even-handed and influential series of editorials commenting on the divisive issues arriving from civil unions for same-sex couples."[61]

Moats said in 2020 that the Rutland newspaper's Pulitzer Prize was a "vindication" for so many in the state who had fought for the issue.[62]

"There was a huge outpouring of support for the newspaper," Moats said. "The outside world had come in on the side of those who had struggled and advocated for civil unions."[63]

As an editor of a small newspaper, I know firsthand what it is like when you do something that offends your readership. But that's what the *Rutland Herald* did with a series of 20 editorials in 2001.

"This newspaper didn't wait to see which way the wind was blowing. It made a decision, and in the face of angry readers, it stood its ground," I wrote to our readers after *Rutland*'s Pulitzer Prize was announced in April 2001. "That's what great journalism is about."[64]

That's courage.

Who will take those courageous stands in the future?

It would be nine more years before New York state would make same-sex marriage legal.

Looking back in 2020, it appeared Sturdevant and Doolittle were ahead of their time in addressing the issue in Glens Falls.

In many ways, the community reaction was discouraging.

"Homosexuality exists in our world. Our story made that plain and obvious," I wrote in the July 28 managing editor column. "Hate, intolerance and homophobia also exist in our world. That was made obvious by the reaction to our story and photo."[65]

But it had been exposed, and I considered that a step forward.

"The story has created a dialogue, a discussion about homosexuality in this community," I wrote. "Hopefully, that leads to more understanding, and most of all, less hate."[66]

Sturdevant would leave *The Post-Star* that November for a three-year stint at the *Caller Times* in Corpus Christi, Texas. He eventually came back east to get a master's degree at Dartmouth College before returning to newspapers in Newport News, Virginia, and the *Hartford* (CT) *Courant* to cover the insurance industry. Along the way he married and had two children.

But after the second child was born in 2015, he left the newspaper business and eventually became head of public relations at an insurance company.

"I really, really tried [to make the newspaper career] work," he said almost apologetically to me in 2020. "I wanted to make it work, but with the cost of day care and student loans combined with my wife's full-time job and weekend shifts at the hospital...."[67]

It was a loss for local journalism.

In February 2018, Moats's job as opinion page editor at the *Rutland Herald* was eliminated, and he was laid off.[68]

It was another loss for journalism among so many in recent years. How do you lay off a Pulitzer Prize winner?

What is left is the legacy of Moats changing his little corner of the world, inspiring Sturdevant to be bold and daring with his reporting and writing to improve another corner of the world. One journalist building on the legacy of the next and improving the world around them one story and editorial at a time.

That's how it worked for generations.

By 2020, that foundation lay in tatters at small community newspapers all across the country.

Bonnie Parker, an RN who was the executive director of HiTOPS Teen Health and Education Center in Princeton (NJ) and who also had a summer home in the Adirondacks, wrote a letter in 2002 that made us feel better about the criticism for "Growing up Gay."

"Congrats on taking this subject on and playing it with great respect and head on," Parker wrote in the letter published on July 23, 2002. "I hope many of the youth in your community read it through and feel the support it is sure to generate for them. Even more, I hope the parents and school officials read it and begin, as Walter Lape says, to little by little change their perspective on gays."[69]

It has been more than ten years since same-sex marriage was made law in New York. Glens Falls and its surrounding communities have changed, too.

Lape, the teacher at the end of Sturdevant's article who foresaw a day of acceptance, did not live to see same-sex marriage become New York state law in 2011. He died in hospice care on April 25, 2010, in St. Petersburg, Florida.

His obituary recognized Lape as a "respected English teacher in Queensbury for 32 years." It also acknowledged his "life partner" and concluded by saying, "Walter was passionate in his advocacy of equal rights."[70]

6

"She has suffered enough..."

Lesley Ingraham awoke in the pre-dawn hours a few days before Thanksgiving in 2002 to a downstairs bedroom filled with black, smothering smoke.[1]

Her four children—three boys and a girl—were upstairs. The 33-year-old mother stumbled out the front door into the frosty November darkness gasping for air and wearing nothing but a long T-shirt.[2]

"I was just screaming for my babies," she said.[3]

Her screams pierced the early-morning solitude of the hardscrabble neighborhood squeezed between the Hudson River down the hill and the Washington County Jail across the street on the other side of the railroad tracks. The General Electric factory was just down the road.

Across the street, Robert Borden was pulling on his boots to go deer hunting when he heard the cries for help. He looked out the window to see big, orange flames shooting out from under the eaves of the yellow house and Ingraham screaming, "Get out! Get out!"[4]

Her oldest son, 12-year-old James Rousseau, appeared at his bedroom window. For a fleeting few seconds, Borden saw the boy, too, as Lesley screamed for him to jump.[5]

Instead, the boy dropped down a small toy and yelled to his mother he was going back to get his two brothers and sister.[6]

Rodney Hatch, who lived two houses away on the same side of the road, heard Lesley's screams, too, and tried to get into the house through a side door.

"I couldn't," he said. "There was just too much smoke and fire. It went up so fast, the whole thing went up in like two minutes."[7]

The old, two-story house was squeezed into a shallow, rectangular lot between two other houses with the front porch close to the road.

From across the street, Borden saw Hatch kick in the door. "But you could tell it was already too late," Borden told *The New York Times*. "It was already up in flames and nobody was getting out of there."[8]

Borden also said he heard the sounds of children screaming.[9]

"All I saw was smoke and fire coming out of the upstairs," neighbor Shirley Pratt said. "Lesley was frantic outside. I asked, 'Where are the kids?' And she said, 'I couldn't get them out.'"[10]

Lesley Ingraham stood helpless in the front yard of the rundown duplex as the flames roared through the house in front of her. It was the Tuesday before Thanksgiving.

Darrin Youker, who had been a *Post-Star* reporter since January and was 25 at the time, arrived at the scene shortly after 9 a.m.[11]

"I was probably there a half-hour when the mom arrived with a group of peo-ple," Youker said in 2020. "She was wrapped up in a dingy blanket and had a 500-yard stare. She looked, well, 'tired' is not the right word. It was more like shell shock. I didn't want to approach her with a large group around her so at one point she walked over toward the house."[12]

A reporter from a larger newspaper stopped her and handed her his business card and walked away. Youker approached and told Ingraham who he was.[13]

"I am so sorry for all you are going through," Youker remembered telling Ingra-ham. "But if you and I don't talk, all I'm going to know about your kids is their names and ages."[14]

Ingraham started to talk.

"After a certain point, I knew that God had taken them," Ingraham said.[15]

She described what happened in the minutes after the fire and lamented she had not moved after being told about previous fires in the house.

"It is hard when you live on $700 a month and try to give your kids some joy," Ingraham told Youker.[16]

The four children were found upstairs at approximately 8 a.m. The three boys were found on top of a bed with the oldest, James, lying on top of his two younger half-brothers, Ky (eight) and Damien (seven). The family dog was under the bed. Nine-year-old Courtney, who slept in another room, was found in the bathroom with a towel wrapped around her mouth.[17]

Then Ingraham told Youker about the children and how James helped with the younger kids. She remembered when he got mad at her he would talk in French, his favorite subject.[18]

She told Youker her daughter, Courtney, wanted to be a nurse, and she helped take care of her sick grandfather.[19]

She said Ky was her little troublemaker, and Damian was always able to bring a smile to her face.[20]

Ingraham smiled for just a second before a tear ran down her cheek.[21]

"They were good kids," Ingraham said. "They've been through a lot. They've had a hard life."[22]

They were small details, but they humanized the story to show a mother's loss. These are the interviews no reporter wants to do, but I wonder all these years later if these interviews provide a triage for the soul in times of tragedy.

"It was one of the most difficult interviews of my career," said Youker, who is now a lobbyist for the Pennsylvania Farm Bureau and has three kids of his own. "It was haunt-ing. I just remember her telling me, 'My kids had a hard life.' That was gut-wrenching."[23]

It's another part of the community newspaper story that goes beyond report-ing the news and selling a few more newspapers because of a tragedy. When it is done properly, the reporting provides a soul to a tragic loss while the heart of an entire community aches.

The front page of The Post-Star screamed the headline "Fire kills 4 children" the next day over a large horizontal photograph of grim-looking neighbors surrounding Lesley Ingraham wrapped in a blanket as she talked on a cordless telephone.[24]

The tragedy at 583 Lower Allen Street in Fort Edward in the hours before Thanksgiving 2002 was epic for the sadness it inflicted on the small working-class town, but it went beyond that. It pulled communities and people together from around the region to help the Ingraham family. And while we all hugged our children a little closer that Thanksgiving, it also tore at the community with rampant rumors that were not true.

The tragedy was recognized as the newspaper's most newsworthy story of 2002, not only because of the loss of life of four children but for the sacrifice of the oldest boy.[25]

"He had more guts, for a 12-year-old kid," the neighbor Borden told Youker, his voice trailing off. "He was a hero, even considering the outcome."[26]

Borden was so moved by the boy's sacrifice, he wrote a letter to the editor that was published a few days later in the newspaper.

"James, the bravest hero I'll ever know, the kid who used to make me wonder, still leaves me in wonderment," Borden wrote. "Please never forget these children."[27]

The day after the fatal fire, a double bunk bed charred black could be seen through a gaping hole in the second floor.

Two days later—on the Saturday after Thanksgiving—approximately 250 mourners gathered at the Gospel Lighthouse Church in Hudson Falls for an hour-long funeral service.[28] *The Post-Star* was there because this is something else community newspapers do in time of grief and mourning. They help their readers grieve, too, even if they didn't know the victims personally.

At the end of the service, each mourner was invited to walk to the front of the church and ring a bell next to each of the four small coffins. The ringing of the bells symbolized the children getting their angel wings in heaven.[29]

As the bells were rung repeatedly, Lesley and Roger Ingraham and other family members broke into trembling sobs.[30]

The headstones for the four children lie flat to the ground on the eastern edge of Union Cemetery in Hudson Falls, New York, the plots side by side so they catch the first rays of sunshine in the morning. It was James who ignored his mother's pleas to jump from the second-floor window. Instead, he went inside to get his siblings. James's body was found spread eagle over his two younger brothers. While all the headstones depict an angel, James's is the only one soaring in flight (photograph by Ken Tingley).

Too often this type of community reporting is looked at as predatory, an invasion of privacy under tragic circumstances to sell newspapers. Too many times, firefighters and police officers have hindered reporters from doing their job to report the news during tragic fires and accidents.

But when the tragedy is community wide, the newspaper becomes the vessel for community-wide grief and a tool for preventing the tragedy from happening again.

The children were buried side by side on the eastern edge of historic Union Cemetery in Fort Edward. Their graves are among the first to feel the warmth of the rising sun. Their headstones are simple and flat to the ground with the essential information from their time on earth. Carved on the left-hand side of the stones for Damien, Ky and Courtney is the same kneeling angel. For James—the boy who went back into the burning building to get his siblings—there is an older angel on the far left of the stone, wings spread in flight and soaring into the sky.

At the burial, 40 mourners watched as Roger and Lesley and other relatives released eight doves into the sky to symbolize "love, peace and unity."[31]

But what followed was far more insidious, with whispers that Lesley Ingraham should have done more.

Lesley Ingraham, in the eyes of some, was guilty of still being alive.

In the days after the funeral there was more criticism of Lesley, as well as other rumors. I finally asked in my December 13 column, "What would you do?"[32]

That became the question, the debate around dinner tables all across the region—and in our own newsroom—about whether you could have saved your own children. I wrote that it wasn't fair:

> You are disoriented. You can smell the acrid smoke choking the life out of you. You start to cough, fighting for breath.
> You make your way out of the bedroom and into the hallway. You can feel the heat. You see the fire.
> You can hardly breathe. Your surroundings look strange. You are not sure where you are.
> Immediately, your thoughts turn to your four children upstairs.
> What do you do?
> We all know what we think we would do. We'd charge up those stairs, through the flames and somehow, in the blackness and thick smoke, find those children—our pride, our job, our reason for being—and somehow get them out of the house.
> Or die trying.[33]

I was asking for empathy. I was asking our readers to walk a few feet in Lesley Ingraham's stockinged feet on that dark November morning when she was turned back by the heat, and her lungs filled with black smoke. I wanted them to feel the heat, to smell the smoke and, most of all, to imagine the fear and panic.

I argued none of us knew what we would do in such a crisis.

This is another part of the community discussion we are losing. It was simply about forgiveness and compassion, and afterward I had readers tell me I was wrong and insist they would have done more. I concluded my column this way:

> We all wonder, we all want to believe that love for our children will keep them out of harm's way, that it will help us to be brave and wise and smart in a crisis.
> We like to believe that this overwhelming love that we possess will save them.
> That isn't necessarily how the story ends in the real world.

Often, it ends in tragedy such as this case.

Often it ends with the parent dying, too.

So don't judge Lesley Ingraham.

Don't think that you could have done better under the circumstances until you have had to face them.

The woman has lost her four children. She has suffered enough for a lifetime.[34]

It got worse for Lesley Ingraham and her estranged husband Roger. One rumor said Lesley was not home at the time of the fire. Another suggested she had time to get dressed and put on shoes before escaping. (She had gone to a neighbor's house for some clothes and a blanket afterward.) And a third rumor had Lesley and Roger fleeing to Florida with donated money for a trip to Disney World.

Letters to the editor critical of Lesley were submitted and rejected as being too harsh for such a tragedy. I considered them heartless. When I told one caller we had checked on the rumors and found them to be untrue, she didn't believe me.

Newspapers don't usually address rumors. They try not to tackle hypotheticals in their news stories, but I believed these needed to be addressed.

"In the course of reporting on these stories, our reporters checked on many of the rumors and innuendo surrounding the tragedy and found the rumors to be unfounded; just people talking," I wrote in my managing editor column. "One woman called the newspaper, livid, and repeated the rumors to me. I assured her that we had looked into them and found them to be untrue."[35]

It was an early version of "fake news." Maybe, it had always been there.

"We often hear that you can't believe everything you read in the newspaper," I said at the end of my column. "But in this case, if you haven't read it in the newspaper, you should question its validity."[36]

For the year-end story, reporter Youker, who was there the morning of the fire, visited with Lesley and Roger in his apartment in Hudson Falls.

"I remember we spent a lot of time on the rumors," Youker remembered 18 years later. "I got the sense, 'bitter' might be the wrong word, but that she was hurt by those allegations that were lobbed against her."[37]

"None of those stories measured up to the police official version of the events," Youker wrote in the December 29 story.[38]

The couple, separated at the time of the fire, told Youker they were trying to reconnect in their marriage and that Lesley had moved into Roger's apartment.

"He's all I have left," Lesley said at the time, but she was also haunted that she wasn't able to do more. "I kind of blamed myself because I could not save my kids."[39]

There was more to the story beyond the rumors.

The building, previously owned by Craig Duell, had been in foreclosure for about a year with Chase Manhattan Bank holding the deed, but it had not been condemned as some neighbors believed. The family had lived there for four years.

Roger Ingraham said the house was in rough shape and had frequent electrical problems. He said he had personally replaced several light sockets and electrical outlets.[40]

After the fire, Youker reported that investigators believed the fire started when sagging floorboards came to rest on the natural-gas-fueled basement furnace and eventually ignited. They also found the furnace had not been serviced in some time, and while floor joists had been repaired in some spots, portions of the floor were sagging. The wiring was also not up to code. Escape from the fire was further hindered by the lack of smoke detectors.[41]

"There were major violations; wires were just hanging out and some were taped together," Washington County fire investigator Kevin Shepherd said. "The construction was in poor shape."[42]

The previous July, neighbors complained to town code enforcement officers there were problems with the home, but when Tom DuFore, a code enforcement officer in Fort Edward, asked to get into the home to see if there were any problems, he was refused entry. In one account, Lesley Ingraham refused to let him into the house. In another published account, it was an unidentified man who would not let him in. Under state law, DuFore could not inspect a home without a tenant's consent.

"It was a total nightmare," DuFore told Youker. "Had they let me in the place, I would have told them to put up smoke detectors or be out of the house in two days."[43]

After the fire, investigators concluded there were violations that would have required immediate attention and forced the family to relocate with the help of social services.

After the fire, the home was demolished.

In a letter to the editor in the days after the fire, Kathy Knights of South Glens Falls suggested that, on Christmas, instead of the drive to buy toys for the less fortunate, the community should instead distribute new smoke detectors and batteries to families in need.[44]

On December 8, editorial writer Mark Mahoney, who had three girls himself, wrote an editorial suggesting a way to avert another tragedy. This is the type of grassroots advocacy we practiced in Glens Falls:

> In our minds, we see James, going to the window then back into his burning home, refusing to leave Damien and Ky behind. His body is found on top of his brothers,' a dying gesture of devotion.
>
> Imagine Courtney, their sister, desperately trying to keep the acrid smoke out of her lungs. Her body is found on the bathroom floor, a towel around her face.
>
> We see their mother, Lesley, outside on the street, helpless, listening as her babies final screams fade into the dawn.
>
> God help us if we ever have to walk that path.[45]

Mahoney bluntly told our readers this tragedy could have been prevented with some basic safety precautions.

He asked readers to check the smoke detectors in their own home, make sure they were placed properly and make sure the batteries were working.

He asked readers to go down into the basement and make sure their furnaces were working properly and schedule inspections. He asked them to be sure there was no flammable material nearby that might catch fire.[46]

If they were out Christmas shopping, Mahoney told readers to buy their family an early Christmas present, an escape ladder for each of the second-floor bedrooms, and maybe a fire extinguisher, too.

And finally, he suggested sketching out an escape route for their family, to practice it and instruct their children what they should do if there is a fire.[47]

This was a call to action. It was the newspaper being a big-brother-pain-in-the-neck for your own good.

"In the time it takes you to do all of these little things, you may be giving yourself and your family the greatest present of all," Mahoney wrote. "Do them today. Not tomorrow. Not after the holidays. Today. Right now. Need a good reason? We can give you four."[48]

Looking back, it was an editorial I'm sure made a difference.

In one final ironic twist, the town of Fort Edward had appointed a Citizen Advisory Committee to improve living conditions at rental properties a month before the fatal fire on Lower Allen Street.

Town Supervisor Merrilyn Pulver said she was putting slumlords on notice to "either clean up your act or you're out of business."[49]

In *The Post-Star* story, it was reported there was no local law that gave the code enforcement officer jurisdiction to inspect rental properties unless a tenant called to complain. That December, the town of Fort Edward proposed just such a law.[50]

Lesley and Roger Ingraham both now live in Avon Park, Florida. It is unknown whether they reconciled.

Driving down Lower Allen Street in the summer of 2020, there was a mixture of homes in various states of repair. It was a sleepy neighborhood without a lot of amenities.

The lot at 583 Lower Allen Street was still empty 18 years later.

7

The Photograph

I was talking on the phone when our assistant city editor David Blow rushed into my office and pushed the photo in front of me.[1]

It was a punch in the gut.

Kevin Kimmerly, 31, was the first local soldier killed in the Iraq War in the aftermath of the 9/11 attacks. It was September 2003, and we had covered his funeral that morning in rural North Creek. He had a wife and nine-year-old son.

It was a public funeral with full military honors that drew hundreds, many who did not know Kimmerly, and media coverage from throughout the Capital District of upstate New York. We had a reporter, columnist and photographer covering the funeral and planned to use it as our lead story the next day on the front page.

I stared at the photograph, but it is better to let our reporter Abigail Tucker describe the scene:

> Army Staff Sgt. Kevin C. Kimmerly "always led from the front," his commanders said.
> It was that way Wednesday when his coffin-led a procession of family, friends and perfect strangers to Bates Cemetery in Johnsburg.
> There they could follow him no farther. At the graveside, Kimmerly's 9-year-old son Christopher looked wildly around him as though he didn't know where to go next.
> His widow, Inge, looked down.[2]

As the uniformed pallbearers approached the grave, they stumbled as they lowered the casket to the ground. It is the final goodbye that is always the most difficult at a military funeral. The final five-shot volley from the honor guard is when emotions are most fragile. Even those most hardened by life can dissolve into tears when the widow is presented the flag from "a grateful nation."[3]

And while the focus is always on the family, it is never more evident than when it is a young widow with a nine-year-old son, as it was in North Creek that day.

"The grave was 50 inches deep, but it may as well have gone down a mile into the earth," was how Sunday editor Will Doolittle started his column about the funeral that day. He was also unable to look away from the young boy sitting next to his mother graveside:

> The 9-year-old boy stared into it, his eyes dull, his face pale.
> Christopher Kimmerly looked like he'd been roused from a dream and shoved into a nightmare, driven on a sunny fall afternoon to a hilltop to stare into his father's grave.
> You could tell from the way he sat, so stiff, with his hands stuffed under his thighs, that he didn't feel the September breeze or hear the leaves rustling with a sound like applause on the trees around the edge of Bates Cemetery.[4]

When assistant city editor David Blow saw this photograph from the funeral of a local soldier killed in the Iraq War, he immediately took it to editor Ken Tingley. It was a gut punch that captured nine-year-old Christopher Kimmerly, flanked by his mother Inge, at the exact moment he dissolved into tears at the funeral of his father, Kevin Kimmerly. The photograph spawned a lengthy debate among reporters and editors in the newsroom about whether a news photograph could be too powerful. Ultimately, it was decided this was the true face of war, and readers needed to see it. It was published as the dominant photograph on the front page. Seventeen years later, the author talked with Kevin Kimmerly's widow, Inge (*Post-Star* photograph by Rick Gargiulo).

The U.S. Army honor guard carries the flag-draped coffin of Army Staff Sgt. Kevin Kimmerly to his final resting place at Bates Cemetery in Johnsburg, New York, on September 24, 2003. Following behind the casket is Kevin's widow, Inge, and their nine-year-old son, Christopher (*Post-Star* photograph by Rick Gargiulo).

Christopher watched intently, and when the five soldiers in their dress uniforms fired their final volley, the little boy began to sob.[5]

Rick Garagiulo, *The Post-Star* photographer, clicked the shutter on his camera from 100 feet away.[6]

"Finally, his eyes grew red and he turned in his seat, twisting his head from one side to the other. Someone put a hand on his shoulder," Doolittle wrote.[7]

It was heartbreaking.

That was the photograph that Dave Blow was showing me that afternoon.

The man behind Christopher with his right hand on his right shoulder was wearing an army uniform. He wore the insignia of a sergeant first class on his shoulder. There were other mourners behind Christopher, but it is the utter anguish of this baby that makes it impossible to look away.

If ever there was an image that showed how much power a single photograph can carry, this was it.

My first reaction was that this was the lead photograph on our front page and that we should run it big, not to sell newspapers, but for the emotional and visual impact of the price of war it conveyed. The Iraq War was a local story now.

As we shared the photograph and asked for feedback from other editors and reporters around the newsroom, some expressed misgivings and concern. They wondered if the photo went too far, if it was possibly too emotionally charged. There was concern the long lens of a photographer from more than 100 feet away might be construed as an intrusion into the privacy of this little boy at the worst moment of his life. There was even concern he might be teased in school.

I ultimately decided this was the "face of war" and that our readers needed to see that, they needed to see the lifetime repercussions on this family, on this little boy. It was not a unanimous decision in the newsroom.

U.S. and coalition forces invaded Iraq in search of weapons of mass destruction in March 2003. You may remember the "Shock and Awe" campaign that quickly overwhelmed Iraq's forces that spring. By May, President George W. Bush stood on the deck of the aircraft carrier U.S.S. *Abraham Lincoln*, and in a nationally televised speech, declared, "Mission accomplished" for the war in Iraq. Our men in uniform were safe.

But the war continued for career solders like Kevin Kimmerly. Four months later, Kimmerly, who had served in the army since high school graduation and did tours of duty in Bosnia and Kosovo, was still in Iraq.

On Monday, September 15, 2003, a vehicle Kimmerly was riding in came under fire from guerrillas in central Baghdad. His wife, Inge, was later told Kevin had been hit in the left side of his abdomen, that his internal organs were gone and his left arm had been blown off.[8] In a late-night phone call from Walter Reed Army Medical Center in Washington, she was told that Kevin was going to die. He had turned 31 a day earlier.[9]

The next morning a chaplain arrived at the military base in Germany to tell her that Kevin was dead. Kevin was supposed to leave for his next assignment in Oklahoma in two weeks. Inge picked out a casket and made arrangements to return Kevin to his little hometown for burial in the Adirondacks.

The community embraced the family and hundreds grieved with them. His death and burial ten days later was a media event, but Inge spurned all interviews. The funeral director asked members of the press to allow the family to grieve in private.

The front page of the September 25, 2003, *Post-Star* was dominated by the funeral coverage. The lead photo of the little boy sobbing was run over four columns and stretched ten inches deep.[10]

The two-deck headline read "A town's hero is laid to rest" next to a smaller photo of the flag-draped coffin being carried to the gravesite.[11] Tucker, who would later go on to work at *The Baltimore Sun* and national magazines, wrote the news story, while Doolittle, who I believed was our best writer at the time, was assigned to write a column that would capture the emotion of the day.

There was also an Associated Press story on the front page that day with a headline that foretold darker days ahead in Iraq, "More reserves may be called up."[12]

The day after the funeral, I received several calls about the photograph of Christopher Kimmerly. I was expecting it.

One woman called and said the photo was "obscene."[13]

I told her I agreed with her. It was obscene that a little boy will live his life without his dad. I can't think of many things worse. I told her it was a grim reminder of the cost of war.[14]

Another woman left me a voice message thanking us for running the photo. She called it "outstanding" and in between sobs told us how much she was touched by the photo of the "sad little boy who had lost his father."[15]

Our community was beginning a conversation about the war, maybe for the first time since the invasion.

I wrote this in my "From the Managing Editor" column that Sunday: "The war in Iraq isn't just about young men dying; it's about little boys and girls losing their daddies. That's something that is horrible to look at. That is something we don't want to see in our morning paper. That is something we don't want to think about. That is something we hope never touches our own families and young ones. But that's what we saw at the funeral. If we ignored that, we would not have been doing our job."[16]

I argued that many disturbing images have made a difference in our history and often altered our view of world and national events.

"Newspapers often have to perform an unpopular role in our communities and shine a light where readers don't necessarily want to look. We'd love to run beautiful hot air balloons every day on the front page to make us all feel good, but that's not realistic," I wrote.[17]

I mentioned the photograph of a naked, young girl screaming after a napalm attack in Vietnam, little John-John saluting his father at President Kennedy's funeral and the photo of an Oklahoma City fireman cradling a deceased baby after the bombing.[18]

I nominated Garagiulo's photo for a Pulitzer Prize the next year. I later had the photo framed and hung in our newspaper's library. Several employees later complained it was too sad to look at, so I took it down.

After the funeral, Inge Kimmerly stayed in North Creek and eventually settled in the town of Moreau in northern Saratoga County where there was a larger school for her son and more work opportunities for her. She got a job as a teacher's aide at South Glens Falls High School where her son attended. Inge is still there.

It would be two years—October 2005—before Inge finally agreed to talk to the newspaper about the death of her husband.

Naturally, it was Thom Randall—the reporter who ventured into New York City on September 12 with the wrong shoes—who was able to coax Inge and Kevin's twin brother, John, into talking while 11-year-old Christopher Kimmerly fished in the Hudson River.[19]

"Kevin and I were close, and I keep things to myself, and Kevin was the same way. I wanted to have my privacy, and I couldn't talk to anybody in the media," Inge Kimmerly told Randall. "I just couldn't. I didn't want the attention."[20]

At the time of that interview, the death count in Iraq had reached 1,962. By 2020, the estimated loss of American life was more than 5,000. There were so many more funerals to come.

"People hear the number of soldiers killed, but every single number represents an entire family that's devastated," Inge Kimmerly told Randall. "It makes me so mad … not just for the loss of my own husband. No good is coming from the war, and it's not getting any better. Every day it goes on, and there's just more pain and suffering. Every time they report that another solider has died, I know what the soldier's family is going through."[21]

The pain that was first broached on the front page of *The Post-Star* with a heartbreaking photo of Christopher Kimmerly was again on full display.

"Nothing has changed," Inge Kimmerly said. "I'm still grieving deeply."[22]

She told Randall that Christopher had excelled as a fifth-grader in South Glens Falls in social studies and mathematics. He had friends and seemed to have adjusted.

She also said she saw many of the same traits, the same outgoing, happy-go-lucky attitudes in Christopher that she had seen in his father.

Seventeen years after the funeral, I talked to Inge Kimmerly about the photo for the first time. I wanted to explain what I was thinking and why we published the photograph the way we did. I hoped it had not caused her pain.

Still sporting a hint of a German accent, Inge Kimmerly said she saw the photo afterward and admitted she was mad at the time.[23]

"I wanted my privacy," she said. "It's why I didn't give any interviews. On the other side, I see what you see. That is the face of war, you are right."[24]

When talking to Randall in 2005, Inge said she hoped Christopher would not become a soldier like his father and put himself in harm's way.[25]

"I hope Christopher takes a different career path," she said.[26]

He did.

By June of 2020, 25-year-old Christopher Kimmerly was finishing up his master's degree at the University of Buffalo in urban planning and had been working summers for a company in Saratoga.[27]

"He is doing very well," Inge Kimmerly said.[28]

Inge Kimmerly never remarried.

On September 14 each year Christopher Kimmerly celebrates the birthday he shared with his father. That is followed the next day by the anniversary of his father's death.

"I can feel it at the end of August," Inge Kimmerly told me. "I can still feel it [the depression] coming, it building. You think about it all the time. You go through all of it again. It is like a flashback."[29]

She has not changed her views on the war that cost her husband his life and her family so much heartache.

That front-page photo is now history, part of the family legacy and part of the newspaper's legacy.

"At the time it was hard to see the picture," Inge Kimmerly told me. "Like I said, I can see it now. You can actually see the pain."[30]

Pain that never, ever went away.

8

Street of Dreams

It was just before 10 a.m. on a sunshine-splashed summer day in July 2011 when the first swipe of the 60-foot boom brought down a street-facing balcony of the Madden Hotel in downtown Glens Falls.[1]

As the Madden came down with an appreciative crowd looking on, a distinctive smell was released, not overwhelming, but like a damp basement or a musty closet. It was the smell of decay.

By noon, work crews had taken down half the building. Two days later, the Madden was a pile of sticks and bricks. The smell was gone, and the future was brighter.

The "Street of Dreams" had changed forever.

The difference made to Glens Falls' seedy, honky-tonk district in the first half of 2011 was dramatic. When the Madden Hotel was finally sold in a tricky real estate transaction that left it in the hands of Glens Falls' hometown bank, it was the culmination of four decades of hand-wringing by city leaders, law enforcement and social services. The Madden Hotel was a blight on the city of Glens Falls.

Every community has one.

Its end was significantly facilitated by a two-part series seven years earlier by an aggressive 56-year-old *Post-Star* reporter unafraid to poke his nose into a flea-bag hotel reeking of cigarettes and urine, to tell the stories of people few others cared about. That reporter was Thom Randall.[2]

Maury Thompson reported in 2011, just months before the Madden came down, its decline could be traced to trends in the hotel industry in the 1970s and 1980s to move away from the centers of small towns to more convenient interstate exit-ramp locations.[3]

By 2000, the Madden did not deserve the label of "hotel." It was a flophouse for those on government assistance, transients and the recently incarcerated who had nowhere else to go.[4]

And for a brief time in the winter of 2003, one *Post-Star* reporter.

By then, Randall already had built a reputation of local community journalism. The newspaper increasingly used him for in-depth projects and stories few others wanted to do.

He founded the *Adirondack Journal* in nearby Warrensburg with his then-wife in 1987 before eventually selling the weekly newspaper. He began taking photographs for *The Post-Star* on a freelance basis and gradually worked his way into a regular correspondent position paid by the story.[5]

Sporting a bushy mustache, chronically uncombed hair and glasses, he was an old-school reporter who still wore a sports coat.

It did not take long for a 60-foot boom to bring down the upper floors of the Madden Hotel on July 19, 2011. The discussion of what to do with the fleabag hotel on Glens Falls' "Street of Dreams" had been ongoing since January 2004 when *Post-Star* reporter Thom Randall published a series of stories about life at the Madden and the people who lived there. The discussions continued over the next seven years before the building was sold to a local bank and torn down for more office space. But it all started with Randall's story (*Post-Star* photograph by Jason McKibben).

Looking more like a rumpled college professor than a go-getter reporter, Randall tended to do things his own way and on his own schedule, testing the patience of editors forced to adjust their deadlines to Randall time. But as a reporter, he had a knack for getting people to open up and invite him into their living rooms. He seemed to be able to get anyone to talk to him.

In June 2002, he convinced the Warren County sheriff to lock him up in the county jail under the guise of a DWI arrest so he could write about the experience firsthand, even though the state had a policy against it. Although Randall had talked about the story idea around the newsroom for months, city editor Bob Condon didn't learn he was actually doing it until he got a call from Randall telling him he was in the county jail.[6]

"The barred steel door slams with a resounding clank and I'm standing in a narrow cellblock with six inmates staring at me. Suddenly, the reality of my situation faces me. I'm locked in with convicts and suspects linked to serious crimes—some violent," Randall wrote as the lead to "Behind Bars."[7]

To get entry to the county jail, Randall agreed to one overriding condition: He wouldn't tell any of the inmates he was a reporter.[8]

"Now I stand here in the narrow cell block catwalk with only a worn sheet, a small dingy towel, two Styrofoam cups, a roll of toilet paper, a stubby toothbrush and a tiny toothpaste tube, all rolled up in a pressed wool blanket—the standard issue for new prisoners," Randall wrote.[9]

He found a half-dozen inmates staring at him as he found his way to Cell No. 2. He described being surrounded by inmates who peppered him with questions while he got increasingly nervous for his safety.

"I feel like a swimmer circled by sharks," Randall wrote. "Immediately, I realize I can't ethically maintain a 'cover' and be able to write a detailed story. Within about three minutes, I'd blown my cover."[10]

Randall remained locked up in his six-foot-by-eight-foot cell for 17 hours, introducing our readers to a colorful cast of characters—Bad Boy, Stalin, The Kid, Farmer, Vanilla—serving time for felony assault, vehicular manslaughter, armed robbery, DWI, burglary—but Randall's true accomplishment was capturing the emotional sense of lost freedom.

From the full-body strip search to sleeping on a rock-hard, steel-plate bed with a thin mattress, he conveyed to readers his total loss of privacy and transported them to life inside the county jail.

"My toilet hangs from the wall, in full view of all who hang out in front of my cell to watch television or talk," Randall wrote. "Thus began a set of discoveries over the next 17 hours. All my choices had been taken away. I can't choose food that I prefer for health reasons. I get what's shoved through the bars on a plastic dish, or I go hungry. I can't follow my own schedule or choose ways to get comfortable."

"I realize that I no longer have any personal space I can call my own," Randall wrote. "Even my own cell door is open to the other prisoners for about 17 hours per day, and new prisoners low in the pecking order don't have a choice about who comes in their cell."[11]

It didn't take long for the prisoners to pass on to the guards they knew Randall's true reason for incarceration. The guards passed it up the chain of command to the sheriff that Randall had violated his one condition for the story. Randall became perhaps the only person to be kicked out of the Warren County Jail.[12]

His "Behind Bars" story earned the top feature-writing honors from the New York State Publishers Association the next year.[13]

"I was really into those emergent journalism stories," Randall said in 2020. "From the ride-alongs I did with the sheriff's officers to the stay in jail, I liked that type of story, that immediate narrative. You were there. This is what it smells like, looks like, the emotion of it."[14]

Amidst the chaos on 9/11, it was Randall who insisted he go to Manhattan the next day to provide firsthand coverage by riding the final Amtrak train into the city.[15]

It was Randall who later got Inge Kimmerly to open up about the death of her husband in Iraq.[16]

Randall's background was unusual even for a newspaper reporter. He grew up in Ohio and spent summers in the Adirondacks at a private Quaker family camp on Indian Lake. He learned photography from his father in their home darkroom as a youngster.[17]

He spent two years at Bard College as an English literature major who roomed with Walter Becker, the lead singer of Steely Dan. After dropping out of college, Randall married and then operated various portrait studios in New Mexico, Colorado, Utah and Arizona, doing studio work and environmental photography.[18]

"This background in portrait photography, I believe, helped a lot later in my reporting career," Randall wrote in an email. "I was trained to scrutinize details in one's expression, presentation, demeanor and also the background details, all of which I found out in various reporting courses are very important in interviewing as well as relating details of a scene in observational reporting."[19]

By the winter of 2003, Randall was an established reporter in Glens Falls, and the Madden Hotel had become the hub for police blotter stories about the residents who lived there.

Randall became fascinated with the dynamic between what the Madden Hotel had once been and what it had become.

"I had heard over and over again about Paul Pines checking in there and writing his poems," Thom said about the local poet who published the work "Hotel Madden Poems" in 1991. "This is the place where jazz musicians would book rooms when they came to visit. But it also had this awful reputation. At the time, there was a lot of talk about drug use, prostitution, desperation and all the crime that was going on in there."[20]

During the winter of 2003, Randall walked into the Madden Hotel and paid $75 cash to rent a room for a week on one of the upper floors.

"It was on the northwest corner of the building and had a view of South Street," Thom remembered. "The place reeked of cigarette smoke, urine. It was disgusting. The linens were unwashed, there was a thread-bare blanket and the sink was falling off the wall."[21]

A couple of hours after Randall checked in, the assistant manager knocked on his door to warn him the last occupant of the room had been a drug dealer known for his bad deals, so if someone knocked on his door in the middle of the night, he should be careful.

"It scared the shit out of me," Randall remembered. "I may have slept one or two hours that whole first night. I didn't want to get stabbed in my sleep."[22]

The next day, he used a washcloth he brought with him to scrub the walls stained yellow from cigarette smoke.

"I was trying to get the cigarette stink off," he said. "The walls were yellow, caked with cigarette smoke. I always slept with the window open because of the stink."[23]

Each day, Thom said he would wander the halls of the rooming house becoming acquainted with one or two people who lived there. One of the first was Skid and his girlfriend, Michelle.

"Skid is hospitable to others. He loves to talk, sharing his experiences and his marijuana," Randall wrote on the second day of his Hotel Madden series. "His door is usually open, and in the Madden, which has no lobby, rooms with open doors attract other tenants hungry for socializing."[24]

Skid told Randall of his tough upbringing by a mother who was a "prostitute and a Harley slut." Skid said he didn't hold her responsible because his grandmother was a prostitute, too. Skid later offered Randall his girlfriend for a night.[25]

"It was crazy," Randall said. "He was trying to pimp her out."[26]

Like a novelist, Randall developed the Madden characters for his two-part series we would publish in January 2004. And just as he had in the county jail, he eventually revealed his real identity to the residents.

"At first, when people would ask what I did, I would change the subject," Randall said. "About a week in, I said I was a writer, then in another week I said I was a news-paper writer, then about five weeks in after I had gotten a lot of material, I told them I was writing a story for *The Post-Star*. They sort of went through phases. When I first told them, they would shut up and go cold on me, then they would relax and open up again each time."[27]

Along the way, Randall tried to live their life. He lined up with others at a day-labor business downtown and spent one long overnight shift stacking magazines at a local plant.

"At the end of my 12-hour shift, my back aches and my wrists ache," Randall wrote. He was paid $75 for his efforts.[28]

Randall spent about three weeks living in the Madden, then gradually balanced other work responsibilities at the newspaper with periodic visits with the residents he knew.[29]

"I didn't know what to do with the Madden story," he admitted. "You gave me the time to mull it. It was like seven weeks and I was waiting for something dramatic, something that people would find gripping."[30]

He found it when Ken Longley, a Vietnam veteran and longtime Madden resident, was found dead in his room. The Hotel Madden series started this way:

> Don Rucker walked up the stairs of the Hotel Madden, sprinkling baking soda on the blood-soaked carpeting where Ken Longley had been found.
> "Kenny used to drink all he wanted in the Saloon, then come back here and drink more until he'd pass out," Rucker said. "There oughta be a law against it."
> Earlier that morning, a middle-aged homeless man named Charlie had found Longley's body in his room.
> Tears falling from his reddened eyes, Charlie stood sobbing in the third-floor hallway.
> Nearby, city police Officer John Norton pulled a tattered bedspread over Longley's body, which was lying facedown on the threadbare, gritty carpet.
> Longley, a 59-year-old Vietnam veteran and longtime Madden resident, had been letting Charlie sleep on his floor. Charlie had nowhere else to go.[31]

"I thought it was really a strong lead," Randall remembered. "The blood running under the door and Don Rucker nonchalantly sprinkling the baking soda on the car-pet to soak up the blood."[32]

Will Doolittle remembered Randall's early drafts of the story as a jumbled stream of consciousness with no context that needed a lot of work.[33] The reporting was great, but without a great editor, the work was worthless.

Looking back, Randall remembered something more about the experience. He remembered sitting on the front stoop of the Madden in old, ragged clothes as the well-dressed professionals from the nearby bank walked past. He noticed when they looked at him in his dirty clothes, they quickly looked away as if hoping he would disappear.[34]

"The look was kind of one of pity mixed with disgust," Randall said. "After [the story] was published, it started the old thing about cracking down by the code enforcement. They had this whole thing, tear it down and that solves our problem. I always felt they needed to create some sort of new facility to deal with the residents and their lack of feeling or self worth, the desperation, the lack of purpose that led them to drug abuse."[35]

Randall's story, published over two days on January 11–12, 2004, got the region's attention with Randall's gritty descriptions highlighting the down-and-out lives of another group of characters—the Sheriff of South Street, Steve, Skid and Michelle—where Randall put readers into their shoes and showed them their lives of squalor.

"Holes about the size of a fist are punched into the bathroom wall. One hole is filled with wadded, soiled toilet paper. Flies buzz around the toilet. One of the flies lands near a handwritten notice scrawled in pencil on the peeling paint. 'Lift the toilet lid, please! Thanks, Larry,'" Thom wrote in the second part.[36]

Don Rucker, a convicted felon who had spent half his life in prison, was now the Madden's manager. He told Randall things were even worse before he became manager. Randall's account was startling:

> Before he got the manager's job about a year ago, Rucker says garbage would be left so long in the hallways it would rot, draw flies and breed maggots.
>
> Rucker says he changed other aspects of life at the Madden.
>
> Homeless street people once would find out about a vacant room and kick the door in so they'd have a place to sleep overnight.
>
> "The Madden's a better place now," he says. "The police are not being called here every night, and there aren't people smoking crack on the landings or sleeping in the hallways."[37]

Remember, this was in "Hometown, USA," where residents took pride in their idyllic little city and its quality of life.

One reader responded that Randall's story was symbolic "of many cities filled with over-populated homeless, forgotten drug addicts. They have no voice and their pleas reach silent ears. Unfortunately, the habit of the privileged people is to turn the other way hoping if not addressed it will go away."[38]

Another letter writer criticized the newspaper for publishing Randall's story about the Madden. The reader wrote that such "bad news" could hurt future business and make our community look bad.[39]

I emailed the reader back, wondering if the newspaper didn't shine a light on the problems in the community, who would?[40]

But the response from Jennifer O'Connor, a former Glens Falls resident who then lived in Newburgh, New York, said it even better. She asked the earlier letter writer how it was living in "La La Land."[41]

"How soon we forget how power of the press has made this country a better place to live," wrote O'Connor. "It was a reporter who exposed the meat packing industry and called for a reform. It was a reporter who exposed conditions in a sanitarium and called for reforms in the mental health industry. It was two reporters who exposed the biggest presidential scandal in history."[42]

The reporting opened the eyes of many others.

Fran Williams of Corinth wrote this in a letter to the editor published on January 14, 2004:

> I just finished reading Thom Randall's article about the Hotel Madden. Wow! What a riveting, wonderful story, gripping and definitely an eye-opener.
>
> How tragic that this story could have been written about any major city, yet it is right in our own backyard. As most of us have had the comforts in life, these poor people scrape together an existence. I am not moralizing drugs/drinking, but well aware on a personal

basis how when caught between the cracks, there is sometimes nowhere to turn and no one who will help.

Thom's firsthand glimpse was poignant, so real and capitalizing. No one knows what it is like to struggle with dependency, loss, poverty unless you walk the walk, see, taste and smell the anguish.[43]

This is what is so valuable about community newspapers. Their work sparks a conversation within the community, and that means there is hope for change.

Sixteen years later in 2020, Randall believed it was more community ignorance than shock.

"They were living with it, kind of ignored it," Randall said. "The underbelly of Glens Falls was suddenly visible because of *The Post-Star* story. Then they really worked on solving the situations. But I think they misplaced their priorities. It wasn't a matter of bricks and mortar, it was the people [at the Madden] who had a lack of purpose."[44]

Several days later, editorial writer Mark Mahoney cut to the heart of the dilemma facing the community as it grappled with what to do next: "That may be the biggest lesson of this story—and the greatest tragedy. We all feel bad. But we don't know what to do about it."[45]

After the story ran, Randall reported in a follow-up that "an unannounced tour of the Madden showed that hallways and bathroom had been mopped and vacuumed and trash had been collected."[46]

By August, city officials said they were looking into developing a facility to provide supervised housing to people who are homeless, recently released from prison or otherwise in need of housing. The discussion was a direct result of the Hotel Madden series.[47]

Mayor Robert Regan, who served as mayor from 1998 to 2005, formed an informal committee of government officials and social workers to address the problem after the Madden series was published. The group concluded this was more a social problem than a building problem.

"It really came down to the fact that if you shut down the Madden, you would throw all those people out of a home," Mayor Regan told *Post-Star* reporter Thompson in 2009. "And at the time it was difficult to place people."[48]

By 2009, Mayor Jack Diamond believed he had discovered a way to not only get rid of the Madden but to clean up the entire bar scene on the "Street of Dreams."

The city took action against the owners of the hotel for code enforcement violations using the city's nuisance abatement law. In June 2009, Thompson found a file one and three-quarters inches thick of building code violations associated with the Madden Hotel dating back to 1987.[49]

The 2000 law addressed activities such as loud noise, disorderly conduct, fighting and lewdness. By taking the Madden owner to court—the first time the city had ever taken action under the law—it hoped to force the owner to sell.[50]

During a political forum that fall, Mayor Diamond said, "The only answer to the Madden Hotel is demolition and closure."[51]

Diamond won reelection.

While touring one of the newly renovated luxury apartments across the street from the Madden in 2009, it was hard not to be impressed with what South Street could become. Developer Michael Kaidas showed a luxury apartment on an upper floor with cathedral ceilings and floor-to-ceiling windows that provided a grand view of a shirtless man drinking a beer on the balcony of the Madden Hotel.

As I left the building, I asked Kaidas if he was concerned about the South Street neighborhood.

Across the street, a small group of people loitered outside the Madden, and two of them started screaming at each other.

"You mean, like that," Kaidas said.[52]

Calling South Street "seedy" was being kind.

Mayor Diamond was not done dealing yet. He dispatched city Economic/Community Development Director Edward Bartholomew, who also served as Glens Falls mayor from 1978 to 1985, to negotiate with the Madden's owner. After initially resisting, the owner agreed to sell the building to the Local Development Corporation for $650,000.[53] The LDC sold the property to Glens Falls National Bank for $500,000 with the $150,000 difference being paid from economic development funds held by the LDC and the city's other two economic development agencies.[54]

By then, getting rid of the Madden had become the key for the city's future economic plans.

On July 9, 2010, *The Post-Star* reported that the Madden Hotel would be demolished to make way for an expansion of Glens Falls National Bank.[55]

After 20 years, through five mayoral administrations, the fate of the once-grand hotel was sealed.

Nine days later, it came down.

In the weeks before the demolition, other accommodations were found for the residents in towns around the region. It was reported residents were relocated to far-better places.

The effect on South Street was dramatic. The Open Door Soup Kitchen, which occupied part of the bottom floor of the Madden, moved its operations across town to Lawrence Street, near the newspaper, and took with it the regular assemblage of sometimes troubled denizens who lined up for a hot meal each evening. Labor Ready, the day labor employment business that many Madden residents counted on for employment, moved to nearby Queensbury.

But the biggest change in the weeks to follow was the quiet.

There was some foot traffic, not much, but no one was screaming. There were no arguments.

As I walked past a cab driver waiting for his next fare later that summer, he gave me a friendly "Hello."[56]

After the Madden came down, Kaidas, the developer who had renovated the Empire Theater across the street, said the change had been dramatic.

"We don't have people hanging out in the street. Not getting that bad element. It really has been a fantastic change," Kaidas said.[57]

Within a few years, the downtown Glens Falls we were so concerned about had been transformed. A new roundabout had been constructed at the troublesome five-way intersection to smooth traffic flow; another downtown building was renovated to house the Wood Theater and draw more people downtown for entertainment. Crandall Public Library, adjacent to City Park, was renovated and expanded and became the city's anchor store.

In 2011, new sidewalk work was put in place on South Street with fancy brickwork that did little to dress up boarded-up storefronts and seedy bars that remained.

That November, Mayor Diamond proclaimed there would be no more new bars on South Street. He made it a city policy and urged the state Liquor Authority to reject any license application.[58]

How many politicians do you know who actually discouraged businesses from coming to their city? It was a small action that sent a big message and in the end made a big difference.

By the end of 2012, Diamond pushed for Glens Falls bars to change their closing times from 4 a.m. to 2 a.m. The newspaper's editorial board endorsed the move, despite expected objections from bar owners. The mayor and bar owners eventually reached a compromise at 3 a.m., and over the next year, police saw a pronounced reduction in late-night problems and arrests.[59]

In the coming years, a vibrant weekend farmer's market was established in the parking lot just across the street from where the Madden once stood. Three other

Post-Star Reporter Thom Randall was always drawn toward participatory journalism like his stay at the Madden Hotel. He was the reporter who caught the last train to New York City on September 12, 2001. He once talked the county sheriff into locking him up so he could write about the jail experience, and another time he spent a weekend embedded in the emergency room of Glens Falls Hospital. On April 17, 2005, former NBC news anchor Tom Brokaw interviewed Randall about a National Guard troop he had covered during the Iraq War that Brokaw was doing a news special about (*Post-Star* file photograph).

prominent bars on the street closed down and the Off Track Betting parlor run by the state was shuttered.

In August of 2016, the state of New York awarded Glens Falls $10,000,000 as part of a Downtown Revitalization Initiative. The city acquired the OTB and bar properties down the street from the Madden, tore them down and planned to build a new year-round farmer's market.[60]

On January 18, 2004, just days after Randall's series on the Madden Hotel was published in our newspaper, our editorial page editor Mahoney wrote this: "The best outcome of a newspaper story like this is that it effects some kind of change."[61]

That's what this story did.

Randall's story put a laser focus on the Madden Hotel, forced community and civic leaders to confront the problem and work toward a solution that would be seven years in the making.

That's the power of newspapers.

Now, even 16 years later, the ramifications of Randall's work are still being felt on South Street and downtown Glens Falls. South Street may again, sometime very soon, be known as the "Street of Dreams" but for different reasons.

Later in the fall of 2004, Randall went behind the scenes again and spent 11 hours in the emergency room at Glens Falls Hospital where he gave readers a glimpse of emergency room medicine in action.[62]

It was vintage Randall as he recounted a woman 30 weeks into her pregnancy with twins who delivered both babies in the ambulance on the way to the hospital. The first baby was breathing normally, but Randall recounted how the second one was in distress:

> One by one, nurses and doctors emerge from hallways leading to the main hospital floors. Breathing equipment, monitors and various medical devices are assembled in Room No. 17. The 40-minute drive from Salem has allowed nurses and pediatricians to fully prepare for an effort to save a life.
>
> The outside doors fly open. Harried and grim-faced ambulance personnel wheel in the mother lying on a gurney. She and one of the twin girls are rushed upstairs. An EMT carries the second tiny pinkish-blue baby, wrapped in flannel blanket, into the treatment room where nurses, equipment and doctor are waiting.
>
> Placed gently on a pediatric bed, she's limp and barely larger than a man's hand.
>
> A pediatrician, Dr. Dedra Flynn pumps the baby girl's tiny chest with her two thumbs. Pediatric nurse Jane Diamond helps out with respiration equipment. Although the baby is surrounded by a flurry of activity, it remains still.
>
> "Come on, sweetheart," Nurse Linda Burrall whispers.[63]

Moments later, Randall reports, a nurse watching a monitor offers good news. "Looks like she's breathing," she says. "We have a heartbeat."[64]

It's the type of narrative reporting that gives a community its heart and soul, and it's the kind of reporting that is almost impossible to do these days with dwindling resources.

The American College of Emergency Room Physicians awarded Randall its national journalism prize in 2005 for the story. The organization honored just one newspaper each year, and it was our small newspaper. It was Randall's 16th award since joining *The Post-Star* in 1995.[65]

Talking to Randall in 2020, we agreed this type of story would never be approved by the hospital today, and communities are the worse for it.

Randall left *The Post-Star* in 2005, took some time off and said he planned on retiring. He eventually went back to work in advertising at a small weekly newspaper in the Capital District.[66]

After dabbling in stock market day-trading for a number of years, Randall said he lost 90 percent of his portfolio in the 2008 financial crisis and eventually returned to Warrensburg where he continues to work at the *Adirondack Journal* as an editor and writer.

At 72, he says he still enjoys the work.

"I miss the old days of journalism when you could really delve into an issue," Randall said.[67]

What I most wonder is whether anyone else noticed it was gone.

9

Monsters After Midnight

Lisa Savard steps onto the stage wearing an elegant black jacket and skirt suitable for an evening out at a nice dinner party. Or maybe that's how you dress when the funeral won't go away.[1]

She gets to the point. She tells the audience in the South Glens Falls High School auditorium the story of her 16-year-old daughter, Joelle Dumoulin, killed in a car accident eight years earlier in 2002. She paces back and forth across the stage, steadily, despite her high-heeled shoes and heavy heart. Her voice is without emotion, oddly matter-of-fact.[2]

Her daughter and a friend met a boy at the Cumberland Farms convenient store in their little town of Corinth. Savard tells her audience they drank some beer and smoked some pot and went for a drive in his pickup truck. Out on the road, the driver began drag racing another car, reaching speeds up to 90 miles per hour, and when he came to a bend in the road, he crashed into a tree.[3]

Savard stops pacing.

It is midnight quiet.

The truck was so crushed that the first police officer on the scene had to crawl on his belly through a small gap in the wreckage to reach Dumoulin. All he heard was gurgling sounds coming from the young girl.[4]

The driver stood a few feet away, smoking a cigarette.[5]

"They told me later, Joelle lived for just a minute after the crash," Savard says. "Sometimes I sit and look at the clock ticking. A minute is a long time."[6]

By the time Dumoulin was pronounced dead in June 2002, it was still not clear our rural corner of northeastern upstate New York had a problem.

The strength of community newspapers—the daily attention to breaking news, accidents, arrests and court cases—can also be a weakness.

They report the horror of a fatality, the tears from a tragedy, even the repercussions for those who did wrong, yet often fail to connect the dots and identify the more enduring problem. It is difficult to see and follow the tentacles that reach out in all directions from one news story to another, and it often takes years to understand the impact.

Newspapers tell big stories incrementally over the course of months, sometimes years, through a variety of perspectives and sources, so it is difficult to see what it all means by reading any one story. Even the facts sometimes change as more is learned.

As Savard lets the seconds tick away on stage, it's hard to believe that eight years have gone by since she broke down in a Saratoga County courtroom.

Classmates of Greenwich Central School's Desmond Ahigian carry his coffin down the steps of St. Joseph's Catholic Church in Greenwich, New York, in April 2002. Ahigian, 16, and Tricia Myers, 17, died in a drunken driving accident that was the first of ten from 2002 to 2004 in the Glens Falls region. The tragedies fueled an underage drinking project by *The Post-Star* and led to the author starting a scrapbook for his five-year-old son that included this photograph and others like it over the next decade. It was this photograph that Joseph Tingley, the editor's son, saw just hours after he passed his driving test, leading to a guest essay on underage drinking (*Post-Star* photograph by Rob Barendse).

Two months before Dumoulin died, reporter Matthew Sturdevant wrote another tragic news story.[7] It is laden with fact after fact to satisfy the "who, what, where, when and how" journalism standards demand, but like most daily newspaper reports, it is deficient in emotion and lacking in context.

GREENWICH—Two local teen-agers died and two others were in critical condition after the car they were riding in crashed into a tree at 12:10 a.m. Saturday on Route 52 about a mile north of the intersection with Meader Road, police said.[8]

A second story two days later described the mourning of classmates,[9] then came another story on the charges of second-degree manslaughter against the 16-year-old driver who had been drinking[10] and, finally, coverage of the funerals for the 16- and 17-year-old victims.[11]

GREENWICH—The rhythm of life seemed to pause Wednesday as people in Greenwich came together to mourn and remember Desmond Ahigian and Tricia Myers.[12]

This was a story that would never go away for the little community of Greenwich, maybe because it had been there before five years earlier when three young people were killed and three injured in another early-morning crash.

Looking back, you wonder if Dumoulin or Savard had heard about the accident in the neighboring county, if they had read the story in the newspaper or seen the young people carrying the casket of their 16-year-old classmate. Or maybe the one before that in February, when a drunk driver crossed over a center line on a rural road in northern Warren County and killed 18-year-old Stephen Cook in another car.[13]

But none of the newspaper coverage at the time asked the most important question: Is there a problem here? That came later after more accidents, more tragedy and a welling chorus of concerns.

After the Greenwich accident, Washington County District Attorney Robert Winn said the underage drinking problem in Greenwich was not any worse there than in any other community in the region.[14]

On one hand, it sounded like he was dismissing the seriousness of the problem, but with the advantage of two decades of hindsight, maybe it was a subtle warning, an alarm that all our small rural communities had a similar problem. Greenwich was no different. It was just the latest to pay the price.

That September, Kaitlin Davis, the driver who killed two of her classmates at Greenwich Central School five months earlier, appeared in court. *Post-Star* reporter Darren Youker reported it this way: "Kaitlin Davis will spend the first day of her senior year of high school in the Washington County jail."[15]

That was the news that day, but what was missing was still how this could happen.

The 17-year-old admitted in court she drank a six-pack of Mike's Hard Lemonade before the crash. The alcohol had been purchased by her 23-year-old brother. While cruising around town, the teens picked up two other classmates and at one point stopped at the home of 16-year-old Desmond Ahigian, one of the victims, to get more alcohol.[16]

Davis said County Route 52 was slick that early April night from snow, and she was driving at a high speed. She did not remember the accident.[17]

"The circumstances do not warrant probation," Judge Philip Berke told Davis in court. "We have two young people that are dead. I don't think you will forget this for the rest of your life."[18]

The judge sentenced Davis to one to three years in jail on two counts of criminally negligent homicide.[19]

She served two years and was released.

Newspapers have a way of performing blunt trauma with their heartless descriptions of tragedies. Readers often asked if we thought about the families, if our reporters and editors had any heart at all.

It was the horrible Greenwich accident that started our campaign on underage drinking in 2002. It left the driver facing vehicular manslaughter charges, families devastated and at least one editor at the newspaper—me—searching for answers.

Over the next few days, the community mourned, the driver was arrested, and I decided to do something.

"Let's learn from this tragedy," was the headline on my column on the morning Desmond Ahigian and Tricia Myers were buried.[20]

I explained I was starting a scrapbook of all the tragic accidents from underage drinking in hopes my five-year-old would learn from it in the future. I urged other parents to start their own scrapbooks and predicted the Greenwich accident would repeat itself in other local communities.[21]

That bleak prophecy was quickly fulfilled.

For the scrapbook, I used an 8½-by-11-inch maroon binder that would traditionally hold the photos of family birthdays and Christmas celebrations. But over a decade, I filled it with 78 pages of newspaper articles that portray a sea of carnage and tragedy.

In the ensuing years, I wrote updates on how fast the scrapbook was filling up, and I continued to follow the underage drinking issue religiously and wrote dozens of columns about it over the years.

I instituted a controversial policy at our newspaper of publishing the names of teenagers arrested for underage drinking, while reporting on the teen parties that police busted, the kids who were caught drinking on senior trips and the schools that tried to keep these incidents out of the public eye.

I criticized parents who hosted teen drinking parties in their homes and supported school officials who suspended student-athletes for drinking.

We covered some trials and some funerals.

At times, I was criticized for being on a crusade. I was told by one young person my views were out of step with modern times.[22] And year after year, I cut out the articles.

A month after Dumoulin died and Davis had been sentenced for the Greenwich crash, an 18-year-old Warrensburg student named Jason Monroe took a late-night joyride on an all-terrain vehicle while attending a party at a cabin in the woods with ten to 15 other underage teens. He wasn't wearing a helmet, and he had a friend riding on the back with him.

Monroe drove the ATV into a tree at 3:30 in the morning. He had been captain of the basketball team, popular and one of the smartest students in his class.[23] His blood alcohol at the time of his death was twice the legal limit. When the other teens at the party were questioned by police, they lied to investigators. That detail came out later, after Monroe was buried, after the mourning was over and the investigation complete.

Maybe that lying should have been the clue that late-night drinking parties were far more insidious and dangerous than we knew. Maybe it deserved more than another shrug that "kids will be kids."

If the lying by partygoers after Monroe's death was not bad enough, then maybe the arrest the next winter of another Warrensburg teen, 17-year-old Jason Daniels, for organizing a keg party for some 40 underage students should have been a red flag that this was a runaway five-alarm fire.[24]

But Daniels's case was handled quietly—as so many of these things are in small towns—and he was charged with a misdemeanor of unlawfully dealing with a child and noncriminal violation of harassment for pushing a police officer who tried to break up the party.[25] The charges, by the newspaper's standards, were minor and not significant enough to be published.

Daniels's lawyer eventually cut a plea deal that all charges would be dropped if he stayed out of trouble for six months and performed 50 hours of community service.[26]

He never made it.

Daniels spent the night after the senior ball at an all-night drinking party at a cabin in the woods. He got so drunk that at 9 a.m. the next day he was killed when his 1989 Ford Ranger pickup truck crossed over the double yellow line and hit another pickup truck head-on. Daniels was on his way to the Warrensburg landfill to serve his community service from the earlier arrest.[27]

Police later reported his blood alcohol level was "well over" the legal limit. Actually, it was twice the legal limit.[28]

A week later, Warrensburg teacher Marc Mularz requested the newspaper publish his guest essay in the newspaper.

"This is an angry column," Mularz wrote. "So for those of you who are looking for some light reading with your Saturday breakfast, I would encourage you to look elsewhere. Furthermore, this column, while filled with my anger, is bound to provoke anger in others as well."[29]

Mularz, who had been teaching 16 years at the time, said he had seen 15 or so students kill themselves in episodes of bad judgment.

"This generation of students has been raised like no other," Mularz wrote. "The message that driving while impaired by alcohol or drugs kills is clear. We have SADD and MADD chapters in every school. We have the DARE program. Yet the message seems to go in one ear and out the other. There can be no excuse that they don't know the perils of their actions. Why then is the message ignored?"[30]

It was the question that needed to be asked of Kaitlin Davis the previous fall and the teenaged driver who smoked a cigarette while Joelle Dumoulin lay trapped beneath a pickup truck, taking her last breaths.

Mularz placed responsibility on permissive parents and a "boys will be boys" philosophy. He called out law enforcement for not making arrests on those who possess alcohol. He called out the district attorney for not being tough in sentencing.

Mularz did not make any friends in the community.

"Over the past few days our school has been filled with memorials to Jason [Daniels]. From posters to remembrances to homemade tattoos to photos on the walls and lockers, everyone has expressed their opinions. My question is this: Where were all of you when Jason was killing himself? Where were you each day when he drove his truck around Warren County like it was the Indy 500? Where were his friends when he was being arrested for supplying alcohol to minors? What were you doing on the morning of his death? You were there with him drinking all night. Did you stop him from driving? He is dead. Will his death cause you to change your own behavior? How long will it be before the next keg party in the woods?"[31]

Not long.

Days after Daniels died, seven teens were arrested in nearby Chester at an underage party.[32]

"The worst part about it is it just continues," said John Goode, a Brant Lake resident who Daniels hit head-on that morning. "The night they buried [Daniels] they had a party in the woods."[33]

The tragedy rattled the Warrensburg community the same way Greenwich was rattled a year earlier. Many began to connect the dots.

Daniels's death led to a county-wide crackdown on underage drinking that brought together police, prosecutors, school officials and parents in an effort to curb alcohol sales to minors.[34]

In June, four Warrensburg students were charged after police saw three cars full of teenagers leaving the woods of a popular party spot in Warrensburg. It was less than a month after Daniels's death. The driver of one car was arrested for driving while intoxicated and the passengers for unlawful possession of an alcoholic beverage.

The newspaper did not publish the names of two of those arrested because of its policy of not publishing the names of those under the age of 18. When a 17-year-old was arrested in connection with Daniels's death, he was granted "youthful offender" status and sentenced to 30 days in jail. The newspaper did not report his name.

After the deaths, Warrensburg stepped up its education efforts regarding underage drinking and instituted a curfew for young people. Community leaders formed the group "Communities Against Youth Substance Abuse" after surveys showed a high incidence of students using alcohol.[35]

Warren County Sheriff Larry Cleveland said he was not surprised after the deaths in Warrensburg.

"There is nothing we can do to totally eradicate the problem," Cleveland said at the time.

We at the newspaper felt differently.

Mularz identified the problem, pointing out that community leaders and parents often shrugged that this was a "rite of passage" for the youths around the region.

"What prompted Mr. Mularz to write his essay was simple. He is tired of seeing his students die," I later wrote in a column.[36]

So was I.

We at the newspaper decided to make our own changes.

When local police made arrests for underage drinking—they were really just a violation—it was the newspaper's policy not to print the names of minors for any infraction that was not a felony. So we changed our policy and said when it came to underage drinking arrests, we would start printing names.

We asked local law enforcement agencies to let us know about any underage drinking arrests through regular press releases.[37]

"We're hoping this keeps the issue in the minds of the public, so we can see how much of a problem is really out there. Maybe it is an epidemic," I wrote to our readers in June 2003.[38]

The Warren County Sheriff's Office followed with a new policy, saying it would contact at least one parent of anyone 16 to 18 arrested for underage drinking.[39] It seemed like a common sense change, but the reality had been that teens were being arrested, going to court on their own and paying their fines without their parents ever knowing.

Officials from neighboring Washington and Saratoga counties praised the policy and said they planned on enacting a similar one.[40]

That July, in a courtroom in Saratoga County, Lisa Savard wept as Christopher Bliss was found guilty of second-degree manslaughter in the death of her daughter Joelle Dumoulin. It took the jury just three hours to convict. Bliss was later sentenced to three and a half to ten and a half years in state prison.[41]

"Joelle's death still has a surreal quality. I still find it hard to believe she is gone," Savard told a *Post-Star* reporter after court. "To have her ripped from my life has left such a void."[42]

That void was never filled, and eight years later Savard was again telling the story of how Joelle died to a group of South Glens Falls students.[43]

She again relived the final minute of her daughter's life as she had done multiple times during the ensuing eight years. I was there when she spoke in May 2010.[44] I called her the next day and asked how she did it. How did she relive the tragedy repeatedly? Where did she put the pain?

"I put the pain where it is manageable," Savard told me. "But there is a refreshing of pain every time I do it. Seeing her [Joelle's] picture on the screen. It is in my throat. I usually cry when I leave."[45]

When Savard got home later that night, she cried again.[46]

By the fall of 2003, we had put together a team of reporters and editors—mostly young people in their 20s—to work on an underage drinking project.

What we did not know at the time was that the issue would become an essential part of what we as a newspaper stood for in our community over the next 15 years. It continues to be and remains one of the core values of the newspaper. We were going after underage drinking because we were tired of seeing young people die needlessly. We were going to do something about it, even if that made some people uncomfortable.

At the time, we didn't even have consensus in the newsroom.

"I think there was differing opinions," Will Doolittle remembered in 2020. "It was right in front of their noses, all these kids dying, but it was also something that was taken for granted, that these things happened. We were going to say these things shouldn't happen and there was some skepticism that was worthwhile. It was an interesting debate as we came along, as the series was produced. As we researched the story, there was more deaths. That helped to convince everyone that, yes, maybe there was a problem here. The newsroom sort of reflected society that way."[47]

As we began our reporting that fall, we found no shortage of material as the carnage continued.

In September, despite the resolve of the Warrensburg Central School, the Warren County Sheriff's Office and teacher Marc Mularz, Warrensburg had a third fatality when 19-year-old Adam Baker of Thurman, a Warrensburg graduate, left a party where he had been drinking to give a young woman a ride home. On the way back to the party, he lost control of his car, hit an embankment and then a tree.[48] His blood alcohol count was twice the legal limit.[49] I couldn't help but wonder if he had read Mularz's guest essay or been at the funerals of Jason Monroe and Jason Daniels.

Later, as part of the "Cost of Fun" project, feature writer Mike Mender wrote a column about the death of Baker, the kid who lived next door to him who he knew as "Buzz":

> It was warm for September that Friday night, almost sticky. Every window in the house was open.
> I couldn't tell at first what I was hearing.
> 2 a.m.
> Maybe some kids sneaked out and were raising hell.
> Maybe my kids.
> The sounds became more defined.

Sounds of panic, terror ... uncontrolled emotion.

I recognized the voice. It was Buzz's mother.

"I need to bring my son home," she pleaded. "We need to make it all right again."

"No, Mom. We can't make it all right."

"But I have to bring him home," she insisted. "We have to make it right again."[50]

It was a heartbreaking account that should have rattled all parents to their core.

Martha Petteys was a 27-year-old feature writer pregnant with her first child when she was given the most important assignment of her newspaper career. Building on earlier project models, we made Petteys the team leader for the underage drinking series.

Petteys always seemed older, a little more mature and serious than the other 20-somethings on *The Post-Star* staff. She was usually the first reporter in the newsroom every morning, put in a productive eight hours and left religiously at 5 p.m. to get home. Even before she was pregnant, you would have more luck finding her in church on Sunday morning than at a bar on Saturday night.

She was organized, hardworking and someone who could be counted on to get things done while bringing a cheerful demeanor and positive outlook to any assignment, something that is rare in the newspaper world.

It was Petteys who was given the first assignment on 9/11 to get to Albany International Airport.

She not only had a way with words, but the previous year she had worked for over ten months on an award-winning six-part series on mental health called "Invisible Prisons."[51]

"I can tell you this about those articles," said Karen Padowicz, the director of development at the Warren/Washington Association of Mental Health. "Every time one appeared, we would receive more phone calls. It reached out to the community and found people who were experiencing some sort of disorder in their lives or in the lives of someone they loved. They felt more alone than they were and called."[52]

That's what small communities will be losing in the future.

Nine reporters and multiple editors took part in the underage drinking project, with Petteys organizing and guiding a bunch of kids fresh out of college who were even younger than herself.

We copied a model we had used three years earlier and organized focus groups with parents, teenagers, members of law enforcement, school officials, community leaders and those on the front lines with social services before establishing parameters and carving up the subject matter to teams of reporters. It was important that community leaders have skin in the game, too.

One mother said flatly during a meeting, "My baby turned into a monster overnight."[53]

One of the teenagers told us that alcohol was much harder to get than drugs. "I can make a phone call and have some [drugs] here in 10 minutes."[54]

We believed him.

What resulted was an eight-part series over four weekends in April and May of 2004 that produced 29 stories. The series was intentionally published at the start of prom season. It was called "The Cost of Fun: Stories of Teen Drinking."

The tentacles of the subject matter took the team in all directions. The goal of the reporting was to provide the big picture of how extensive the region-wide problem was, how it could be addressed and the impact the tragedies had on local communities.

It was Teen Drinking 101.

Our goal was simple. We wanted to save lives. We wanted to shine a spotlight on an issue that had been around since I was a teenager 25 years earlier, and probably even before that.

Petteys provided this introduction to the series: "In the coming weeks, we will learn about what parents can do to keep their kids safe, the impact of tougher drinking laws and the culture of acceptance that has left a wake of tragedies. Area young people will be attending proms this month and graduations the next. The unfortunate reality is drinking will be part of many of these celebrations. Perhaps by educating our community, we can make a difference. Perhaps, we can keep the flowers and the tears for graduation ceremonies, not roadside memorials."[55]

I also challenged our readers: "We urge you to set aside time from raking the yard, grocery shopping or watching the ballgame to immerse yourself in what at times will be an uncomfortable read filled with waste and tragedy. The life of someone close to you may depend on it."[56]

When I contacted Petteys about her work on the series 16 years later, I realized her three children were at, or near, the age when they would be most at risk.

Petteys was 43 and her children were ten, 13 and 15. She said she was worried more about vaping and smoking pot than alcohol in her children's lives. I briefly considered that was what parents told us while doing the series 15 years earlier.[57]

What stood out to her all these years later was her reporting on the science regarding the development of the teenage brain.[58]

"That is something that has stuck with me over the years," she said. "At that age, they are not capable of making those decisions. They are incapable of mentally managing risk."[59]

It was perhaps the most important reporting in the series. It was not the parents, the schools or law enforcement that was the problem. It was not that the kids were bad or stupid or that teen drinking was an inevitable evil; it was simple science that the teenage brain was still developing and not capable of handling the lethal cocktail of alcohol and risk. That was important new information.

"Poor judgment, a lack of self-control, emotional outbursts, experimentation with alcohol and drug use and other common teen woes are now being linked to developmental changes in the teenage brain," Petteys reported in 2004.[60]

This was the science behind the teen drinking problem. If the average teen brain is not fully developed, it explained teens' propensity for risky behavior, whether that was driving fast or drinking too much.

It helped to explain the tragedy from the previous August when a 19-year-old Ticonderoga man was killed while lying in the middle of the road with his brother after a night of drinking. Police did not know why they were lying in the road.[61]

I wondered if local high schools had considered teaching this science to teens.

Looking back all these years later, the scope of the series is startling and thought-provoking.

Following a Friday night football game, several of our baby face 20-something reporters were told the location of a party in the woods. They crashed it and later identified themselves as newspaper reporters.

Throughout the series, the team tried to get teens to explain why they did what they did.

"The teenagers of Fort Edward come here without flashlights and with few words, stepping through the matted grass and over mud puddles and crushed empties to a bonfire tucked at the end of about a half a mile of trails. 'The Pasture' is an underage drinking spot that has been passed down for decades," wrote Abigail Tucker to open "The Cost of Fun" series.[62]

She described a scene of some 35 teens cradling six packs and cardboard cases of beer while others carried bottles in book bags. By midnight, the young people in hooded sweatshirts and letterman jackets were more talkative as they huddled around a fire.

"There is nothing wrong here," one young man told Tucker. "This is just what we do."[63]

Tucker described a scene as the evening wore on when some of the teens excused themselves to urinate or vomit in the darkness. The teens claimed they never drove. Some walked home; others had their parents pick them up.

Our reporters found drinking had become a problem with many teens as early as middle school, while law enforcement officials complained of being handcuffed by laws and sentencing guidelines that were too lenient.

We looked at the culture of drinking around sports and included a profile of a former star athlete who admitted he was an alcoholic by the time he left high school. We later did a story on his need for a liver transplant.

Ryan Brainard, a 2003 graduate of Warrensburg, told *Post-Star* sportswriter Brett Orzechowski that "drinking was everywhere" at Warrensburg when he was in school. He said the problem was not getting any better in 2004.[64]

"At first, Jason's death had a huge effect," Brainard said. "[The effect] has subsided considerably since then. A lot of athletes just continue to drink like they did before."[65]

Warrensburg basketball Coach Doug Duell also believed not much had changed.

"The effect of those deaths have worn off a long time ago. The Jasons [Daniels and Monroe] were popular athletes," Duell told Orzechowski. "If it doesn't change after this, I don't think it ever will. I don't know how many times a program can be hit with this before the message sinks in."[66]

The reporters looked at the role parents play in their children's lives and consulted parenting experts. Some parents let their children drink at home; others had imposed strict punishments; others ignored the problem entirely.[67]

Ultimately, we wanted to bring the readers' attention back from all the journalism and remember the personal toll.

On each of the four Sundays during the series, we ran a segment titled "Flashback" that told the story of a teenager who had died tragically.

It was the most difficult reading all week—none more than Petteys's "Flashback" about the 1990 death of Robert Wheaton, an Adirondack Community College student from Lake Luzerne:

> Edward Litwa Jr., 19, arrived at Robert's house in Lake Luzerne.
> "Don't worry Mr. Wheaton, I'll bring Robert home safe," Litwa called from the driveway.
> Robert and Edward visited a house party and a drinking party in the woods. Then, around 12:30 a.m. they went to pick up friend Karen Allen in Corinth.

After leaving Karen's Eastern Avenue home, Edward lost control on a curve.

They hit a telephone pole. The silver transformer box fell on the car, spilling oil across the hood.

Edward and another passenger crawled from the vehicle as the oil fire spread. Edward tried to pull Robert out, but his legs were crushed under the dashboard. Karen, who was in the backseat, was already dead.

"Please, don't let me die," Robert pleaded.

After trying in vain to free his friend, Edward ran into the woods to hide.

An 8-year-old boy watched the scene from his bedroom window.

Smoke filled the vehicle.

Minutes later, Robert was dead.[68]

Petteys, who was eight months pregnant at the time, remembered being tired all the time that spring and finding herself reading stories for the series in the newsroom library where she could prop up her feet.

"As I was reading, people were writing these different columns and stuff," Petteys said in 2020. "And it occurred to me that I could write about my own experience."[69]

On Friday, September 30, 2005, the national Mothers Against Drunk Driving organization honored *The Post-Star* in Washington, D.C., for its newspaper coverage of underage drinking. "The MADD Media Awards program allows us to celebrate the media who share stories of victimization and survival, heartache and triumph," MADD's national president Wendy Hamilton said. Martha Petteys, the team leader of the project, accepted the award on behalf of the newspaper and had her photograph taken with former CBS anchorman Dan Rather. It was one of several national awards the newspaper received for the eight-part series (photograph by Martin Petteys).

On May 17, 2004—in the third weekend of the series—the newspaper published Martha's column, "It happened to my family," on the front page of the newspaper.

"My brother had come home drunk again. He was 16," Petteys wrote. "I found out later that he had banged up the side of my parents' truck driving through the woods where he liked to party."[70]

Martha Petteys was an expert witness. We had not realized that when we made her team leader.

"It can happen to anyone's family. I know because it happened to mine," Petteys told our readers.[71]

The woman who always had a smile on her face, who was always so positive at work, also had a personal story to tell.

"It felt cathartic to write about it," Petteys said in 2020. "My brother's first drink was when he was 9 years old and my parents were good, good parents, so how did that happen?"[72]

Petteys opened the curtain to a family once in turmoil, to a family scarred by the experience.

"Mom cried a lot," she wrote of her early childhood memories. "Dad got quiet."[73]

Petteys, the mature, straight arrow in our newsroom, was showing us why she was so mature, why she was so serious and why she was the perfect person to lead this project.

"I am no longer that 6-year-old crying in my sister's bed. I am now married and am expecting my first child, but I am still scared. And I still cry sometimes. The fear is the same for all of my family. It's the fear of the late-night phone call. It's the fear of hearing the person on the line tell you, it has started again."[74]

Telling those personal stories is a part of journalism that does not get the credit it deserves, especially in small, rural communities where the readers know the journalists.

Revealing those personal challenges in print allows those in the community to understand they are not alone. While the facts are critical, the experiences are often just as vital to report.

When I asked about her brother, Petteys asked me how she left things in the original column.[75]

I reminded her it was hopeful; she wrote her brother had found sobriety.

"That's what I thought," she said.[76]

It did not last.

Petteys's brother eventually went back to drinking and died when he was 40.[77]

Not surprisingly, Petteys found the positive in how her experience with her brother changed the way she lived her life.

"Yes, I have thought about that," she said 16 years later. "I was the polar opposite because I saw the hurt it did to my family. I will never do that. There is a part of me that is thankful for that. I am this way because of my brother. My choices were different because of him. That is a positive."[78]

After the teen drinking series was published, Petteys started writing a column about her pregnancy that morphed into a freelance column about her family after she left the newspaper. It lasted another 16 years. She left the newspaper as a full-time writer soon after finishing the teen drinking series.

We found out through our underage drinking series there are lasting effects on the people and communities.

Those close to the victims—like Lisa Savard—looked to find a positive through the tragedy by becoming advocates.

Annette Wheaton, the mother of Robert Wheaton who died in that horrific car fire that Petteys wrote about, became a speaker for Mother's Against Drunk Driving.[79]

Anne Ahigian, whose 16-year-old son Desmond died in the Greenwich crash, said in 2004 it seemed that hardly a day had gone by since the crash two years earlier.

"I feel I am stuck at that same place," Anne said. "It is impossible to describe the feeling."[80]

Shortly after the crash in 2002, a group of concerned citizens in Greenwich got together to form Greenwich-Easton Community Cares group.

John Goode, who survived the head-on collision with Jason Daniels, still cringes when an oncoming car approaches the double yellow line.[81]

Daniels died that day, but Goode, a professional firefighter in Albany, survived. He suffered eight bone fractures that day and required multiple surgeries. He was out of work for six months after the accident.[82]

"I'm fortunate I'm back to work, but I'm never going to be the same," he told reporter Don Lehman in 2004. "I deal with pain every day, emotional ups and downs every day. I wonder what my life is going to be like in 10 or 20 years."[83]

The 17-year-old who hosted the drinking party the night before Daniels died was later arrested and sentenced to 30 days in jail. Because the charge was not a felony, the newspaper did not report his name.

When Larry Cook was contacted by one of the reporters nearly two years after his 18-year-old son Stephen was killed by a drunk driver, he said he was saddened to learn about the recent spate of alcohol-related crashes. He said he often wants to contact those involved to let them know that they are not alone in dealing with such a staggering loss.[84]

As the parks and recreation superintendent in the town of Johnsburg in northern Warren County, he said he often had teens assigned to his staff to fulfill their community service after getting in trouble drinking, but many don't take it seriously.[85]

"As soon as they're done [with community service] they're looking to figure out a way they can get away with it again. These kids don't think it can happen to them," Cook said.[86]

Cook pointed out that the man who killed his son, 20-year-old Winstin Hayes of Minerva, was sentenced to two and a third to seven years. He said that was not nearly long enough. He wondered aloud if Hayes was still in prison. When the reporter checked, he told Cook that Hayes would not be released for another year at the earliest.[87]

"I'm glad to hear that," Cook said.[88]

Those on the front lines of the problem described a bigger problem in the rural communities where nobody was immune.

"It's not the kid on the other side of town," said Chris McCormick, a community educator for the Council for Prevention of Warren and Washington counties. "It's the kid next door. It's the baby-sitter."[89]

"This is so serious that people need to get P-O-ed," said John Underwood, an Essex County alcohol prevention educator in the opening part of the series.[90]

Every athletic director who sportswriter Brett Orzechowski contacted about the series refused to let him talk to a high school athlete about drinking at their schools.[91]

Underwood said that is part of the problem, "People are in denial." He said parents have to stop pretending there is not a problem, and they should be talking to them rather than deny it's an issue, thinking that it's everybody else's kid.[92]

The "Cost of Fun" would go on to win state and national awards. I hoped it would be used as a tool for schools and civic groups to warn parents and teens about the dangers.

The Post-Star made one final plea to the community in an editorial by Mark Mahoney on Sunday, May 23, 2004, as the series concluded:

> We can stop alcohol abuse among our teenagers. We have the ability. And we have the support. All we need is the will. Start making the effort, a little bit at a time. Once we start addressing this enormous problem, we'll be able to sleep a little easier at night.[93]

We reprinted the series in a special tabloid edition and printed several thousand copies in August 2004. We announced we would give the special section away to anyone who wanted to educate young people.

Over the next six months, I got just two requests. Stacks of the section, still bundled, were still in The Post-Star's warehouse in 2020. I kept one bundle in my office, just in case.

Shortly after the series concluded, the South Glens Falls Superintendent of Schools, James McCarthy, invited Petteys and I to speak to the district's Safety/Security Committee to talk about the series.[94]

A couple of dozen people were at the meeting, including teachers, town officials, members of law enforcement and one student representative. We talked about the depth of the problem facing local communities. Many concurred, giving their own impressions and experiences and what they thought needed to be done.[95]

It was a good discussion. We told the group we were trying to figure out where to go from here. We told them about reprinting the special edition. McCarthy said he wanted to work with us and distribute the series to students and parents at freshman or junior high orientations.[96]

At the end of the meeting, I asked the student representative who was present what kind of buzz the series had generated with her classmates. I wanted to know their reactions.

"I'm sorry," she said politely. "I don't know what you're talking about."[97]

10

9-1-1

It was a cold Sunday in late February 2005, and it was Mark Mahoney's day off. He had spent the morning with his three young daughters packing for a move.

Mahoney, *The Post-Star's* editorial page editor, had been working at the newspaper since 1988. He divorced in 2000 and was moving in with his fiancée, Lisa. He was hoping to get the kids' stuff packed and moved to Lisa's house for their visit later in the week. For Mahoney, this time with his daughters was the best time of the week.[1]

Like most small cities, Glens Falls is a sleepy little place on Sunday afternoons. Mahoney and his girls stopped at the Cumberland Farms on Bay Road shortly after 2 p.m. to pick up some snacks after leaving the home of the girls' mother in nearby Moreau. Cumberland Farms is a couple of blocks from downtown Glens Falls.

Laurie DiLorenzo, a 42-year-old local nurse who worked at Glens Falls Hospital, had pulled in to the Cumberland Farms and parked next to the gas pumps with her 13-year-old daughter Christin at about the same time.[2] She had just come from the Glens Falls police station, less than a half-mile away, where she talked to officers about her estranged husband following her and her boyfriend in recent days. She believed her husband had also vandalized her car. Before leaving, she told police she did not want to file a complaint or have him arrested and that she did not believe she was in danger.[3]

While Mark's eight-year-old twins, Chelsea and Christa, reviewed snack options at the back of the convenience store, Mahoney and 11-year-old Caitlin made their way to the potato chip display near the counter.[4]

Christin DiLorenzo, Laurie's 13-year-old daughter, had gotten out of the red car, leaving the passenger door open, and was pumping gas for her mother.

There was a commotion at the front of the store. At first, Mahoney wasn't sure what was happening.

Raymond DiLorenzo, a former Glens Falls Hospital security guard and Laurie's 48-year-old husband, pulled his silver Nissan Pulsar into the parking lot at an angle to Laurie's car.

The clerk at the counter started shouting.

"I looked out the window of the store and saw a white car parked angled toward a red car," Mahoney wrote in his account published in the next day's newspaper. "I thought there might have been some kind of car accident, but then I noticed the bumpers weren't touching."[5]

Mark and Caitlin saw a man standing next to the car. He was holding a rifle, and he was firing shots down into the driver's side of the car.

"I could hear shots muffled through the store window," Mahoney wrote. "I saw something appear on the windshield, but I thought it was the window shattering from the gunshots."[6]

Caitlin later told her father that when the gunman was done shooting, he turned and looked right at her from 30 feet away. She wondered if he might come back to harm her.[7]

"He looked into the store at me and the clerk and a few other people through the glass windows," Mahoney said 15 years later. "He took a couple of steps toward us. I don't think he was trying to be intimidating, I just think he was walking."[8]

Mahoney did not see anyone inside the red car. He thought the man was just shooting up the car.[9]

Mahoney was always one of those reporters who was the first to dash out the door when news was happening on the police scanner. He was that way as city editor, too, always unafraid to get in the middle of the action.

He called 9-1-1.

Caitlin had just learned in school about what to do if you witness violence. She memorized the license plate number and kept repeating it out loud while planting a description of the shooter in her head. She then told her father the license number while he talked to the 9-1-1 dispatcher and slowly walked out the store door and into the parking lot.[10]

Mahoney heard someone outside say that someone had been killed.

"I told the dispatcher—probably shouted to him—to get someone to the Cumberland Farms on Bay street, that someone had just been shot to death. I told him the shooter had fled in a white car, and I gave the license number. [It later turned out the car was silver.]"[11]

The dispatcher asked what direction the car had gone.

Mahoney frantically asked others in the parking lot if they knew which direction the man in the car had fled. Someone yelled, "North!"[12]

Mark noticed a young woman, a teenager just a year older than Caitlin, walking around the red car, shouting into a cell phone that her mother had just been shot. He heard someone else say it was the girl's father who had done it.[13]

He later learned the girl was Christin DiLorenzo. He would see her again eight months later in court.

"I walked closer to the car and saw a woman slumped against the wheel," Mahoney wrote in his published newspaper account. "I realized then that the windshield was not shattered, but splattered with blood. I didn't try to take a closer look. It was clear the woman was dead."[14]

Mahoney was working a crime scene like he had done many times before because that's what journalists do in an emergency, even if it is your day off.

His next phone call was to *The Post-Star* newsroom just a half-mile away, where, of course, it was reporter Thom Randall who answered the phone and found himself in the middle of another big story. He was on the scene within minutes.

Mahoney turned his attention back to his daughters, who were still inside the Cumberland Farms.

"When I was sure it was safe, I told them to get into our car, which was parked just outside the store and to sit tight," Mahoney wrote. "They were kind of panicky, and a little worked up. You could see it on their faces. They got in and ducked down low in the seat."[15]

Events had occurred at breakneck speed.

There were sirens as police cars arrived within a minute or two. Officers rounded up witnesses, yellow tape was strung around the crime scene and a white sheet was thrown over the front of the red car while Mahoney's three children looked on from inside their own car.

Mahoney wrote this chilling passage: "It was apparent they wouldn't need to provide the woman with medical attention, and none was given."[16]

When we talked later that week, Mark told me proudly, "My first call was 9-1-1. My second call was to the newspaper."[17]

There are generally two or three people in the newsroom on a Sunday, but there were more later that afternoon as news of the murder spread. Our police reporter, Don Lehman, joined Randall at the scene along with staff photographer Erin Coker. Lehman, in more than 25 years at the newspaper, was never more than a phone call and a few minutes away from covering breaking news, even on a weekend.

Murders are rare in quiet little cities like Glens Falls where random violence is almost nonexistent. Public violence, beyond your run-of-the mill bar fight, is rarer still, so for a staff member to witness a murder was unprecedented.

"To me it was a crime scene thing," Mahoney said in 2020. "I had covered those things before. It was just hard to believe what I was seeing."[18]

Later on the day of the murder, I asked Mahoney if he could write an eyewitness account.

Mahoney said he knew that was coming. He didn't want to do it, but he knew it was important for readers to know exactly what had happened at the convenience store, and he was in the best position to report the facts accurately.[19]

"Afterward, I was amazed at how few details I remembered. You always hear people say, 'It just happened so fast.' And it's true. It was over, literally, in seconds," Mahoney wrote in his account of the shooting. "I couldn't give the police a great description of the shooter. All I remember was the first moment of panic inside the store, the image of this guy firing into the car, a moment of uncertainty about whether he'd come inside, the relief that he was leaving and that lasting image in my head of the terrible tragedy that my daughter and I'd just witnessed."[20]

He later told the district attorney his 11-year-old daughter would have made a better witness than him.[21]

Looking back 15 years later, Mark's account was more than just a description of a heinous act of violence; it was also an account of how a father reacts, worries and deals with his children when there is danger. Any reader would have related, and ours would get a front row seat as that played out.

As Mahoney waited for the police to talk with him, his girls just wanted to go home, so he called his fiancée, Lisa, to come and pick up the girls since his ex-wife was out of town.

"I worried the whole time about how the girls were reacting," Mahoney wrote. "I called home and they seemed to be fine. Lisa said they were cleaning the house. The twins, who are 8, didn't see the shooting. But Caitlin did. And I wondered if the whole thing will hit them later."[22]

It did.

That fall, some eight months after the killing, Mahoney made a Sunday morning doughnut run into Glens Falls with the girls. After picking up the doughnuts, he told the girls he needed to stop at Cumberland Farms to pick up some orange juice.[23]

He remembers a "howl" from the back seat and being startled by the noise. "What's wrong?" he asked.[24]

"Cumberland Farms," one of them said.[25]

Mark said it hadn't occurred to him.

Raymond DiLorenzo fled the scene of the murder, abandoned his car ten miles away in rural Lake Luzerne[26] and for three days remained at large as police conducted a statewide manhunt.

Capt. Joseph Bethel, left, and Capt. Stanley Wood, right, of the Glens Falls police lead accused murderer Raymond DiLorenzo into the Glens Falls police station on Wednesday, February 23, 2005, after DiLorenzo was apprehended in Syracuse, New York, earlier in the day. Three days earlier, Mark Mahoney, *The Post-Star*'s editorial page editor, had witnessed DiLorenzo shoot his wife with a rifle in the parking lot of a local convenience store (*Post-Star* photograph by Erin R. Coker).

After finding the car, police got a call from a man who said he believed he had picked up the short, squat former security guard hitchhiking at about 3 p.m. Sunday. He said he dropped the man off at the Mobil gas station at Exit 21 off the Northway.[27]

Laurie DiLorenzo's family was given police protection and moved to a safe house.[28]

By Monday, a steady stream of gawkers was visiting the Cumberland Farms. The store manager said customer after customer wanted to talk to the staff about the killing.[29]

"This never happens here in Glens Falls," one resident said. Another said they would "definitely lock my door tonight."[30]

Mahoney's daughter, Caitlin, would hang on every televised news report and read every story in the newspaper about the manhunt for the rest of the week.[31]

"She tried to convince herself, with some parental help, that if he had wanted to eliminate witnesses, he would have shot them while he was still at the gas station," Mahoney would write later in October. "Or maybe he had killed himself. Either way, she talked herself into believing he was no longer a threat to her, even though the words that came out of her mouth were far from convincing."[32]

Fifteen years later, Mahoney remembered the manhunt lasting for weeks. He was surprised to learn it was only three days.

Lehman learned from Laurie DiLorenzo's sister, Gail Duncan of Whitehall, that Laurie had long been a victim of domestic violence at the hands of her husband.

"There was lots of domestic violence over the years—years of abuse," Duncan told Lehman the day after the shooting. "But she didn't believe he could do this. I would read [his behavior] and say, 'Laurie, you really need to do something,' but she'd say, 'Oh, he'd never hurt me.'"[33]

The couple had split up the previous May and were in the process of getting a divorce while working through custody issues with their 13-year-old daughter. Her sister said that Raymond DiLorenzo had been stalking and harassing his wife for months, but it had intensified in recent weeks when he had been sending her defaced family photographs.[34]

On the Tuesday after the killing, Glens Falls police revealed that Laurie DiLorenzo had been at the Glens Falls Police Department ten minutes before the Sunday killing to report her husband had been following her.[35]

Police Chief Richard Carey said she did not express concerns for her safety at the time, and she did not want to file a complaint or have DiLorenzo arrested.[36]

"We consulted her, and there wasn't anything criminal," Carey said. "They had a Family Court appearance upcoming and we encouraged her to get an order of protection through Family Court because we didn't have anything criminal."[37]

Police also revealed two different portraits of the alleged killer, Raymond G. DiLorenzo.[38]

"To his fellow co-workers at Glens Falls Hospital and many police officers who came in contact with him there, he was simply Ray or 'Rosy,' the roly-poly affable security guard who had worked at the hospital for years," Lehman wrote in the lead for his story that Wednesday. "Raymond G. DiLorenzo was the guard who insisted on holding open the door for female employees and always cheerfully cooperated with police whenever they needed assistance in the emergency room."[39]

"Before Sunday, you couldn't really find many people who could say anything bad about him," Glens Falls police Detective Sgt. Lloyd Swartz said at the time.[40]

But a search of the couple's suburban Algonquin Drive home in Queensbury revealed a disturbing alter ego.[41]

Police found the home filled with debris and garbage, defaced family photos and graffiti on the walls denigrating Laurie DiLorenzo, including threats against Laurie, her sister and Laurie's boyfriend, saying they would all "die in 2005."[42]

Police allowed reporters and photographers inside to photograph the graffiti, and the newspaper published three of the photographs, including one that shows a cabinet spray-painted with the message "Laurie the slut" and the satanic symbol "666" underneath.[43]

Warren County Family Court Judge Timothy Breen told Lehman no domestic violence allegations had been brought up in court.

Police finally arrested Raymond DiLorenzo in a Syracuse homeless shelter on Wednesday morning after a waitress at a restaurant, who had read about the case in the Syracuse newspapers, recognized him. It was another reminder of the reach that newspapers still had. Raymond DiLorenzo was arraigned later that day in Glens Falls City Court.[44]

When Caitlin learned the killer had been caught, Mahoney said she let out a heavy sigh. But even then, it wasn't really the end.[45]

In August, Raymond

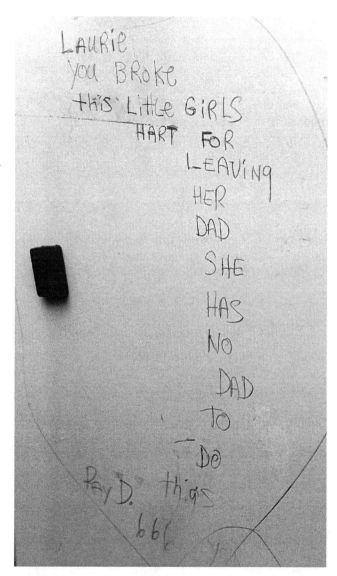

Inside the DiLorenzo home at 5 Algonquin Drive in Queensbury, New York, police found a disaster. There were defaced family photographs, graffiti scrawled on the walls of four different rooms denigrating Laurie DiLorenzo and trash scattered everywhere in the house. This photograph shows a message Raymond DiLorenzo wrote on an inside wall circled by a heart (*Post-Star* photograph by Erin R. Coker).

DiLorenzo pleaded guilty to murdering his wife, even though he claimed he had no memory of the killing. He faced 25 years to life in prison.[46]

"I'm very sorry for what happened," DiLorenzo told Warren County Judge John Hall.[47] Neither Mahoney nor his daughter Caitlin would have to testify.

The guilty plea came a day after DiLorenzo and his lawyer viewed the convenience store surveillance camera video that caught the shooting on tape. DiLorenzo told the judge he wanted to spare his daughter from having to testify in the trial.[48]

"She's had enough trauma these last few months," DiLorenzo said. "I don't want to put her through any more."[49]

The judge asked him if he had heard the tape of his daughter's 9-1-1 call after the shooting.[50]

DiLorenzo said yes.

"Did she say someone shot her mother?" the judge asked.

"Yes," he replied.

"Did she say that someone was you?" the judge asked.

"Yes," he said.[51]

Later that day, Christopher and Christin DiLorenzo faced their father a second time in Warren County Family Court. Raymond DiLorenzo was barred from having any further contact with his daughter until she was 18.[52]

After the neglect hearing, the Department of Social Services asked Breen to give custody of 14-year-old Christin to her 22-year-old brother, Christopher. She had been living with her aunt, Gail Duncan.[53]

Breen gave Christopher temporary physical custody, pending a hearing in October, then called him to the front of the court gallery.[54]

"Chris, are you ready for this?" Breen asked.

"Yes, your honor," Christopher replied.

"Are you going to do a good job for me?" Breen asked.

"Yes, your honor," Christopher replied.[55]

On October 26, 2005, Raymond DiLorenzo was sentenced in Warren County Court, and Mark Mahoney was there just as he promised his daughter Caitlin.

"Going to the sentencing was important for me," Mahoney explained 15 years later. "Caitlin had been upset by the manhunt and she wanted to know if he was ever going to get out. We sat down and talked about it. I told her I was going to go to the sentencing so I could tell her myself if he is ever going to get out."[56]

Raymond DiLorenzo apologized to his children and other relatives in court that October day, but it did not lead to forgiveness.[57] His two children spoke calmly as they stood just feet from their handcuffed, manacled father.

"I hope you rot in jail for the rest of your miserable life," 14-year-old Christin told her father.[58]

"No one can bring back what you, Raymond DiLorenzo, stole from my sister and I [sic]," his 22-year-old son Christopher said.[59]

There was nearly an hour of victims' impact statements. District Attorney Kate Hogan concluded by saying that a young girl witnessing her mother being shot to death by her father is "a horror beyond imagination."[60]

Hogan asked to play the surveillance camera video of the shooting, but the judge denied the request after watching the footage before the hearing. Judge Hall then imposed the maximum sentence of 25 years to life in state prison.[61]

After the sentencing, Mahoney called Caitlin and told her that Raymond DiLorenzo had received the maximum sentence.[62]

He told her he would never get out.[63]

That afternoon, Mahoney came into my office and asked me to read something he had written from the sentencing. Eight months after his forensic "just the facts" account of the killing he had witnessed, Mahoney emptied his emotions in a rare commentary that we published on our front page.[64] He was writing more as a father than a journalist.

"I went because I wanted to see them put the bastard away," is how Mahoney started the commentary. We allowed the profanity to be published because it seemed appropriate.[65]

"For my sake. For my kids' sake, I had to see this with my own eyes," he wrote.[66]

When I talked to him in 2020, I told him the difference between the eyewitness accounts of the murder and courtroom sentencing were startling in their emotional impact.

"It bothered me as time went on," Mahoney admitted. "I'm not a victim like these people in court were. I didn't see my mother killed. But I'm part of it. I think a lot of witnesses feel that way too."[67]

And then it was like Mahoney was back there again.

"It makes you angry," he said. "There is this teenage girl just standing there pumping gas. Her door is open. She saw it all. She was on the phone with the cops crying. He could have gone on a shooting spree and killed 10 people. He could have gone crazy. I was surprised at how he hesitated, how he took his time.... I live my life, but it comes back to you."[68]

Mahoney said that after I was done reading his commentary from court, I scrawled one word at the top and left the pages on his desk.[69]

"Wow!" I had written.

Mahoney's emotions had been buried for eight months as a father still fretting about his children's safety in a violent world. His feelings went to the heart of the matter for all of us:

> After something like this, how do you ever convince a child that there's not a murderer lurking around every gas pump?
> How do you comfort a daughter who keeps her thoughts and fears to herself until something unexpectedly triggers them loose?
> How do you assure your kids that if they one day do something to anger someone that person, won't do the same horrible thing to them?
> And how do you get past the implied understanding that no matter how much he tries, there are circumstances in which Daddy can't always protect his babies from harm?[70]

It's what we all grapple with, isn't it?

I think that came through to our readers that day.

"As I fought back tears, I understood that no one could put themselves in this family's place," Mahoney wrote after court. "But Raymond DiLorenzo's actions also touched my life in a permanent way by ripping a hole in my children's trust in the world. My daughters may relegate the details of this nightmare to the recesses of their minds. But it will always be there—the fear that there are people out there capable of doing horrible things and destroying innocent lives. And some future event in their lives may bring it all back."[71]

In February 2007, Raymond D. Lorenzo appealed his conviction, arguing he was not properly told of all his options to defend himself. Two months later, the Appellate Division of the state Supreme Court denied his appeal, saying he had adequate representation.

At the end of the first account of the killing of Laurie DiLorenzo, the newspaper reported this was not the first time we had seen lethal domestic violence in our community. It was actually the third such killing in the past four years.

In November 2002, Fort Ann resident Heath Russell had beaten his girlfriend's mother to death in Lake Luzerne. Three months after that, Queensbury resident Bryan Al-Dijaili stabbed his girlfriend to death in their home.[72]

But Laurie DiLorenzo's murder was witnessed firsthand, not only by one of our editors but all our readers because Mahoney just happened to be buying some snacks that afternoon. They saw the threats spray-painted in her home and surely imagined her terror.

That is the power of community journalism and the dedication of those who practice it.

The case and its aftermath spurred a community-wide conversation on how the region's criminal justice system handles domestic violence cases. But that October morning in the Warren County Court, Mahoney was not so sure anything would change.

"I wanted to think that being there [in court] would do us all some good," Mahoney concluded that day. "Somehow, though, I knew that it wouldn't."[73]

11

Breaking Their Silence

Konrad Marshall was a 27-year-old Australian with an easygoing presence, sharp wit and a disarming accent that seemed to put anyone he talked to at ease.

It was his job to talk to the victims—all of them.

The very public killing of Laurie DiLorenzo in February 2005 opened up a spigot of raw emotion in our community unlike anything seen before. Because it was so public, because there were so many details of the abuse in the public realm, it demanded our attention.

Before there was a trial, we assembled a group of editors and reporters to look into domestic violence locally. Our goal was to drag the dark realities into the open where they could be witnessed by our readers. That reality had already been witnessed by one of our editors.

The goal was to show the face of domestic violence, but to do that we needed our readers to trust us. We needed them to reach out to us, to come forward and tell us their stories of abuse as they had with the "Growing up Gay" story. We didn't know if they would.

We published a short notice in the newspaper urging readers to contact us and tell their stories of domestic violence.

The team we assembled was again made up of young reporters in their 20s. Our team leader on the project was Sunday editor Betsy DeMars, a 29-year-old who was married with two children. We asked readers to call DeMars and tell her their stories. Since we expected most of the victims to be women, we believed it was important a woman be the first contact. DeMars was also the editor in charge on the Sunday when Laurie DiLorenzo was murdered.

"Going through that in the newsroom, something that happened in broad daylight, it just kind of struck deep in my soul," DeMars remembered 15 years later. "You knew there were so many things that did not happen in broad daylight that these victims were enduring. You just knew that there was no way this was the first time he was violent with her. That ended in terrible tragedy, but there had to be stuff that led up to that."[1]

In the following weeks, DeMars listened to heartbreaking story after heartbreaking story. It was her job to review the stories first, explain the project to the victims and assure them their stories not only needed to be published but would be handled with the utmost care.[2]

"That is my personality, to put people at ease," DeMars said. "When people were calling, you had to make them feel comfortable that what they were doing had value and they were doing the right thing.[3]

Sunday editor Betsy Demars and reporter Konrad Marshall both worked the phones, asking the domestic violence victims they had interviewed if they would go one step further and have their photograph taken as a group for the story. Photographer T.J. Hooker brought along a stepladder to take the photograph of seven women in a wooded area of Glens Falls' Crandall Park. We agreed not to identify them by name in the photograph, and the photograph was published on the front page (*Post-Star* photograph by T.J. Hooker).

"I don't think it was that hard," she said. "The reason I wanted to be the project manager, I felt so passionate and deeply about what we were doing. That's what I wanted to come through when I talked to these women, that it was really important for people to hear their stories."[4]

That's what gives projects on a subject like domestic violence their heart and credibility. DeMars fielded dozens of calls, and by the time we were ready to begin reporting the story, she had already become an expert on the issue.

Twenty-three victims came forward and agreed to talk to a reporter. Konrad Marshall was selected to handle all of the interviews.

Marshall interviewed some of the victims in their homes, others by phone in the newsroom, but gradually he developed a routine. After working his regular day shift, he went home for dinner. Afterward, he would return to the newsroom when it was quieter, with fewer distractions.[5]

"Once I had all the names, I interviewed each one of them at length," Marshall remembered 15 years later from Melbourne, Australia, where he now works as a senior writer for *Good Weekend* magazine. "I didn't want to do it in the bustling *Post-Star* newsroom or at home. So after most people had gone home, I would come back to *The Post-Star* and do it in the quiet of that big empty space."[6]

Perhaps, he didn't want others to hear the horror in his own voice or see him beating back his own tears. Or maybe it was a more intimate way to make a connection.

"I have vivid recollections of driving in there with virtually no one else there," he said. "This big empty room and listening to people cry ... listening."[7]

Night after night, Marshall chronicled the nightmares and asked the questions few dared to ask before.

"There was just some wrenching and horrible stuff," he remembered.[8]

Even 15 years later, Marshall could still recall many of the stories. He remembered Melanie of Corinth.[9]

She was 27 at the time when he interviewed her. She told him about being eight months pregnant with her second child. Her kidneys had shut down, she had a catheter hanging out the back of her and she was worried about losing the baby.[10]

"I wasn't allowed to have intercourse, and he raped me in front of my 4-year-old son," she told Marshall. "My son was watching, and I was screaming, and he closed the door in his face."[11]

Marshall described it this way when he recounted it in 2005: "But the image of the door closing on her son, when he raped her, pregnant, sick and screaming will always be with her."[12]

It stayed with Marshall, too.

"She just looked so..." Marshall said over the phone in 2020, before pausing and gathering his words again. "She was a really pretty young girl and she looked so broken down by life. You couldn't help but see this relationship had broken her. She seemed so brave to me, to be speaking to me and agreeing to be photographed. There was lots of courage and resilience that was coming from a dark place."[13]

You could tell, Marshall was back there again, too.

This is what you have to remember as well: communities like Glens Falls are the real-life incarnation of Bedford Falls, the perfect little town from *It's a Wonderful Life*. It is a lovely little city where the anchor business downtown is the public library. The side streets are lined with the two-story homes with friendly front porches and fragrant flowers you usually only see on make-believe Hollywood backlots. People move to Glens Falls because they want their families to be safe while watching their children walk to the neighborhood school around the corner.

In some ways, the DiLorenzo murder shattered that illusion or, at the least, questioned it for a time.

Communities like Glens Falls are made up of a series of institutions—the hometown bank, local businesses, the local hospital, the library and a daily newspaper that has been publishing for over 100 years. They all have a stake in its quality of life, in making it a better place to live. I think they take that role seriously. This was another conversation the community needed to have—like it or not—like underage drinking, same-sex marriage or the tragic effect of a foreign war on a little boy.

So when we at the newspaper saw a problem, an issue that was not being addressed, we picked at the scab, pulled off the Band-Aid and exposed the wound for all to see. No other business is quite like it. Most prefer a broom to deal with the problem.

When DeMars handed off the interviews to Marshall, it was unclear if he was ready for the project.

He had met his future wife Nicky, a Glens Falls woman, when she was studying in Australia. When she finished her studies, Konrad followed her back to the United

States. He tried to cobble together a living with various freelance writing gigs before landing a job as a part-time night cops reporter with *The Post-Star*. About five months later, at Will Doolittle's insistence, we hired him full-time in the features department over Thom Randall, who also wanted the job. That tells you something about Doolittle's eye for talent, or maybe the concern about working with Randall.[14]

This was Marshall's first big project. He remembered hearing so much about the underage drinking series from a couple of years earlier. He wanted to be part of something like that. It was the kind of journalism he wanted to do.[15]

Marshall, with his charming Australian accent and easygoing manner, seemed perfectly suited to putting the victims at ease while visiting their homes and talking on the telephone late in the evenings. What he endured was a relentless stream of unimaginably sadistic acts that would leave anyone shattered.

Over three days, Marshall told those stories in short vignettes accompanied by a collection of quotations from the victims that often left you with a hopeless feeling. The first part of "Breaking Their Silence" was published on July 10, 2005.

> *The last time he beat me, he showed up and broke down the door of my house. A neighbor saw me fly past the window, he threw me so hard, I don't remember anything after that. I found myself wandering the woods. I don't know where I was. I was just bleeding and walking.*[16]

We set out to tell the story, as much as possible, from the point of view of the victims. Marshall organized the interviews into three categories.

The first part was about their first experiences with domestic violence and how it all began. The second part described the violence at its worst. And the third part showed how the victims eventually got away.

Twenty-two women and one man came forward to tell their stories. The victims were often nervous, sometimes crying, but told their stories in agonizing detail. They were of all ages, backgrounds and education levels. Most of all, they wanted the community to know how common domestic violence was in our community and that it had no socioeconomic limitations.

Most of the women agreed to let us use their full names, but for legal reasons and in the spirit of protecting their identities, we decided to print only their first names, ages and the towns they were from. DeMars remembered that was important to many of the victims.[17]

The stories that Marshall reported were so long, so detailed in the abuse that often lasted years, we decided to write abbreviated vignettes for each of the 23 victims to be published in the newspaper over three days. We published longer stories for each person online.

Looking back 15 years later, the brutality described in the accounts is striking in how relentlessly matter-of-fact the stories are. In some ways, this was reader abuse, especially over three consecutive days of coverage, as we subjected our readers to one terrifying tale after another—much like the victims who lived it.

The repetition of one atrocity after another and the brutality of the words left you exhausted and sometimes not wanting to read any further. Maybe that's what gave it power.

> One night he woke me with a machete to my throat. He'd be in a fit of rage for no reason, saying, "I'll kill you, you're no good." We hadn't even fought or anything.[18]

Marshall told the story of 50-year-old Janet, who got pregnant and dropped out of high school at 16: "But the girl who had always been so strong-willed began stubbornly to take his abuse. He beat the resistance out of her. The pain became habit. Janet would show up to work with a black and blue face, telling stories of the stairways and doorways she misjudged."[19]

There was 56-year-old Kathy from Warrensburg who said the abuse started two months after she was married: "Then he stood, picked up his chair and brought it down on her head. She doesn't remember much of the rest of the night. All she remembers is coming to on the floor of the dining room and cleaning up the mess. Then cleaning up her wounds—in that order."[20]

Kathy's husband was a successful engineer.

Marshall remembered her, too.

"I remember sitting at her dinner table and she explained to me a memory of the guy roaring in and screaming and breaking a chair over the top of her head. I was just shocked," Marshall said 15 years later. "She was this incredibly put together, well-to-do woman. This was a real eye-opener that domestic violence crossed over all strata of people."[21]

> It was the week after our wedding. He was jealous of somebody. He walked in and killed my kitten. He just grabbed my kitten and chucked it at a wall.[22]

There was 42-year-old Dan from Saratoga: "She came in and started screaming at me. Next thing I know she's hitting me. She just lit into me with a golf club. The neighbors called the police, who arrived to find her holding the golf club, while Dan sat in the corner nearly unconscious and bloodied. They wouldn't even take a police report. They told me to get out, or they'd arrest me. And the shelters wouldn't help."[23]

There was 38-year-old Angela from Lake George: "He pounded me with the vacuum over and over. He told me I was used goods, that no one would want me."[24]

As part of the first day of coverage in "Breaking Their Silence," reporter Bonnie Naumann rode along with Glens Falls police to chronicle their response to real domestic violence calls and find out the challenges they faced. She found officers often played the role of marriage counselors and mediators after violence was threatened.

Naumann learned the statistics did not tell a complete story, writing, "Society doesn't seem to have a grasp on the definition of domestic violence. And the details of cases that are reported get buried in filing cabinets and computer systems. Local law enforcement agencies catalog criminal offenses, not people's relationships. Databases may be able to tally stabbings, assaults or robberies, but they can't easily retrieve all the crimes that began as a domestic dispute and escalated."[25]

Consider the story of 50-year-old Crystal who Marshall wrote about in Part 2:

> They were coming down from a binge together one night and he wanted to make love. She did not.
>
> He took an elbow to her face, and had his way with her all the same.
>
> "I couldn't fight back," she said. "I felt cold inside, dead inside. It was the first time I hadn't fought back."
>
> She limped to the bathroom to get dressed, still naked. But he came after her, knocked her to the floor and took her by the hair, dragging her up and down the hall.
>
> Crystal screamed, but no neighbors came to her aid in the efficiency apartment. By the end of the beating, she had urinated and defecated on herself.

She slowly got up and walked to the kitchen, grabbed a chef's knife, raised it to stab him. He backed into a corner and said she was crazy, looking panicked.

With that, she dropped the knife and ran into the warm night air, crying to neighbors who called the police.

"The police came, and he was a big old fat cigar-chompin' good ol' boy," Crystal said. "He spoke to my husband before me and he looked at me, told me to turn around, and I did, and he laughed and laughed and said, 'Little lady, you look like you been in a car accident.'"[26]

"Only 5 percent of victims get help in any way," Maggie Fronk, executive director for Domestic Violence and Rape Crisis Services in Saratoga told Naumann.[27]

"This is part of the picture of why it is hard for our society to see domestic violence," Jeanne Noordsy, coordinator with Catholic Charities' Domestic Violence Project, told Naumann.[28]

Our readers needed to understand why this continued to happen over and over again.

> He smacked me across the face and I started crying. He told me to stop crying. When I couldn't, he put a pillow over my face and pushed down.[29]

In the second part on Monday, reporter Kate Perry painted a picture of the ordinary batterer while struggling to find a psychological profile the experts could agree upon.

Perry found even the experts on the front lines disagreed about the root causes of the aggression and obsession with control.

Robert Davis, a Saratoga Springs clinical social worker who counsels more than a dozen people with aggressive problems at any given time, told Perry society had shaped what it envisions an abuser to be.[30]

"Over the course of three months in the making of this series, *The Post-Star* was contacted by domestic violence victims who say they were abused by people from all walks of society. Among the abusers who were named were a sheriff's deputy, an engineer, a naval officer, a church elder, a firefighter and a lawyer," Perry wrote.[31]

We were asking our readers to understand it was some of their neighbors sitting on those friendly front porches who were often guilty of abuse.

On the second day, Marshall chronicled the most horrific of deeds.

He told Janet's story of being dragged from her car by her husband on a country road and beaten up. When the couple returned to his parents' home that evening with her bloodied and covered in road dust, her mother-in-law asked her what happened. When she told her what her son had done, she said, "No, you must be mistaken."[32]

> He wanted me to say something, but he was choking me. I could not even breathe. I thought my life had come down to that moment. I thought I would never be all of the things I have dreamed of being.[33]

Marshall told the story of 48-year-old Carol being whipped with a belt and choked until she passed out. When she called 9-1-1, she was told her injuries weren't that bad.[34]

"He's good at that, at things that don't leave marks, except on the inside," she told Marshall. "That's the kind of person he is. He left a lot of marks on the inside."[35]

By the third part on Tuesday, reporter Don Lehman returned us to the beginning, to the killing of Laurie DiLorenzo that previous February, and gave our readers new details about footprints in the snow that Laurie had found outside her apartment window, repeated incidents of stalking and the photo her husband had stuck a knife through that was found in her former home.

Warren County District Attorney Kate Hogan said that Laurie DiLorenzo's path to leaving her husband was like that of many others. Hogan said not every abusive relationship ended with a beating or assault.[36]

"Every DV [domestic violence] survivor is different," she told Lehman. "Sometimes one event makes them walk away; sometimes they just reach the breaking point when it has just gone on for so long."[37]

In some ways, how the victims got out of their relationships was the most difficult to read, the final straw, the breaking point that sometimes came with broken bones and permanently damaged psyches.

Marshall brought readers back to the story of Kathy of Warrensburg, who had the chair broken over her head when she was first married and who Marshall remembered 15 years later as being so professional and together.[38]

Kathy had started to gather her belongings and her money and began making plans to leave when he took her to dinner at the fanciest restaurant in town.[39]

"He seemed menacing then, said that he'd been thinking about killing himself. He told her his plan like it was dinner conversation. He would drive his car into a bridge abutment with Kathy and the kids there with him," Marshall wrote. "A final warning came while talking to her daughter on the phone. 'Daddy called,' her young daughter said. 'Why do I have to go on a trip with him. You said I could stay here.'"[40]

Kathy called the police, raced around the house packing clothes, birth certificates and other important files. Other friends helped her to find a place to live as she hid in another town with her children.[41]

She later discovered after speaking with many other victims, there was nothing unique about her case.[42]

In the days before "Breaking Their Silence" ran, we realized we had a problem. We did not have a lead photograph for a project of this magnitude. Because of the delicate nature of the story, we did not feel comfortable asking any of the victims to pose individually for portrait-style photos. We doubted any would agree anyway.

Someone posed the idea of a group photograph. Perhaps, there was strength in numbers. Perhaps, that would make the piece more powerful.

While the stories remain difficult to read all these years later, the photos taken by our young photographer, T.J. Hooker, remain inspirational.

"I can still see that photo," our team leader DeMars said 15 years later.[43]

DeMars and Marshall called around and got nine of the victims to agree to be photographed. If they had gone this far, maybe they would be willing to go a little further.

The logistics were difficult and several who agreed to be photographed could not make it, but seven women showed up for the photo shoot in Glens Falls' Crandall Park. DeMars made sure to be there to put their minds at ease. She had to finish the job she started. So was our editorial page editor Mark Mahoney, who I suspect was also looking for closure after being an eyewitness to Laurie DiLorenzo's murder.

"They are members of an uneasy sisterhood," Mahoney wrote in the Sunday editorial after watching the women gather for the photo. "They smile and talk casually about a darkness few of us will ever know. Though they've never met, a group of domestic violence survivors gathers for a *Post-Star* photo shoot to share stories as if attending their high school reunion. Only these stories aren't of favorite subjects and first kisses. These are stories of terror, of fearing for their lives at the hands of their spouses. Of bare-fisted beatings and murderous fingers gripping their throats. About getting shot at and being stalked and being told that if they ever left, they and their children would be hunted down and killed."[44]

Mahoney had become a dazzling master of advocating for our community and a better way of life.

The photo was taken in a grove of evergreen trees in Crandall Park, a lovely green space where families picnic, children are pushed on swings and taught to fish in a nearby pond. It was a half-mile from where Laurie DiLorenzo was murdered at the Cumberland Farms five months earlier.

The giant pines cast shadows across the grassy undercarriage with the seven of them spread out among the trees, alone, yet with the commonality of a dark past.

Hooker, our photographer, was atop a stepladder.

None of the women are smiling.

One had her hands behind her back, two clenched their hands in front of them, another leaned against a tree while another seemed ready to bolt.

There is a loneliness about the group, an uneasiness that they all seem to share, but also a defiance that they are unafraid to stand there together, united as survivors.

All these years later, I still find it remarkable.

"What do we have to be ashamed of?" one of them says out loud.[45]

"For being stupid too long," another answers.[46]

The July 10 editorial from Mark Mahoney goes on to say:

> We hope that this series opens some eyes to the serious and pervasive nature of this problem. We hope that by sharing the stories of the domestic violence survivors, it will encourage more victims to come forward and take action to help themselves and their children. We hope some abusers will recognize themselves in these stories and get the help they need. And we hope that in educating the general public about the signs of domestic abuse, fewer people will be able to turn their backs on the problem.[47]

"These were men and women from our communities, not from some far-off place and they came forward to shine a light on a dark spot in our community," I wrote after the series had been published. "They should be commended. Seven agreed to stand together and have their photograph taken. It added a reality to the series that these people were flesh and blood and had survived a traumatic ordeal."[48]

In the aftermath of the series, the newspaper received calls and messages from approximately 20 more people who wanted to tell their own stories of domestic violence. Some wanted information on how the court system works. Others criticized the judges who did not take abuse into account enough during custody hearings. Others called asking for help because they were in an abusive relationship, too.[49]

Years later, I wonder if this work helped others to escape their abuse.

The next year, the New York State Associated Press Association named Konrad Marshall the "Young Journalist of the Year."[50] He is now recognized as a top journalist in Australia.

"They're caught up in this cycle and they can't escape," Marshall told me in an email after the series ran. "They've been calling me crying for weeks, and that's just as hard to leave at the office as women telling you about beatings and rapes."[51]

If he was looking for that small bit of hope, it was elusive as he described the lasting impact from Jodie, whose boyfriend used to tailgate her so closely she couldn't see the front of his car in the rearview mirror.[52]

"At red lights, I'll still think of him," Jodie said of the threats by her boyfriend to kill her. "The fear will come over me, and I'll lock my doors."[53]

After all those lonely nights in the newsroom, Marshall finally offered that one nugget of hope, that possibility of a happily-ever-after that had remained elusive.

"Her man told Jessica of Hartford to pack her stuff and leave like he had done many times before," Marshall wrote in his final account. "This time, she did it.[54]

"As she loaded up a suitcase, she found her pride," Marshall wrote. "As she brought them to the car, she found her self-esteem."[55]

12

"I don't know where my husband is"

It was 2:55 p.m. on a sun-splashed Sunday in October 2005 when the call came into the Warren County police dispatcher. There was something happening on Lake George.

CALLER: Oh my god! Oh my god! A boat, a boat, a boat went over, the *Ethan Allen* just outside of Green Harbor! It tipped right over.
DISPATCHER: How many people are in the boat?
CALLER: Oh, a lot of people. They were hanging onto the front of the boat when it went over! Oh please, hurry![1]

Twenty-five minutes earlier, a senior citizen tour group from Michigan had boarded the *Ethan Allen*, a 40-foot tour boat that sat low in the water with two sets of bench seats running across the deck divided by a center aisle and a canopy overhead[2] to keep its passengers out of the sun. The wooden benches, bolted to the deck, seated three on the left side of the boat and two on the right side, giving it a slight 2.2-degree tilt when full.[3] Most of the tour group's passengers were in their 70s.

It was one of those perfect autumn days in the Adirondack Mountains of upstate New York. By October, the 32-mile-long lake is peaceful and quiet compared to the bustling tourist center that attracts so many from New York City, Long Island and New Jersey during the bustling summer months. It was sweater weather.

The Michigan seniors boarded the small boat at the southernmost tip of the lake with a breathtaking vista of mountains, lake and foliage before them as they headed north. It was Lake George in all its pristine glory.

There were 47 passengers and one crew member,[4] the captain, on board as the boat left the dock. There was no requirement for a safety briefing. Life preservers were stored in plain sight overhead.[5]

Richard Paris, the 74-year-old captain, held the wheel while standing at the stern. Conditions were calm as Paris provided narration about the history of the lake as the vessel poked along at an estimated eight miles per hour. He had more than 20 years experience as captain.[6]

Paris took the vessel north up the east side of Lake George and was nearly halfway through the one-hour cruise when he made an abrupt turn to the right after encountering a "wave or waves" just south of Cramer Point. He later said he was trying to avoid being swamped by the wake of another boat.[7]

Margie Kidon, a 65-year-old chaperone with the Trenton Travelers seniors' group, was sitting on the left side of the *Ethan Allen*—the side closest to the shore—when

Warren County Sheriff's Department Sgt. Steven Stockdale takes a moment as the enormity of the tragedy before him sinks in. Stockdale was among the first on the scene after the *Ethan Allen* tour boat capsized and sank on Lake George with nearly 50 senior citizens aboard on October 2, 2005. Some of the 20 who died are covered by sheets in front of him (*Post-Star* photograph by T.J. Hooker).

she felt the boat rock. Passengers slid off their bench seats, and the boat overturned. Kidon hit her head on a swinging plexiglass window next to her.[8]

Loretta and Lowell Peacock, 78 and 79, said the boat just kept tipping, and as it tipped, the people on the benches all slid to one side.[9]

Anna Mae Hawley, 74, said the boat tipped over suddenly.[10]

Jeane Siler, 76, said she was sitting on the right side of the boat when she was jolted. "I don't know if I jumped out of the boat or I was thrown," she said. "I was on the boat one minute and in the water the next."[11]

As the *Ethan Allen* rolled onto its left side, Siler instinctively held onto her purse.[12]

Brian Hart, who was canoeing nearby, saw the boat capsize and called 9-1-1. He told them to hurry. He paddled back to the dock to drop off his children, then called his brother. The two went out to the scene in a motorboat.[13]

Loretta Peacock said she was temporarily trapped under the boat, but when she finally found her way to the surface, she was right next to her husband, Lowell.[14]

"I was in a washing machine-agitating atmosphere where I was swimming for my life," 67-year-old Carole Mahalak said.[15]

The *Ethan Allen* capsized several hundred feet from shore where the water was approximately 60 feet deep.[16]

An emergency radio call went out to all first responders, but when Bruce Kilburn, the chief of the Lake George Fire Department, heard there were 50 casualties, he asked for it to be confirmed.

"I thought it had to be 15. It couldn't be 50," Kilburn asked.[17]

Like most Sundays at small newspapers, it was a slow day in *The Post-Star* newsroom ten miles south of the lake in Glens Falls.

Amanda Bensen, a 26-year-old Columbia journalism school graduate, was the general assignment reporter that day when the police scanner came to life. She normally writes features, not news.

T.J. Hooker, a 23-year-old full-time photographer at the newspaper, was editing photos near the end of his eight-hour shift. He heard the call that a boat had overturned on Lake George and people were in the water.[18]

"I thought that is a pretty good-sized boat," Hooker remembered 15 years later.[19]

Almost immediately there was another call saying that 14 people were in the water.[20]

"That isn't a small vessel," Hooker remembered thinking. "I realized that something must have gone terribly wrong."[21]

Hooker grabbed a telephoto lens, walked the short distance into the newsroom and said to the only reporter in the room, "Amanda, come with me."[22]

It is a scene that is repeated daily in newsrooms all the around the country where professional journalists practice their craft in tandem with the crackle of a police scanner. The best reporters and editors can read the inflections or word choices of the dispatcher to decipher how serious the emergency might be and whether it warrants news coverage. But neither Hooker nor Bensen had ever covered anything like this. None of us had.

The pair climbed into Hooker's Chevy Cobalt for what is normally a 25-minute drive when there is not much traffic. Hooker said he got there a lot quicker.[23]

Warren County sheriff's sergeant Steve Stockdale heard the alert and hopped on a patrol boat with Sgt. Michael Webster in the village of Lake George just south of the incident.[24]

Back on the lake, people noticed a commotion off Cramer Point.

"I heard all these people screaming," the canoeist Hart said later. "It was like the Titanic. It was awful. It was hard to pull people out because they were so frantic. Some couldn't swim and grabbed me so hard that it's a good thing I was wearing a life jacket, or I'd be another casualty."[25]

Hart eventually pulled six people from the water. Two were already dead, and one died later.

"One gentleman saw me pull his wife onto my boat after him and die right in front of us," the canoeist Hart said. "He said it was their 50th wedding anniversary last week, and this was like a honeymoon cruise for them."[26]

Mounir Rahal, a nearby Queensbury resident and jewelry store owner, was out on the lake with his wife and five children when they saw the commotion. He was one of the first boats on the scene. They pulled six passengers from the water, including Anna Mae Hawley.[27]

Giselle Root and her husband John Root, owners of the nearby Brookside Motel, got in their boat and pulled eight of the passengers from the water. Giselle Root said none of the victims knew how to swim and had to be coaxed to their boat while clinging to the hull of the *Ethan Allen*. As other boats arrived at the scene, they tossed life preservers into the lake.[28]

As the two sheriff's officers approached Cramer Point, they spotted the overturned hull of the boat with "debris" all around it.[29]

But it wasn't debris.

It was bodies.

Frank Sause, whose family operates Cramer Point Motel, rushed to the scene with his daughter, hoping to help. He tried to help one man as he watched his unconscious wife being removed from the water and realized she appeared to be dead.

"I just couldn't calm him down," he said later.[30]

Kidon was picked up by Larry Steinhart and Joyce Cloutier.

When the two sheriff's officers arrived, Stockdale pulled two women who had drowned out of the lake.

By 3:10 p.m., witnesses said the *Ethan Allen* was submerged as boats converged from all around the lake. But little more could be done.

On shore, ambulances were on their way to the scene.

Post-Star reporter Don Lehman was at home watching the Philadelphia Eagles' game on television when Warren County Sheriff Larry Cleveland called to tell him at least 12 people had died in the accident.[31] Lehman, who had been our cops reporter for a decade, was so well respected the police often called him directly when there was breaking news. Lehman did not see the end of the game and would be our lead writer on the *Ethan Allen* story for the next ten years.

Lake George's longtime village Mayor Robert Blais was golfing when he heard whispers about a massive tragedy on the lake. He rushed into town to organize assistance for the survivors and others with the tour group.[32]

Dorothy and David Warren, who had lakefront property near Cramer Point, also rushed out to see if they could help as the nearby shoreline was transformed into part triage center, part temporary morgue.[33]

Sgt. Stockdale called Glens Falls Hospital and told it to activate its disaster plan. Hospital personnel got a page at 3:26 p.m. signaling "code yellow" at the hospital—all hands on deck.[34]

The Warren County dive team—a group that photographer Hooker had coincidentally been working with for a photo story—had been training nearby and responded as well.

Hooker does not remember much about the drive to the lake, just that they got there quickly.

"I think I beat a bunch of the first responders," he said with some pride in his voice in 2020. "I just followed the ambulances."[35]

Pulling in off of Route 9N, he parked his Chevy on Cramer Point Road near a small general store.[36]

As the boats brought in victims, emergency crews began to line up the bodies in a neat row along the shore. Someone finally covered them with some sheets.

Within minutes, Hooker arrived at the scene.

"I walked with a wide angle lens on because I didn't know what was going on," he said. "I walked down this one concrete path and I saw all the victims covered with sheets."[37]

Hooker stopped in his tracks.[38]

The atmosphere was busy but quiet as emergency personnel went about the grim task of recovery.

Realizing he had the wrong lens on his camera, Hooker stepped back several steps and saw Sgt. Stockdale crouching on the lawn on the other side of the bodies.[39]

He squeezed off two images.[40]

He counted the number of bodies. There were 14 at the time.[41]

Within minutes, he was asked to leave by one of the emergency responders, who took him to the other side of the building where some of the survivors were waiting for ambulances.[42]

Bensen began to gently interview some of the survivors. Earlier in the day, she had finished up a feature story on a driving instructor's commitment to safety. This was a different type of reporting.

She approached Anna Mae Hawley, a 74-year-old from Trenton, Michigan, who appeared dazed, and noted a tag on her right wrist where her name and age were scrawled, along with one word, "Cold." She began to ask her questions about what happened while observing how Anna Mae was clutching a soft, yellow blanket.[43]

She looked at Bensen and said, "I don't know where my husband is."[44]

"He's probably at the hospital," said Rahal, the local jeweler who had pulled her out of the water.[45]

But he wasn't.

Her 84-year-old husband, Earl, was one of the 20 victims.

"I could see my husband, and I called to him," Hawley told Bensen, "but he didn't respond. I don't know where he is now."[46]

The couple had been married 49 years.

"Amanda was interviewing people who had just lost loved ones," Hooker said. "It was done with as much respect and tact as could have been done. It has got to be one of the most difficult things you can do as a journalist and you have to do it right."[47]

At one point, Sause, the Cramer Point Motel owner who had come to help took a step back to look at the scene around him, and, like Hooker, he was shocked.

"When I saw all those bodies, I couldn't believe it," he said.[48]

Hooker and Bensen, two of the youngsters in our newsroom, were the first two members of the media to arrive. Their descriptions and first impressions from the victims right after the accident provided perhaps the only clear context of the scope of the tragedy. Both would later be interviewed repeatedly by members of the national media about what they saw.

When Lehman got to the scene, he found all access denied.[49] There were no woods to sneak through like during the railway tanker accident in 1999.

Still, with his vast local contacts among police and first responders, he would deliver an unparalleled account of the tragedy, a first draft of history that mostly matched the conclusions the NTSB reached after a ten-month investigation.

This was also one of the first times our newspaper used the power of its digital product to cover a breaking news story in real time.[50]

As word spread about the tragedy, city editor Bob Condon and news editor Pat Dowd rallied newsroom resources with reporters covering the unfolding story at the hospital and around the village of Lake George while also continually updating the website with the latest information.

The newsroom was inundated with calls from news outlets around the world.

Hooker was heading back to his car about the time other members of the media were first arriving.

"I remember seeing my friend and competing photographer Brian Feulner from the Saratogian," Hooker remembered. "He was arriving as I was leaving. We saw each other in passing. I don't recall what we said, but I remember I just indicated it was bad."[51]

Back at the office, Hooker began going through his digital photographs.

He had two photographs of Sgt. Stockdale kneeling in back of the sheet-covered bodies. You could see a foot sticking out from beneath one of the sheets.

Dowd, who had also come in on his day off after hearing the news, came into the photo department and looked over Hooker's shoulder at the photographs. He was preparing to design the front page.[52]

"Jesus Christ," he said in horror, immediately rushing back to his desk in the newsroom.[53]

"I didn't know if I had done something wrong or what," Hooker said. "I knew it was a powerful image."[54]

Other editors came in to review the photograph as well and began discussing if we should publish it and, if we did, how prominently it should be played. We talked about our responsibility to tell the story of this tragedy but to also be sensitive to the victims. Like most newspapers, we had a policy of not publishing photographs of dead bodies. On 9/11, we decided not to run photographs of people jumping out of windows.

"The discussion of that photo was thorough," Hooker remembered. "The editors took the time to discuss the impact. I remember it being a long and difficult conversation as we decided how we would play it on the page. The general public doesn't necessarily know the level of debate and contemplation that goes into running a graphic image or a name or any of the nuances of the editorial process. With regards to scenes like this, I don't know if that is happening as robustly anymore."[55]

The next day's front page had a large two-deck headline that stretched across the top of the page. It was the kind of treatment big news stories received in another era but rarely do today:

> At least 20 dead after tour boat
> capsizes, sinks in Lake George

Below the headline, Hooker's photo would run five columns wide and nine and a half inches deep. It dominated the page and told the story of an overwhelming tragedy.

At the bottom of the page, Bensen's story ran with the heartbreaking headline, "I

While most newspapers have a policy against publishing photographs of bodies, *Post-Star* editors made an exception for the front page of October 3, 2005. They believed the story of this unprecedented tragedy could not be told without the reaction of Sgt. Stockdale at the scene. It was published the next day in other major newspapers across the country (front page courtesy of *The Post-Star*, Glens Falls, NY).

don't know where my husband is" that I suggested. There was also a map of where the sinking happened on the lake.

Hooker's lead photo was picked up by the Associated Press wire service and transmitted around the world.

The story about the sinking of the *Ethan Allen* would run on the front page of *The New York Times* and New York *Daily News* the next day. Hooker's photo ran on inside pages in both newspapers.

By 4:41 p.m., five injured victims arrived at Glens Falls Hospital where our business reporter, Scott Donnelly, was reporting. A total of 27 would eventually be treated at the hospital by the time the last ambulance arrived at 5:25 p.m.[56]

There were 20 dead.

The label on our second section Monday was changed from "Local" to "Tragedy on the lake" where we ran two more of Hooker's on-the-scene photographs.

For our newspaper, this was first a story of tragic proportions, but it quickly became a story about the safety of tourists coming to Lake George, the number one industry in our region.

The safety question had come up before.

Six years earlier, a 1940s era touring boat—the same approximate age as the *Ethan Allen*—sank in Arkansas where a canopy was blamed for pulling some of the passengers to their deaths.[57]

It was logical to ask Lake George tour boat operators at the time about their own safety concerns.

The *Ethan Allen*, rising in the background, was raised from the bottom of Lake George a day after it capsized and sank, costing 20 visiting senior citizens their lives. A Warren County sheriff's department officer rescues one of the life preservers as the boat surfaces (*Post-Star* photograph by T.J. Hooker).

Immediately after the Arkansas accident, *Post-Star* reporter David Blow, who would later become our assistant city editor, approached the owners of Lake George's two tour boat companies. William P. Dow, owner of the Lake George Steamboat Company said curtly that his boats met Coast Guard standards and are among the "safest in the world."[58]

James Quirk, Shoreline Cruises owner and the operator of seven boats including the *Ethan Allen*, was more realistic, saying he was confident but not overconfident. "I worry all the time [about potential accidents]. We have storms and the potential for accidents. We just have to be careful."[59]

Warren County Sheriff Larry Cleveland, who would make that phone call to Lehman six years later to tell him the *Ethan Allen* sank, said in 1999, "I don't worry about it. These companies are super careful in what they do, and New York State has a complete inspection program in place."[60]

On May 9, 1999, I wrote in my managing editor column, "We read the story of the tragedy in Arkansas of a small tour boat with a canopy that sank and led to the drowning deaths of 13 people. We thought it sounded remarkably similar to some of the tour boats we had seen countless times on Lake George."[61]

I went on to chastise the owner of the Lake George Steamboat Company for being so curt, asking if he had ever heard of the "unsinkable Titanic."[62]

The initial reporting of the *Ethan Allen* sinking indicated it was a perfect storm of events that led to a tragic accident.

By Monday morning, the tragedy had become a national story with reporters from New York City and Detroit arriving in Lake George.

Konrad Marshall, the features writer who played such an important role in our domestic violence series, was on vacation, but remembered driving across the desert out West and hearing the news on the radio.[63]

With Lehman's local contacts, we continued to stay ahead of the other national media in providing new, important details as everyone tried to answer the question of why a tour boat with a perfect 40-year safety record had sunk in perfect weather conditions.

We learned on Monday that Shoreline Cruises should have had a second crew member on board,[64] but our most important reporting came when one of our editors remembered the investigation of a fatal sinking in Baltimore's inner harbor a few years earlier in which the National Transportation Safety Board concluded the Coast Guard's formula for calculating passenger capacity was based on outdated data.

One of our former reporters happened to work at *The Baltimore Sun*. She got us the name of the reporter who had worked on that story.

Will Doolittle, our features editor, reported the previous formula dated to 1960 and set the average weight of a passenger at 140 pounds. It had never been updated. It was concluded the outdated formula allowed far too many people on board the water taxi that sank and killed five people. We wondered if the same thing had happened with the *Ethan Allen*.[65]

Warren County Sheriff Larry Cleveland said the passengers he saw appeared to weigh more than 150 pounds.[66]

The NTSB investigation later concluded the average weight of a passenger on board the *Ethan Allen* that day was 178 pounds. The investigation into the accident concluded the weight to be a significant factor in the capsizing of the vessel.

When a canopy was added to the vessel in 1989, it added 2,000 pounds of weight. The boat was never retested for stability by the Coast Guard. The canopy made the boat sit lower in the water, making it more vulnerable to tipping over.[67]

The NTSB later concluded the boat should not have had more than 14 people on board. It had 48 that day.[68]

Mark Mahoney, our editorial writer, called on the state to fix the problem.

"In the wake of this tragedy, there are many aspects of boat safety that should be reviewed—placement and requirement of wearing life jackets, the required number of crew members carrying elderly or handicapped people, etc.," Mahoney wrote in Wednesday's editorial. "But there's one factor—one that's a proven contributor to boating accidents—that can make an immediate and significant contribution to boat safety. And that is the revision of the weight limit formula."[69]

It was a call to action.

The New York State Legislature did just that. The changes included increasing the penalties for violations of state Navigation Law, requiring at least two exits for a boat that can carry more than 20 people, prohibiting operation of a public vessel with insufficient crew members and a criteria for boat owners to notify the state when they modify a vessel.[70]

James Quirk, the owner of the *Ethan Allen*, said at the time he didn't think the laws went far enough. He said that vessels could come in from out of state with Coast Guard certificates of inspection without a new stability inspection.[71]

The *Ethan Allen* accident scene, just off Cramer Point on Lake George, is shown on Monday, October 3, as dive teams work to raise the boat from the bottom. The boat was eventually raised from the depths late on Monday (*Post-Star* photograph by Erin R. Coker).

While Doolittle worked on the weight issue on Monday, Hooker and news editor Dowd were back on the lake. We were fortunate that Dowd's parents had a boat he could use.

The pair stayed on the lake for most of the day as authorities labored to raise the *Ethan Allen*. When the vessel finally popped to the surface that afternoon, Hooker delivered another poignant photo of a man fishing a life jacket out of the lake while the *Ethan Allen* rose out of the water behind him.

Another one of our photographers captured the scene with an aerial photograph over Cramer Point.

We would not be done with the story for a long time.

There were ongoing questions of why the captain, Richard Paris, was not given a sobriety test after the accident. Paris had retired from the state police and was known to many in the Warren County Sheriff's Office.

Sheriff Cleveland later claimed he had Paris breathe into his face after the capsizing, and there was no odor of alcohol.[72] Paris voluntarily gave blood and urine samples on Tuesday after the Sunday accident[73] while our reporters explored other possible reasons for the accident.

On Monday, I made it a point to talk to Bensen about what she had seen. I asked her if she had anyone to talk to about the experience. Reporters can experience post traumatic stress, too.

"I called my mother last night," she said. "I always talk to my mother." Bensen eventually moved on to *Smithsonian* magazine and married another reporter from our staff, one of several newsroom romances over the years. They later had a little girl named Eleanor.

I also asked Hooker how he was doing after two long days in Lake George and advised him of the counseling, too, then sent him home for two days.[74]

It had been a long and trying week for many on our staff, I wrote to our readers a week after the accident.

"Reporting on tragedies such as these is always a difficult and emotional experience, and one we hope we never have to do again," I wrote.[75]

In early February, more than 600 people turned out at the Glens Falls Civic Center for a "Service to Community" ceremony to honor the emergency personnel, civilian rescuers and local officials who responded to the tragedy.[76]

Brian Hart, the East Greenbush electrician who had been canoeing that day at the time of the accident, was among two dozen civilian rescuers recognized with a certificate and a medallion for "heroic actions and service to the community."[77]

Hart was one of the rescuers mentioned in a letter from one of the survivors, Carol Carlton. She called Hart "my angel."

"That afternoon is etched into all of our minds, memories, and spirits," Carlton wrote in the letter. "You humans, you beautiful people, became for a time our angels, our means of being given a second chance at life.... Please know that on that afternoon, you superseded what man can do for man. My love transcends into your world every second."[78]

Rahal, the jeweler who pulled Anna Mae Hawley out of the water and kept in contact with many of the survivors afterward, said he was planning a summer trip to Michigan to visit one of the people he saved.[79]

It wasn't until February that a Warren County grand jury indicted the captain and the company that owned the *Ethan Allen* for not having a second crew member on board as required by law. But the grand jury concluded it could not bring weightier charges such as homicide because it could not find "criminal negligence."[80]

At the end of March 2007, Paris and Shoreline pleaded guilty to the misdemeanor charge. Lehman reported Paris was sorry for the accident, but he did not believe he was responsible for it. He wrote he pleaded guilty to "get it over with."[81]

"As far as I was concerned, I did nothing wrong. It was strictly an accident," he told television station WNYT in Albany. "It's something I have to live with for the rest of my life. But if it's boiled right down, it was not my fault."[82]

Paris also admitted that he was still having trouble sleeping.

Shoreline owner James Quirk was in court with Paris but did not speak during the hearing. Judge John Hall imposed $250 fines—the maximum—on both Paris and Shoreline and community service to Paris.[83]

By then, more than a dozen lawsuits had been filed in federal court naming Shoreline, Paris and others as defendants.

Warren County District Attorney Kate Hogan acknowledged the victims were angry with the outcome of the criminal case.

"The victims of the case expected more out of the criminal justice system," Hogan said. "But the facts of the case did not allow us to charge more than the violation of the certificate of inspection."[84]

The *Ethan Allen* case would be a campaign issue in the 2007 Warren County Sheriff's race when Sheriff Larry Cleveland was criticized for not formally testing the *Ethan Allen* captain for alcohol. Cleveland lost the election to Nathan "Bud" York.

Shoreline learned two weeks after the accident that the $2,000,000 liability insurance policy on its boats was fraudulent and never existed.[85] The insurance scam later became the basis of a 2019 movie by director Steven Soderbergh that starred Meryl Streep and recreated the sinking of the *Ethan Allen* in the opening scenes.[86]

Later in the film, Matthew Quirk, the son of Shoreline Cruises owner, James Quirk, is portrayed as the person responsible for purchasing the fraudulent insurance policy.

The Albany *Times Union* reported in April 2016 the man responsible for selling the fake insurance policy admitted to "conspiring to launder premiums from a scheme that sold fake liability insurance policies over the course of more than 10 years to Shoreline and other business[es] throughout the U.S."[87]

The man pleaded guilty and was sentenced to eight years in prison. But as part of the sentence, the court said it would not determine how much restitution would be due his victims until after the accountant had served his eight-year prison sentence. Considering the age of the victims, that seemed particularly odd.[88]

It was later revealed the five defendants in the case were part of a Panamanian-based law firm that crafted a global money-laundering and tax evasion scheme known as the "Panama Papers."

"This is one of the saddest, most complicated cases that I have ever handled in 30 years," lawyer James Hackler, who represented the families of *Ethan Allen* victims, told the *Times Union* in 2016. "The only reason this scam came to light was the magnitude of this disaster."[89]

Without insurance, Shoreline Cruises reached an undisclosed settlement with some of the victims and their families in May 2009.[90] The *Times Union* reported owner James Quirk had to mortgage property to settle lawsuits with the victims' families to keep his business afloat.[91]

In September, Matthew Quirk took one of Shoreline's boats out on the lake on a Saturday afternoon. Later that evening, his boat was found adrift in the southern basin of the lake without any sign of Quirk. His body was found at the bottom of the lake the next day. Lehman later learned the divers who removed Quirk's body from the lake found a boat anchor tied to his body.[92]

The New York State Court of Appeals dismissed the last lawsuit in the case in November 2012 when it ruled the state should not be held liable for the actions of the inspector who certified the boat.[93]

The New York State Associated Press Association honored *The Post-Star* with its highest honor—Newspaper of Distinction—for the third straight year in September 2006. Its coverage of the *Ethan Allen* accident received top honors for continuing coverage.[94]

That night in the ballroom at a Saratoga Springs hotel, T.J. Hooker's photograph of Sgt. Stockdale kneeling behind the victims of the *Ethan Allen* hushed the crowd as it was projected onto the big screen.

Hooker was honored with the Bruce Cromie Award for excellence in news photography for the best news photo of the year.[95]

"I felt uncomfortable benefitting in any way from the tragedy," Hooker told me in 2020. "Gaining notoriety as a journalist? I strove for that. I was good at what I did, at least at the time. As a news photographer, I wanted to show the world around me. Getting the award was bittersweet. Yes, I was at the top of the game, but benefitting from that still wears on me a bit."[96]

In 2015, reporter Don Lehman revisited the tragedy on its tenth anniversary and talked to victims and rescuers.[97]

Lehman hoped to get Paris on the record about his memories of that day and to see how he was holding up. When he knocked on the door of his Queensbury home, his wife said he did not want to talk.[98]

Richard Paris died in August 2016 at the age of 85.[99]

Rahal, the jeweler who was out on the lake with his family that day, kept in touch with several of the victims' families. He still has the thank you notes he received in the months after the accident.

"It still haunts us," Rahal said in 2015. "I remember Allie [his daughter], she was just 13 years old, using CPR she had just learned. I remember talking about the smell of gasoline."[100]

Kidon, the chaperone on the trip, said she had health problems for years that she blamed on the accident. She lost her job after the city in Michigan discontinued the senior travel program. She also remembered how the people of Lake George and Glens Falls were so kind and helpful to the survivors.[101]

The NTSB investigation went on for nine months and led to a 3,300-page report that concluded a number of factors played a part in the accident, but stopped short of placing blame.[102]

A year after the report was issued, the lead investigator at the NTSB quit his job over concerns about the way the investigation was handled. He told Lehman in June 2007 that evidence was ignored about the boat's raw water coolant pump, which he believed leaked significant amounts of water into the boat's hull that could have also affected its stability.

"They [the NTSB] basically thought it was going to be a slam dunk, and they stopped investigating," Robert Ford told Lehman. "They just drove it [the final report] right through."[103]

James Quirk, the owner of Shoreline Cruises who feared a boating accident as early as 1999, still did not want to talk about the accident in 2015.[104]

Kidon, who survived the sinking, said the fines paid by Quirk and Paris were "a slap on the wrist."[105]

Anna Mae Hawley, the woman who Bensen interviewed minutes after the accident, died in August 2015. She was 84.

Amanda Bensen, the young reporter who interviewed Hawley, died in January 2017 after a two-year battle with colon cancer. She was just 37.

"A lot of the things that we saw, they stick with you," Hooker said. "It's kind of inevitable that it will have an impact on you. This was specifically one of the most shocking that I came across in my career and it accumulates over time, seeing so many of these things rather routinely. It has an impact."[106]

Hooker left the newspaper in 2012 after surviving multiple rounds of newsroom layoffs. He went back to school and became a registered nurse but left that job because of the stress. He later did a stint as a fishing guide in Alaska before returning to his native Vermont. In 2020, he was back shooting freelance assignments four days a week for the Rutland, Vermont, newspaper and guiding rafting trips in the Adirondacks two days a week.[107]

"The continuing coverage of this, the way we covered every aspect of it from the initial response to the regulations that were changed to the memorial that was put up was something," Hooker said. "It isn't often that small newspapers have that type of expertise and tenacity and full-throated coverage, at least this day and age. I was proud to be a part of it."[108]

"The *Ethan Allen* was the biggest story we had in my tenure there," Lehman said in 2020. "It was long hours and lots of stress with a CNN truck sitting there every day with these massive news conferences. It went on like that for months. I ended up with pneumonia. I wouldn't want to go through that again."[109]

On the first anniversary of the sinking in 2006, Lake George village officials marked the day by dedicating a monument to acknowledge the tragedy that had occurred on the lake.

On the large stone was an inscription from a Bret Harte poem written in 1797:

> We hear from the misty
> troubled shore
> the voice of those
> gone before
> drawing the soul to its
> anchorage

A lone singer quietly, sweetly began to sing "Amazing Grace" after the names of all the victims were read by Lake George Mayor Robert Blais.[110]

One person in the crowd began humming the familiar hymn, then more joined in quietly until all were humming.[111]

When the ceremony was over, it began to rain.[112]

13

"Was that Vito?"

Even at age 55, Jim Marshall had Robert Redford good looks and a vitality that had him competing in professional team roping at his own charity rodeo in Glens Falls.

This was Butch Cassidy with a tie.

By 2006, Marshall had been publisher of *The Post-Star* for 21 years, raised his family in the area and had become a city father in many respects. He was not only publisher, he was also a part-owner of the Howard Publications chain that owned the newspaper. His father and the Howard brothers had started out in the oil business together,[1] and it was well known Marshall was a millionaire many times over. He eventually bought a small farm in nearby Queensbury where he bred and later owned and raced thoroughbred horses.

There is often an uneasy relationship between editors and publishers, as editorial content sometimes undermines business interests. That can lead to tension or something far worse—war.

The publisher is responsible for keeping the newspaper profitable while editors can be unyielding in upholding editorial standards. At good newspapers, there is a strict line between advertising and editorial content that is never crossed, especially by the publisher.

Marshall was a champion in that regard. He rarely meddled in the newsroom and was supportive of even our most controversial stories and editorials.

Business-wise, Marshall had a simple roller-coaster philosophy: Sometimes you had good years, sometimes you had bad years as newspaper revenues fluctuated with the health of the economy.

"There is no manual," Marshall said when I interviewed him in 2004 as part of the newspaper's centennial celebration. "A former publisher told me to just do what you think is right for the paper."[2]

Because of Marshall's ownership stake in Howard, he had more independence than most publishers, and our newsroom benefited from that. That changed when Howard Publications sold its community newspapers to Lee Enterprises in 2002 at the height of their value. Marshall was no longer an owner, just another publisher with a corporate boss.[3]

Marshall benefited financially when Lee bought Howard, but he soon chafed at the oversight that a publicly traded company brought to the way he ran his newspaper. He was soon butting heads with Lee management.

"With Howard, I was an owner so I was making the decisions," Marshall said in 2020. "But Lee wanted me to call them with every decision. They wanted to feel important by babysitting me."[4]

Jim Marshall, who was publisher of *The Post-Star* for 21 years (1985–2006), is shown in his office in January 2004 as the newspaper was about to celebrate its 100th anniversary serving the community (*Post-Star* file photograph).

During our weekly department head meeting in March 2006, Marshall told us Kevin Mowbray, the regional vice president in charge of *The Post-Star*, was coming to Glens Falls for a Friday morning meeting. Mowbray would later become publisher at the *St. Louis Post-Dispatch* and then CEO of Lee.

Mowbray's visit was not planned like most corporate visits, and it seemed particularly odd for him to visit on St. Patrick's Day, a big day of celebration in Glens Falls.

The other department heads were concerned and asked Marshall if he was worried. At the time, he said he was not, but 14 years later, he told me, "When they scheduled the meeting on a Friday, I knew something was up."[5]

When Mowbray arrived that morning to see Marshall, I was surprised to see another man with him. Within minutes, our Production Manager Dave Guay was in my office asking the question: "Was that Vito?"

Vytenis P. Kuraitis was a gregarious presence on the Lee Enterprises management team who was also the head of human resources. But you didn't want to see Vito unexpectedly, and he looked undertaker-serious that morning.

We were about to see corporate politics play out in real time.

Next, I saw David Stoeffler heading into Marshall's office. Stoeffler was a past editor of the *Journal-Star* in Lincoln, Nebraska, and had been Lee's vice president of news when I met him four years earlier. When Lee bought Howard Publications, Stoeffler asked me to help with editor training. He was a colleague I liked and respected.

Stoeffler, seeing the puzzled look on my face, smiled as he walked past my office and said, "We'll talk later."

A short time later, we gathered the staff from our two buildings in the middle of the newsroom where Marshall announced his retirement after 21 years as publisher. He did it matter-of-factly, as if it had been planned for months.

"This newspaper has a truly outstanding staff, and I'll miss all of the great people here," Marshall told reporter Erin DeMuth for the story in the next day's newspaper, "but I'm looking forward to the next stage of my life."[6]

A day earlier, the next stage of his life was the horse he had running at Aqueduct Friday afternoon.

Stoeffler was named our interim publisher.

Mowbray and Kuraitis, their work done, left soon afterward. The department heads, with Stoeffler looking on, gathered in Marshall's office as he packed his things.

"You know, I've pretty much blocked it out," Marshall told me in 2020, pausing, then saying, "I still don't like the way it was handled. They just walked in and said I was gone. There was no conversation to say what I did or how it could be fixed. To this day, I have no idea why I was let go. I was totally blindsided."[7]

I guess you could say it was just business.

"You know, I had just been diagnosed with prostate cancer and was going to work with a bag on me," Marshall said. "I was in there every day giving it my all."[8]

I never looked at my job quite the same way after that and certainly not with any sense of security.

Marshall didn't need to work. He was financially secure, but he had been a prominent leader in the community who regularly donated thousands of dollars in newspaper advertising to good causes like Glens Falls Hospital and the Glens Falls Family YMCA. He was one of the city fathers.

Later that afternoon, his horse won at Aqueduct and paid $15 to win. It was the one bright spot on a dismal day.

Marshall had hired me as managing editor seven years earlier after I had been sports editor for 11 years. As far as I was concerned, he was a great publisher. He was hands off in the newsroom but locked in with what was going on in the community. He let me do my job, and when one of our news stories cost the newspaper some advertising dollars—as it did from time to time—I rarely heard about it. He had our back.

With Marshall at the helm, I gradually added staff and resources that made the newspaper better, the journalism more ambitious and the community better served.

What I did not realize about the newspaper business until I became a managing editor was how much money it generated. While attending an American Press Institute training seminar in 2011, I learned the 1980s and 1990s were golden years for newspaper revenue.

Most small newspapers had ungodly profit margins—often 30 percent and sometimes more at small community newspapers—and could have paid the men and women reporting the news far better for the professional work they did, especially considering that many were struggling to pay off college loans.

Marshall's retirement was the end of an era at *The Post-Star*. It was the beginning of a revolving door of six more publishers over the next 15 years—all from outside the region—who often challenged my news judgment and ideas about running the paper.

Each time the word came about another publisher leaving, I would head out to where the editors were sitting and announce, "Well, I survived another one."

After Marshall left, I wrote a column—which Stoeffler was obliged to read first and approve—about Marshall's service, his departure and the legacy he left behind.

"Over those two decades, the newspaper expanded to a four-section newspaper, began publishing in full color, started a Sunday newspaper and adopted the latest computer layout technology. The newspaper grew into a two-building campus and circulation often exceeded 40,000 in the summer months while expanding into communities over a three-county area."[9]

By the time he left, we had nearly 50 people in the newsroom, had opened a four-person bureau in downtown Saratoga Springs to compete with the other Capital District newspapers and introduced a separate weekly product to compete with the regional weeklies.

We believed we had a good future.

In my column, I wrote that Marshall created the Adirondack Charity Rodeo to benefit local nonprofits and to provide a connection to the agricultural community in rural Washington County.[10]

That fall, *The Post-Star* was honored by the New York State Associated Press Association with its "Newspaper of Distinction" for the third straight year. We had become a small newspaper with a big reputation for doing great journalism, and Marshall had given us the resources to do that.[11]

Two years later, Jim Marshall and his wife, Tina, were honored by the Adirondack Regional Chamber of Commerce with the prestigious J. Walter Juckett Award for exemplary community service.[12] It was kind of the lifetime achievement award for local leaders.

Marshall's former colleagues from the newspaper filled a table at the upscale Sagamore Resort on Lake George to see him receive the award. Afterward, he came over to talk. He mentioned how the recent financial collapse had dramatically eroded Lee's stock value.

He said he lost a lot of money as the stock depreciated, but he cheered the decline every step of the way, knowing the folks who let him go had lost a lot more.

In 2004, as part of *The Post-Star's* 100th anniversary celebration, I had done a feature story on Marshall.

"I've always felt that the paper should be a mirror to the community," Marshall said. "If you see something negative in the paper, then you probably need to fix it. … I think the newspaper needs to keep people informed of what government is doing, but it also has to let us know what our local people are doing. I think we do a good job of that."[13]

It was a reminder of what community newspapers—and publishers like Marshall—did all across the country. There was no reason to believe he wouldn't continue in the role for a long time.

I was wrong.

I look back at those times as "the good old days."

"You can open doors and go to places that maybe someone else in a different line of work couldn't go," Marshall said about being publisher in a small city. "Everyone's business is my business. I like doing what I do. I like coming to work every day and being part of things. I like this area. It is home."[14]

None of Jim Marshall's successors ever really called Glens Falls home. It was just a stepping stone to somewhere else. Marshall later split his time between Las Vegas and Queensbury, but when I talked to him in 2021, he acknowledged they had put the farm up for sale in Queensbury to be closer to their children.

Lee Enterprises later added the Pulitzer newspaper chain as part of a blockbuster billion-dollar deal in 2005. It was still paying off that debt in 2020 when it acquired all of Warren Buffett's Berkshire Hathaway newspapers to become the fourth-largest newspaper group in the country.[15] As newspaper revenues began to erode, Lee continued to pay down the Pulitzer debt while slashing resources in newsrooms.

By 2021, Lee Enterprises had eliminated the publisher position in Glens Falls and the newsroom had been reduced to eight.

14

Congressman Kick-Ass

Rep. John Sweeney navigated his 2001 Jeep Laredo down a dark, two-lane road on his way home from the Willard Mountain ski area late on the night of Tuesday, January 23, 2001, when he said he reached down to adjust the radio. The road was wet but not slippery.[1]

It was the beginning of a series of events, one piled on another that chronicled the downfall of a public servant who had, up until that moment, unlimited potential.

Rep. Sweeney, 45 in 2001, was starting his second term as congressman of the 20th Congressional District and was a season pass holder at the rural Washington County ski area in Easton New York.

He must have felt good that night about his career and future in the Republican Party. The new president, George W. Bush, had been inaugurated three days earlier and had christened him "Congressman Kick-Ass" for his actions the previous fall in shutting down the recount by Miami–Dade County election commissioners in Florida. Sweeney and his cohorts reportedly banged on the doors where the commissioners were doing the recount and, when inside, screamed, "Shut it down!" His intimidation tactics helped halt the recount and earned the admiration of the new president. The scene was later recreated in the 2008 HBO movie *Recount*.[2]

Rep. Sweeney was our congressman and a political star on the rise.

Before leaving Willard for the evening that Tuesday night, he stopped at the ski area bar and had "one or two glasses of wine" according to the bartender who worked that evening.[3] He talked to one other patron about politics who did not think he was intoxicated.[4]

As he drove down the hill from Willard and turned onto Vly Summit Road in Easton, he said he reached for the radio and failed to negotiate a turn, slipped off the side of the road and sliced a utility pole in half. Sweeney, who was wearing his seatbelt, was not hurt.[5]

The lights went out at the ski area, and some skiers were briefly stranded on the lifts before power was restored with an emergency generator.

Donna English, a local woman who lived nearby and was a Republican councilwoman in Easton, offered assistance. Standing uphill from the crash, she turned back traffic from the scene. Another neighbor, Edward Lundberg, brought up some emergency road flares, then left to alert another neighbor, Easton Fire Chief Steve Bott, about the accident and the live electrical wires in the road.[6]

When Trooper Kevin Saunders arrived at the scene, the accident was handled in some unusual ways. The trooper did not give Rep. Sweeney a field sobriety test, and when the Easton Fire Department asked if assistance was needed, it was refused by the state police. English, the neighbor, continued to direct traffic from 10 p.m. until midnight. The new Jeep, which was registered to Sweeney's campaign, had to be towed from the scene.[7]

Sweeney was not charged or ticketed for the accident, and it took four hours to open the road and another eight hours to restore power to the ski resort.

Even a minor fender bender involving a local congressman was news but even more so for a congressman who was making national headlines in recent months. When *Post-Star* reporter Don Lehman made his regular "cop checks" the next morning, state police made no mention of the incident. Nor did they mention it the next day or the day after that.

It would be more than a week before *The Post-Star* was able to confirm the accident even happened.

Newspaper reporters and editors have a reputation for cynicism, even under the best of circumstances, but this story stank from the beginning. It would not have been unprecedented for someone in local law enforcement to grant a politically connected individual a break by keeping something out of the newspaper.

Not only was Sweeney a sitting congressman; he was a political insider in the state Republican Party. He had served as the executive director and chief counsel of the New York Republican Party from 1992 to 1995 and was instrumental in helping to get the sitting Governor George Pataki elected in 1995. He was Governor Pataki's first commissioner of the State Department of Labor and later moved into Pataki's inner circle as deputy secretary to the governor before resigning to run for Congress.

The newspaper reported the bare-bones details of the accident eight days later on February 1 before pursuing the reasons the accident had been kept quiet.[8]

In reporter Don Lehman's February 2 story with the headline "Police: No bias in crash," the regional commander of the state police, Capt. Frank A. Pace, denied the congressman had received preferential treatment.[9]

"He was treated just like any other citizen," Pace said. "It was a minor accident. The only thing notable about this was the power outage."[10]

And it involved a sitting congressman who had close ties to the governor.

Despite what was characterized as an innocent accident, Rep. Sweeney did not return repeated phone calls from *The Post-Star*. His Chief of Staff Brad Card (his brother was Andrew Card, chief of staff for President George W. Bush who would famously tell the president on 9/11 that the country was under attack) said he would not discuss the crash and referred all calls to Pace at the state police.[11]

Pace said the trooper saw no sign Sweeney was drinking prior to the crash.[12]

Trooper Saunders, who was the first on the scene, first told reporter Lehman he did not contact a state police supervisor about the crash,[13] but Pace said a day later that Saunders did in fact notify a sergeant because of the power outage.[14] Pace said that was standard procedure. Five years later, anonymous sources with the state police told Lehman that Trooper Saunders had contacted Pace that night, and it was Pace who decided no tickets would be issued.[15]

That's the thing about bulldog reporters like Lehman. You fudge one fact and he will find out about it, even if it takes years.

Lehman continued to follow leads on the case, and the owner of the Willard ski area confirmed that Sweeney had been seen drinking "one or two glasses of wine" in the bar before the crash.[16]

When he heard about the drinking, Washington County District Attorney Robert Winn, a Republican, said that the state police should investigate their handling of the matter.[17]

State police did not allow Trooper Saunders to talk to a reporter, and Sweeney's office said it would not comment on the drinking allegations.

It all stank of a cover-up, especially to our Sunday editor Will Doolittle.

Doolittle, who grew up in the Adirondacks in the small town of Saranac Lake, had newspaper ink in his veins. He was a Stanford graduate, had sound journalistic instincts and could write like a dream.

In his Sunday, February 4, column, Doolittle demanded answers regarding the Sweeney accident.

"Questions are hovering over John Sweeney's car crash on Vly Mountain Road like fruit flies over a stale glass of wine," Doolittle wrote.[18]

Doolittle wanted to know if Trooper Saunders had asked Sweeney if he was drinking and why no sobriety test was administered.

He wanted to know why the Easton Fire Department was called off with live electrical wires in the road and one lone civilian directing traffic.

He wanted to know what instructions Trooper Saunders was given about issuing tickets.

He wanted to know why the congressman had not given his side of the story.[19]

It was a reminder of how important commentary and editorials can be in giving context to the news events of the day by asking important questions not answered in the original reporting.

"But I guess Mr. Sweeney's spokesmen aren't thinking about anyone else's inconvenience. I guess they're thinking only about Mr. Sweeney and how they can manage things so his reputation survives this crash along with his good health," concluded Doolittle.[20]

This was just the first entry in Sweeney's increasingly murky reputation. It became clear in the months and years ahead that Sweeney would not forget the criticism.

The Glens Falls region, like most of upstate New York, is bloodred conservative Republican. That was true in 2001, and it is still true today.

After becoming managing editor in 1999, I was struck at how vicious the letter writers were to President Bill Clinton and later to his wife, Hillary Clinton, when she ran for the U.S. Senate in New York. I was a registered Republican at the time.

For two decades as editor, I reiterated that reporters report the news fairly and accurately, and the editorial board tries to take common sense positions on local issues.

"The trouble is that many readers seem to want to pigeonhole newspapers, their columnists and maybe just about everyone who votes into a category," I wrote to the readers before the 2000 election. "Are we right or left, conservative or liberal, Republican or Democrat? I think at various times we are each of those things."[21]

It is a reminder our political divisions did not appear overnight during the 2016 presidential election.

The Post-Star editorial board endorsed Rep. Sweeney for reelection in 2000, but when we reported on his accident the next February, many saw it as a political attack by the "liberal media."

What I naively didn't know then as an inexperienced editor was the extent politicians would go to discredit anyone perceived to be an enemy, including members of the press.

Few people in Glens Falls knew anything about Sweeney when he first ran for Congress. The Troy native graduated from Russell Sage College in Albany in 1981. During college, he was arrested twice, once for pulling a fire alarm and a second time for driving while intoxicated. It was written off as youthful indiscretions when he ran for office.

Sweeney was running to replace the locally revered Gerald Solomon, a longtime local Republican leader who had served four years as supervisor of the Town of Queensbury and five years in the state assembly before serving in Congress from 1979 to 1999. Solomon eventually became chairman of the House Rules Committee.

When Solomon announced his retirement, Sweeney was anointed as his successor, an obvious nod to his inside connections with Governor Pataki and the state GOP. He did not even live in the district at the time. With Republicans holding a two-to-one advantage, there was little doubt he would be elected.

As expected, Sweeney defeated Democratic challenger Jean Bordewich with 55 percent of the vote. It was a modest triumph, considering the overwhelming margins Solomon had previously run up.[22]

By the end of his first term, Sweeney had more name recognition and was bringing federal money into the district. He won reelection in 2000 with nearly 68 percent of the vote.[23]

The January 2001 crash did not damage his reputation. He won reelection in 2002 with 73 percent of the vote,[24] then got 66 percent of the vote in 2004. *The Post-Star* editorial board endorsed him each time,[25] but because of the accident coverage, the relationship simmered with acrimony from the Sweeney camp.

I wrote this about Rep. Sweeney in November 2005: "When Congressman Sweeney gets angry at something that is written about him in the newspaper, he lets us know by cutting off direct access to the newspaper. At least, that's the way it seems. We'd ask him, but I'm pretty sure he's not talking to anyone here right now. We talked on the phone earlier this year because he was mad about something one of our columnists wrote about him. It was good to talk to him. I wish he would call more often to complain."[26]

I never heard from him again, but our new publisher did.

Five months after Jim Marshall abruptly retired on St. Patrick's Day, our new publisher, Rona Rahlf, was dropped into the middle of a contentious congressional race between Rep. John Sweeney and Kirsten Gillibrand.

It was not long before Rep. Sweeney reached out to Rahlf and told her our news coverage was partisan. In future years, this scenario would repeat itself whenever we had a new publisher. Those who believed they were unfairly criticized hoped to set the record straight with a new boss.

Rahlf called me into her office and told me Sweeney had accused editorial page editor Mark Mahoney and me of being on the payroll of the "D-Triple-C." She did not smile.

Sweeney told her our editorials mirrored the Democratic Congressional Campaign Committee press releases.

These were serious, end-of-your-career-type charges, and Rahlf was taking the accusations seriously. I told Rahlf I would review every story and editorial we had done about Rep. Sweeney in recent months to see if the charges had any merit and give her a full report. Rahlf could not imagine a sitting congressman was lying to her.

After reviewing all our news stories and editorials, Rahlf backed off.

This was payback for the ski area accident coverage and all those questions from Will Doolittle.

Kirsten Gillibrand's entry into the congressional race as a legitimate Democratic challenger was unexpected, but she was still considered a long shot.

I wrote this in February 2006 after meeting Gillibrand: "People in the 20th Congressional District are going to find out in the coming months that Gillibrand is a refreshingly passionate novice politician who really believes she can pull off a miracle on ice."[27]

Over the next nine months, she got a lot of help from Sweeney.

In the spring of 2005, Rep. Sweeney's 18-year-old son was indicted on felony charges, including gang assault for a group fight the previous August. Young Sweeney was facing 15 years in prison.[28]

Rep. Sweeney vigorously defended his son and criticized the police investigation. Coincidentally, it was Capt. Pace from the Willard ski accident who investigated young Sweeney's case.

That fall, the New York *Daily News* reported Rep. Sweeney had gotten into a fight in a Washington, D.C., bar with a Red Sox fan who didn't like the way Sweeney was rooting for the Yankees.[29] Reporters increasingly heard whispers about Sweeney's drinking.

Then, on December 2, 2005, police responded to Rep. Sweeney's home in Clifton Park after his wife, Gayle, called 9-1-1, telling the dispatcher Sweeney was "knocking her around the house."[30]

The Post-Star and media outlets around the Capital District heard rumors about the incident for months but could not confirm its authenticity. State police refused repeated requests to release information. The state's Committee on Open Government later ruled the state police wrongly denied that request.[31]

A Freedom of Information Law request by *Post-Star* reporter Brendan McGarry in March 2006 redacted the names of all the people involved in the complaints on the night in question, making it impossible to know whether there was an incident involving the Sweeneys.

Two weeks after the 9-1-1 call in 2005, Sweeney's son and a friend were placed on probation for five years and sentenced to 240 hours of community service for their role in the assault of another teen who was left with chipped teeth and long-term vision damage.[32]

Both defendants had their six-month sentences in the Saratoga County Jail suspended and were granted youthful offender status after pleading to a reduced charge of second-degree felony assault. They were also ordered to pay restitution totaling $18,000 for the victim's medical bills. The two men were accused of punching and kicking the victim while he was on the ground.[33]

"I think the sentence is totally unjust," victim Matthew Brady told *Post-Star* reporter McGarry. "They just walked away with a slap on the wrist. The thing that bothers me the most is, if you have money you have power."[34]

Or if your father is a congressman.

By January 2006, when Gillibrand entered the race, Sweeney was taking heat from his opponent over a $2,000-per-person "Skiing with Sweeney" weekend in Park City, Utah, that included a private dinner at the home of a lobbyist who represented Boston Scientific, a local medical device manufacturer.[35]

Gillibrand continued to criticize Sweeney for his ethical lapses. That October, Sweeney conceded he may not have properly reported a 2001 trip with a lobbyist to the Northern Marianas Islands in the Pacific. The congressman's financial forms were reviewed by the Department of Justice, but Sweeney insisted it was just a mistake.[36]

Later, it was learned that Sweeney was part of a group of lawmakers who regularly made trips to the Caribbean[37] for elaborate receptions. A wedding reception was held for Sweeney and his second wife, Gayle Ford, in Antigua by financier Allen Stanford after the couple was married in 2004. Stanford would be convicted of charges in 2012 that his investment company was a massive Ponzi scheme. He was sentenced to 110 years in jail.[38]

In April, Sweeney got more bad press when he was accused of getting a no-show job for his wife. In April 2003, Sweeney began paying a company called Creative Consulting for fundraising. Ford had founded the company a day before she was married to Sweeney. Ford was to get 10 percent of any money raised, even though she had no experience with fundraising.[39]

Photographs also emerged in April that showed a red-faced Sweeney at an Alpha Delta Phi fraternity party at Union College in Schenectady after the college's student newspaper reported that Sweeney appeared at the party "intoxicated."[40]

John Tomlin, the student who reported the story for the college newspaper, told *Post-Star* reporter Maury Thompson, "Everything that's written is based on facts."[41] Tomlin said he based his report on accounts of seven or eight students who attended the party, including two who were named in the article. Tomlin said he personally saw Sweeney outside the fraternity house on his way into the party, and the congressman appeared intoxicated.[42]

It led Doolittle to write a tongue-in-cheek satire about an imaginary conversation between Sweeney and House Majority Leader John Boehner that went back and forth between the two men as they fictitiously discussed how to repair Sweeney's reputation.

The column was a sharp rebuke to Rep. Sweeney's growing reputation as a hard-partying congressman whose ethics were repeatedly being called into question.

Here's an excerpt:

> **BOEHNER:** Maybe frat parties aren't the best place for you right now, John. Do you like bridge? Or knitting?
>
> **SWEENEY:** I wasn't doing anything at that frat party that I wouldn't do every night in my own home.
>
> **BOEHNER:** That might not be the best way to put it, John.
>
> **SWEENEY:** I like young people, darn it. I like the way they drink.... I mean think.
>
> **BOEHNER:** Now, that's what I mean John.[43]

I suspect that was another reason for Sweeney's later call to Rahlf.

Thompson, who had covered Sweeney since 1998, remembered a campaign event that summer at the Fort Hudson Nursing Home in Hudson Falls where Sweeney spoke to residents and the media. When it was time for questions, Sweeney turned to Thompson and told him sternly, "I'll talk to you later."[44]

"Later outside, he lambasted me for about 10 minutes about a column Will Doolittle had written," Thompson said in 2020.[45]

Things just got worse for Sweeney from there.

That September, the Citizens for Responsibility and Ethics in Washington released its second annual report on the members of Congress with ethical issues. Sweeney was ranked as one of the 20 most corrupt members of Congress.[46]

In October, challenger Gillibrand sent a 275-word letter to Sweeney asking him to release records about his previous run-ins with police. She said it was about transparency. Gillibrand rubbed it in by admitting she had once received a traffic violation for going through a stop sign.[47]

As Election Day got closer, internal campaign polls revealed the race was tightening.

In late October, *The Post-Star* organized a debate between the two candidates at Heritage Hall at the Glens Falls Civic Center. On the Monday before the Thursday debate, Melissa Carlson called from Sweeney's office to say the congressman would not participate unless Gillibrand released copies of her personal income taxes.[48]

"We're big proponents of the voters getting a chance to see the candidates debate the issues," I said in the news story. "So it's the voters that are losing out."[49]

On Sunday, October 29, *The Post-Star* editorial board endorsed Rep. Sweeney's reelection with a lukewarm editorial. The headline read "Sweeney's record overshadows his shortcomings."[50]

We lauded the millions of dollars he had brought to the district in federal funds and his more progressive stand on same-sex marriage, but we criticized his use of untrue attack ads and his lack of transparency regarding past encounters with the police, late-night appearances at frat parties and questionable fact-finding jaunts with lobbyists to exotic islands and ski resorts.[51]

Ultimately, the editorial board decided Gillibrand did not have enough experience.

The bombshell came a few days later when the Albany *Times Union* reported that state police had gone to the Sweeneys' home in Clifton Park nearly a year earlier on December 2, 2005, after his wife called 9-1-1.[52] The *T U* was finally able to confirm the visit by the police based on a police report given to the newspaper.[53]

The newspaper reported Gayle Sweeney, the congressman's 36-year-old wife, called 9-1-1 at 12:55 a.m. on December 2, 2005, to report a domestic violence incident. The police report stated that the responding officer was told by Gayle Sweeney that "she and husband got into a verbal argument that turned a little physical by her being grabbed by the neck and pushed around the house."[54]

The report said Gayle Sweeney told police her husband was "knocking her around" and that he had grabbed her by the throat and was pushing her around the house. Police also reported the congressman had scratches on his face when police arrived to investigate.[55]

No charges were filed because Mrs. Sweeney refused to press charges.

The police report the *Times Union* obtained said the following.

"Female caller stating her husband is knocking her around the house," the dispatcher wrote. "Then she stated [from the phone call], 'Here it comes, are you ready?' And disconnected the call. Upon the call-back, the husband stated no problem ... asked the wife if she wanted to talk. Wife [caller] then got on the phone and states that she's fine and she's drunk. Caller sounded intoxicated. She advised that she was endangered for a moment, but everything is fine."[56]

On Wednesday, November 1, with Election Day less than a week away, *The Post-Star's* Maury Thompson followed up with his own coverage as Rep. Sweeney and his wife acknowledged in a conference call that state police had come to their home the previous December, but denied it was an incident of domestic violence. Gayle Sweeney called the published report a "completely false allegation against my husband."[57]

At a press conference outside their home a half-hour later, Rep. Sweeney said he did not hit his wife. Neither the congressman nor his wife took questions from reporters.[58]

A day earlier, Sweeney's campaign office issued a statement to the *Times Union* calling the police report a fabrication and "campaign propaganda."[59]

"The real incident report has nothing in it like the salacious words in this concocted document," Gayle Sweeney said on a conference call. "I don't know if it is possible, but I give permission for the State Police to release the real report for all to see."[60]

Rep. Sweeney also called on the state police to release the report.

When Thompson contacted Sgt. Kern Swoboda at the state police, he responded that by law, he could not release the report without a notarized waiver from the Sweeneys.[61] The Sweeneys said they would do that, but they never did.

By Thursday, the congressman and his wife still had not given notarized authorization for the police report to be released to the public, despite offers from the editorial board of the Albany *Times Union*, the Associated Press and the New York *Daily News* to provide the congressman and his wife the paperwork.

We reported the congressman had angrily refused.

Instead, Sweeney appeared with Governor Pataki and former New York City Mayor Rudy Giuliani at a campaign event, and when reporters asked about releasing the police report, he said, "Talk to my lawyer."[62]

By then, the domestic violence charges had reached full throat, and our editorial page editor Mark Mahoney asked me if we should withdraw our endorsement.

Mahoney and I took the proposal to publisher Rahlf. We argued that because of the accusations against the congressman, we should withdraw the endorsement and not endorse either candidate.

We were surprised when she agreed.

"There is a time when you have to say, enough," is the way Mahoney started the editorial published on Friday, November 3, 2006. "Here is one such time."[63]

Pulling back our endorsement became a news story as well. Rep. Sweeney earlier told *Times Union* editors the incident at his home was a "non-issue."

Mahoney wrote this in the editorial withdrawing the newspaper's endorsement:

We don't think it's a non-issue. And we're sure many of our readers don't either.

In May of last year, 25 courageous victims of domestic violence came forward and told their compelling stories of abuse as part of a series in this newspaper on domestic violence. They told of violence and fear, and of shame and humiliation they felt when they failed to remove themselves from their abusive situations.

The congressman's curt dismissal of a domestic violence incident as a non-issue demonstrates that he either doesn't understand the seriousness of this matter as it relates to his role as a member of Congress, or that he simply hopes to divert attention from it so he can win the election.

His response to this incident reflects disturbingly not only on his character, but on his credibility to serve effectively as a representative of all the people.

There are still three days until Election Day, and we urge the congressman to release the police documentation he says will unveil the truth about what really happened that night.

Given this situation and Congressman Sweeney's unacceptable response to it, we can no longer stand behind our earlier endorsement of his candidacy.[64]

The day before the election, Rep. Sweeney appeared in Milton to announce a $1,000,000 grant for the town to fund road improvements. He also said he would not continue to answer questions about the controversy.[65]

"I don't want to answer. I'm really done with this," Sweeney told reporters.[66]

The next night, four-term Congressman John Sweeney took the stage at the Holiday Inn in downtown Saratoga Springs and conceded defeat.

Democrat Kirsten Gillibrand had received 53 percent of the vote in a district that had been in Republican hands for all but four years since 1913.

"I'm only sorry that I let you down," Sweeney said, while clutching his wife Gayle's hand.[67]

Moments after he left the stage, *Post-Star* reporter Konrad Marshall described a scene of Sweeney in the hallway, "shaking hands, kissing faces, hugging bodies and receiving thanks while offering nothing but apologies."

"I'm sorry, I'm so sorry," he said.[68]

Emily's List later reported Sweeney had taken more campaign contributions from special interest groups during 2006 than any other of New York's 29 members of Congress. He was also the seventh-largest recipient of contributions from lobbyists out of the 435 members of the House of Representatives.

Twelve years later, Sweeney told the *Times Union*, "When I lost in 2006, I was as depressed as I'd ever been, but I was detached from myself. I looked at it as being a victim."

The whole sordid affair was far from over. After first insisting the 9-1-1 report had been "fabricated" by political operatives, Rep. Sweeney's charges morphed into "who" had released the report.[69]

The Albany *Times Union* reported in the weeks after the election that there were "dueling" state police incident reports about the 9-1-1 call.[70]

T U columnist Fred LeBrun said this in a November 19 column: "At the very least, this broadly suggests efforts were made at the top echelons of the State Police to deflect attention from the initial, complete report, or to bury that first report to protect the Sweeneys."[71]

On the same day, *Post-Star* reporter Don Lehman—he never, ever really goes away—reported that the state police captain who commanded the agency's investigators in the region had been reassigned and his salary lowered as a result of a state police investigation into the handling of records related to the Sweeney 9-1-1 call.[72] That state police captain was Frank A. Pace, the commander of troopers in Washington County the night of Sweeney's Willard Mountain ski accident and the man who had investigated his son's arrest for fighting.

Lehman reported that Pace had been accused of leaking a state police blotter report regarding the incident at Sweeney's home.[73]

But the police union's president told Lehman state police documents were apparently altered and that was not getting enough attention. Others did not believe Pace had leaked the report.[74]

"They're ignoring the cover-up," PBA president Dan DeFedericis said.[75]

Five years after the car accident, Lehman reported that "sources familiar with the matter" said Pace was contacted by troopers at the scene that night and decided no tickets would be issued. Lehman was still reporting on an accident from five years earlier.[76]

Things did not get much better for Sweeney after his defeat. He filed for divorce from his second wife, Gayle, who told the *Times Union* that Sweeney had physically and verbally abused her and that she had made a "coerced" statement to rebut the police report before the election[77] in 2007.

A year after his defeat, Sweeney was arrested for driving while intoxicated on the interstate at 1:19 a.m. He failed a field sobriety test and was administered a breath test. His blood alcohol reading was 0.18, more than twice the legal limit. Police had no comment about where Sweeney was driving from or where he was headed, nor did they comment about whether there was a passenger in the vehicle. Even as a former congressman, Sweeney appeared to be getting special treatment.[78]

Court documents later revealed Sweeney had a young woman in the car with him who was reportedly sitting on his lap. His lawyer later confirmed a young woman was with him,[79] but denied she was sitting on his lap. Sweeney was fined $1,000, and his license was suspended for six months.

On April 6, 2009, Sweeney was charged with a felony count of driving while intoxicated when state police pulled the 53-year-old over at 3:30 a.m. on Route 9 in Clifton Park. Sweeney refused to take a sobriety test.[80]

He later told reporter Paul Grondahl of the Albany *Times Union* in 2018 that was the last time he took a drink.[81]

It was more than a year later before Sweeney was finally sentenced on the drunken driving conviction, although later downgraded to a misdemeanor as part of the plea deal. Sweeney was sentenced to serve 30 days in Saratoga County Jail, do 300 hours of community service and wear an alcohol-detecting ankle bracelet for at least one year. In an unusual arrangement, Sweeney began serving his time a week before sentencing.[82]

Wearing a suit and tie—and cuffed at the wrists and ankles—Sweeney addressed the court, "The last year has been a year of recovery for me," Sweeney said. "Moving forward, I hope that I may be a positive role model for others."[83]

A week later, Sweeney was released from the county jail ten days early for good behavior.[84]

He remarried and had two more children before getting divorced again in 2018.

Times Union reporter Carol DeMare profiled Sweeney in a 2011 story, "Sweeney talks of loss, healing," where he admitted he had become a "professional alcoholic."[85]

"Losing a seat in Congress wasn't my biggest loss," Sweeney told DeMare. "It was the loss of myself and the loss of everything that went with it, the harm and hurt I created for people around me who I love and love me. At the end of the day, in a very ironic way, it's what saved me. You decide to live or die. What made me want to live was my kids."[86]

For many, that accident coming back from Willard in 2001 was the first sign, yet it was one the newspaper was criticized for covering.

"I lost everything, destroyed my family, served a jail sentence and went through the shame of all my mistakes in the public eye," Sweeney told *Times Union* reporter Paul Grondahl in 2018. "I decided to get sober for my kids."[87]

Sweeney said that of the 38 people who completed a residential drug and alcohol treatment program with him in Florida, only two were still sober. Twenty were dead.

"Over the period of my life, there were consequences, bad things would happen, and I would always blow it off to something else," Sweeney said to DeMare in the *T U* article. "I've come to the realization alcohol was always involved and when you have that kind of awakening, it helps in recovery."[88]

But Sweeney was never too far from the next headline.

In October 2014, the *Albany Business Review* reported that a strip club in Colonie, New York, patronized by boxer Mike Tyson and other celebrities—had been sold. Sweeney, who allegedly had been a patron of the club over the years, was the club's attorney.[89]

After his third marriage ended in divorce in 2018, the *Daily Freeman* in Kingston, New York, reported in August 2018 that a private investigator was suing the former congressman for lack of payment after he hired him to follow his wife in a child custody matter.[90]

During the 2016 presidential election, Sweeney found his way back into politics when he was hired by Donald Trump's campaign in New York.

After Trump's election in November, "Congressman Kick-Ass" reprised his role on the ground in the swing states of Michigan and Wisconsin during recounts.

In December, Sweeney was appointed to the executive committee on President-Elect Trump's transition team. He was at the center of vetting candidates for posts throughout the Trump administration.[91]

In September 2019, *Post-Star* reporter Michael Goot reported that Sweeney had signed a $750,000 contract with a Kremlin-controlled investment bank to lobby against any new sanctions imposed by the United States. Sweeney would reportedly be paid $62,500 a month.[92]

The bank had been sanctioned in 2014 by President Barack Obama as part of the U.S. response to Russia's annexation of Crimea. The bank's previous chairman, Sergei Gorkof, met with President Trump's son-in-law, Jared Kushner, in December 2016, according to *Mother Jones* magazine. The meeting was investigated as part of the Robert Mueller probe into interference in the 2016 presidential election.[93]

While cleaning up my office at *The Post-Star* in 2020, I found an old T-shirt.

Mark Mahoney, my close colleague and the editorial page editor, gave me the T-shirt sometime after the 2006 election. The white T-shirt with black sleeves has a photograph of a red-faced Sweeney taken at the Union College fraternity party that is now part of his legacy.

"I got ripped with John Sweeney," it reads over the top of the former congressman's photo. Underneath the photo it reads, "Alpha Beta Booze."

It was a reminder that over the long haul, newspapers usually get it right.

15

Not Again...

Our reporters and editors were back in front of the newsroom television in April 2007 as we watched the coverage of the Virginia Tech slaughter that claimed 32 students. It was a new level of violence that shocked us.

The communities that surround Glens Falls in upstate New York are mostly rural with a strong conservative point of view. Gun clubs dot the landscape, and hunting is a family pastime. More people own firearms than do not. If you want to run for public office, you better be for the Second Amendment, and packing a pistol wouldn't hurt.

In the years since the 13 murders at Columbine, the National Rifle Association had become the most powerful lobbying organization in the country.

Looking back at any list of mass shootings today, I find shockingly few even made the front page of our newspaper. To even display such an act of violence prominently on the front page might lead to a backlash from readers sensitive to attacks on the Second Amendment. It was always in the back of my mind in those early years. Should we rock the boat?

What happened next was even worse. We gradually became numb to the mass shootings, to the problem of gun violence around the country, and perhaps the danger to our own communities. After each shooting, we posed the question again about whether it could happen in our idyllic little world, where murders and random crime were rare.

Each time we saw another shooting on the newsroom television, we'd mutter, "Not again," and walk away. We failed our community in that regard.

By 2008, filing Freedom of Information requests had become routine for reporters and encouraged by editors.

In January 2008, Nick Reisman, a 23-year-old University at Albany graduate who had started at the newspaper the previous September, filed a Freedom of Information Law request with our three local counties asking for the names and residences of all pistol permit holders.[1]

He knew it was public information and didn't think much about the request. I was not aware he had even made the request, which is not unusual when a reporter is just starting the reporting process.

One morning in early February, I got an unusually angry phone call, demanding to know why we had published the names and addresses of local pistol permit holders. At one point, I asked the caller if they were sure they had the right newspaper because I did not know what he was talking about.

More phone calls followed and accusatory emails laced with profanities came in bunches for the rest of the day. As the calls and emails escalated, I learned that many of the callers and writers were from different parts of the country and had seen information online that we were putting gun owners in jeopardy by publishing their personal information. Remember, this was in the early days of the internet before anyone had uttered "fake news," and Facebook was still a novelty.

I asked around the newsroom and discovered Reisman had filed FOIL requests in hopes it would lead to a story. He had not received any of the information at that point.

I was getting so many emails, I composed a form-letter response saying we had not published the information in question and had no plans to do so. Apparently, this was posted on message boards around the country.

Some were happy to hear the story was not true, while others said they did not believe me. Reisman was having the same experience.

"A lot of brain power was spent responding to people on this," Reisman said 12 years later in 2020.[2]

Years later, I found this online on one of the gun websites: "Earlier this month, *The North Country Gazette* learned that *The Post-Star* had filed Freedom of Information Law requests with the town clerks of Warren, Washington and Saratoga Counties for a list of names and towns of concealed carry permit holders in the three counties and had plans of publishing those names in a database on their website."[3]

While it was true we had filed the FOIL requests, there was no truth we intended to publish the information online. The other problem with the report was the source. *The North Country Gazette* was not a real printed newspaper. It was one woman writing a blog in the Adirondacks who had repeatedly criticized our reporting over the years and regularly threatened to sue us.

The online report was quickly passed around the country to websites advocating gun rights such as righttobeararms.com, guns.com, highroad.com and AR15.com. It was an online community that many of us did not know existed. These were message boards where like-minded people could talk about issues they were concerned about. It was the forerunner of what would become social media.[4]

Over the next few days, so many phone calls came in I started a list of who had called. I recognized a few as regular letter writers, but not many of the others. After several days, the number of calls had reached 70. There were probably just as many emails.

Handling the fallout from something we did not even do was frustrating and continued to consume most of my day for the rest of that week. It trickled down to other editors in the newsroom, and the publisher. Some callers threatened newspaper employees with harm; others talked of organizing a boycott of the newspaper and its advertisers. We all felt uneasy in the newsroom. I just wanted it to stop.

I can't emphasize enough the effect this had on me as editor, and the newsroom as a whole. We were under attack because a reporter had filed a Freedom of Information Law request—any citizen's legal right—for public information. It was a chilling insight into the fanaticism of the gun rights supporters and their level of organization.

What I didn't know at the time was that three years earlier an Orlando television station had published the identities of central Florida gun owners on its website, raising hell among those named.

A small newspaper in Virginia had done the same thing, and gun owners said their families were being put in danger.[5] Gun rights supporters argued criminals could use the databases to target their homes and steal their weapons, or criminals might use the database to target homes of residents who did not have guns. Both arguments seemed hollow—perhaps even laughable—in our region where random burglaries were rare and home invasions nonexistent.

While trying to figure out why so many people were upset at us and so paranoid about having their names published for owning a weapon, I learned that the *South Florida Sun Sentinel* had also acquired the state's database for gun licenses in June 2006, just before the state put into effect a new law that ended access to gun license information without a court order.

The *South Florida Sun Sentinel* put the Florida database of gun licenses to good use, comparing it with a felony database. That was the basis of the January 2007 story, "License to carry," that found the state of Florida had given concealed weapon gun licenses to hundreds of people with a past criminal history.[6]

The Florida newspaper found more than 1,400 people who pleaded guilty or "no contest" to felonies had qualified for a gun license because of a loophole in the law and that another 216 with outstanding warrants also had gun licenses. The reporting also showed another 128 people with active domestic violence injunctions against them. So while our reporter did not have a purpose for the databases initially, he did now.[7]

Perhaps the more disturbing issue was the total lack of trust that gun owners had for the media, even small newspapers like ours that had not taken any type of stand on gun control measures. They characterized all reporters and editors as liberals attempting to take away their guns. That characterization would continue and escalate in future years.

Later, after we received the gun ownership data from Washington County, several callers wanted to know what precautions we had taken to keep the information from being stolen.

I argued we did not need to do that since the information was available legally from the county clerk to anyone who wanted it.

On February 5, 2008, at the height of the controversy, we took the unprecedented step of addressing our readers on the front page of the newspaper about something we had not even published.

> To our readers,
>
> We here at The *Post-Star* find ourselves in the unusual position of responding to the concerns of our readers about something that has not even been published in our newspaper or on our website.
>
> In the past week, the amount of emails and general conversation in the community—and in some cases around the state—has reached such a pitch that we felt it was in everyone's best interest to address the concerns directly.
>
> About a month ago, one of our reporters submitted a Freedom of Information Law (FOIL) request to the county clerks in Warren, Washington and Saratoga counties, asking for the names and towns of residence of all gun permit holders in their counties.
>
> This immediately drew great concern from members of gun clubs and people with gun permits in general, a concern we totally understand.
>
> FOIL requests are a regular part of the reporting process, especially when government bodies are reluctant to give up public information to which any citizen is entitled. It is the law of the land.
>
> In this case, just filing the FOIL request seems to have touched a nerve.

We want to assure our readers that this newspaper takes its community service responsibility seriously when it comes to sensitive and private information. We always have and we always will.

Many have contacted us wanting to know what we are going to do with this information and why we wanted it.

We listened to those concerns and want to assure each and every person that we would never, ever do anything to endanger private citizens or make information conveniently available that might lead to a safety concern.

One potential story that could come out of this is finding out whether there is a database of convicted felons. We would run that database through the gun permit database in each county to find out if there are people who shouldn't have guns.

This is a somewhat new development in journalism called computer assisted reporting. We think it would be an important story if it turned out that convicted felons showed up with gun permits. But we can't do that story without the gun database.

We have served communities in Warren, Washington and Saratoga counties for more than 100 years. We consider this newspaper an institution that is an important part of each and every community as a news source, a watchdog of government and an entity that seeks to serve our readers and make our communities better.

We also expect our government leaders to enforce the laws they were elected to uphold. We will continue to hold them to that standard, especially when it comes to the Freedom of Information Law.

We hope that our readers will support us in these endeavors and we promise that we will continue to do our jobs responsibly and only for the greater good of the community.

Ken Tingley
Editor[8]

Over the next few days, there were more than 50 reader comments evenly split about our intentions for acquiring the pistol permits.[9]

The website thehighroad.com ran a headline without any punctuation or capitalization that read "another paper in NY state wants to publish concealed carriers" with a link to *The North Country Gazette* website's initial report and my note to the readers addressing the issue.[10]

One person commented on thehighroad.com, "Sounds like a good story, if they stick to the stated parameters."[11]

Another said, "Problem with that is that reporters don't always get it right."[12]

On the AR15.com website "223Rem" posted this comment: "If I lived in NY, I'd want to be on that list. Gives me more legal protection when a dumbass MF'er comes through the front door and gets two in the chest. It was public knowledge that I owned a handgun, yet the dumbass did not heed the warning."

I'd like to say that was just the mentality at the time, but I believe it is just as pervasive today.

The experience showed us that gun rights activists were organized and ready to pounce on any media outlet that dared to file a Freedom of Information request. It also showed that within local counties our FOIL requests were being shared by government officials as part of the political game.

In late February, reporter Reisman heard from Saratoga County Clerk Kathleen Marchione that the FOIL request was ready, but he would have to pick it up at her office.

"It was so strange," Reisman remembered in 2020. "She had me pick it up in her office in Ballston Spa. She kind of marched me into her office, handed me the CD and read part of the letter to me in front of the people in her office. I wouldn't be surprised if she recorded the conversation. Quite frankly, she was ambitious and she saw this as a way to show she was the face of gun owners and gun rights advocates and that she had their backs."[13]

Gun rights would actually be the focus of one of her later campaigns for the state senate.

"As I have previously stated, I would not be providing you with this information except that Penal Law requires me to do so," Marchione wrote in the letter to Reisman. "Although I firmly believe that open government is extremely important, I also believe it needs to be balanced when the safety and security of residents may be at risk. The publication of Pistol Permit holders' names and/or addresses may put those individuals in danger of being burglarized by criminals seeking hand guns. Conversely, criminals might target where they know the household does not possess a hand gun. Senate Bill 2733 amends the Penal Law in relation to confidentiality of information contained in an application for a Pistol license and has now passed out of the Senate Codes Committee and awaits debate on the Senate floor. I respectfully request the above safety and security concerns be considered when utilizing the enclosed Saratoga County Pistol permit holders' list."[14]

Also enclosed was a bill for $1.24 for the reproduction of the disc.

Marchione had been chosen president of the New York State Association of County Clerks a year earlier, and in 2007 she led a group of county clerks in opposition to Governor Eliot Spitzer's plan to allow undocumented immigrants to obtain driver licenses. Governor Spitzer eventually withdrew the plan after criticism from the public.[15]

When we finally heard from Warren County Clerk Pam Vogel, she said there would be a delay in getting us the information because some of the database would have to be redacted.

After my "To the readers" response was posted on the AR15.com website, someone with the handle "Outdoor1894" posted that Warren County Sheriff Nathan "Bud" York began "sending emails to his department employees in an attempt to remove their names from the list of pistol permit holders because the Warren County attorney has stated that the information cannot be withheld."

It was months before Vogel made the database available, writing us that it had taken some time to redact information from the database. She enclosed a bill for that work. Neither Washington County nor Saratoga County redacted any information.

I told Reisman not to pick up the Warren County database, and we never did the story on possible felons with legal gun permits in our communities. I regret that decision today. I had been cowed by bullying tactics of the gun rights activists who made our communities less safe. We let the pistol permit issue die off by doing nothing. I suspect that was the intent. It would not be long before we would all be in front of the newsroom television shaking our heads, "Not again."

"I guess, ultimately, I learned not to stick my head into a beehive," Reisman laughed during a 2020 interview. "I gained a certain amount of wisdom from it going forward. If you are going to go after an issue like gun rights, an issue that is controversial, be prepared for blowback. Be prepared for people to get whipped up in a frenzy."[16]

"I think my big regret was not being able to think what we were going to be able to do with this to turn it into a story that is useful for people to read," Reisman said.[17]

Sadly, we would all have another chance.

Parents Still Don't Get It

The party was in Putnam, New York, a tiny rural community of about 500 in the most northern reaches of Washington County. Putnam is so small it does not have its own high school or downtown. Most of the 20 to 30 teenagers gathered around the bonfire that Sunday night in April 2008 went to Ticonderoga High School about eight miles north of Putnam. The teens drank beer and smoked marijuana.

By 2:15 a.m., the outdoor party at the residence of Jimmy Joe and Kellie St. Andrews was starting to break up. The two adults were in bed. Their son, 16-year-old Dustin St. Andrews, borrowed his uncle's Cadillac STS without permission to give four other teens a ride back to Ticonderoga.[1]

You know how this ends.

Route 22 north to Ticonderoga is a two-lane road lined with dense woods on each side. Police say Dustin St. Andrews accelerated the car to speeds north of 130 miles per hour.[2]

Even now, if you stare at the photograph of the wrecked black Cadillac, it's hard to imagine that any of them survived. The luxury automobile is crumpled like a bad first draft of a letter. The vehicle could pass as a compact rather than a luxury sedan. Each side of the car has collapsed into the middle while the trunk is intruding into the backseat.[3]

Dustin St. Andrews had a compound fracture to his wrist. Two of his friends were taken to the hospital but survived.[4]

The two 16-year-old girls in the car—Shannon James and Michaella Lopes—were not wearing seatbelts.[5] They must have been like rag dolls on impact. Amazingly, James lived until the next day. Lopes was dead at the scene.

Dustin St. Andrews pleaded guilty to first degree vehicular manslaughter six months later. In court that day, Bill James, Shannon's father, told how he buried his daughter in the prom dress she never got to wear.[6]

Danielle Lopes recounted how 200 friends and family members sang "Happy Birthday" to her daughter during a memorial service on what would have been her 17th birthday.[7]

Dustin St. Andrews, dressed in a black-and-white jail jumpsuit with his hands shackled, sobbed.

"If I could take it back I would," he said in court. "Not a day goes by that I don't think of Shannon and Mika."[8]

Judge Kelly McKeighan imposed a two and a half- to seven and a half-year prison sentence on St. Andrews.[9]

But this was not the conclusion of another tragedy; this was the beginning of

Jimmy Joe St. Andrews, 41, and his wife Kellie St. Andrews, 40, look on during their trial in Washington County court in February 2009. After two teens died in an accident in which their son was the driver, the couple was charged with some 30 counts of unlawfully dealing with a child and criminal nuisance for looking the other way while a late-night drinking party was going on in their yard. They became the face of all permissive parents. The jury found Jimmy Joe guilty of endangering the welfare of a child but not guilty of two other endangering charges. Kellie was found guilty of endangering the welfare of a child and unlawfully dealing with a child. She was found not guilty of six other charges. Two years later, the verdict against Jimmy Joe was overturned. Despite being sentenced to 60 days in jail, they served just a few days each (*Post-Star* photograph by Jeffrey Fehder).

another discussion in the debate about underage drinking.

Newspapers and the words they publish rarely have the power to solve complicated societal problems overnight. Even ambitious projects like *The Post-Star's* eight-part series on underage drinking four years earlier are soon forgotten with another week's worth of news. But in the months after "The Cost of Fun" was published, there were two encouraging developments: Readers were talking about the problem, and there had not been any more fatalities.

We at the newspaper were feeling good about our work and the impact it seemed to be having. That ended in the early morning hours of February 20, 2005, when two young people died in an early-morning accident in the rural town of Jackson in Washington County.[10]

David Saffer, local executive director of the Council for Prevention, had been an integral source and cheerleader on the underage drinking series. In the days after the crash in Washington County, he stopped by for a chat.

Saffer pointed out that Warren County had gone eight months without an underage drinking fatality.[11]

"That is an eternity for around here," he said.[12]

While young people continued to drink and party, there was now a loud and public discussion. Most local communities had already reached a consensus that drinking and driving were unacceptable; what was under discussion now was whether teen drinking was an acceptable rite of passage.

Seven Warren County communities and another in Washington County banded together with a federal government initiative called Communities that Care, while seven school districts in each county agreed to a comprehensive survey on teen attitudes.

The newspaper adopted a controversial policy of printing the names of those arrested for underage drinking. There was support for the initiative, until it was your kid.

After we printed the names of some Lake George teens, one parent called me and wanted to know why her son's name was published. She argued he only had a couple sips of beer.[13]

"I suspect we all have a blind spot when it comes to our kids," I wrote on April 24, 2005. "The more we talk about the issue of teen drinking, the more I'm convinced it's the parents we have to reach—not just the teens."[14]

As we approached the one-year anniversary of our series, the teen drinking issue became part of the daily diet of news in the spring of 2005. Teens in Lake George, Fort Ann, Whitehall and Granville were all caught having parties. Some were arrested, some disciplined by their schools after being caught on class trips.

Glens Falls High School was one of the first to promote an after-prom party that would keep kids safe. The goal was to keep kids away from alcohol and off the road. Glens Falls officials reported that 270 of the 278 students attending the junior prom also attended the after-prom party. It is a tradition that continues to this day all around the region.

In June 2005, the Washington County Sheriff's Office conducted a sting using an underage volunteer to buy alcohol from grocery, convenience and liquor store clerks around the county. Of the 22 stores visited, the 20-year-old volunteer was shockingly able to buy alcohol in eight stores. Three of the clerks were over 30.

More importantly, five months after "The Cost of Fun" was published, it was clear there was a new problem.

In October 2004, a Queensbury couple hosted a birthday party for their 17-year-old daughter and dozens of her friends. Soon afterward, photos appeared online of the mother posing with underage teens holding alcoholic beverages. This was at the dawn of social media, and most didn't know any better.[15]

A link to the photos was sent to Glens Falls High School Principal Jeffrey Ziegler. He contacted the police.[16]

The mother and father were charged with a misdemeanor charge of unlawfully dealing with a child in connection with the October 9 party in which police believed dozens of underage students were allowed to drink alcohol.[17]

Police were able to identify only 13 of the students holding alcoholic beverages. They were all charged with underage drinking, and this time their names were published in the newspaper.[18]

In Saratoga County, there was enough of a worry that nearly 100 members of law enforcement, alcohol prevention specialists and educators gathered to kick off a 12-county initiative to educate parents and arrest those who threw parties and served alcohol to underage students.[19]

But it was the death of the two girls in Putnam that put the parental responsibility issue front and center.

In the days after the fatal crash, Jimmy Joe St. Andrews, 41, and Kellie St. Andrews, 40—Dustin's parents—faced 30 counts of unlawfully dealing with a child and criminal nuisance. They became the face of all permissive parents.

Authorities believed the St. Andrews's residence had become a gathering place for teen parties on more than one occasion. But more importantly, they accused Kellie St. Andrews of buying alcohol for the party the night of April 20, 2008. The St. Andrews were also accused of allowing children as young as 13 to drink alcohol at their home.[20]

As Danielle Lopes spoke at Dustin St. Andrews's sentencing, she lashed out at his parents: "You raised this little monster," Lopes said, glaring at Jimmy Joe and Kellie St. Andrews sitting in the back of the courtroom. "He's a victim of you."[21]

She then turned back to Dustin St. Andrews, "You're better off in jail than you would be with those parents."[22]

Jimmie Joe and Kellie St. Andrews stood trial in February 2009 for their role in the underage drinking parties at their home between 2005 and 2008.[23]

Rarely do newspapers—even small community newspapers—provide coverage of misdemeanor trials, but this was different. This was an integral part of the community conversation about why teenagers were dying in our communities and what the responsibility of parents was.

The Post-Star's Mark Mahoney continued to set new standards of persuasion with this editorial the day before the trial started in Washington County Court:

> Parents, pay attention to this one.
>
> On trial in a court of law are the parents of a teenage boy who's in prison for killing two children in a car crash that started at a party in which alcohol was served to minors, one of several parties that these parents may have hosted or at least condoned over a period of years.
>
> Put yourself in the position of any of the participants—the parents who are on trial, the son who is in prison, the parents of the other kids who attended the parties, the parents of the victims.
>
> This is something any parent could face. This is something any family could face. ... And then consider how far you'd go to avoid walking in any of their shoes.[24]

Jimmy Joe St. Andrews and Kellie St. Andrews testified they didn't know about their son's underage drinking parties, and they did not provide alcohol to anyone under age. Dustin St. Andrews also testified his parents did not know about the drinking and drug use.[25]

Then, 16-year-old Bryant Austin of Ticonderoga testified. He was one of the teens who survived the 130-mile-per-hour crash almost a year earlier.[26]

Washington County District Attorney Kevin Kortright asked Austin whether Kellie St. Andrews had ever purchased alcohol for him.[27]

"Yes," he replied, then described how she purchased a 30-pack of Keystone beer before the April 20 party. He said that Dustin St. Andrews then took the beer from the truck for them to consume at the outdoor gathering.[28]

Austin testified that Jimmy Joe St. Andrews came outside the Putnam home during the outdoor party and that no one made any effort to hide their beer.[29]

Four other teens testified that Kellie St. Andrews briefly visited the April 20 party, and no one hid their drinking.[30]

When Schroon Lake Fire Chief Larry Shiel arrived at the St. Andrews's home at 3 a.m. on April 21, 2008, to tell the couple their son had been in an accident, Shiel testified there were beer cans and bottles all over the yard and a couple of young people still around the bonfire.[31]

"This is the party house in Washington County," District Attorney Kevin Kortright said in his closing argument. "This is where the kids go to do what they want to do when they want."[32]

"They should have known," was how I opened my column on February 15 about Jimmy Joe and Kellie St. Andrews.[33]

"This is what parents are up against if you want to keep your sons and daughters alive past the age of 21," I wrote. "Overstated? Well, remember the horrible reality—two 16-year-old girls never made it home from that party."[34]

I argued to *Post-Star* readers the problem was bigger than this one case. One week after Dustin St. Andrews's deadly joyride, a 16-year-old from Greenwich had crashed and died while driving home from another parent-hosted party that included alcohol. Charges were being considered against that parent.[35]

"There are others just like them who believe underage drinking is no big deal and they would rather have parties under their supervision. This case paints a picture that raises so many questions about the parenting of so many, it should leave us all shaking our heads as we wonder, not only if we can trust our own kids, but if we can trust the parents of their friends. If at any time on the night of April 20–21, the St. Andrewses had ventured out into the yard, if they had checked on the group for a minute or two, if they had shown the least bit of curiosity about what was going on around that bonfire, perhaps two young people would still be alive."[36]

The case went to the jury at 2:30 p.m. on a Friday. The jury did not return a verdict until nearly midnight. One juror later told *The Post-Star* reporter that two jurors wanted to declare the jury hung.[37] That says a lot about the perceptions of regular people at the time when it came to underage drinking issues. They were ready to let Jimmy Joe and Kellie go.[38]

I wished I could have asked how many of the jurors had read "The Cost of Fun."

Hours before the verdict, Judge McKeighan dismissed many of the criminal charges against the couple, saying that the prosecution had not proven its case.[39]

The jury found Jimmy Joe St. Andrews guilty of endangering the welfare of a child but not guilty of two other endangering charges.[40]

Kellie St. Andrews was found guilty of endangering the welfare of a child and unlawfully dealing with a child. She was found not guilty of three other counts of endangering the welfare of a child and three additional unlawfully dealing with a child charges.[41]

Neither showed any emotion when the verdict was read,[42] and they were later sentenced to 60 days in jail, three years probation and 100 hours of community service.[43]

Two years later in March 2011, Jimmy Joe St. Andrews's conviction was overturned on appeal on grounds of insufficient evidence. He had served just seven days in jail.[44]

Bill James, who had buried his daughter in her prom dress nearly a year earlier,[45] was in court for the initial guilty verdict.

"I truly hope this is the first step to making change in the community," James told a *Post-Star* reporter. "We've had so many tragedies."[46]

That fall, 13 young people were charged with underage drinking in the same Putnam community, and one 21-year-old was charged with endangering the welfare of a minor for supplying the alcohol.[47]

If ever there were two communities where they should have known better, it was Putnam and Ticonderoga.

But it gets worse.

Kristopher Wilson, 18, was one of those arrested at the later party. Wilson had gone on that wild joyride with Dustin St. Andrews that reached speeds of 130 miles per hour and killed two 16-year-old girls two years earlier.[48] Authorities said the only reason Wilson was alive was that the two girls plugged the sunroof, preventing him from being thrown from the car.

And it gets worse still.

William James, the 21-year-old arrested for providing the alcohol to the teens in the more recent case, was the older brother of Shannon James, one of the 16-year-old girls killed in the accident and the son of Bill James, who had been so vocal about putting an end to the tragedies.[49]

I wrote this at the time: "If your mouth just dropped into your cereal, I don't blame you. I'm speechless as well."[50]

Washington County District Attorney Kevin Kortright, who had prosecuted the case, said this, "These kids should know better than anyone. They are the ones that cry at the funeral, and now they are partying at the house."[51]

Things did not turn out any better for Jimmy Joe and Kellie St. Andrews.

The couple eventually separated, and there were accounts that Jimmy Joe made threats against his estranged wife. News reports said that on Friday, July 13, 2012, Jimmy Joe St. Andrews approached a group of six people gathered at an apartment attached to a salon where Kellie St. Andrews worked in Ticonderoga.[52]

He fired six shots into the group, wounding a 45-year-old man from Hudson Falls, but police believed his intended victim was Kellie.[53]

Jimmy Joe St. Andrews fled on foot and 20 minutes later called a family member to say he was going to kill himself. His body was found in a wooded area next to the Mount Hope Cemetery in Ticonderoga, with a self-inflicted gunshot wound.[54]

Dustin St. Andrews got into more trouble in prison and was prosecuted for possessing contraband. That added an additional one and a half to three years on top of his original prison sentence of two and a half to seven and a half years. He was finally released on March 19, 2018, after more than nine years in prison.[55]

He was sent to jail again less than six weeks later for a parole violation. While surrendering to authorities at the Washington County Jail, police found he had secreted a pack of drugs in his rectum. He pleaded guilty to a felony for trying to smuggle prescription drugs, marijuana and tobacco into the jail.[56]

Washington County Judge Kelly McKeighan sentenced him to another one and a half to three years in prison.[57]

Eight months after the convictions of Jimmy Joe and Kellie St. Andrews were splashed across the front page of *The Post-Star*, a local businesswoman, who had previously owned a bar in downtown Glens Falls, was arrested when police broke up an underage drinking party in a suburban, upscale Queensbury residence on Halloween night. Police believed there were as many as 75 young people at the party.[58]

The woman's lawyer said she had hosted a non-alcohol party for her children, and "swarms" of teens with alcohol crashed the gathering. One 16-year-old girl required treatment at Glens Falls Hospital, and two other teens were arrested for underage drinking.[59]

The excuses often stretched the bounds of believability.

"It started out fine, but within 30 minutes the house was overtaken by a bunch of marauding teenagers, a swarm of total party-crashers," lawyer Greg Canale said in defense of the 47-year-old woman.[60]

After receiving a tip about the party, officers arrived at the scene just after 11 p.m. to find dozens of young people running from the home into the nearby woods. It seemed more like a scene from the movie *Animal House* than a respectable suburban neighborhood.[61]

Seven months later, Queensbury Town Justice Robert McNally dismissed the misdemeanor charge against the local businesswoman and parent, saying there was no evidence she provided alcohol to any of the underage drinkers at her home. The town justice pointed out that just knowing there was underage drinking in her home did not support the charges brought against her. It may not have been morally appropriate, but it was not against the law. The judge wrote in his six-page decision that addressing the law was the work of the state legislature.[62]

"If the Legislature wishes to criminalize the knowing, passive hosting of parties at which alcohol is served to minors, it certainly may and probably ought to do so," McNally said.[63]

It sounded like even the town justice still needed to be convinced.

At another event in October 2010, community leaders determined to fight the underage drinking problem gathered at Hudson Valley Community College in Troy, New York, to talk about solutions.[64]

Saratoga County District Attorney Jim Murphy summed up the problem perfectly: Parents still don't get it, he said.[65]

Looking back, I can't help but wonder if Jimmy Joe and Kellie St. Andrews actually helped the cause. By taking their case to trial, they directed a spotlight, not only on underage drinking, but parenting.

Some parents complained when their children's arrests appeared in the newspaper for underage drinking. They argued the newspaper was ruining their kids' chances of getting into a good college or a job later in life.

Others said the newspaper should not be preaching its values.

But if we didn't do it, who would?

It turned out some brave adults were willing to take a stand, and others were not.

Greenwich Principal George C. Neisse, who had seen his share of tragedy in his town, told about tipping off the police to an underage drinking party only to be chastised at the next Board of Education meeting by angry parents.[66]

In Ballston Spa, school officials asked authorities not to tell the media that more than 30 students were busted at a party in Warrensburg when they were supposed to be in school.[67]

In Glens Falls in January 2010, police received a call just after midnight that an underage drinking party was going on at a house on New Street. When officers arrived, they found 25 or so people at the house where an 18-year-old woman lived. Many fled, and one teenager was found hiding in a closet with an alcoholic beverage.[68]

Who dropped the dime?

The 18-year-old girl's father.

The father had warned his daughter not to have a party while he was out of town.

He told her if there was a party, he would call the police. On Saturday, January 16, the daughter held the party. And the father called the police.[69]

How many of us would do that? How many of us would back up our words with actions and give one of our kids a record with the police? I'm guessing not many.

Others were taking a stand, too.

In March 2010, Dan Davis addressed the students at Lake George Central School about his life experiences with drug and alcohol abuse. After a morning assembly, Davis spent the rest of the day interacting with students in breakout sessions where they could talk intimately about their own lives and community.

At the end of the day, Davis sat down with Lake George Principal Fran Cocozza and told him, "You guys have a problem."[70]

Davis told Cocozza that the students had unloaded about all the issues facing the school and the community. Cocozza sent home a letter to parents with a sledgehammer in it.[71]

This is what he told parents:

- Students continue to come to school drunk or high. They are just hiding it better.
- All types of drugs are easily accessible within the village and school.
- Some parents are aware their children are drinking alcohol or smoking pot, but do nothing.
- A few parents host parties at which drugs or alcohol are present.
- Several students indicated there was nothing wrong with abusing pot or drinking alcohol because it is not harmful.

Even after talking to Davis, several students indicated they were going home to drink or get high that night.[72]

Cocozza implored parents to talk to their children and to work with him to help solve the problem—together. It was refreshing to see a public official address the problem quickly, aggressively and publicly. Instead of whispering about it behind closed doors, he chose to shout it out so all could hear. Cocozza later said a majority of the community was in his corner.[73]

Not only did Cocozza send the letter home; he shared it with the faculty, the support staff, the elementary schools and the bus drivers. He wanted everyone on board. He was not afraid of hurting the school's reputation or drawing fire for the job he was doing.[74]

"The only thing I hear sometimes is, 'This is not your issue, but my issue at home,'" Cocozza told me at the time. "My perspective is, 'No, we have to work on this together.' I think a lot of parents are shy or fearful of the punitive measures. If you reach out for help we are going to help your child."[75]

At almost exactly the same time, the local Council for Prevention released a survey on alcohol and drug use at local schools. Nearly a third of Lake George students in grades 7 to 12 admitted to drinking in the past 30 days. About 17 percent said they had smoked marijuana.[76]

"That is significant," Cocozza said then.[77]

It was April and prom and graduation celebrations were just around the corner.

"So many said this is just a rite of passage," Cocozza said. "But I am not going to sit back and let that be our excuse."[78]

Maybe our message was getting through.

It had for Nick Fitzgerald in South Glens Falls. He reached out to me that spring. Fitzgerald was the athletic director at South Glens Falls and was in charge of the school's annual health fair, one of those school events nobody else wants to do because students rarely take it seriously.

Fitzgerald wanted to go beyond the lectures and panel discussions that leave teens rolling their eyes. He wanted something real, something that would linger and remind teens that tragedy can knock on your door at any time.

It was the same mission our newspaper had been on since publishing "The Cost of Fun" six years earlier.

Fitzgerald said, when he talked to teachers, they whispered about the drug and alcohol problems in their schools. They told him about the students in the parking lot changing their shirts and squirting Visine in their eyes to cover up the signs and smells of marijuana use.[79]

Fitzgerald said teachers often feel they are losing the battle, especially when there are parents ready to argue this is a rite of passage for all young adults.

Fitzgerald conjured up a presentation that was part docudrama and part movie of the week. He had done the impossible. He filled the South Glens Falls auditorium with hundreds of tittering adolescents and silenced them. He used the resources of the drama club for an opening scene in the auditorium in which a mother talks her husband into letting their daughter have a drinking party at their home so kids "will be safe."[80]

This was a story ripped right from *The Post-Star* headlines. The party unfolds on stage with 25 or 30 students acting out a Saturday night blowout worthy of a college fraternity, complete with simulated games of beer pong and youngsters acting drunk.[81]

"When the party scene was going on, the kids were all cheering and chanting," said Fitzgerald about the afternoon performance during school. "But pretty soon, you could hear a pin drop."[82]

What unfolds is as close to being there as you can get.

On stage, the teens have a party; then a video produced with the help of a local television station shows a carload of boys wearing letterman jackets drinking beer, swerving down the road and finally hitting a little girl crossing the street to the haunting sounds of a song called "Too Late to Apologize."[83]

The video shows the teenager being arrested, handcuffed and taken to the real Glens Falls jail to be fingerprinted. John Gray, one of the news anchors at Fox 23 News in Albany, cuts into the proceeding to describe the breaking news like a real local news telecast. Headlines from *The Post-Star* are shown chronicling the event.[84]

When the action returns to the stage, the partying teens are at a funeral, and a small coffin is carried to the center of the stage.[85]

That's when Lisa Savard appears.

You remember Joelle Dumoulin's mother Lisa, who brought the audience to its knees with the ultimate reality. She had lost her own daughter eight years earlier. You remember the story about Joelle and a friend meeting a boy and going for a ride. He hit a tree while drag racing, leaving Joelle pinned in the wreckage.

Joelle lived only another minute, Lisa was told. It was supposed to be comforting for her, so she knew her daughter did not suffer. Instead, it haunts her.

"They told me later Joelle lived for just a minute after the crash," Savard said quietly that evening eight years later. "Sometimes I look at the clock ticking. A minute is a long time."[86]

This was a new tactic for fighting underage drinking. Give Nick Fitzgerald a lot of credit for not only taking on the fight but finding a new way to reach the young adults at his school by making it real.

"The combination of re-enactment and reality drives home the possibility of tragedy, leaving those of us who are parents wondering how long we should lock our sons and daughters in a closet," I wrote after seeing the production.[87]

The conversation had been taken to an entirely new level by Fitzgerald, a guy passionate about his cause, about the future of not only his own two kids but other people's kids as well.

Fitzgerald later told me he had kids coming to his office at the end of the day to tell him they cried, to tell him they were moved. They showed their emotions, let their guard down and admitted they learned something.[88]

I believe Fitzgerald saved lives that day.

It was another step.

Another example of the conversation taking place that would make a difference.

Leaders with that type of passion don't stay athletic directors for long. Fitzgerald became principal at Cairo-Durham in 2015, then superintendent of schools at Canajoharie in 2019. I suspect he brought his idea of dramatic production to save teen lives at each stop along the way.

At least, I hope he did.

Two years later on a gray February day, my 16-year-old son passed his driver's test. It had been 11 years since I started the scrapbook after the two fatalities in Greenwich.

Later that evening, he asked if he could drive the car to his rehearsal for the high school musical.

I told him he had to read the scrapbook first.

I hoped the headline, "16-year-old girl killed in Corinth," the 2002 newspaper clipping when Joelle Dumoulin died would have a profound impact on this 16-year-old teenager in 2013.

I hoped the scrapbook filled with the victims from familiar neighboring towns over the past ten years—and real people his own age—would scare him for life.

"You know what really gets me," he said a little later that evening. "It's not the photos of the wrecked cars. They are bad and all, but it's the photos of the kids. They are my age. Some of them are only 16, like me."[89]

"They will always be 16," I said.[90]

After he returned from rehearsal that night, I learned he spent more time with the scrapbook in his bedroom. Before going to bed that evening and saying good night, he brought up the scrapbook again.

"The thing that really got me is that you took the time to cut out every one of those articles over the past 10 years and put them all in the scrapbook," he said.[91]

"And why do you think I did that?" I asked.

"To save my life," he said.[92]

I was unable to speak.

He got it.

A few weeks later, Joseph Tingley, that little boy I had repeatedly used as the reason behind the scrapbook and my crusade against underage drinking over the past 11 years, wrote a guest essay that was published in *The Post-Star* with a photo of him holding the scrapbook.[93]

"So when my dad told me as we drove home from my driver's test I had some reading to do, I knew what that meant," he wrote.[94]

In the fourth paragraph, he wrote this about the Greenwich accident from 2002: "A few pages later, there is a color image of a coffin being carried down the steps of a church. The students carrying the coffin of their friend are my age. If they sat down in my chemistry class, they would fit right in with us."[95]

It was the same photo that appeared the day after I wrote about starting the scrapbook.

"Ten years is a long time to keep anything going, but my dad kept going. I realized then more than I ever have before how much my dad loves me and the measures he would take to keep me alive."[96]

Those words still choke me up. There are tears in my eyes right now.

"As I continued to flip through the scrapbook," my son wrote in his essay, "I started to understand my dad's anger over this issue and why he takes it so seriously. I knew before, but reading the scrapbook brought me greater clarity. All I could think was: Why do we keep doing this? Can we not learn from our mistakes?"[97]

I like to think I passed the torch to another generation. I often argued that if we saved one life with our stories, it was all worth it.

I had found that one life.

17

"You won it, buddy"

Mark Mahoney was down the street at Burger King when he got a call from the new publisher telling him to return to the office immediately. There was going to be an "all-hands-on-deck" meeting in the conference room.[1]

Mahoney feared the worst. Just a month earlier at the last "all-hands-on-deck" meeting, the staff was told that 11 full-time employees had been thrown overboard. It was the Great Recession, and business was not good for small community newspapers like *The Post-Star*.[2]

"I think I freaked him a little bit," publisher Rick Emanuel said in an interview in 2011.[3]

"It scared the shit out of me," Mahoney remembered more bluntly.[4]

The Post-Star has a large rectangular conference room more reminiscent of a Fortune 500 boardroom than a small community newspaper. A muscular wooden table with a dark finish stretches from one end of the room to the other. Along the walls are framed *Post-Star* front pages from significant local news events like presidential elections and the *Ethan Allen* tragedy. The table stretches 20 feet from one end of the conference room to the other, and 15 people can sit around it comfortably.

As sullen-faced reporters, editors and support staff filled the room for the unscheduled afternoon meeting, Mahoney took a seat on the one side of the table while Emanuel fiddled with a speaker phone at the middle.

Most of the newsroom staff stood, hoping the meeting would be short.

The phone rang in Florida where I was on vacation.

Speaking into the phone, Emanuel said to me, "OK, I'm going to put you on speaker phone."

How did this happen, I wondered?

How did we get here?

"Go ahead, Ken," I heard Emanuel say.

It was April 2009.

In 2008, I was asked to be a judge for the Pulitzer Prizes in New York City. I spent several days at Columbia University that February judging column writing. From my conversations with others who were judging editorials, it was clear they were disappointed in the entries. It convinced me that Mark Mahoney, and small newspapers like ours, could compete in the editorial writing category.

"You can play in that league," I told Mahoney when I returned.

In January 2009, Mahoney put together an entry heavy on open government and Freedom of Information editorials but refused to write the nomination letter. That

Post-Star editorial page editor Mark Mahoney is stunned after being told by editor Ken Tingley he had just won the Pulitzer Prize for editorial writing in April 2009. Weekly editor Nancy O'Brien (behind Mahoney) is equally surprised by the announcement. Mahoney is one of the few to win a Pulitzer at a small newspaper. It was the first Pulitzer Prize for *The Post-Star* (*Post-Star* photograph by Derek Pruitt).

was Mahoney. He would enter the contest, but he didn't feel comfortable selling his work, so I wrote it.

In February, I returned as a Pulitzer judge for the second year. While judging editorial cartoons, I noticed the editorial writing judging was going on at a table close by. In those days, you submitted your Pulitzer entry—ten clipped editorials from the newspaper—in a large scrapbook. As the entries were reviewed, those rejected by three or more judges were put off to the side, while those still in the running were put in the middle of the round table for further review. For Mahoney's entry, I purchased a scrapbook with a bright blue cover that stood out.

After the second day of judging, the bright blue scrapbook was still in the center of the table. By the last day of the judging, I was repeatedly distracted by the discussions at the editorial judging table. I was starting to get excited.

"These are the kinds of editorials that make a difference," I heard one of the judges arguing passionately. He had the blue scrapbook in front of him.

When I left at the end of the day, the big blue scrapbook was one of three still in the middle of the table. Leaving nothing to chance, I opened the scrapbook before leaving and confirmed it was Mahoney's entry.

Pulitzer Prize judging is done in two stages. The entries are first whittled down to three finalists in February before the Pulitzer Prize Board selects a winner and two finalists at a second meeting.

We had a chance.

The *Rutland Herald*, a neighboring Vermont newspaper about our size, won the Pulitzer Prize in 2001 for editorial writing.[5] I called their editorial writer, David Moats, after he won, telling him he needed to know all of us at small newspapers shared in his triumph. It was an affirmation of the type of work being done every day in small communities across the country.

In those early years as editor, the Pulitzer Prize was something I whispered about when talking to editors, and sometimes to reporters. We were doing some good work, so I pointed to Rutland's Pulitzer and said more loudly, "If Rutland can win one, so can we."

When I returned to the newspaper from the judging at Columbia in 2009, I met with our new publisher Rick Emanuel and told him I was pretty sure Mahoney was one of three Pulitzer finalists. We swore each other to secrecy. It would be a long seven weeks.

The Pulitzer Prizes were announced on Monday, April 20, the same week I had planned a Florida vacation.

Pulitzer Day is just another day at small newspapers like ours. Few in the newsroom were aware the prizes were being awarded that Monday, including Mahoney.

As the time of the announcement neared, Emanuel repeatedly refreshed his computer screen to see who had won. He had told no one else.

In Florida, I was trying to do the same with my laptop, but I could not get on the Pulitzer website.

The phone rang.

"Go ahead, Ken," I heard Emanuel say.

The trouble was that I did not know whether Mahoney had won the top prize or was just a finalist.

"Is it what we thought," I asked Emanuel. But he just told me that everyone was gathered in the conference room and to go ahead.

I had not rehearsed what I would say.

"Mark," I said. "We've talked about this for a long time. I have some news."

I paused again.

"I'm like, 'What news?'" Mahoney remembered.[6]

Then, Emanuel busted in, "Tell him!"

Those in the room looked at each other, confused about what was happening.

"You won it, buddy," I said, then realizing that was not official enough, started again and said, "Mark Mahoney has won the Pulitzer Prize for editorial writing."

Mahoney, wearing a collared striped shirt and a blue tie, sat with his hands folded in his lap and gradually turned his head to the left as he tried to process the information. Sitting behind him was the editor of our weekly newspapers, Nancy O'Brien. Her mouth fell open in amazement. Scott Donnelly, our assistant city editor, looked the same on the other side of the room. Mahoney's head gradually tilted back.

"I just remember the blood draining from my face," he said.[7]

To his left, Mahoney saw our chief photographer, Derek Pruitt, sitting on the floor with the motor drive purring. Over the phone, I heard cheering and screams.

Gradually, there was a hint of a smile on his face, and it appeared he may have been looking to the heavens as his colleagues leapt to their feet to give him a standing ovation.

In Florida, my wife Gillian, our 13-year-old son Joseph and I hugged and began bouncing up and down in delirious unison.

When *Post-Star* publisher Rick Emanuel called for an "all hands on deck" meeting in April 2009, many—including editorial page editor Mark Mahoney (seated right)—feared it was bad news. Instead, Mahoney was stunned to learn he had won the Pulitzer Prize for editorial writing, and his colleagues rose to give him a standing ovation (*Post-Star* photograph by Derek Pruitt).

Mahoney remained seated at the conference room table, gradually bringing his arms up with his palms turned upward at the impossibility of it all. His face was one of stunned amazement, as if he still questioned what he was hearing. This is what it looks like when your dream comes true.

You've got to remember small community newspapers like ours don't win Pulitzer Prizes.

It's a pipe dream.

It's a somewhere-over-the-rainbow possibility when most of the time your readers are telling you how bad you are.

On this day, editorial writers from the *Chicago Tribune* and *The Washington Post* were looking up at Mark as runners-up.

Across five columns at the top of *The Post-Star* on Tuesday, April 21, 2009, is the headline "*Post-Star* Pulitzer" in big, bold type. A framed copy remains on display at the center of the newsroom not far from where Mahoney had his desk.

The lead photograph is of a smiling Mahoney on the phone at his desk as his 12-year-old daughter, Christa, gives him a hug. Below that photo is one of Mahoney in shock after hearing my words over the speaker phone, his colleagues in the background standing and clapping.

It had been ten years since Mahoney lost the city editor job sending him down a new career path. The Pulitzer confirmed he had found his true calling.

Unlike my announcement over the phone, I had prepared what I wanted to say for the news story:

Editor Ken Tingley said Mahoney's win made him think of the line from the movie "Hoosiers" when the basketball coach is urging on his small-school team to the championship.

"This is for all the small newspapers out there that never got to play in the game," Tingley said.[8]

After stammering through an interview with the Associated Press, Mahoney said he needed to get some air. He went outside and called his fiancée, Lisa, on his cell phone, but she didn't answer. He made the obligatory calls to his three daughters and his parents while leaning on a car in the parking lot. Mahoney said he does not remember how he celebrated that evening.

That's Mahoney, too.

Oddly, there was no quote from Mahoney in the story the next day. The Pulitzer had rendered him speechless.

On Wednesday, for the first time in a long time the lead editorial was not written by Mark Mahoney. Since this was one of my first editorials, I asked our readers for forgiveness, not only for the quality of the editorial but for taking a break from the issues of the day to pat ourselves on the back.

This was the Academy Award of newspaper honors and a first in our 105-year history, I wrote:

> What raises Mahoney's prose to a level of Pulitzer consideration is his ability to find a voice, an argument that is always passionate and persuasive, and brings it to the people so they understand why they should care.
>
> His Pulitzer Prize-winning entry was heavy on freedom of information issues that fought for your right to know information that the government was keeping from you.[9]

But I also wanted the readers to know that they were part of the equation:

> But this is not just an honor for this newspaper. This is a pat on the back to this community and this region as well. Any reader who has called to complain, written a letter to the editor, commented on a story or simply been a dedicated subscriber to this newspaper year after year, you deserve a piece of this as well. This is about community conversation and this community loves to converse.
>
> It inspires us daily, drives us to lend our voice to make this community better, to hold it to the highest possible standards and to look out for all its citizens.[10]

Mahoney was swamped by emails and phone calls for days.

When I returned from vacation, I printed out all the congratulatory emails we had received and wallpapered the newsroom bulletin board for all to see. I left it there for a few weeks, too.

"I remember that for like two weeks, every one was nice to me," Mahoney said. "I would be walking down the street and people would stop me and congratulate me."[11]

When I returned from vacation my first stop was at Mahoney's desk where I gave that big bear of a man a Pulitzer Prize-winning hug.

Several days later, Mahoney dropped his Sunday editorial on my desk. It was his first effort since winning the Pulitzer.

I started to read it, at first perplexed, then after I read some more a smile crept across my face and I started to laugh. I walked out of my office directly to Mahoney's desk at the center of the newsroom.

"This has got to be the worst editorial you have ever written," I said loudly in front of everyone. And it was, too.

Mahoney couldn't escape the shadow of the Pulitzer. All the editorials would have to be great now, and it was freaking him out.

"That was a real challenge," Mark admitted.[12]

A couple of days later, Mahoney stormed into my office and threw down the front page of the newspaper and pointed to an article, "Do you believe this shit!" he screamed.

"Oh, thank god," I exclaimed with relief. "You are back."

At the end of May, Mahoney and his fiancée, Lisa, traveled with my wife, Gillian, and me to New York City where he accepted his Pulitzer Prize at a luncheon at Columbia University.

The citation read as follows:

> Awarded to Mark Mahoney of The *Post-Star*, Glens Falls, N.Y., for his relentless, down-to-earth editorials on the perils of local government secrecy, effectively admonishing citizens to uphold their right to know.[13]

In the next day's newspaper story, we finally heard from Mahoney for the first time. "It is just an incredible honor to be in this company," he said. "It also says a lot about the value of small newspapers and the ability to make a difference in our communities."[14]

After the luncheon, the Pulitzer Prize class of 2009 gathered on the steps of the Columbia library to have a group photo taken. At one point, Mahoney dropped his Pulitzer scroll on the steps. Jon Meacham, the Pulitzer winner that year for his biography on Andrew Jackson, picked it up for him and with a big smile said, "I think you dropped something."

After returning to midtown, the four of us adjourned to a rooftop bar at the Peninsula Hotel on East 55th Street. Lisa bought champagne, and we toasted Mahoney's amazing accomplishment. We were literally on top of the world.

We eventually found our way to a small Italian restaurant nearby. As Mahoney and I waited for the women to come back from the restroom, former Secretary of State Colin Powell was leaving.

"How ya doing," Powell said, giving us a nod.

"Pretty good," said Mahoney. There was never a greater understatement.

Mahoney was now a celebrity in our little city, and he couldn't go anywhere without people telling him how proud they were of him.

Later that summer, Glens Falls Mayor Jack Diamond proclaimed it "Mark Mahoney Day" in the city of Glens Falls. The proclamation read in part: "Throughout his tenure at the helm of The *Post-Star* Editorial Page, Mark has established a legacy of consistent quality and thoughtful opinion through his writing."

And yes, he had criticized the city of Glens Falls more than a few times.

In the months afterward, Mahoney received job feelers from much larger newspapers, but as a divorced father of three daughters, he knew he couldn't leave.

We framed the Pulitzer Prize along with a photo of Mark's shocked expression and hung it behind the reception desk for every visitor to see. It is still there today.

Two years later in October 2011, Mahoney came into my office and closed the door. It had been 12 years since he had walked angrily out of my office, leaving me uncertain of his return. Now, it was official.

He said he had accepted a position with the New York State Bar Association in Albany to serve as its associate director of media services. He would be doing public relations work but advocating for causes he cared about.

"I'm sad to be leaving. *The Post-Star* has been like a family to me," Mahoney said in the story announcing his departure. "I have learned so much and met so many terrific people over the years. I'm going to miss everyone. But I'm also excited about my new opportunity at the bar association and I hope to apply what I've learned here in my new position."[15]

Mahoney had worked for the newspaper for 23 years, but he had not had a raise in five. This was the new normal.

"I was just looking for something different to do," Mahoney said.[16] But a pay raise was important, too.

Three days later, I shared my farewell with the readers and admitted that Mahoney's decision to leave struck me harder than most.

The front page for the April 21, 2009, *Post-Star* was framed and is still displayed in the newsroom near where Mark Mahoney had his desk (front page courtesy of *The Post-Star*, Glens Falls, NY).

"We didn't know each other very well until I became editor 12 years ago and I made Mark our editorial page editor," I wrote. "We were ambitious and we wanted to make a difference in the community. ... We fought a lot of battles and sometimes made a difference.[17]

"I wish Mark was not leaving," I wrote. "It is a loss for *The Post-Star*; it is a loss for journalism. But I wish my friend well and hope he continues to slay the dragons in Albany and around the state."[18]

We all owed him a lot.

This was the guy who stuck it out after being demoted in 1999, who built *The Post-Star* brand with hard-hitting editorials that made a difference, organized political forums and built up the reputation of our editorial board until it was clear it was a rite of passage for any politician wanting to serve.

This was the guy who called 9-1-1, then the newspaper after he witnessed a murder, but his legacy would always be the Pulitzer Prize. The first line of his obituary had already been written.

How do you replace someone like that?

You don't when business is not good.

When Mahoney left *The Post-Star* in 2011, he was not replaced. Will Doolittle and I took over writing the editorials, and before long the two of us were writing just as many editorials as Mahoney, but it did take two of us.

More importantly, we both took the job seriously because Mahoney had set the bar so high. We were determined to maintain the same quality of editorials and continue his legacy of making a difference. In the coming years, we expanded our editorial board to three citizen representatives and interviewed more political candidates than at any previous time while continuing to take strong and important stands as the times became more and more tumultuous. Mahoney had showed us the way.

Each April, I still peruse the latest Pulitzer winners looking for the next "Hoosiers" moment that will make us little guys proud all over again. They still pop up from time to time, and I usually send a congratulatory email to welcome the new member to the club. I remind them that all of us at small newspapers are proud of them.

Mahoney and I talked from time to time over the next few years and occasionally got together for a beer. He joked about the slow pace of his new job compared to the daily deadlines of a newspaper. I wasn't sure he was happy.

In March 2014, Mahoney got a phone call from Judy Patrick, the editor of *The Daily Gazette* in nearby Schenectady, New York.

"Did you ever want to get back into newspapers?" Patrick asked him.[19]

"Every single day of my life," Mahoney responded.[20]

That was it.

Mahoney was hired as *The Daily Gazette*'s editorial page editor. In the announcement, Mahoney was described as "Pulitzer Prize winning editorial writer Mark Mahoney."

That was his for life.

Just this past year, Mahoney was laid up with the flu for a few days. On Valentine's Day morning, he realized he had not gotten his wife, Lisa, anything.

"It was 6 in the morning and I dragged my ass out to Price Chopper to get some flowers," Mahoney remembered. "I was in sweats, had a three-day beard and I go up to this young cashier and he says, 'Hey, you're the Pulitzer winner.' I was like stunned. 'Thank you for remembering' I said. And he says, 'Well, that was quite an accomplishment.' You just never know when you are going to have your 15 minutes and 20 seconds of fame again."[21]

Mahoney was still at *The Daily Gazette* in the summer of 2020 banging out daily editorials from his home during the pandemic and still trying to make a difference.

"I was working in my office the other day, the Pulitzer on the wall and I fucked up an editorial," Mahoney said.[22]

You could tell he was kicking himself for his sloppiness.

"It was a reminder to me this job is day to day," he said. "Every day, you are starting from scratch."[23]

Mahoney, 56, was back where he belonged—at a newspaper—still fighting the good fight.

I asked him why he went back.

"Because every day I come to work and find something to piss me off," he said. "Newspapers out there are getting rid of their entire opinion sections. We've had 1,500 letters to the editor this year [through August 2020] and we still have the big election season ahead. People are really into it. People are using the newspaper to express their opinions. I find that encouraging."[24]

That's what keeps so many of us going.

I'd like to think that every once in a while when Mahoney can't find the right word or the inspiration demanded, he stops a second, takes a peek at the Pulitzer on the wall and remembers my words:

"You won it, buddy."

"There are kids in there"

Mark Bosford was up early on the morning of Saturday, June 26, 2010, to pick up his brother from work, leaving behind his girlfriend, Mary, and five-year-old son, Noah, slumbering in a downstairs bedroom. He shared the four-bedroom residence with another couple, Lewis "Carl" Smith and Samantha Cox, and six of their children.[1]

The couple was a blended family that included three children the couple had together, along with their other children from previous relationships.[2]

Neighbors said it was a nice house and not run down.[3] Burgoyne Street is a pleasant residential neighborhood, quiet, and just a block removed from busy Route 4 Fort Edward.

The fire broke out in the living room of the two-story home shortly before 7 a.m. Confronted with flames in the living room downstairs, Mary pushed out an air conditioner in the ground-floor bedroom window and placed Noah safely outside before climbing out herself.[4]

Carl and Samantha, both 34, awoke about the same time in the other downstairs bedroom where they were sleeping with their one-year-old child.

A 9-1-1 call was made at 6:51 a.m.[5] When Carl Smith opened the bedroom door, he was met by a wall of fire and had to retreat into the bedroom.[6]

Gerryanne Spring, who lived across the street from the home, looked out her front door and saw flames shooting up through the house. She also saw a woman, who she said was burned, sitting cross-legged on her lawn holding a child, while nearby, a man who was also burned was trying to get back into a house engulfed in flames.

"He kept yelling, 'Save my kids,'" Spring said. "They were trying to get back in the house, but they couldn't. The heat, it was horrible."[7]

Lydia Wheeler was just 22 years old and had been a full-time general assignment reporter for less than a year, but she had plenty of experience. She was a local Queensbury kid who had worked for the newspaper since her junior year in high school. We were hoping she would be the rare, young reporter who would make a career with her hometown newspaper.

As the new reporter, Wheeler drew the weekend shift. She remembered waking up that morning, flipping on the local radio station and hearing a report about a fire in Fort Edward.[8]

"It sounded like it might be bad," Wheeler said.[9]

Fort Edward is a 15-minute drive from Queensbury, and Wheeler got to the scene at about 9 a.m.

"I'll never forget that day," Wheeler said in 2020. "When I got there, I remember

I approached one of the firemen. 'I can't talk on the record, but there are kids in there,'" he said.[10]

It did not take long for the fire to gut the house after Carl and Samantha escaped. The six children left inside were between the ages of one and 12.

The rest of the day was a long, agonizing vigil for those waiting for official word.

"I started talking to extended family members," Wheeler remembered. "There was a lot of people crying. I remember going up to the grandmother of one of the girls, and then a cousin, and they were just hysterical."[11]

Here is the other part about community newspapers that most don't consider. This was a 22-year-old woman who had little experience with breaking news, reporting under the worst possible conditions, but she delivered the story with respect to the victims and family alike.

"The thing that I will never forget was the look on the fireman's face," Wheeler remembered a decade later. "That blank disbelief. Some scenes, you pull up to as a reporter and the firemen don't seem fazed at all. But this was a really bad one. You could just tell. He looked like a ghost."[12]

About 8 p.m., they brought out the six bodies.

The house on 40 Burgoyne Street in Fort Edward was just a mile from where the four children had died on Lower Allen Street eight years earlier.

One-year-old Abbigayle Smith was found in the bed where Carl Smith and Samantha Cox had been sleeping on the ground floor.[13] The other five children were found upstairs, with several huddled around the oldest, 12-year-old Hope Palazzo-Smith.[14]

"She was trying to protect them," Wheeler remembered. "I will never forget that one detail."[15]

The couple had one other child, seven-year-old Rose Smith, who was sleeping at a friend's house the night of the blaze. She was now an only child.

Both Carl Smith and Samantha Cox were taken to the Westchester County Hospital burn unit—nearly three hours away—where Cox was listed in critical condition. Noah Bosford and Mary, the first two out of the house, were taken to Glens Falls Hospital where they were treated and released.

It had happened again in the community of Fort Edward.

Investigators later concluded an improper fuse had failed to trip a circuit breaker, causing the electrical fire. A nearby couch in the living room helped fuel the blaze. The house, which was built in 1900, did not have a history of building code violations and was owned by a limited liability company based in Santa Cruz, California.

Washington County District Attorney Kevin Kortright eventually concluded, "This was just a horrific accident."[16]

It was determined the children all died of smoke inhalation, most likely before the fire department arrived.[17]

One working smoke detector was found in a stairway to a basement and one without batteries was found in the basement. Carl Smith told investigators the house had smoke detectors on the first and second floors, but he did not hear them activate. No devices were found anywhere else in the house, but fire officials said they could have been destroyed by the fire.[18]

"When there is a tragedy of this magnitude, you want more," I wrote to our readers. "You are looking for something or someone to blame. You want to know why. You want to believe that someone must have made a mistake, or was careless, or else none of us are really safe in our homes. But there is no one to blame here."[19]

It would be ten days before the six children would be mourned and buried at Evergreen Cemetery in Lake George.

Once again, the Gospel Lighthouse Church in Kingsbury was the location of the funeral service, with 150 in attendance. At the rear of the church were the children's class portraits, family photos and certificates of achievement.

We chose Wheeler to cover the funeral. This was her story now. I was there, too.

I didn't want to go to the church that day and be put through the emotional ringer of seeing six little caskets, but I made myself go. I believed it was my job to help provide emotional support for a community's breaking heart and to put another tragedy in context.

"I remember having the overwhelming feeling of not being wanted there," Wheeler remembered.[20]

On our way into the church, one of the funeral directors approached me and asked me not to interview anyone from the family. I assured him we would respect their privacy. We were there to report on the service.

The two of us took a seat in the back left corner of the modern church as we tried not to draw attention to ourselves. We kept our notebooks out of sight as we scribbled notes in our laps.

It was a scene of unimaginable grief at the Gospel Lighthouse Church in Kingsbury, New York, as the funerals were held for six children killed in a fire in nearby Fort Edward in June 2010. Six sets of pallbearers were needed, and when the name of each child was called, their father, Carl Smith, led them on their final journey to the hearse and then the cemetery (*Post-Star* photograph by Jason McKibben).

"At the same time, I also felt I had a duty to report this event," Wheeler said. "I was feeling a little bit like a pariah, but it was important that we cover not only the fire, but the aftermath as well."[21]

Not bad for a young kid.

Richard Yancy, minister at the Faith Baptist Church in Queensbury, described Carl Smith as "rough around the edges" that day "but he has a big heart, an enormous heart."[22]

Yancy described how Samantha Cox comforted people at the wake more than she herself was being comforted.[23]

Funerals are designed to comfort loved ones in the family. I looked at our reporting of these tragedies as comforting the whole community:

> When the hour-long service had concluded, they called up the pallbearers to the sanctuary in groups of four. One group for each of the six caskets.
>
> Twenty-four of them to take "Car Car," Mackenzie, Emilie, Abbigayle, Paige and Hope to their final resting place in Lake George.
>
> The call went out six times.
>
> Each time a group of four would arrive by the side of a casket, and Carl would shake their hands, pat them on the back and thank them for their service. Each time, he would get behind the small coffin and push it to the waiting hearse with pallbearers on each side.
>
> Each time another set of pallbearers would wait for Carl to return.
>
> Each time, that big heart had to be breaking a little more.
>
> Samantha's too.
>
> And so many others.
>
> It was as if Carl refused to let those children take another step in their journey without him. It was as if he was trying to make the most of their time left together before that final goodbye.
>
> Nearby, as they were moving away the final coffin, Samantha, the mother of four of the children, was dissolving into tears, her left arm still bandaged from the fire.
>
> And all around her, an entire community's heart was breaking.[24]

The most heartbreaking scene of all was seeing six-year-old Rose Smith walking hand in hand with her father, Carl, looking lost, before taking her brothers and sisters to the cemetery. Ten years later, I found Rose Smith had attained academic honors at Argyle Central School.

Just like eight years earlier, the horrific tragedy was selected as the most newsworthy story of the year by the newspaper, but the story was not yet complete.

Wheeler had taken us this far, so she was chosen to do the year-end story on the fire and interview Carl Smith, who said he could not "legally" talk, but it was clear he had something to say.[25]

"The only thing I can really tell you is that we're still trying to get Rose through it, and it never gets any better due to Florence Palazzo," Carl Smith said.[26]

Palazzo was the mother of two of the children with Carl Smith—12-year-old Hope Palazzo-Smith and six-year-old MacKenzie Palazzo-Smith—and she was still inconsolable. She called for a grand jury investigation of the fire and the actions of Smith and Cox. She asked why the couple was unable to rescue any of the children, including the one-year-old who was in the bedroom with them.[27]

I suspected Lesley Ingraham from the fire eight years earlier might be able to provide an answer.

"I can't defend myself with the stuff she's said," Carl Smith told Wheeler. "She's

Carl Smith (at the very back behind the casket of one of his six children) helps the pallbearers as they prepare for the trip to the cemetery. To the right is six-year-old Rose, the only one of Carl Smith's surviving children. She was sleeping over at a friend's house the night of the fire (*Post-Star* photograph by Jason McKibben).

called me a murderer because I didn't try to save my kids. She has no clue on that day, no clue. No one does, and now I have to get a 6-year-old through it. I don't know how I feel about it, I don't know what she's feeling."[28]

A 309-page report from the state Office of Fire Prevention and Control revealed that one-year-old Abbigayle Smith was found on the remains of the couple's bed in the first-floor bedroom.[29]

"She was found in the same bed as them," Palazzo told a *Post-Star* reporter while sharing part of the report.[30]

Neither Carl Smith nor Samantha Cox was ever able to recount exactly what they did in the moments after discovering the house was on fire. Palazzo said charges were warranted.

There was another enormous outpouring of community sympathy and support to help the family pay for the funeral expenses of the six children.

Robin Renaud, whose daughter knew the parents, told the newspaper she was already planning a spaghetti dinner to raise money for the family in the days after the fire. She set up an account for donations at a local bank.[31] The various fundraisers eventually raised $50,000 to help the family with funeral expenses and find them a place to live.[32]

In the weeks after the fire, Carl, Samantha and Rose lived in a camper on a relative's property in the town of Argyle. By August, Carl and Samantha were planning to buy a modular home and some land with the money that had been raised.[33]

But lawyers for Carl Smith and Samantha Cox noticed money appeared to be unaccounted for when Renaud turned over $20,000 that remained after funeral expenses were paid.

The next spring, the 44-year-old Renaud was accused of stealing $7,329 from the charity. About $30,000 had gone toward funeral expenses, but the indictment alleged more than $7,000 was unaccounted for when the bank account was closed. Another Hudson Falls resident, Tina Goodall, 41, was also named in the indictment. Both pleaded not guilty.[34]

Three months later, after moving to North Carolina, Renaud pleaded guilty to misdemeanor petit larceny as part of a plea deal. She agreed to repay $4,829 and spend three years on probation after she was able to prove she made a $2,500 payment to the Fort Edward Fire Department.[35]

Renaud's lawyer later said in court she was overwhelmed by the fundraisers and was not aware of all the bookkeeping rules. Goodall pleaded guilty to a noncriminal count of disorderly conduct. She had received $500 from the fund, which her lawyer said was a legal payment for her expenses in helping with the fundraising.[36]

Just over a year after the fatal fire, Carl Smith and Samantha Cox received a $485,000 settlement from the insurance company of the home's owner, KFNY0504 LLC of Santa Cruz, California. Carl and Samantha's lawyer, Michael Martin, said they planned to build a memorial playground for the children, but as of April 2012, it was unclear whether those plans had ever progressed. The couple eventually separated.[37]

In July 2012, Fort Edward police received an early-morning call about a man not breathing in a vehicle on Lincoln Street.

It was Carl Smith II.

He was stricken while hanging out with a group of young women around his parked car. Officers performed CPR, but Smith later died at the hospital. He was 37 years old. An autopsy concluded he had heart disease and died of a heart attack. Since separating from his wife, Samantha Cox, he had been living in his car.[38]

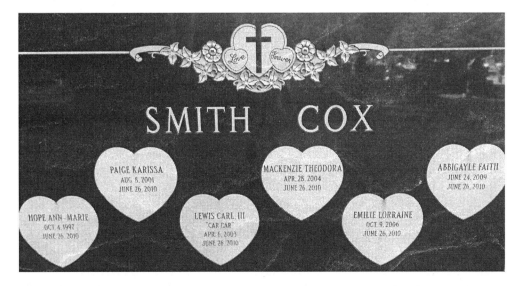

The six children—Hope Ann Marie, Paige Karissa, Lewis Carl III, MacKenzie Theodora, Emilie Lorraine and Abbigayle Faith—are buried at the back, northwest corner of Evergreen Cemetery in Lake George beneath an enormous granite monument. Carl Smith and his mother are buried on the other side of the stone, too (photograph by Ken Tingley).

It seemed fitting it was his heart that broke in the end.

Beneath an enormous black granite monument at a back corner of Evergreen Cemetery in Lake George, the six children are buried with their names etched within small hearts on the front of the stone.

On the back of the black granite, a scene of a small cabin on an Adirondack lake is carved with four more names beneath it.

Carl Smith and his mother, Lorraine St. Clair, are buried here, too. Carl Smith's death came just six weeks after his 62-year-old mother's. Next to Carl's name is Samantha Cox and their lone surviving daughter, Rose, who was 16 in 2020. It appears the plan was for them all to eventually be together again.

When Carl Smith died, it had been two years since the fire.

Over the next two years, having working smoke detectors became a community cause, not only in Washington County but throughout the region because of the tragedy.

Only one working smoke detector was found in the house; Carl Smith insisted there were ten at the time of the fire, but none went off. A 2003 state law required homeowners to have smoke detectors that are audible in each room where people are sleeping.[39]

After the fire, Washington County was awarded a state grant that provided 655 smoke detectors for free distribution around the community.[40]

"We are giving them out to people in the communities that can't afford to bring their houses up to code on their own," Washington County Public Safety Director William Cook told Wheeler. "Some houses we've been in are receiving up to 10 to 12 smoke detectors to make that happen."[41]

Included in the article was contact information in Washington County on how residents could get a smoke detector. We were hoping to save lives, too.

Cook said he also believed the county needed to take a closer look at code enforcement.[42] That November, *Post-Star* reporter David Taube wrote a story about a Fort Edward eighth-grader, Caitlyn Hunt, who was trying to prevent other tragic deaths. She had been friends with Hope Palazzo-Smith, the little girl who had tried to protect her siblings in the upstairs bedroom at 40 Burgoyne Avenue.

Hunt led an effort in her school district to bring fire detectors and batteries to homes that needed them. The newspaper covered that story, too.[43]

Project Hope/Fort Edward not only secured $5,000 from an online contest run by PepsiCo; it also was given a $1,000 grant from the local Stewart's Shops.[44]

On October 1, 2011, the father of a small family on 14 Case Street in Fort Edward heard the piercing sound of a smoke detector. The house was a half-mile from where the six children died on Burgoyne Avenue.[45]

The father leapt out of bed and found a fire on the first floor of their home. He alerted the rest of the family and led them out through a second-floor window onto the porch roof where they all jumped safely to the ground.[46]

"The smoke alarms saved their lives," Fort Edward Fire Chief Matt Hurlburt said at the time.[47]

I couldn't help but wonder if the smoke detector was one of those given away in the wake of the fire that killed the six children, one that had been purchased with the money raised by eighth-grader Caitlyn Hunt, the friend of Hope Palazzo-Smith.

I'd like to think so.

In the summer of 2020, I drove down Burgoyne Avenue and stopped in front of the empty lot where the six children died.

A large maple tree, filled with leaves reaching into the late afternoon sky, sat near where the house once stood.

It was quiet.

There was not a single sound of a child playing.

19

Profile in Courage

In the eight years since *The Post-Star* ran its "Growing up Gay" story and suffered the ire of conservative readers, the same-sex marriage debate gradually became an issue no one could ignore in the state.

In 2004, the mayor in New Paltz, New York, married 25 same-sex couples in front of the New Paltz City Hall to draw attention to the issue. The local district attorney charged him with 19 misdemeanors. Several other mayors said they would conduct same-sex marriages in their cities.[1]

In 2006, the New York Court of Appeals ruled the state constitution did not recognize same-sex marriage and left the question to the state legislature to decide. The state of Vermont had done the same thing five years earlier. Following the ruling, the New York Assembly, made up predominantly of liberal Democrats from downstate New York, passed same-sex marriage legislation in 2007 and 2009, but the state senate, under Republican control, voted against it both times.[2]

Local state senator Roy McDonald had voted against the bill both times, once as a member of the assembly and the second time as a member of the senate.

McDonald was an upbeat and enthusiastic self-promoter who unapologetically boasted of his numerous accomplishments as supervisor in the town of Wilton and then in the legislature. He regularly filled reporters' notebooks with colorful quotes and insights from a single question.

But when I interviewed McDonald on Election Day 2010, he was subdued. Sitting within the quiet confines of the newsroom's library that afternoon, he seemed off his game. Maybe he was just tired from campaigning, but he didn't seem to have a lot to say about his first term in the state senate.[3]

The 63-year-old, who had served in Vietnam with the U.S. Army's First Air Cavalry, seemed resigned, beaten down by the dysfunction in the legislature.

If you were an idealistic patriot wanting to make a difference in your state and community—as McDonald liked to portray himself—the New York State Legislature was not the place to be.

He seemed beaten.

That Election Day, the word "beaten" stirred some life into him.

"No, not beaten," he said. "Not at all. My life has always been about challenges."[4]

At first, McDonald struggled to find the right words for the challenge of working with New York City representatives, but he quickly found his footing.

"As I've gotten older, I have evolved. I like people, I really do, and I'll work with anyone, but I'm also very candid. What's scaring me is they are not competent. These are fourth-stringers coming out of the city. I had a higher expectation for the people.

Some of these people are terrible. The Senate is supposed to be this elite body. You want some people with wisdom and vision. What I saw was appalling. I saw a bunch of hustlers."[5]

It was the most honest and forthright evaluation of state politics I had ever heard, and the police blotter in recent years had confirmed McDonald's observations over and over again. It was clear this was what was bugging him. This was not Republicans against Democrats or even upstate versus downstate; this was simply right versus wrong.

"We have to get away from the personal attacks, the lies," said McDonald. "It is a freak show. One guy beats his girlfriend on tape, another is rigging bids, and another is arrested for assault for the second time. This is out of control. Twenty million people are looking at us, and you need to have a certain amount of respect. It drives me crazy when they say they are a 'public advocate.' I want to ask them, 'Did you ever have a job?' because that's how my dad measured people."[6]

McDonald railed about a bloated state government where political patronage runs rampant, and handouts in the form of "member items"—or pork—are routinely used to get incumbents elected.

"We've got to start whacking the hell out of the top," McDonald said. "We've got to get it under control."[7]

McDonald easily won reelection that night with 58 percent of the vote without any voter in his district hearing those words. Andrew Cuomo was elected New York's new governor that night, too, setting in motion an unexpected fate for McDonald.

The new governor made it clear he wanted a same-sex marriage law passed before the end of the legislative session in June 2011.[8]

With 32 votes needed to pass the law, initial tallies showed 26 state senators supported same-sex marriage, 29 opposed and seven were undecided.[9] After voting against the measure twice before, McDonald said he was uncommitted.

At the end of May, *The Post-Star* editorial board decided to take a stand on the issue for the first time. On May 27, 2011, the newspaper editorial board of publisher Rick Emanuel, editorial page editor Mark Mahoney and me, endorsed gay marriage.[10]

Mahoney, our Pulitzer Prize winner from two years earlier, wrote this:

> What the entire debate over New York's same-sex marriage bill boils down to is something that the most brilliant minds of the 18th century American found to be self-evident.
> Equality of rights.
> It's the bedrock on which this nation was built. It's why we fought a revolution. It's why we fought a civil war. It's why Martin Luther King lost his life and why Susan B. Anthony is an American hero.
> It's what defines us as a nation and what we strive to achieve.
> Equality of rights.[11]

McDonald had a much-more-difficult problem. He became the subject of an intense lobbying campaign and the center of the Albany debate. A billboard went up on I-787 in Albany urging McDonald to "support all loving couples."[12]

Governor Cuomo called him several times.[13]

A Quinnipiac Poll released on June 2 said 58 percent of respondents supported gay marriage nationally.[14] In 2002, when the "Growing up Gay" story was published, national approval was under 40 percent. There had been a dramatic shift nationwide in attitudes, but maybe not locally.

On June 11, McDonald said, "I will be doing what I think is right."[15]

As the vote neared, Monroe County Republican James Alesi, who also voted against the legislation in 2009, became the 30th vote.[16]

On June 14, with the vote nearing, McDonald announced he would become the 31st vote, despite objections from the Roman Catholic Church, religious groups and conservative Republicans across his district.[17]

McDonald sounded like the man I had interviewed seven months earlier in the newsroom library, and his words became a "Profiles in Courage" moment in a place—the New York State Legislature—where taking the moral high ground was unheard of.

"You get to the point where you evolve in your life, where everything isn't black and white, good and bad, and you try to do the right thing," McDonald said to reporters. "You might not like that. You might be very cynical about that. Well, fuck it. I don't care what you think. I'm trying to do the right thing. I'm tired of Republican-Democrat politics. They can take the job and shove it. I come from a blue-collar background. I'm trying to do the right thing and that's where I'm going with this."[18]

It was the type of truth you don't see from politicians anymore.

"I'm not one of these guys that lives and dies, at this age of my life, for politics," he told Jimmy Vielkind of Politico. "I've accomplished more than the average guy around here. I'm going to go and see my family when I leave here. I'm going to go, turn around, and if I get out of politics I'll be a professional like I've been in the past. I'll make money. My grandchildren will have money to help through the problems they have. I'll go play golf, see my wife and spend time with my three kids and grandkids."[19]

Four days after McDonald announced his decision, I told our readers to consider Roy McDonald's rare courage.

To remember he did it because he thought it was the right thing.

To acknowledge this was what true leadership looked like.

Two more Republicans defected, and on June 24 the Marriage Equality Act passed 33–29 in the Senate with four Republicans joining the Democrats. Governor Cuomo signed it into law the same day.[20]

New York became just the sixth state to legalize same-sex marriage and give gay couples the same rights as straight couples when it came to health insurance, hospital visiting rights and income taxes.

"New York has always been a beacon for the country on LGBT rights," Governor Cuomo said in a statement.

The next month, McDonald visited with our editorial board again. It was in this room where I first met McDonald a decade earlier as part of a community meeting to debate urban sprawl. During one heated exchange, McDonald asked another panelist if he wanted to step outside and settle things. There were plenty of contentious discussions in that room over the years, but that was the only time we almost had a fight.

As we began the meeting in 2011, McDonald said he didn't want to talk about the gay marriage vote, but then he did, because guys like McDonald can't stop from charging forward.[21]

He talked about his military service, his record as Wilton supervisor and his work in the assembly and all the good he tried to do as a state senator.

In the month since the vote, conservatives—his people—had vowed to work against anyone who voted for gay marriage. These were constituents willing to toss out every bit of good he had done because of this one vote. Some voters began saying they would never, ever vote for him again.

McDonald was feeling the wrath our newspaper had felt nine years earlier when we published "Growing up Gay." It was as if the community had not evolved at all.

McDonald held firm against the criticism.

"If they want to vote against me, that is their right," he said.[22]

But I wondered if there was a different reason McDonald didn't want to talk about the aftermath of his vote.

I wondered if he found the ugliness of it so disheartening, just as he found the ugliness of the corruption in the Senate disheartening on Election Day 2010, that he just didn't want to be part of it any more.

I wondered if it made him question his own sense of community, his own sense of what America is supposed to be and who he was representing when state police were needed to stand sentry at the end of his driveway in the weeks after the vote.

Like we said when we concluded our editorial two months earlier: "How can we live in a nation founded on the principle that everyone is equal, when we live in a state in which one segment of the population clearly is not?"[23]

McDonald may have wondered if his constituents believed that, too.

"Give me 100 Roy McDonalds who are willing to stand up to their own political party, who are willing to reconsider a position he has held for most of his life," I wrote on July 26.[24] There were many who disagreed with me.

Just a week earlier, *Post-Star* reporter Maury Thompson reported the National Organization for Marriage sent a mailing to households in McDonald's district comparing him to Benedict Arnold.[25]

It was part of a $2,000,000 initiative to defeat McDonald and six other New York senators in the 2012 election[26] because voting your conscience has consequences, too.

As promised, conservative Republicans found a candidate to oppose McDonald in Saratoga County Clerk Kathy Marchione. She was best known for leading a group of New York county clerks in opposing Governor Eliot Spitzer's 2007 plan to allow undocumented immigrants to obtain state driver's licenses. After the backlash, Governor Spitzer withdrew his plan.

We knew her for the tongue-lashing she gave Nick Reisman when he asked for the county pistol permit database.

Marchione's campaign centered entirely on McDonald's vote on gay marriage and McDonald's blunt talk that voters could "take the job and shove it."[27]

That didn't sit well with rank-and-file Republicans and the committees that are the heart and soul of local politics.

McDonald had raised close to $1,000,000 for the race to Marchione's $100,000, but maybe McDonald's heart just wasn't in it anymore.

Republican committees in his district were split evenly among McDonald and Marchione, and the race was getting statewide attention because of McDonald's vote on same-sex marriage.

"People feel betrayed," Marchione told *The New York Times*. "I've heard that a lot— that they feel betrayed by our senator, that you said one thing, you do something else."[28]

But of course, McDonald did not back down.

"I'm in the party of Abraham Lincoln—I'm very proud of that," McDonald said in the *Times* article. "I'm not in a party of a bunch of right-wing nitwits. It's Abraham Lincoln. It's everybody included. And I feel that's very important."[29]

Two days before the September primary, the two candidates met in Troy for their only debate. Marchione supporters packed the hall, and she repeatedly questioned McDonald about his vote, to the cheers of her supporters.

"I would ask them, 'Do you want me to tell you what you want to hear or do you want me to tell you the truth?'" McDonald told me in 2020. "They didn't want the truth."[30]

When the votes were counted at the end of primary night, Marchione led by 107 votes.[31] Absentee ballots cut the lead to 99.

McDonald could have continued the fight. An endorsement from the Independence Party meant McDonald would be on the ballot in November. Many encouraged McDonald to keep going, including Governor Cuomo.

"You stood up for your principles, for equality and for a population long victimized," Governor Cuomo wrote in a two-page letter to McDonald. "It is now evident that you paid a political price for your convictions. You should not be left to stand alone now."[32]

Governor Cuomo told McDonald he had his endorsement. But in McDonald's district, that would probably cost him votes.

Within days, McDonald said he was dropping out of the race because it was in the best interests of the Republican Party. His concern was that if he stayed in, it would split the Republican vote in his district and allow the Democrats to gain the seat and take back control of the Senate.[33]

"I believe maintaining the Republican majority in the New York State Senate will continue to positively change state government. It is important to recognize the need for checks and balances in our democracy, which can only be assured by a multi-party system," McDonald said in a statement.[34]

There was some truth to that, but it didn't sit well with me. I knew how rare it was for a politician to stand for a cause because it was right.

"On Thursday, he gave up that fight for the worst possible reason: the party," I wrote on September 30. "Just like any run-of-the-mill political hack, he caved to party pressure."[35]

Then I concluded: "Roy McDonald was the one guy I thought wouldn't do that."[36]

I suspect if I had told him that face-to-face, he would have asked me to step outside.

A year later, a young woman from Homestead High School in Fort Wayne, Indiana, was chosen the winner of the John F. Kennedy Profile in Courage Essay Contest for high school students.[37]

The award recognized a public official at the local, state or federal level whose actions demonstrate the qualities of politically courageous leadership in the spirit of John F. Kennedy's book *Profiles in Courage*.

Jamie Baer's subject was Roy McDonald.

She concluded her essay this way:

McDonald's leap of faith in June 2011 came at a steep price. Although his vote in favor of same-sex marriage cost him his reelection to the state senate, it was a worthy sacrifice. In the words of Mayor Bloomberg, McDonald walked away from the state senate with the "satisfaction of knowing for the rest of his life he stood up and voted his conscience." McDonald reaffirmed America's "faith that the people will not simply elect men who will represent their views ably and faithfully, but also elect men who will exercise their conscientious judgment." During his first and last term in the state Senate, McDonald achieved a feat most politicians do not accomplish in a lifetime—he embodied true democracy.[38]

Between 2012 and 2014 more than 10,000 same-sex couples were married in New York.[39]

Four years after McDonald's vote helped make same-sex marriage legal in New York, the United States Supreme Court made same-sex marriage the law of the land.

In 2016, a man killed 49 people in a gay nightclub in Orlando, Florida. Our country still had a long way to go.

McDonald faded away from local politics. I reached out once for an interview on the current state of politics, but I didn't hear back.

During the 2018 election for his old seat, McDonald backed a Democrat named Aaron Gladd over Marchione.[40]

He had good reason.

After interviewing Gladd, our editorial board believed he was one of the best candidates we had ever met running for state office and endorsed him.

"You know, I never was bitter over losing a primary," McDonald told the Albany *Times Union* when endorsing Gladd. "I did the vote and I would do that again. There are independent votes that are very important and I will continue to always admire the men and women whether they're in Washington or Albany and say I don't agree with that and I'm going to do what's best for our community."[41]

Aaron Gladd was resoundingly trounced by Senator Marchione.

When I had lunch with Roy McDonald in July 2020, he told me off the record, "I don't consider myself a Republican anymore."[42]

A couple years earlier, he had gone down to the Wilton Town Hall where he served as supervisor for 23 years.[43]

He told the woman at the Board of Elections he wanted to change his political affiliation.

"I don't think she even knew who I was," McDonald said.[44]

I emailed him later and asked if he would be willing to go on the record about changing his affiliation.

"The answer is yes to go ahead," he wrote in an email. "I am not a Republican or Democrat, I am an American first and foremost."[45]

As usual, Roy McDonald got it right.

20

You Don't Want to Read This

It would take the local tragedy of Nicholas Naumkin to finally get our attention regarding the gun debate.

Naumkin was a seventh-grader at Maple Avenue Middle School in Wilton visiting a friend a few days before Christmas in 2010. The two were left alone for more than three hours to play video games.[1]

They found a handgun and ammunition in the father's bedroom. The two boys were handling the gun at about 7 p.m.—loading and unloading the clip—when it fired and struck Naumkin in the head. He was taken to Albany Medical Center and pronounced dead.[2]

The gun was registered to 56-year-old Edward O'Rourke. He had hidden the weapon in one bureau drawer and the ammunition in another. He thought he had been safe. He later pleaded guilty to a misdemeanor of endangering the welfare of a child, but he did not serve any time in jail. He was banned from owning a firearm.[3]

His son later admitted in Saratoga County Court that he was holding the gun when Naumkin was shot. The boy received probation in Family Court.[4]

This time we responded with an editorial, but even then we tried not to offend gun owners. I thought it was the best way to move forward and not be accused of being the "liberal media."

"Before we get started, here is what this editorial is not about: It is not about gun control. It is not about Second Amendment rights. It is not about restricting anyone's right to protect themselves and their families from harm. It's not about inviting Big Brother into our homes and it is not about perpetuating the 'nanny state,'" we wrote in the editorial.[5]

It took us seven long paragraphs before we even got to the essential point that this was a terrible tragedy that could have been prevented with a simple device known as a trigger lock.[6] I suspect we were still traumatized by the pistol permit controversy from 2008. We did not want to antagonize gun owners.

But, of course, this tragedy doesn't end there. They have a way of branching out and spreading.

A week after the tragic accident, Naumkin's maternal grandparents visited Nicholas's grave before going grocery shopping. When they were finished, Nicholas's 77-year-old grandfather, Oleg Moston, walked away from his wife outside the store.[7]

"My mom said she was yelling at him, but he just kept walking," Nicholas's mother told *Post-Star* reporter Thomas Dimopoulos. "From what my mother is telling me, he was going through the motions after what happened. The last few days, she said he was doing really, really bad."[8]

Nicholas's grandfather walked the half-mile to Interstate 87 where police said he tried to run across the southbound lanes of the busy highway near Exit 15 and was killed when he was struck by a car and two tractor-trailer trucks.[9]

Moston was a pianist who graduated from the Moscow Conservatory in 1957 and toured throughout the Soviet Union before emigrating to the United States in 1979. He was a member of the Skidmore College faculty.[10]

"I am in complete disbelief and very scared right now," Nicholas's mother, Oksana Naumkin, said. "I just don't know why this is happening to my family."[11]

Families all around the country continued to ask the same question.

In December 2012—nine years after the pistol permit controversy—we were once again in front of the newsroom TV with our mouths agape at the news coming out of Newtown, Connecticut, a small community not far from where I grew up.

There had been a mass shooting at Sandy Hook Elementary School, and 26 were dead.

Twenty of them were first-graders.

"Maybe we are not as civilized as we thought." I opened a column that Sunday before I knew the horrible details of what happened to those babies.[12]

This was the breaking point for many of us. Nine years after being cowed by the gun rights crowd in the pistol permit controversy, I was ready to lead a conversation on guns in our communities.

I hoped our readers and the local gun rights activists were ready for the conversation, too.

At our next editorial board meeting with publisher Rick Emanuel, projects editor Will Doolittle and citizen representative Robert Sledd, I proposed we lead the community discussion on all aspects of the problem laid raw by Newtown. I suggested a series of editorials to be published on successive Sundays on various aspects of the firearm debate—gun control, mental health and school security—over the next month.

I believed we had been silent for too long and needed to lead, even if the conversation was uncomfortable and controversial. I was ready to take on the gun lobby, the gun rights activists and anyone else who believed the Second Amendment was more important than the safety of young children in schools.

On December 23, 2012, the conversation began with an editorial on our Sunday opinion page that I wrote:

> Surely, we can agree the conversations should take place.
> That mass murder of innocent children, like what occurred in Newtown, Conn., needs a full-throated response from all of us so it never happens again.
> Surely, we can agree that would be a start.
> The difficulty is identifying the conversation that needs to take place.
> From what we know—and we may never know the most important details, including the motive behind the crime—there is no one clear response, no obvious course that would have prevented what happened at Sandy Hook Elementary School.
> It is bits and pieces of society's ills meeting at a crossroads to form a perfect storm of evil.
> But it must be addressed.
> Beginning today and on succeeding Sundays for the next few weeks, this newspaper plans to instigate a discussion in our community of what happened in Newtown, of what is the proper response, of how far we go and what we need to do to make our communities safe.[13]

That's what a community newspaper does in a time of crisis. It rallies its citizens to discuss the issue and advocate for needed change.

This time, I did not get 70 calls or emails from gun rights advocates challenging the newspaper's motives. This time, we were ready to lead, and we hoped the community was ready to take part. Maybe some attitudes were changing.

"What happened in Newtown can never happen again," we wrote in our conclusion to that first editorial after the shooting. "But if we don't have the conversation, it surely will."[14]

Most editorials receive just two or three online comments. This one received over 100. It was a start, but there are 60,000 people who live in Warren County and another 60,000 in Washington County.

Our "After Newtown" series ran for five consecutive Sundays as we addressed gun control, school security, the care and treatment of those with mental illnesses and the effect media and video games have on our children.

We desperately wanted to make a difference.

Our segment on gun control that ran on Sunday, January 13, reached a new crescendo for debate among our readers and preceded Governor Andrew Cuomo's controversial announcement of a new gun law—The SAFE Act[15]—that would aggravate gun rights activists upstate for years to come.

Any gun owners who were open-minded toward some restrictions changed their minds when Governor Cuomo, using a little-known legislative maneuver known as "a message of necessity" to bypass a three-day waiting period for the public, passed sweeping gun control measures in the middle of the night.

The New York Senate passed the law on January 14, 2013, with nine Senate Republicans voting in favor. Senator Kathy Marchione, who had written her objections to us while turning over the pistol permit information as a county clerk ten years earlier, was one of 18 Republicans who voted against the measure.

The passage of the SAFE ACT—which our editorial board criticized because of the use of the "message of necessity—made the discussion of gun control even more difficult.[16] The comments and remarks on our editorial far outnumbered any previous discussion. But it didn't appear we were changing any minds."

"As we wrote when we started the [After Newtown] series, no one thing was to blame for the Newtown shooting," I wrote in my managing editor column to the readers on January 26. "No new law or procedure by itself would have saved those 20 children. They all needed to be analyzed and debated. We all needed to look deep, because this was who we as a people had become, and we should be scared by that."[17]

The discussion covered a lot of ground, from constitutional rights to the cultures of other countries, to our own history and violent tendencies, with many readers pledging to do anything to keep their families safe. A few brave souls said they were rethinking their beliefs, but only a few.

I'd like to think we moved the needle a little, but it was hard to tell.

And, of course, the mass shootings continued while shattering any notion we were a civilized society of caring people. From the slayings of a prayer group at a church in Charleston, South Carolina, to the mass executions at the gay nightclub in Orlando, Florida, and the outdoor concert in Las Vegas, there appeared little hope of solving the gun issue.

After 27 were massacred in another church shooting in Sutherland, Texas, in

November 2017, I warned my readers in the headline to my November 12, 2017, column, "Trust me, you don't want to read this."[18]

"It will disturb you. You will have nightmares, if you can sleep at all," I wrote to the readers. "You will be angry at me for giving you the front seat to unspeakable carnage, for providing images no human should ever conjure up."[19]

After reading the responses, I gave up. I concluded further gun control was impossible because the monsters in our midst were looking back at us in the mirror. We were all accessories to the carnage for not demanding change. We had become an evil and violent people for accepting this.

Then, I asked readers to consider this one detail the Associated Press reported from the Sutherland, Texas, church shooting: "Kelly [the shooter] went aisle by aisle through the pews and shot dying children at point blank range."[20]

And then I demanded, "You should be forced to see what an AR-15 will do to the head of a crying baby."[21]

After the killing of all those children in Newtown, the Connecticut state legislature passed a law prohibiting the release of crime scene photographs.[22] The goal was to protect the families of victims. I wasn't so sure.

I believed the law was to protect the gun lobby,[23] and I went back to the words in the police report from the first officer who arrived at the Sandy Hook Elementary School. And I warn you, too: You do not want to read this.

> At first glance it did not appear that there were any casualties. To the left of the room as you walk in there was a bathroom in the corner. There was a massive pile of bodies in this room. At the time, I did not know this room was a bathroom and wondered how the suspect had time to kill that many people and stack them in the corner of the room. There appeared to be about 15 bodies in the small room and several bodies, including two adults near the entrance to the room.
>
> All the other bodies were inside the bathroom or in the entrance to the bathroom. An adult victim was lying across the mass of bodies inside the bathroom. ... Sgt. Carrio began to lift bodies off of the top of the pile [redacted] and many of the bodies had injuries that were obviously fatal. As Sgt. Carrio began to empty out the bathroom, it became apparent what had occurred due to how efficiently packed in the bathroom the children were. It appeared as if the teachers in the room immediately upon hearing the gun shots began to pack the children into the bathroom. The children that were sitting on the floor of the bathroom were packed in like sardines.
>
> One little girl was sitting crouched in between the toilet and the back corner of the room. I thought that she might have the best chance for survival. As the pile got higher it appeared that there was a mad scramble to get into the bathroom with people stepping on one another and climbing on top of each other. The teachers appeared to have been shepherding the children into the room and were then probably gong to shut the door.
>
> They did not close and lock the door to the classroom for some reason and were interrupted by the shooter as they attempted to fill the bathroom with children. The shooter then opened fire on the mass of children and adults. As Sgt. Carrio got to the last bodies, it was clear that no one had survived.[24]

Medical examinations of the victims revealed each had been shot multiple times. These were first-graders.

Three months after I wrote that column, 17 students were killed at a high school in Parkland, Florida, and a new generation rose up to challenge why we needed guns and why the laws were not stronger. These young men and women did not seem afraid of the gun lobby or the National Rifle Association. Their protests were all across the country, but more impressively, the Florida Legislature approved stronger gun laws.

After Parkland, there was a call to arm teachers, so I called my younger cousin Nancy, a longtime elementary school teacher in Connecticut. She taught school just 15 miles from Newtown.[25]

"It actually infuriates me," Nancy Tingley told me. "That's not my job, It's not why I went to school. You know I love my job, but the day I have to carry a gun is the day I will quit. I will stand in front of a bullet for your child, but I won't shoot a gun."[26]

Nancy was not afraid of the gun activists and lobbyists either.

She told me about a recent lockdown at the school. She got her second-graders up from their desks and they filed into the bathroom as they had done in previous drills. Nancy closed the classroom door, locked it and turned out the lights before joining the children in the bathroom.[27]

I thought about that bathroom at Sandy Hook where the teacher never got a chance to lock the door.

Nancy and her kids stood quietly in the bathroom for ten to 15 minutes.

Fifteen minutes is a long time to be scared to death.

This was the new world for our children.

In June 2018, gun violence struck a newspaper in Maryland, and five people were killed at the *Capital Gazette*, a newspaper similar to ours in size and mission. The attacker was a man who was upset with the newspaper's coverage of past complaints against him.

I was not surprised by the shooting.

We addressed readers with a rare front-page message to explain this new world for newspaper employees and how personally we took the *Capital Gazette* murders. We were no longer going to be cowed.

I explained to the readers the realities of our daily world:

As our staff talked yesterday, we recounted dozens of instances of relentless harassment by someone who felt they had been done wrong by the newspaper.

The behavior that preceded Thursday's shooting in Maryland is also commonplace here in this community.

We've had death threats, been told people were going to get us and, earlier this year, someone left our newspaper on the porch rolled up in dog feces.

Consider that type of harassment for a minute. The harassment got so bad for one of our reporters six years ago, we filed charges and that person went to jail.

I had one person leave me critical voicemail messages daily for nearly a year.

Last month, I received an anonymous threatening letter, telling me not to write about a certain subject or else.

The accused killer had a beef with a newspaper that is a community institution. And he finally acted.

I was shocked but not surprised by yesterday's murders.

I knew it was only a matter of time, considering the written and verbal attacks on journalists.

But yesterday morning, everyone in my newsroom showed up to work, talking about their kids, what they planned to do this weekend and what stories they were working on. They were ready to go back on the front lines.[28]

In my Sunday column, I summed up the attacks—verbal and otherwise—that our reporters and editors received.[29]

"We're seeing something more devious and evil than we've seen before," I wrote. "Our critics aren't throwing sticks and stones anymore, they've begun to shoot bullets."[30]

One reader responded I should arm myself. I replied I did that daily with my words.

There were occasional signs of encouragement.

By July 2019, Nicholas Naumkin—the victim in that accidental shooting in 2010—would have been 21 years old. The father of his friend, whose gun was left unsecured, never received any punishment. But on July 29, 2019, Governor Cuomo signed into law a measure that required gun owners to secure their weapons if they have children under the age of 16 living or visiting in their home.[31]

It was one of those you-can't-believe-it-isn't-a-law-already measures that only took nine years for the legislature to pass.

In response, local Assemblyman Dan Stec, a popular local Republican who had been supervisor in Queensbury, released a statement that cuts to the heart of the work that lies ahead in making any headway on gun violence: "Since taking office I have been a strong advocate of Second Amendment and protecting rights of gun owners in the North Country. Yesterday [Monday] a bill was brought to the floor that I had serious concerns with that would restrict law-abiding gun owners' rights when it comes to how they can store their firearms in their homes. This legislation unnecessarily puts more restrictions on gun owners and is unenforceable by law enforcement."[32]

The National Rifle Association might as well have written the statement for him. It spoke to another generation before mass shootings were commonplace.

"It turns out that a survey done by the Johns Hopkins School of Public Health found almost 50 percent of gun owners already secure their weapons in a gun safe, cabinet or with a trigger lock, because I suspect it is the pragmatic thing to do to keep their children safe," I wrote after the legislature passed the bill and Stec objected. "This ridiculous notion that there is an assault on the Second Amendment has got to end. We are better than that."[33]

An investigation by *USA Today* and the Associated Press found that 113 children and teens were killed by unintentional firearm discharges in 2014, much like Nicholas Naumkin in 2010.[34]

So I let the assemblyman—and any other gun owners who were cheering him on—have it: "If gun owners want to be reckless because of irrational fears of criminals coming through the window at night, I suppose that is their right, but if the troubled teen living under their roof goes on a rampage, or decides to end their own life, or if a curious 9-year-old shoots their best friend with dad's pistol found unsecured in a nightstand drawer, then there needs to be consequences. I doubt that Assemblyman Stec's thoughts and prayers will mean much to the family."[35]

I never would have written that in the days right after Columbine.

Without community newspapers, I don't know who does.

21

Who Will Take Care of Us?

There is some truth that news is what the editor sees on his way to work. In my case, it was on my way home from work.

In the fall of 2012, my daily schedule was dramatically altered. When I was done at the newspaper each evening, I stopped on my way home at the Stanton, a nursing home where my 84-year-old mother now lived.

It was usually dinnertime when I arrived, and my mom's eyes brightened as she introduced me around the dinner table for the third time that week. There were 50 to 60 other residents having their evening meal in the large dining hall. Mom and I would talk—sometimes she just complained—but she eventually reveled in each detail of her 16-year-old grandson's life. It was not unusual for us to be the last two to leave the dining room.

"Kenny, please take me upstairs," she would say in that irresistible Irish brogue. Of course, there was no second floor in the building.

What was so sad was how few residents had family there at dinnertime, or really any time.

Over the previous months, my brother and I had received a crash course on how nursing homes work, the mountain of paperwork required to qualify for Medicaid and the emotional toll it took on nursing home staff, residents and the family, my own included.

This was life.

This was a story our readers needed to hear, especially with so many Baby Boomers retiring every year. Our readers needed to understand the challenges they would face and what each of them could do to prepare themselves if a loved one needed long-term care.

In this case, I was a valuable asset for our reporters with my experience with my mother acting as a touchstone for what our readers needed to know and what I wished I had known.

As we had with many of our past projects, we reached out to local professionals to be our eyes and ears. Donna Balcomb, the administrator at the Stanton who I first met when looking to get my mother care, helped me to put together a forum of nursing home experts.[1]

We invited more than a dozen health care professionals to the newspaper to meet with our reporters, talk about their jobs, the challenges they faced and what the future looked like for the industry. We had administrators, nursing directors, aides, nurses, social workers and a county ombudsman in attendance.[2] I also invited all our editors and reporters because the only previous experience most of our young journalists had at nursing homes was covering the 100th birthday parties staged for residents.

I assured our guests everything they said was off the record. I wanted them to express themselves frankly and without fear of losing their jobs. What followed was a two-hour discussion that could have gone on much longer. We talked about the business of nursing homes, the difficulty of retaining aides and nurses and the heart and soul so many brought to their jobs.[3]

As the meeting was winding down, I asked one of the nurse's aides what she wanted to see us write about.

She said we shouldn't make nursing homes out to be bad places. She said there was a lot of good there. I told her I couldn't make any promises, but we would try to tell that story, too.[4]

Over the course of nine days in May and June, we published the series "Who will take care of us?"

"Over the past eight months, I have gotten to see what life in a nursing home is like firsthand," I wrote, introducing the series. "It is obvious they struggle with staffing levels and it is obvious most people work very hard. I have seen some of the most heart-wrenching scenes there, but I have also seen some of the most extraordinary acts of kindness and love from staff members."[5]

Meg Hagerty, our features writer, immersed herself in the daily rhythms of life at the Stanton and painted a vivid picture of what life was like every day for the elderly who lived there. It was a scene I was familiar with:

> The dining room at the Stanton Nursing and Rehabilitation Centre was decorated like a 6-year-old birthday party. Brightly colored crepe paper flowers hung from fluorescent lights and draped the entrances to usher in the arrival of spring.
>
> About a dozen residents were spread among four tables for the Wednesday morning craft class. Activities assistant Cookie Jones circulated to make sure everyone was busy with their markers and paints.
>
> Across the room, a sleeping woman lay sprawled under a blanket in a lounge chair, while a gentleman wearing a gray knit cap began softly crooning a tune. A nurses aide sat with them, drawing a design on a white pillowcase.[6]

Over the next five weeks, our reporters established that the crushing weight of the aging Baby Boomers would strain the limits of elderly health care in the years to come.

"This is a generation that has changed much about the U.S. society—from music to sex, to how Americans consume goods and services—and as its members flood into retirement and trickle into nursing homes, they will change how the country cares for its old people," *Post-Star* reporter Jon Alexander wrote in Part 1.[7]

This was a warning shot across all our bows, a call to action that if we wanted grandma and grandpa, mom and dad, and eventually each of us to truly have golden years, we needed to address it now.

Alexander reported the elderly would have more needs in the coming years than in the past because they were living longer. He acknowledged the current model for nursing homes was not sustainable. There was not enough capacity.[8]

Alexander reported the eight nursing homes in our region accounted for 930 beds, but the homes were regularly short-staffed and needed nurses from private agencies to fill staffing gaps.[9]

Some homes were already developing services so more of the elderly could remain in their own homes longer with partial care.

At the heart of the series was a demand for our readers to pay attention to something—their own mortality—that they probably didn't want to think about.

In the editorial after Part 1, we were direct in describing what was coming: "As distasteful as it is to think about, short terminal illnesses will be displaced by gradual deterioration in health and lifestyle. Who will take care of the boomers? But what we are really asking is, who will take care of us?"[10]

We were hoping to make our readers think about a future where their health would be compromised.

Over the coming five weeks, we explored economic, emotional and political challenges that elderly care presented. And we didn't pull any punches.

"We believe this will be the next great crisis our country must face as we struggle to care for our fathers, mothers, grandmothers and grandfathers," the editorial predicted, "as they once took care of us."[11]

Jamie Munks, a young reporter who covered Washington County government, embedded herself with a nurse to see firsthand the challenges they faced on a daily basis. She spent an entire shift with Diana Conte, a licensed practical nurse at Tri-County Nursing & Rehabilitation Center in the small town of North Creek in northern Warren County.[12]

Looking back, the access our staff received was extraordinary and something you would not see today. The difference was we were trusted then. Many of the health care professionals had been part of the early meetings about the series where relationships had been established. They wanted, and needed, the issue to be addressed, too.

Munks reported the nursing home "always had [job] vacancies" because of a nationwide nursing shortage. Munks captured the difficulty of the work:

> When Conte makes her medication pass, she is administering eye drops and insulin injections and changing oxygen tanks. She works quickly and efficiently, talking to residents as she goes.
> Conte gets emotional when she talks about watching residents struggle at the end of their lives. When nurses see a significant change in a resident's quality of life, they start pain management. Their only recourse is to make the person as comfortable as possible. When residents die, the nurses often feel relieved.
> "Some are so sick and they're fighting," Conte said. "We see them every day, struggling."[13]

Munks went on to profile one family and its journey of caring for an elderly father that was equal parts emotional, physical and economic: "As Mike O'Connor cared for his ailing father, he was also preparing to do something he never thought he would do—move his father into a nursing home."[14]

The story was familiar. It was the same journey my brother and I had made the previous year.

Munks was able to chronicle not only the physical and emotional demands of caring for a parent but the financial repercussions if you waited too long to protect your assets.

"Medicaid wasn't meant to cover the size and scope of people it covers today," Andrew Cruikshank, CEO of Fort Hudson Health System told Munks.[15]

To qualify for Medicaid, a person must have exhausted all of their assets, including selling their home. In other words, they needed to be broke. New York state required a five-year look-back period to make sure that assets had not been given away to relatives to avoid having to pay for nursing home care. The small inheritance many people expected to get after their parents died ended up paying for nursing home care.

Qualifying for Medicaid was a ruthlessly forensic economic ordeal in which families had to document the smallest of expenses during the look-back period. It could feel like an accusation of wrongdoing.

"In most cases, it's the first time people are hitting the health care system head-on," Jack Coburn, chief financial officer at Fort Hudson, told Munks. "The families that have it all together are in the minority. It's always somewhat of a mess; in some case, it's a disaster."[16]

By 2013, nursing home care cost about $10,000 a month for a resident in our community, so even if they had some money saved, it would not last long.

Cruikshank told Munks if you make it to age 70, there's a good chance you will require long-term care at a skilled nursing facility at some point during the remainder of your life.[17] Reading that as a 63-year-old in 2020 took on new meaning.

The work we did on that series was more intensely personal than perhaps any previous in-depth project. And maybe even more useful. It was information readers could immediately use.

The Local Media Association, a national journalism organization for smaller newspapers, honored the series with a first place for in-depth reporting,[18] as did the New York State Associated Press.

"It's the type of community journalism that *The Post-Star* is known for," publisher Rick Emanuel said. "The story addressed deeply emotional family issues that many of us would prefer not to confront until it's too late. I think it was a real service to our community."[19]

Lee Enterprises, our corporate owner, honored the series with a President's Award that fall.

"I was very taken by their ability to speak to issues that I think are on the minds of so many readers and they addressed it in ways that people could act on. That was very impressive. This is a subject I think that is often overlooked and I've rarely seen it so very well explained," wrote one of the judges.[20]

"Who will take care of us?" became more personal the next spring when publisher Rick Emanuel told me five more people in the newsroom needed to be laid off.[21]

"Regretfully, we had to let some of our colleagues go today," Emanuel said in a prepared statement published in the newspaper. "The economic conditions have steadily declined over the past few months and this has left us with no other choice than to make these necessary cuts. The remainder of *The Post-Star* team will work together to make our way out of the roughest business climate we have ever encountered."[22]

Over a two-hour period we repeated the sad ritual with each of the five employees.

Munks, the young woman who had so deftly characterized the challenges of one family putting their father in the nursing home the previous year, was one of the casualties. When the meeting was over, she asked for a minute in the conference room, then broke down in tears.

We were cutting at the core of the newspaper and the work we did by letting great reporters go. Not surprisingly, Munks found another newspaper job and was working for the *Chicago Tribune*, covering Illinois state government, in 2020.

Previously, our goal was to do at least two large community journalism projects each year, but with reduced staffing, we were now struggling to do one.

"Who will take care of us?" was an important piece of journalism in our community but only the beginning of the community conversation about nursing homes.

Four years later, Warren County and Washington County both sold their nursing homes to a private, for-profit company, Centers Health Care. By 2017, most of the local nursing homes were operated by the company. By 2018, Centers Health Care owned 53 nursing homes across New York and the Northeast.

In February, there was a full-throated uproar about the conditions and staffing levels at the Warren Center in Queensbury.

In a July 16, 2017, editorial, I told the readers I had reached out to Centers Health Care and asked if CEO Kenny Rozenberg would meet with our editorial board. Rozenberg quickly agreed to meet with us the next month.[23]

In preparation for that meeting, I asked readers of their local nursing home concerns.[24] The reaction was immediate. Over the next few days, I received a steady stream of emails describing conditions and incidents that, if true, bordered on neglect.

On August 13, 2017, *The Post-Star* editorial board, which had grown to seven members with three citizen representatives, sat down to meet with CEO Rozenberg and five members of his management team.[25]

Centers was taking the meeting seriously and was prepared. It set up a laptop and walked us through a PowerPoint statistical analysis of its operation and the type of quality care it provides.[26]

We reported back to our readers we had engaged in a productive back-and-forth with the Centers team for nearly two hours. We found them to be passionate and compassionate about their mission. We liked some of the things we heard, but other explanations did not pass muster.[27]

They argued the federal quality ratings almost always went down after they took over a nursing home because they were meticulously evaluating the care of their patients. They believed the ratings would go back up over time.[28]

In this case, the newspaper editorial board was representing the communities and families with loved ones, just as we had done four years earlier. We were standing up for them and their concerns because that's what community newspapers do.

There was one telling moment during the meeting when we asked if staffing was a problem at places like the Warren Center. While Warren Center's Director of Nursing Jennifer Burnham and the social worker who worked there, Robin Chiaravalle, both nodded vigorously, the corporate officers said staffing was not an issue.[29]

When we brought up the complaints our readers brought to us, the Centers executives said they were being addressed. We passed on a list of complaints from the Warren Center's Family Council to the CEO and his team.[30]

Rozenberg appeared to be insulted when we suggested he might be cutting corners because it is a "for profit" business. He denied it, saying they always put quality care first.[31]

Our editorial board was not entirely convinced: "We know that caring for the elderly is enormously challenging and more needs to be done," we concluded in our editorial. "It is obvious to us—and we think to the management of Centers Health Care—that they need to do better."[32]

Because of our nursing home series in 2013, we knew something about the nursing home business.

Because of the severity of the complaints we heard, we assembled another team of reporters to look into the allegations of neglect. This time there were just three reporters and me. We did not have the staffing to do more.

One especially brave nurses' aide contacted me personally to tell me about the poor conditions and staff ineptitude at one local nursing home. She sent me a video recording of a nurse sleeping at her desk during one overnight shift. She said it happened regularly. No one on the staff even bothered to wake her up.

It got my attention.

But we never did the story.

"There never seemed to be enough time," reporter Kathleen Moore lamented in 2020.[33]

Our staff levels continued to erode, and so did our ability to do in-depth projects. Gradually, I acknowledged it was impossible to assemble a large team of reporters to address important issues like we once did. We were relegated to assigning one reporter or editor to do the best they could. It still produced important work, just not as good as before.

We compromised quality because of staffing levels. It was the exact same problem nursing homes were having.

That December, a resident at the Warren Center in Queensbury died while being transported in his wheelchair because he was not secured properly in the vehicle. Centers was fined $17,023 by the state.[34] That was the going rate for the life of a 94-year-old at the time.

"Five years after we first asked the question 'Who will take care of us?' we still do not have an answer," we reminded our readers in an editorial.[35]

By 2018, Don Lehman was able to take a deeper dive on nursing home conditions. He reported on one case in which a wife found her 94-year-old husband had bedsores and was regularly left in a soiled diaper for hours at a time. She was part of a group of residents that took the issue to the newspaper as a last resort.[36]

Staffing was again at the root of the complaint, especially on weekends. Lehman was told residents who could not feed themselves had to wait until a staff member was available to eat. By then, their meal was often cold.[37]

Centers now operated seven local nursing homes, and Lehman found the complaints about its care increasing. In 2018, a male resident was charged with sexually abusing a female resident. At the Washington Centers, a staff member was convicted of sexually abusing a resident.[38]

Centers Health Care also saw its federal ratings improve. But Richard Mollot, the head of a nonprofit watchdog organization that monitors the nursing home industry, told Lehman nursing home operators could "game" the ratings because they were based on self-reported data.[39]

One family member told Lehman she wasn't surprised the home got an improved rating. "They told us they knew the state inspector was coming," she said. A family member of another resident told Lehman the same thing.[40]

Apparently, annual inspections happened about the same time each year, so administrators could prepare for them.

"I've seen homes that are disasters get four or five stars [ratings]," Mollot told Lehman.[41]

In 2016, three years after our first nursing home coverage, the New York comptroller's office criticized the Department of Health for nursing home oversight problems. It found the department was short-staffed on enforcement referrals and was unable to process complaints in a timely manner.[42]

"The state Health Department needs to strengthen its enforcement policies to better protect the health and well-being of nursing home residents across the state," State Comptroller Thomas DiNapoli said when the report was released. "DOH is not using the full array of enforcement actions available and this trend has recently worsened, taking the teeth out of a significant deterrent to unsafe practices and conditions. DOH officials deserve credit for their timely inspection of nursing homes but more must be done. Families need to know their loved ones have safe accommodations and providers are being held accountable when problems are found."[43]

It was not surprising that nursing homes suffered so many deaths when the pandemic struck in the spring of 2020. If staffing levels were a problem before, it was worse during the pandemic.

By then, staffing levels at the newspaper had dwindled so much, any in-depth look at the problems caused by the pandemic was almost impossible.

On March 30, 2020, Lee Enterprises announced each employee would be furloughed for two weeks over the next three months.[44] The newsroom was doing little depth reporting. There were only ten of us left.

Bill Toscano, one of the reporters assigned to the original nursing home project in 2013, suffered a stroke in 2018. I eventually went to see him at what had been the Stanton in Glens Falls. His room was across the hall from where my mother died in 2013. He was in a wheelchair and receiving rehab but was in great spirits. He never returned to the newspaper work he loved.

Toscano's wife later moved him to another nursing home in Massachusetts where he died on May 13, 2020, from the coronavirus.

When I checked the nursing home ratings for the Warren Center and the Glens Falls Center, formerly the Stanton, that summer, they were both one star.

We had let our community down.

The Evil Librarian

Like so many newspaper stories, it started with a phone call from a proud mom.

Katie Weaver's nine-year-old son, Tyler, had just won the Hudson Falls Public Library's summer reading contest for the fifth straight year. Between June 24 and August 3, 2013, Tyler had read 63 books. His seven-year-old brother, Jonathan, was second.[1] Since kindergarten, Tyler had read 373 books during the summer reading contest. He appeared to be the Babe Ruth of summer reading.

This is the bread and butter of community journalism, those little "feel-good" stories that parents and grandparents clip out for their scrapbooks and people talk about at work. Newspapers like *The Post-Star* publish dozens of them each month.

But when features writer Meg Hagerty called the Hudson Falls Librarian Marie Gandron, she was startled by her response.

Instead of further accolades for the young bibliophile, the librarian told Hagerty Tyler "hogs" the contest every year and he should "step aside."[2]

Hagerty was neither Woodward nor Bernstein at our newspaper, so she reminded the librarian she was talking "on the record" to the newspaper. The librarian said she knew that. Hagerty, who could have played the librarian in the movie, was mortified and didn't know what to do.

As a 40-something mother of two grown children, Hagerty was new to the journalism profession. Now, she was staring down her first controversy.

A year earlier, Hagerty was looking for something to fill her days as an empty-nester. Her son was a senior in college in Virginia and her daughter two hours away at boarding school. She made no apologies for being more June Cleaver than Lois Lane.

By her own admission, Hagerty loved being a wife and mother, going out to lunch, skiing, playing tennis, bicycling on sunny days and spending summers with her retired husband, George, at their home on Lake George.[3]

But there was a hole left with the children gone. She was another example of a reporter who had found her way to journalism by an unusual path.

Hagerty took a features-writing class at the local community college—George talked her out of taking Mandarin Chinese—where she found writing sparked something inside her. Her professor encouraged her to submit samples to the newspaper's features editor Doug Gruse. She became a regular freelancer in features that summer, and when there was a full-time job opening that fall, Gruse hired her.[4]

Hagerty was meticulous, organized and generally filed her stories days before they were due. Writing on deadline scared the bejesus out of her, a source of frustration for Gruse, but she had a nice writing touch and was a good interviewer. I think it was easy for people to trust her, and I don't recall ever getting a complaint about her.

Hagerty was such a vanilla milkshake that when we needed someone to do a profile on a young woman running for Congress for the first time, Elise Stefanik, I chose Hagerty because I knew there was absolutely nothing political or controversial about her.[5]

We tried to broaden her experience and pushed her to do more expansive and in-depth journalism that led to several feature-writing awards. While she had a reputation for doing nice, positive stories, she gradually became a professional journalist, whether she wanted to admit it or not.

So on that summer day in 2013, she was flummoxed by what to do with something mean.

When her editor Gruse asked Hagerty if she was sure that was what the librarian said, Hagerty was adamant because she had gone back and listened to the tape.

"She tape-recorded the conversation?" I asked Gruse incredulously.

While news reporters routinely tape-record interviews (in New York, it is legal to do so as long as one party in the conversation knows it is being done), it can be a time suck to transcribe. On shorter, less in-depth stories it is often easier to take notes or type out your notes during a phone interview. Most reporters don't tape-record puff pieces, but that was not Hagerty. She was always careful.

"Other kids quit because they can't keep up," the librarian told Hagerty in what she described as a "rant." Gandron said she planned to change the rules of the contest so that instead of giving prizes to the children who read the most books, she would draw names out of a hat.[6] Essentially, everyone would get a prize who competed.

Gandron admitted to Hagerty she had an "attitude" about the contest because one little girl had been caught cheating a few years earlier. New rules were implemented to test the children with random reader comprehension questions to ensure they had read the books. Gandron also said there was no indication young Tyler cheated.

Hagerty also interviewed Lita Casey, an aide at the library for the past 28 years who oversaw the contest. Casey said she didn't want her job to be in jeopardy, but she thought Gandron's plan to change the rules of the contest was "ridiculous." She called a member of the library board of trustees to complain but was told the board stood behind Gandron.[7]

Hagerty's story was published on the front of the local section on August 15, 2013:

> HUDSON FALLS—Tyler Weaver calls himself "the king of the reading club" at Hudson Falls Public Library. But now it seems Hudson Falls Public Library Director Marie Gandron wants to end his reign and have him dethroned.[8]

I blogged about the story the next day, saying it was a "feel-good" story that had turned into a "minor" controversy.[9] I thought that would be the end of it, but by 2013 social media was beginning to be a force as blogs and media websites picked up silly little controversies as "click bait" to drive online traffic.

That's what happened here.

"Evil librarian tells kid who loves books to stop reading so much," read an online headline on Gawker.[10]

"World's worst librarian wants nine-year-old kid to stop winning reading contests," read the headline on Yahoo/News.[11]

As the story went viral across the country, Hagerty was assigned to do a follow-up on the publicity. Tyler's mom, Katie, told Hagerty the attention had been "insane" as she and Tyler did phone interviews with reporters across the country. The mom also told Hagerty she had contacted the library's board of trustees, asking them to leave the contest rules as they were.[12]

The day Hagerty's follow-up was published, Katie and Tyler did an interview at their home with Jennifer Lee, a reporter at WTEN-TV in Albany. In that piece, Lee reported that the Hudson Falls librarian, Marie Gandron, told her she had been "misquoted" (by *The Post-Star*) and that her words were "taken out of context."[13]

Gandron sounded like a politician who had been caught saying something stupid.

I responded with a pointed blog post that defended the story while reminding readers the reporter had tape-recorded the interview. By then, my blog had become an important tool to talk to readers.

The television reporter never asked for our side of the story.

"When you are called a liar, you have to respond. After all, a newspaper's credibility is essential in any community," I wrote on my blog the next day. "As part of a story we ran on the 9-year-old's appearance on national TV, I explained our reporter got it right and did not misquote anyone in this story."[14]

This was hardly a life-and-death First Amendment issue, but I believed our reporter should be defended. I also wrote the librarian owed Hagerty an apology.[15]

That same day, the library's board of trustees released a statement with board president Michael Herman suggesting, "Let's turn the page on this unfortunate controversy."[16]

But this story had legs.

It grabbed the attention of the folks at "Fox and Friends" in New York City. They whisked Tyler and Katie down to their studios for a live three and a half-minute interview on the national morning show.

"I just wanted a picture of him buried in the Sunday paper, so [*Post-Star* reporter] Meg [Hagerty] called the library director and that's when all the comments came out and that's how I found out that they weren't happy," Katie told Steve Doocy during the interview.[17]

"The winner is the winner," Doocy said to Tyler. "Not only did you work for it but ... you could have been doing other things at the time but you set aside special time to read 63 books, right?"[18]

Tyler said he just wanted a response from the librarian. "I want an apology and an explanation for why they thought that I should stop reading to let other people have a chance to win," Tyler told Doocy.[19]

Tyler and Katie also did a phone interview with the *Today* show on NBC.

Then one of our letter writers asked that Hagerty be fired.[20] Hagerty was mortified.

"I think what was really hard was the letter to the editor asking to take my job," Hagerty said in 2020. "What the heck. This is the features writer. It is ridiculous that it had gone that far. I remember going into your office and almost bursting into tears. This is not what I signed on for. This was supposed to be a fun job."[21]

The library board said it would review the reading program.[22]

It appeared everyone could finally put this silly little controversy behind them and get back to more important issues. Instead, things became more controversial.

On September 13, reporter Amanda Mae Metzger reported Marie Gandron no longer worked at the library. She had been employed there for 41 years.[23]

"The only thing I can say is Marie is no longer employed by the library," board of trustees president Michael Herman said.[24] When the board's minutes were finally made public the next month—perhaps prompted by two Freedom of Information requests by *The Post-Star*—it was confirmed Gandron was fired on September 12.[25]

A week earlier, Katie Weaver said she received an email from the library's board with a scanned letter from Gandron attached. Weaver said Gandron wrote in the unsigned letter she wanted to express "regret for any confusion or misunderstandings that occurred." Katie Weaver said it did not sound like an apology.[26]

"I honestly thought she was going to apologize," Katie Weaver said. "I was under the assumption she wasn't going to be happy about it, but I never saw this [the firing] as an end result."[27]

When the winners of all the summer contests were posted on the library bulletin board, no winners were listed for the reading contest, Katie Weaver said.[28]

Four days after Gandron was fired, it was learned library aide Lita Casey, who had called Gandron's views on the reading contest "ridiculous" the previous month, also was fired by the library's board. She was 79 years old and had worked as an aide at the library for 28 years.[29]

Casey told reporter Bill Toscano she was told about her termination over the phone by board member Michael Mercure, a Washington County public defender.

"I asked why I was being terminated, and was told the board would not give a reason," Casey said. "I asked if I could come down and talk to the board. He went away for a minute, came back and said no. I worked there for 28 years without a complaint. I have to believe it was related to the whole reading controversy.[30]

"I am so disappointed in the board for failing to recognize the years I have put in," Casey said. "I am going to miss it."[31]

"Her whole life has been given to the kids at that library," Katie Weaver said. "For them to do that to her is just awful."[32]

Each new development brought renewed national attention to the library.

The events sparked a Facebook group called "Find Tyler Weaver a New Library" that had 119 likes in October 2013.[33]

We hoped to bring the whole sordid affair to a close with an editorial with a clever headline: "Hudson Falls Library Board wrote the book on what not to do."[34]

I thought the editorial gave the needed context. "We agree with many of you this story deserves an award for the size of the mountain created out of the molehill. It ended up being Himalayan in scope, with young Tyler appearing on national television and Gandron and the library board smeared with egg."[35]

We acknowledged that the editorial board is usually hesitant to jump into the middle of personnel issues, but as the leaders of a community institution, the library board of trustees needed to be more accountable to the community, even if it did not have to legally.[36]

The editorial also acknowledged it was clear why Gandron no longer worked at the library and that she had only herself to blame, but Casey was a different story.

"What concerns us most—and certainly we have a stake in this—is that Ms. Casey was fired because she spoke to the newspaper," our editorial said. "Freedom of speech is an important part of our democracy and her comments were only made in response to the questions posed to her by a reporter. In this world of regular 'no comments,' Casey spoke her mind and ultimately righted a wrong. She should be applauded for that. From what we know, she should get her job back."[37]

That October, the Hudson Falls Free Library board of trustees received a petition circulated on change.org that called for it to apologize to former aide Lita Casey and offer to reinstate her. The petition was signed by 242 people from 20 states and three countries in the two weeks it had been online.[38]

Board president Michael Herman told a *Post-Star* reporter it had received the petition, but it would not be on the agenda for the next meeting.[39]

In the minutes of the board of trustees September meetings, Herman said the library board members had been instructed not to comment further on the issue. Two members of the board later resigned.[40]

The controversy over the reading program was voted as the third biggest story of 2013 by *The Post-Star* staff.[41]

The next summer, features editor Doug Gruse took over as online editor, a position with a more secure future. I was told not to replace him in features.

The move left Hagerty feeling rudderless as the lone remaining features writer. It was no longer a "department." The woman who went from housewife to award-winning professional journalist, and weathered the evil librarian storm quietly, stepped away from the newspaper in January 2015. She said it was not fun anymore.[42] In a farewell blog, she called the story of the reading controversy "the defining moment" of her time at the newspaper.[43]

"I remember you [Tingley] saying at the time that we did a service, that we cut out a cancer at the library," Hagerty remembered. "She had her own little fiefdom and was showing favoritism to certain employees in there. Maybe the story helped restore some order."[44]

It appears Tyler kept on reading. He graduated from Hudson Falls High School in May 2021 as a member of the National Technical Honor Society. He sang in the choir, played trumpet in the various high school bands and participated in the drama club. He entered a technical program in ninth grade that allowed him to take college courses throughout high school. He completed the Early College Career Academy at SUNY Adirondack. He planned on continuing his education there to complete his degree in advanced manufacturing and engineering.[45]

One thing is for certain, Tyler can handle the reading.

23

Heroin Hits Home

Will Doolittle found himself sitting in the small trailer in Kingsbury listening to a story unlike any he had heard before.[1]

Nancy Derusha handed four-month-old Leland to Doolittle to hold. She had potatoes to peel.

Around him were Derusha's three nieces—Kiara, 15, Coralee, 12, and Keeley, 10—listening and filling in details to the story, their story.[2]

It started when a ringing telephone awoke Derusha from slumber on the morning of November 8, 2012. Her sister-in-law, Rebecca, was on the line. She asked Derusha to make the hour's drive to Poultney, Vermont, to pick up Rebecca's three daughters.[3]

DeRusha's brother, Chris, was already in Washington County Jail. Rebecca told Derusha she had left her children and wasn't coming back. They were alone.[4]

That's what heroin does to you.

The girls filled in the blanks as Doolittle cradled little Leland while trying to take notes. This was not Doolittle's first visit to the trailer.[5]

The girls had been alone in the Poultney house for three days, eating whatever food they could find—mostly ramen noodles and hotdogs—12-year-old Coralee said.[6]

They were sleeping with the four dogs for warmth because the furnace had been ripped out of the house and sold for scrap to buy drugs. The girls were using a garden hose for water because the copper pipes had been torn out of the house and also sold to buy drugs.[7]

The toilet would flush only a cup or so at a time, so the girls had to reach into the back and pull the chain over and over. The entire house smelled of urine from the dogs relieving themselves inside.[8]

DeRusha arrived about 4 p.m. to find the girls waiting in the cold on the porch, surrounded by broken appliances. She described to Doolittle garbage bags piled in a heap in the yard six feet high. A tarp covered dozens of gas cans. Dishes spilled from boxes, covered in mold.[9]

"It looked like the garage had puked into the driveway," Derusha told Doolittle. "It was unreal. I could not believe the conditions in that place."[10]

Doolittle summed it up in his story this way: "The girls were abandoned by parents drawn to other, darker places."[11]

The parents were heroin addicts.

The girls came back to Derusha's trailer in Kingsbury where they shared a single bedroom. They had missed a lot of school, so Derusha enrolled them in Hudson Falls schools and tried to restore some normalcy to their lives.[12]

Nancy DeRusha and her three nieces became the face of the opioid crisis in Glens Falls when *The Post-Star* did its series "Heroin hits home" in June 2014. DeRusha adopted her three nieces when her sister and husband abandoned the children after becoming addicted to heroin (*Post-Star* photograph by Steve Jacobs).

They were thin and in bad health, so Derusha took them to the doctor. She eventually received custody when their parents failed to show for the court hearing.[13]

The girls had been through a lot. They had seen the needles their mother kept in her shoes. Kiara, the oldest daughter, would go with her mother on late-night drug runs. Sometimes, before the parents went out at night, they would load the children up on Benadryl so they would sleep through the night and not know they were away.[14]

The story Doolittle eventually published in the newspaper was a horror, but it revealed that Hometown, USA, had a problem.

At first, we didn't want to do these stories.

David Saffer, local executive director of the Council for Prevention, had been an integral source and cheerleader on the underage drinking series ten years earlier. His organization took the pulse of local schools in the region, offering us statistics and real-time reporting of what his organization was seeing in the community.

About a year after the "Cost of Fun" was published, two young people were killed in a car crash in Washington County, and we wondered if our work had made any difference at all.[15]

A few days after the crash, Saffer visited us at the newspaper for a chat. Perhaps he knew what we were feeling because he had been there before, too. He pointed out that Warren County had gone eight months without an underage drinking fatality.[16]

"That is an eternity around here," he said.[17]

Saffer visited us often after the underage drinking series. We had an unofficial partnership with the Council for Prevention, and Saffer and his staff knew they could count on us to help them with their message.

During the spring of 2014, Saffer again asked to meet with me. He told me the drug problem had escalated locally. He hoped we would take a close look at the problem and produce a journalism effort the equal of our underage drinking series.[18]

Our staff was already shrinking a little bit each year, especially after the Great Recession, so I zealously guarded our resources when it came to big projects. It had to be the right project.

I was skeptical about taking on the drug problem, but out of respect for Saffer, I told him I would pitch it to our editors. They agreed with me. They felt we had already covered the problem significantly and our resources could be better spent elsewhere. Saffer refused to accept that and asked if he could meet with the editors. Saffer passionately explained what he was seeing in the community and why our help was desperately needed.

He changed our minds.

Not long afterward, Nancy Derusha called the newsroom and talked to Will Doolittle. While speaking to Doolittle about another complaint, she mentioned she had custody of her three nieces because her brother and his wife were addicted to heroin.[19]

That got Doolittle's attention. Four interviews followed with Derusha and the girls at the small trailer in neighboring Kingsbury. It was a humbling existence, but at least the girls had someone looking out for them.[20]

Derusha told Doolittle she hoped telling their story would help in some way. One of the girls hoped the story would inspire her parents to get clean.[21]

We hoped so, too.

Don Lehman, our cops and courts reporter, kept close track of the overdoses police reported. He found at least seven confirmed or suspected heroin deaths in the Glens Falls region over the past year. None had drawn much notice. But he also learned some deaths were not officially classified as overdoses.[22]

Washington County Undersheriff John Winchell told Lehman heroin overdoses were often covered up by police, coroners or others to spare the victims' families. He said the number of overdose deaths were underreported.[23]

Washington County Sheriff Jeff Murphy told Lehman of affluent parents going to pawn shops to buy back items their addicted children had stolen and sold. Others told of parents quitting their jobs to stay home to protect their property from their own children.[24]

Saffer helped organize a forum that included members of law enforcement, the judicial system, hospital employees and social services. We met in late April with 20 people in attendance.[25]

Saffer also invited one mother whose son was in jail because of drugs.

Judy Moffitt, a schoolteacher in South Glens Falls, sat at *The Post-Star*'s big conference room table listening to all the experts talk about their experiences and what they believed needed to be done.[26]

She had been at another meeting like this.

No one knew her there either.

She sat quietly, saying nothing. She remembered thinking, "These people don't know what they are talking about."[27]

The conversation drifted to finding a public spokesperson, someone prominent from the region, like local professional basketball player Jimmer Fredette or television personality and Lake George native Rachel Ray, to be the face of addressing the addiction issue.

Saffer stared at Moffitt and nodded. It was her turn to talk.

Moffitt stood up tall and straight and told how her son had ruined his life and almost ruined hers.

"This is the face of addiction," she said staring back at the experts around her. "This is what it looks like to have your only child dying of addiction."[28]

You don't forget those moments when someone bares their soul.

It was one of the bravest things I ever saw.

Meg Hagerty, who had found a second career as a features writer after her children went off to school, was assigned to tell Moffitt's story. It was about as far from Hagerty's life as anything she could have imagined.

In many ways, the story was typical, at least for drug addiction.

As a high school kid, Judy's son Nick was smart and articulate with a bright future. He began using marijuana at 16, graduated to cocaine in high school, and as his relationship with Judy deteriorated, he moved out of the house.[29]

There were calls to Judy after he was arrested, attempts at rehabilitation and counseling, second chances, third chances and so on. You've heard the story before.

And yet Judy remained resolute: "I vowed to do everything in my power to not let Nick feel alone or abandoned."[30]

There was a stay in the county jail, shock incarceration and an inpatient stay in rehab, and Judy stood by her son. He was beaten up by drug dealers, and Judy stood up to them and told them of the consequences if they touched him again.

"I was the momma tiger who would do anything to protect him," she told Hagerty.[31]

But as Hagerty unraveled the story of Nick's continued drug abuse, it became clear this was also a story about Judy and her journey and what she had to endure to survive.

At times, Judy blamed herself, sank into depression and couldn't sleep.

"What had we done wrong to have a child so out of control?" she asked Hagerty.[32]

Getting her son back would be a marathon.

In 2007, Nick was arrested by Glens Falls police on a felony count of selling drugs. He never finished his senior year of high school. On the day he was sentenced, Judy watched as he was handcuffed and shackled, and felt guilt.[33]

"I felt no mother should have to do this," Judy told Hagerty.[34]

In some ways, Judy was serving time, too.

She wrote to Nick in jail every day. She tried to inspire him with stories of others who had worked through their addictions. She made the 12-hour round trip drive to western New York every other week to see him in jail. She worried about how he was being treated, and when she left jail after those visits, she cried.[35]

When Nick got out, a relative gave him a job at a contractor supply business. Nick enrolled at SUNY Adirondack, but it lasted less than a year. Judy saw him become more withdrawn, going into work late, and her son told her he thought about suicide. A marijuana plant was found in a closet, and Judy kicked him out.[36]

It was happening all over again.

In May 2010, Nick was arrested for possession of OxyContin. His girlfriend told Judy a couple months later Nick was using heroin.[37]

"That made me fall to my knees. I had talked with him before and he promised me he would never be involved with heroin," Judy told Hagerty.[38]

When Judy got Nick Suboxone to keep him off heroin, he sold it to buy more heroin.

She got a call from the public defender's office when Nick missed his court date and was told the police were looking for him. She left work and found him in bed at home, his face beaten to a pulp by drug dealers.[39]

When the state police called later, Judy feared Nick was dead. Instead, she was told he had been arrested for shoplifting at the Polo Ralph Lauren outlet. Police found a heroin needle in the car.[40]

"I was done being used. I was done being an enabler," Judy said. "I was detaching. I was not going down with this disease."[41]

Nick was sentenced to eight months in the county jail for possession of Oxy-Contin. When he called from jail, Judy refused to pick up the phone. She told him he couldn't come home again.[42]

After getting out of jail, Nick got his life back on track. He got counseling and started his own business. He seemed excited about the future. Judy felt like her own life was back on track, too.

She was told about a counselor who understood addiction.

"It was my last ditch effort to tell me how to fix it," Judy remembered in 2020. "I went to his home office and started to tell my story with the hope he could give me the answer nobody else could give. As I talked, he started to fill in the story for me. 'How does he know this?' I wondered. It's because all our stories are the same story. His words were empowering. He said, 'Your son won't get better until you get better.'"[43]

Judy turned to her faith and started going to Nar-Anon meetings. She began speaking in public to share her experiences with others. She moved into a new house.

"I felt like I had finally found Judy," she told Hagerty.

In August 2013, Judy got a call that Nick had been arrested for selling Suboxone and was in jail again.[44] He was eventually sentenced to five years in prison and a couple more miles were added to the marathon as Hagerty explained Judy's typical weekend:

> Many weekends Moffitt awakes at 3:30 in the morning and is on the road an hour later, headed to Bare Hill Correctional Facility in Malone. She checks in at 7:30 a.m. and waits to see her son. A few hours later, she is seated with Nick in a big room with small tables. She has to face the guards. Lunch is whatever comes out of the vending machine. At least she can hold his hand and give him a hug.
>
> She's on the highway again when visiting hours are over at 3 in the afternoon. She gets home close to 7 p.m. This has been her routine for close to a year now and it will continue for as long as Nick remains in prison. His sentence is 5 years.
>
> Moffitt has been on a harrowing journey with her son since he was a teenager battling drug addiction. Still, she considers herself lucky.
>
> "He is alive. If it's this or the morgue, I'm taking this," Moffitt said.[45]

The story took you inside one parent's nightmare, but after the interview with Hagerty, Judy remembered sending her a 2 a.m. email that bared her soul again.

"I was petrified," Judy admitted. "I didn't know how she was going to write this. I didn't know what my estranged husband would do after reading it. I didn't know if my son would be upset."[46]

After the article came out, Judy was inundated with emails and phone calls thanking her for telling her story. Some asked her for help in addressing problems with their own relatives.

"I was so grateful to Meg," Judy said. "She really did reflect what I was thinking. I didn't want to be a victim. I wanted people to know the raw, honest truth that this could happen to anyone, but I also didn't want to be a victim of this. I wanted to use this [the story] to get healthier and help my child."[47]

When Judy visited Nick in jail, she slid the article across the table for him to read.

When he finished, he looked back at Judy and said, "They are starting to understand."[48]

We hoped our readers were, too.

But there was more.

Reporter Michael Goot sat down to talk to Sean and Tricia DeMerchant about the knock on the door we all fear in the middle of the night:

> At a quarter to 2 in the morning, Sean DeMerchant heard a knock on the door of his Halfmoon house.
>
> When he answered, a Saratoga County sheriff's officer handed him a piece of paper and told him to call the number on it to reach Oswego Police Department. DeMerchant knew it would be about his son.
>
> "I was out of my mind at the moment. I didn't know what to think. I was hoping he was arrested," he said.
>
> But his son, Sean Jr., had not been arrested. On April 24, Sean, a 22-year-old student at SUNY Oswego died of a heroin overdose. It happened a month before he would have received his bachelor's degree in marketing.[49]

Sean DeMerchant Jr.'s obituary only confirmed what had already been reported.

It said he had "died on Thursday, April 24, 2014 after losing his courageous battle with addiction while attending SUNY Oswego."[50]

The family directed that instead of flowers, donations be made in Sean's name to the Addiction Care Center in Albany or the Hudson Mohawk Recovery Center in Troy.[51]

His parents told Goot their son had struggled with addiction since high school. And even while using hard drugs in college, he had maintained high grades.

The parents blamed their insurance company for demanding outpatient treatment before agreeing to cover inpatient care at a 30-day treatment center.

It was Tricia DeMerchant who suggested making his problems public in the obituary.

"The heroin problem is all middle-to-upper-middle class college kids," Tricia told Goot. "They're not bums on the street."[52]

The Council for Prevention saw the same thing.

"We still get calls from white middle-class college-age kids' families saying, 'My kid is using. My kid went away to college and came back addicted, and there's no halfway houses here,'" Saffer told Goot. He said the number of heroin cases had been building for four or five years.[53]

In the final two parts of our series, reporter Bill Toscano talked about how addicts struggle to get clean.

"Getting addicted to oxycodone or heroin can take as little as a week or two. Getting clean can take the better part of forever," Toscano wrote in his lead.[54]

A couple years earlier, there was community outrage in Glens Falls when a local treatment facility tried to place a methadone clinic in the city. Citizens recoiled in horror at the prospect of bringing addicts into their community.

"It turns out they were already here," we wrote in an editorial. The community needed to accept it had problems, too.[55]

What we learned again was shining a light on a problem can change attitudes and perspectives.

Just two weeks after we published the last part of our "Heroin Hits Home" series, a group of community leaders held a public forum to address the problem. They asked me to be the first speaker.

I wrote this on July 26:

> By the end of the evening, it was clear our series had opened an important portal, and it became increasingly obvious many had already walked through it.
>
> I've been to plenty of these well-intentioned community forums, but this one was different. It wasn't the power in the PowerPoint, or the expertise of the professional panel or even the magnitude of the drug problem facing our communities. It was the audience that was different.
>
> They didn't need to be convinced there was a problem.[56]

The 150 people in attendance didn't need to hear the details of addiction and recovery. Many were already living it.

This was the beginning of the "Hometown vs. Heroin" effort that Judy Moffitt was part of. And as the evening wore on, those people began to share their personal stories.[57]

There was the grandmother taken aback when her toddler granddaughter asked her imaginary friends to "take a hit," then showed how mommy took her medicine by putting it up her nose. The daughter eventually abandoned her child, leaving the grandmother to raise her.[58]

There was the woman whose sister was an alcoholic and desperately wanted to know how she could have helped her. The sister had died at 39.[59]

There was a woman who had been ruined financially by her husband's drug use, and whose son was now caught up in selling drugs, too. She wanted people to learn from her experiences.

It was as if those 150 people were learning for the first time they were not alone anymore, and they could share their own ordeal and warn others of the insidious nature of the drugs that were everywhere.

There was plenty of anger to go around.

Some wanted to blame doctors for overprescribing pain medications, others the police for not locking up the addicts their family members had become, or politicians for failing to fund adequate recovery programs. But maybe most of all, people were blaming themselves.

Tears were shed.

The professional panel sitting at the long table on the stage desperately tried to help, to guide them toward solutions and offer comfort, but the nature of the problem was so complex that by the end of the evening it was clear few would go home with the answers they sought.

They were ready to deal with this problem. They just didn't know how.

A year later, Doolittle went back to visit Derusha and her nieces to see how they were doing.[60]

"I remember feeling a big sense of responsibility for that story," Doolittle said in 2020. "Some stories, you really question yourself. Am I doing this family any favors? Am I exploiting this situation? So many questions about that. I wanted to do it right.[61]

"In the end, I don't think it made a difference for them," Doolittle said. "There was so much going against this family, and Nancy had her own really bad health issues. She was nice and doing her best, but it was kind of impossible. So many headwinds."[62]

DeRusha said she was proud of the girls because none of them had missed any time in school. Their story did elicit sympathy from the community. People called, asking how they could help. Strangers sent checks. A woman came by with a $575 check for school clothes for the girls. The same woman raised money from co-workers to buy Christmas gifts. She continued to help them in the years to come and kept Doolittle updated, but things never got that much better.[63]

DeRusha continued to struggle with her own health issues. She had diabetes and heart problems. She did not know where the children's parents were, although Kiara did hear from her father once on Facebook, but after Derusha asked her about it, Kiara blocked him.[64]

The heroin series was honored with several national awards and was a finalist for community journalism in a contest sponsored by the Scripps Howard Foundation.[65]

Lee Enterprises honored the newspaper with a prestigious "President's Award" for excellence in news. Judges called the heroin series "a sobering revelation of local heroin use and the destruction it has caused in the community."[66]

The Local Media Association honored the series with a first place for Best In-Depth Reporting.[67]

"Sometimes, as a journalist you wonder who gets anything out of this story," Doolittle said. "I write a compelling story, and get some praise and recognition, but what has been accomplished here? I think it is part of the profession."[68]

What was more satisfying was hearing praise from local law enforcement and public health officials who said the series had made a difference.

In the Washington County town of Greenwich, where three people had died from heroin overdoses before the series, Supervisor Sara Idleman said coverage of the issue resonated.

"It was an amazing series and people are stepping up to the plate, talking about this and what needs to be done," Idleman said.[69]

Washington County Sheriff Jeff Murphy said he heard doctors were being more careful about the painkillers they prescribed following the heroin articles.

"Doctors read that. Medical people see that," Murphy said. "A lot of nurses told me there are a lot of Advil and Ibuprofen [prescribed] when it used to be hydrocodone and other things."[70]

"The awareness has been raised significantly in the community," Saffer said at the heroin forum. It was Saffer who was instrumental in pulling together a group called "Hometown vs. Heroin" to educate the public and mobilize a response to the problem.

The task force started with four people, but after *The Post-Star* series was published, it grew to 40.[71]

"The goal was to inform the public about what is going on," Sheriff Murphy said. "And I think with the help of *The Post-Star*'s series, we were able to do that."[72]

State officials jumped on board and a program was created to acquire the drug Narcan, a drug that reverses overdoses, for police departments in New York.

The drug was used at least five times in the months after the series to reverse overdoses.[73] Unfortunately, we continued to hear overdose calls on the newsroom scanner for years to come.

By January 2016, a Saratoga Springs organization sought hundreds of thousands of dollars in state funding to create a network of "recovery community centers" in the region, including one in Glens Falls.[74]

By 2017, a collaboration between the Council for Prevention and Glens Falls Hospital's Centers for Recovery was being explored to put together an opioid diversion program with Saffer again in the middle of the effort.[75]

By the end of 2019, 30 people had graduated from the one-year diversion program with a success rate of 87 percent. It led to the state Office of Court Administration to expand the program so it could accept defendants from criminal cases in other courts in Warren County.[76]

It all started with Saffer's visit to the newspaper and his insistence that we act. But it was also clear the problem remained.

Halfway through 2017, Don Lehman found 11 people had died of drug overdoses at Glens Falls Hospital. There had been only four in 2016. Warren County Undersheriff Shawn Lamouree told Lehman there may have been as many as 35 uses of the drug Narcan to revive those who had overdosed.

After 17 years at the Council for Prevention, Saffer retired in December 2017 at the age of 72. There was no parade or day in his honor. There should have been.

Judy Chittenden Moffitt created a Facebook page to tell her story and offer advice, called "The Addict's Mom." She had 35,000 followers in 2020 and remained active as an advocate for others facing addiction.[77]

"When I began my journey with what happened to my family, I thought I knew what addiction was," Judy said in 2020. "Everyone has an opinion of what it is, but you don't know what it is until you know what it is."[78]

It is an illness. she said, and part of the problem is that many still refuse to accept that.

"It's like telling your kid not to have cancer," Judy said. "It doesn't work."[79]

Judy said she still receives at least one message a day asking her for help. She retired from teaching in 2020 and is busier than ever with her advocacy work as a recovery coach. I asked her how important the newspaper series was in battling the problem.[80]

"It was critical," Judy said about the initial reporting and the later updates. "*The Post-Star* was so instrumental in all that. They never failed once to share that type of information. It was truly instrumental and I still talk about the article. We need the media to promote what we are doing."[81]

It is another part of community journalism we are losing.

Ultimately, Judy said she was just "trying to save her son."[82]

After getting out of prison, Nick, now 31, became a personal trainer and power lifter and moved back in with Judy.[83]

"He became the man of the house," Judy said. "This is a lifetime battle. I don't anticipate anything changing [with Nick], but it is what it is. It doesn't go away. There are success stories. I'm a success story. I've gathered tools to have a peaceful life. But you never reach the end."[84]

But maybe our community reached an understanding.

It was people like Judy Moffitt, Nancy Derusha and Sean and Tricia DeMerchant who made our readers pay attention to their stories by trusting our reporters and editors.

These were difficult, time-consuming stories to do. Finding the people who were willing to talk about being to hell and back is never easy, but it struck such a chord in the community and made such a difference it was worth that effort. Stories like these saved lives. That is the power of community journalism. That is the legacy of community newspapers.

Sadly, it was our last major team project.

24

The Difficult Mr. Lehman

There had to be a hundred reasons to fire Don Lehman over the years.

He was a difficult, headstrong reporter who criticized copy editors for their headlines, editors for their editing and reporters for the quality—or lack of it—in their reporting and writing, and he regularly said it out loud in front of the entire newsroom.

He scared half the newsroom to death.

The other half asked for a desk as far away from him as possible.

I suspect most of his sources were scared of him, too, and they were cops.

He was also the best reporter we ever had.

"In the office, he noticed what everyone else was doing, or not doing, and made acerbic comments," said Will Doolittle, who worked alongside him for more than 25 years. "He had no patience for people he felt were lazy or incompetent, and his comments were public and often pointed."[1]

Lehman didn't just want to beat the weeklies and small dailies to a story; he wanted to beat the bigger newspapers in Albany, Schenectady and Troy and all the television stations, too.

When we did get beat, Lehman could be heard bellyaching about the latest embarrassment throughout the newsroom and then assigning blame.

During one sit-down, I lauded him for his great reporting and prolific output as a reporter, but when he asked if his last raise would have been better if he wasn't such a pain in the ass, I said, "Absolutely."

Our editors—Mark Mahoney, Will Doolittle, Bob Condon and myself—all learned to separate the brutal honesty of his personality with the quality of work he delivered every single day of the week and a couple more times each weekend.

There were so many "What are we going to do with Lehman?" meetings, that we eventually just gave up trying to change him. Maybe that was bad management, but it paid dividends over three decades with a parade of impeccably crafted crime and court stories that kept us football fields ahead of the competition.

Lehman was the absolute standard for great cops and courts reporting. He was a fighter, a scrapper, someone who hustled from one story to the next and refused to accept being stonewalled by the sheriff, a beat cop or the district attorney. God help the person trying to hide something from him.

Every complaint about Lehman ended with a "but."

But he turned out so many stories.

But he had such great sources.

But he went the extra mile every day whether it was getting up in the middle of the night to chase a fire or coming home late to dinner after a day in court.

Don Lehman spent 28 years as the consummate bulldog reporter for *The Post-Star*. He is shown here in 2007 reporting on a press conference. He was at the center of almost every significant news event for three decades. He finally resigned his post at the very start of the pandemic in March 2020, saying he didn't think he had a future at the newspaper anymore (*Post-Star* file photograph).

What may have been the most difficult thing to accept was his strong opinions and observations about how the newspaper was being run were often right on the mark.

If you could live with that, you could live with Lehman and hope the news of the day kept him too busy to complain. The rest of us just tried to keep our heads down.

"I let a lot of things go without comment and sometimes even joined in," Doolittle said. "Bob [city editor Condon], to his credit, often called Don out and demanded he stop it."[2]

Doolittle thought Lehman could be too dismissive of the people who had hard lives and gotten in trouble with the law.

"His attitude was sometimes like the attitude of the police officers he covered," Doolittle said. "It could seem heartless."[3]

It wasn't unusual for Lehman to slam the phone down, sometimes after a few colorful expletives, when fielding a complaint from a reader or someone who had turned up in one of his stories from the police blotter. I wondered if it was his way of dealing with the horrors he wrote about every day.

As the commander of calm in our newsroom, the few times I ever saw Condon lose his temper was usually over something inappropriate Lehman had said. Fuming, Condon would tell Lehman to follow him into the conference room for a behind-closed-doors meeting.

"On the other hand, Don often called Bob out on things he should have been confronting or complaining about, but wasn't," Doolittle said. "They were opposites: Don the one who took legitimate criticism too far, and Bob the one who always sought to keep things smooth, even when he should have been pointing out problems."[4]

Over three decades, Lehman's reporting on the police beat became newsroom lore, not because of any one story or scoop, but because he was relentless in his mission and unafraid to ask anyone anything while regularly skirting the protocols set by the police and courts.

"You don't want to break the law, I tell my students," said David Blow, the former *Post-Star* reporter and editor who is now a professor at Castleton State in Vermont. "But it is OK to trample on it a little bit."[5]

One time at the arraignment of an accused killer, Lehman leaned over the rail in the courtroom and struck up a conversation with the distraught accused murderer when his lawyer briefly left the room.

"His lawyer was not happy when he found out his client had confessed to me, too," Lehman wrote in an email to me in 2020.[6]

"He was the epitome of a cops reporter," Blow said. "He was taking shit every day from people who were arrested. He had the perfect temperament because he gave it right back. Nobody ever came away feeling good about criticizing Don."[7]

Lehman chalked it up to a simple desire to get the story.

"So much of a reporter's job came down to effort, and a willingness to get to the bottom of the story," he said.[8]

Lehman was relentless in that mission every day. He was at the center of every major accident, crime or court case from the tanker spill in Fort Edward to the *Ethan Allen* sinking on Lake George to every murder in three counties over three decades.

"It was exciting," Lehman said. "It was different every day. You weren't sitting in a meeting every day, and as you know, I've always been very competitive."[9]

As newspaper jobs were eliminated, Lehman stepped into new responsibilities because he believed it would help the newspaper.

As we pushed to develop a digital presence online, Lehman got up each morning before sunrise and did early cop checks to get overnight arrests and accidents on the website before breakfast time. His stories often drew more page views than any others.

He began shooting his own photographs way before the other reporters and then videos from fires and accident scenes. He was the first reporter to totally embrace the online reporting and blogging, including play-by-play descriptions of what was going on during high-profile trials.

After a staff layoff in 2008, Lehman volunteered to take over the Warren County government beat. Sitting through boring government meetings was now part of his job, too.

With the loss of each newsroom position, Lehman worked even harder, regularly producing twice as many stories as other reporters. He was always the first person in the office every morning. Over the years, editors learned that if Lehman wasn't in the office when they arrived, there was a good chance something happened overnight.

Lehman's world was a barrage of the worst humanity had to offer. There were times after especially graphic reporting I asked him if he needed to talk to someone. But Lehman was a tough guy.

Once, as a visitor to Blow's college journalism class at Castleton, Lehman offered a peek at the toll reporting can take.

"He showed a little bit of the softer side," Blow remembered. "When the kids asked him if he found any of the reporting difficult, he said that after he had kids, writing about child abuse and babies getting killed was very difficult."[10]

Lehman never told any of us at the newspaper.

In the spring of 2017, Lehman got a call from a reader who had stumbled on a homeless man living in the woods. Lehman had heard about the man before but thought he was a seasonal drifter.[11]

This time, he asked around.

The local SPCA president said he knew about the guy and his camp in the woods and volunteered to take Lehman there.

On a rainy April morning, Jim Fitzgerald and Lehman went into the woods, and Lehman met Gregg Burdo for the first time.[12]

It did not go well. Burdo was angry Fitzgerald had brought this stranger from the newspaper to see him. Lehman believed Burdo might attack him, but the homeless man eventually calmed down. Lehman asked he if could come back and see him again another time.[13]

When Lehman returned, the 69-year-old Burdo was just as combative. He was a Vietnam veteran who had been a local high school sports star. Lehman brought up the local sports scene, and Burdo calmed down. Burdo eventually confided in Lehman some of the graphic details about his service in Vietnam.[14]

"I was amazed at the life he was living and the camp he had created," Lehman later wrote in his blog, "and as I did some background checking about him, I was finding that police, fire officials and others knew he was living where he lives, despite years of offers of help for him and his cats."[15]

Burdo's biggest concern was his privacy, and Lehman promised not to reveal where his camp was in the woods. Lehman reported Burdo was a skilled "dumpster diver" and had plenty of clothes, supplies and food for him and the cats.

"I don't need help," Burdo repeatedly told Lehman.[16]

When Lehman told Burdo he was writing a story about his life, Burdo again was angry.

"I told him I found his life fascinating and that I thought the public would too," Lehman wrote in his blog. "He is one of the most intelligent people I have met in years. Even living in the woods with no electricity, TV or cellphone, he is more informed about the world and local events than the vast majority of people I deal with every day."[17]

The Sunday, July 16, profile, "Decades in the woods," was published on the front page with two photos of Burdo at his camp. It was the type of story neither the editors nor *Post-Star* readers were used to seeing from Lehman.

It had a heart.

Lehman chronicled a story of a Vietnam veteran who lost his way after returning home from the war, then retreated into the woods where he had lived with a dozen or so cats for the past 36 years.[18]

It was a tale of survival and solitude but, most importantly, a story about a man living his life differently.

I think this spoke to Lehman.

I wondered if he saw a little of himself in the sometimes combative Burdo, who was so determined to live life his own way. If that wild child at Castleton had not found a passion for journalism in college, maybe he wouldn't have met his wife in the Glens Falls newsroom, had those two kids and carved out a pretty good life.

"There were some nights I thought I was going to die," Burdo confided to Lehman about the brutal winters. "If I wasn't living here, I would be dead or in jail."[19]

What Lehman revealed in this tale was more than just a story of a man who had fallen through the cracks in society; it was also about a network of quiet helpers behind the scenes making sure Burdo was okay.

This was another part of the community we served.

"One of the things I got from [military] service was courage to do what I want to do," Burdo told Lehman. "I don't know what the future brings. I could stay here until I'm 80."[20]

After the story was published that Sunday, Lehman received more than a dozen inquiries from readers who wanted to help Burdo and his cats.

He told them Burdo said he didn't need any help.

"One side that you never saw of Lehman was that human side," Blow, his old friend from college, said. "You never saw that in 30 years. He never gave a glimpse of himself. But the Burdo story, the Vietnam veteran living in the woods, all of a sudden you saw a side of Don Lehman we hadn't seen."[21]

And the story didn't end with that front-page article in July 2017.

Lehman continued to go back and check on Burdo every few months. He told us it was because readers were concerned with how he was doing. I thought it was something more. I wondered if Lehman had found a kindred spirit out there in the woods.

In November 2017, Lehman visited Burdo on a cold and rainy Friday. He found him layered up in warm clothes.

"I asked him if he needed anything, and he said he was all set," Lehman wrote in the blog. "I reminded him that there are organizations that can get him indoors for the cold weather, but he said he has made it though plenty of winters and thinks it will be another mild one."[22]

Burdo also told Lehman his bicycle had broken down. Lehman arranged to get him another one. After all, Lehman's son was off in college and would not need it.[23]

In December 2019, Lehman reported on his blog that readers had paid thousands of dollars worth of Burdo's veterinarian bills for his cats and assisted the man with clothing.[24]

That was because of Don Lehman.

Another woman reached out to donate a tent, sleeping bag and cot.[25]

Also because of Lehman.

On March 20, 2020, I got an early-morning email from Lehman saying he was resigning his position to take a job with Warren County. He apologized for not being able to give two weeks' notice. It was typical for Lehman to just move on.

He addressed his leaving with readers on his *Post-Star* blog without clearing it with any of the editors. When the publisher saw the post, he made me take it down, even though there was nothing controversial or derogatory about the newspaper or its staff. It was a simple farewell to readers.

I was surprised and a little annoyed Lehman didn't give me a heads-up after all those years. I often told Lehman he would be the last guy to turn out the lights. He saw it differently.

"I saw the writing on the wall with the pandemic," he said in 2020. "I thought it would be the death knell for many newspaper jobs."[26]

He was right again. Within six months, the newsroom staff would be cut by another third.

Different reporters chronicled the arrests and important court cases, but there were fewer scoops and a lot fewer stories.

Perhaps the biggest loss was we no longer knew how Gregg Burdo was doing.

When I asked Lehman in September 2020 if he still checked on the old homeless man, he said, "I do. Just saw him last night. Took him over some sweatshirts and blankets."[27]

I'm guessing his son had grown out of them.

The Great Email Caper

Tony Metivier became that rarity among those holding public office in 2017. Someone who made a difference by doing the right thing.

I'd like to think part of the reason was his dad, Don Metivier, had been a long-time reporter at *The Post-Star* and some of that pursuit-of-the-truth DNA that is part of every good reporter's moral compass rubbed off on him. While I never worked with Don, his columns about everyday people and life in Glens Falls maintain a special place with *Post-Star* readers. Being a "Metivier" meant something here.

Tony Metivier, a local real estate agent and businessman, had quietly served on the Queensbury Town Board since 2008.

By 2017, the Town of Queensbury had grown larger than the city of Glens Falls and was a bustling hub of retail shopping centers and big-box stores. Queensbury was Glens Falls' suburban bedroom community.

Metivier was part of a Republican block that controlled the Queensbury Town Board for as long as anyone could remember. He had mostly flown under the radar as a councilman during his four terms without a hint of controversy or political ambition.

John Strough, a former Queensbury High School history teacher, had served for nine years as a Town Board member before being elected supervisor in 2013 and reelected in 2015. He was the rarest of commodities in Warren County political circles. He was a Democrat.

In late 2016, there were four Republicans on the Town Board with Democrat Strough. Up until then, the board had functioned effectively with little controversy. Strough was a Democrat, but he was no liberal. He regularly voted with Republicans on the county board and was a staunch fiscal conservative. It was often hard to tell Republicans and Democrats apart around the county.

But that didn't eliminate the politics. The presence of a Democrat, leading the county's largest town, was a source of annoyance to some county Republican leaders.

Metivier later characterized that annoyance as something greater.

"They [the Republican leaders] really want John [Strough] out of office and will do everything they can to make the next six months as miserable as possible. This is very unsettling," Metivier told me in June 2017 as Strough faced reelection in the fall. "It's about the Republicans winning. It's not about John. I've sat there in Republican meetings in the past, and I don't understand how Republicans winning will make much difference here in Queensbury. I'm left scratching my head."[1]

It was as if the same type of national political furor—just win, baby—was seeping into hometown politics. It would soon have the same ugly ramifications.

What transpired between election days in 2015 and 2017 is a lesson in the pitfalls of small-town politics run amok, the influence national politics had locally, and a reminder of how one newspaper's aggressive coverage could make a difference for the voters it served.

Doug Irish, one of the four Republican members on the Town Board, informed Metivier on the Friday before the regular Monday meeting in November 2016 that he was resurrecting a two-year-old bid that would change the Town of Queensbury's legal representation.[2]

Metivier said the proposal made him "uncomfortable."[3]

Irish wanted to replace a respectable law firm the town had used since 1996 with one run by John Aspland, who was vice chairman of the Queensbury Republican Party.[4] Irish was the chairman and Bill VanNess, another Republican on the Town Board, had previously been chairman. The fourth Republican on the Town Board, Brian Clements, also served on the committee.

Irish said the move was to save the town money, which it appeared to do, but it also sounded partisan.

"John Aspland and Doug Irish are tight," Metivier told me. "Huge conflict of interest there. That is underhanded, no other word for it."[5]

Before the vote, Michael Grasso, chairman of the Warren County Republican Party for more than a decade, left Metivier a message on his phone, saying, "You will vote for this, or you will pay."[6]

At the meeting, Strough and Irish argued bitterly over changing the town's lawyers, with Strough accusing him of political "cronyism or pay to play."[7]

Strough said at least three lawyers at Aspland's law firm served on the Warren County Republican Committee and contributed to Republican political candidates. Aspland had also served as Irish's lawyer in an election dispute against a Democratic rival in 2015. VanNess had received a campaign contribution from Aspland's law firm in 2015.[8]

"I think they have to make up their mind if they want to be a political organization or a law firm," Strough said about Aspland's law firm.[9]

Queensbury's current firm had a policy of not allowing its lawyers to serve on political committees or make political contributions.[10]

Metivier tried to delay the vote, arguing with Irish there was no advance discussion, which was customary. He told Irish he wanted to review the two-year-old proposal again.[11]

Irish balked, telling Metivier he already had the votes.

"My point was that we should discuss it again and interview [the law firms] again," Metivier said. "Of the six attorneys we talked to at the time [in 2014], four were no longer with the firm. My argument [at the meeting] Monday was we don't know who we are dealing with and what kind of experience they have. It wasn't about the money, it was about are you qualified to do the job. I just wanted an extra week."[12]

The Town Board voted 3–2 during the Monday meeting to switch law firms, with Strough and Metivier dissenting. Metivier knew his "no" vote would not make a difference, but he voted against the proposal anyway.[13]

"I am not going to be anyone's puppet," Metivier said later. "I probably voted no just to prove a point."[14]

Things then got petty. Two weeks later, Strough announced he was replacing

VanNess as deputy town supervisor and appointing Metivier. The three other Town Board members responded by voting to eliminate the deputy supervisor position.[15]

Ultimately, the question that needed answering was: Who was calling the shots when it came to the Town of Queensbury business—the Town Board or the Republican leadership in Warren County?

The next spring, VanNess, who had cast one of the decisive votes to switch law firms, resigned from his Town Board seat and was appointed Republican commissioner to the Warren County Board of Elections over an experienced longtime deputy at a salary of $64,500.[16] That is the value of being a good soldier in party politics. There are rewards when you do what you are told and consequences when you don't.

Metivier was about to find that out.

Early in June, 41 members of the Queensbury Republican Committee met with Town Board candidates to decide who to endorse in the fall election. Metivier was an incumbent in Ward 1, where he had served for ten years.[17]

"I went before the Republican committee to ask for the nomination," Metivier related. "I told them that someone in this room told me that I had to vote for the new law firm, or I would pay. Doug Irish spoke up and said no one in that room would do that. Then Grasso chirped up and said, 'I said that.'"[18]

Metivier said he was told the vote was 41–0 for Hal Bain, a 72-year-old who had never held elected office.[19] "I was disappointed, let down and frustrated," Metivier said, "but I wasn't surprised."[20]

Then Metivier said the words that should be mandatory for anyone running for political office: "I am not a politician, I am a public servant. I am not here for the party, I am here for the people of Queensbury. I think there are people out there that actually appreciated that."[21]

That made Metivier a dinosaur because elected officials just don't say those things anymore.

Faced with going door-to-door to get the signatures needed to get on the ballot for a Republican primary, most figured Metivier would quietly bow out, but this was the son of a newspaper man for whom doing the right thing and standing up to the bullies meant something.

Metivier went door-to-door without help from Republican volunteers and got the signatures needed to get on the ballot. "Not a single person has said they will not sign," Metivier said after getting on the ballot. "People have been telling me to stick to my guns."[22]

Looking back, the actions of these small-town politicians mirrored what we were seeing nationally as they became more aggressive, unafraid of dirty tricks while portraying the local newspaper as "fake news."

It was about winning, not serving the people, as Metivier pointed out.

During a Town Board meeting on June 5, Doug Irish went on a tirade against the newspaper and its editorial board's position on a state audit that Strough may have mishandled. The Republican board members accused Strough of being involved in a cover-up.[23]

Then Irish attacked the paper's news coverage. In a blog post the next day, *Post-Star* reporter Kathleen Moore said Irish described the paper as "akin to fiction."[24]

"You can't believe half the things that's in it," he said in the public meeting.[25]

We responded in an editorial: "The anonymity of the internet has eroded not only our manners, but our ability to conduct vigorous debate in any sort of civilized manner. The rise of social media as a staple of our culture has encouraged an ugliness in our debates, as half-truths and outright lies have become accepted norms in the political arena."[26]

Our credibility was being questioned by Irish, and we couldn't let him get away with that. The editorial pointed out that if Irish didn't believe half the stories in our newspaper (about 300 a month at the time), he should contact the editor immediately and identify the 150 stories he believed to be "fiction" so that he could correct the record.[27]

"We know he won't do that because none of it is true," the editorial said. "Our reporting is solid and so are our facts."[28]

It was a debate that mirrored what was going on nationally.

We never heard from Irish. In July, he accepted a job in North Carolina but continued to serve on the Town Board while living out of state.

The spiderweb was stretching into all corners of local Republican politics as the race for Queensbury supervisor heated up.

Rachel Seeber, a former victim's advocate in the Warren County District Attorney's Office, served as an at-large supervisor for the Town of Queensbury on the Warren County board. She was another rarity in Warren County politics, a young woman who was a Republican. She was considered a rising star in local politics. With Republicans holding a 2-to-1 advantage in the town, she was expected to give Strough a strong challenge. She was also close to Irish.

On September 11, 2017, Queensbury Republicans went to the polls in Ward 1 and rejected the Republican-endorsed Hal Bain, 200–95.[29] Rumors swirled during the summer that Bain was not running, but Bain never responded to reporter Kathleen Moore's inquiries.

What was not known was that Doug Irish and the town's lawyer, John Aspland, had cooked up another scheme.

Hearing that Irish was using his town email for political work, the Queensbury Democratic Committee filed a Freedom of Information request to see all of Irish's emails between July 10 and September 25. After reading the emails, the Democratic Committee filed an official complaint with the state Attorney General's Office, alleging Irish had misused government resources by using his town email account for personal business. Specifically, political business.[30]

Among that business was a proposition made in an email exchange between Irish and Aspland, the town attorney, in which Hal Bain, Michael Grasso and a third Republican Town Board member, Brian Clements, were copied to address Bain's reluctance to continue his campaign. Irish suggested that Bain should continue his run for Town Board, then resign after getting elected so the Republican-dominated board could appoint a replacement.[31]

"That would be optimal," Aspland responded.[32]

On October 15, the newspaper published an editorial titled "Emails reveal dirty politics in Queensbury."[33]

"Even worse than the misuse of time, however, is the way Irish and Aspland abandon all pretense of working in the best interests of the town and engage in raw political scheming," the editorial said. "Here we have two Town Board members

[Irish and Clements] discussing with a town employee [Aspland] the running of a sham candidate [Bain] in a shameful attempt to manipulate the election system."[34]

Irish justified the emails as politics as usual.

"I'm sorry people don't like to see how sausage is made, but this is how sausage is made," he said.[35]

The emails became a local scandal and an important issue, not only in the Town Board races, but in the supervisor race between Strough and Seeber.

At the regular Monday Town Board meeting on October 16, Metivier read a statement from one of his constituents, saying he was "embarrassed" to live in the town because of the political shenanigans.[36]

Metivier called out Irish for not being at any Town Board meetings for the past four months, as well as fellow board member, Brian Clements, and supervisor candidate, Rachel Seeber, for supporting Irish's decision to keep his position while living in North Carolina. Metivier also wondered if more town business decisions would be based on political affiliation.[37]

It was a legitimate question.

"It is embarrassing to live in this town right now and be affiliated with members of this Town Board that continue to behave the way they do," Metivier said. He suggested voters should not vote for anyone who supported Irish, including Clements and Seeber.[38]

The events in Queensbury continued to escalate as the paper played a larger and more aggressive role in holding politicians accountable.

I wrote in my column that Queensbury residents should be proud to have someone like Metivier standing up for what is right.[39]

Earlier in the week, before Metivier spoke at the Town Board meeting, *Post-Star* publisher Robert Forcey was served with seven counts of "throwing refuse on highways and adjacent lands" in connection with the delivery of a free weekly newspaper. It appeared the newspaper was being sent a message by local Republicans, as well.[40]

Forcey was ticketed for the delivery of a *Post-Star* product after Seeber brought the issue to the attention of the Sheriff's Office, where her husband, Kevin Conine, was an investigator.[41] One of the littering complaints came from Joanne Irish, the wife of Doug Irish.[42]

Don Lehman, our longtime police reporter who usually steered clear of politics, said in a blog post after the election, he had never seen anything like it.[43]

"I personally thought the littering case that just concluded was one of the most moronic misuses of police, prosecutor and court time I have seen in years," Lehman wrote. "I tried to play it as straight as I could. To be clear, don't blame the Warren County District Attorney's Office for this waste of time, I was told that the office's prosecutors made it clear to the Warren County Sheriff's Office that the charges were not viable before the police pursued their 'investigation.' But they did so anyway."[44]

Warren County Sheriff Bud York, a Republican who had endorsed Seeber, admitted this was the first time his agency was asked to investigate a "littering" case. He still allowed it to go forward.[45]

"This seems like we were being targeted," Forcey said.[46]

He now knew how Metivier felt.

Earlier that week, I called Bain to confirm he was running for the Town Board and that he would serve if he won.

I got no response.

In my column on October 18, I said the Republicans were trying to perpetrate a fraud on the voters of Ward 1, and called Irish out on his political dirty tricks[47]:

> It is sad there are people like Irish who believe conniving shortcuts are acceptable virtues when you want your own way.
>
> What he especially doesn't understand is most people don't think the way he does. They believe voters should make up their own minds and candidates who are elected should serve.[48]

On Sunday, October 22, reporter Moore received an email from Irish, saying he would resign from the Town Board—not because he no longer lived in the town—but because it was affecting Republican support for Seeber.[49]

On Tuesday, Bain walked into the newspaper's office and asked to speak with me.

Bain told me he was not a candidate for the Town Board and that Republican officials had known that since July. Bain said it was the Republican leadership (Michael Grasso) in the county who forced him to be a middleman in a scheme in which Republicans would appoint a successor if he was elected.[50]

"I will not accept that position if I were to win," Bain told me. "People should vote for whoever they believe will do the best job in any race."[51]

Bain told me he was upset his name was being dragged through the mud. I told him it was because he had not returned phone calls to set the record straight.

"I'm at fault, too," Bain said. "I should have come out and said something."[52]

The dominoes continued to fall. A day after Irish resigned from the Town Board, town lawyer Aspland resigned his political position. He said his "dual roles" with the town and political committee led to an "unnecessary distraction."[53]

He also said the newspaper had misconstrued his advice to the town.

"Regrettably, *The Post-Star* has chosen to misconstrue my advice and malign me," Aspland said. "A simple phone call or question could have resolved their concern, but there was no phone call and no question."[54]

In the news story by Moore reporting Aspland's resignation, I responded, "John Aspland's accusations about the quality and accuracy of *The Post-Star*'s reporting are an outrage and an obvious attempt to deflect from his own ethical shortcomings and political dirty tricks. *The Post-Star* stands by its reporting and commentary on this ongoing issue in Queensbury, and the fact Mr. Aspland has not made any mention of specific factual errors speaks volumes."[55]

My favorite part of the story was the next paragraph from Moore: "Aspland did not return two calls Wednesday, asking him why he had not returned three previous calls, which were placed to both his office and cell phones."[56]

In the editorial board's endorsement in the Queensbury supervisor race, we summed it up like this:

> John Strough is a hard-working supervisor who occasionally fails to keep his fellow board members as informed as he should.
>
> Rachel Seeber is a hard-charging candidate who is too political by half.[57]

The endorsement editorial concluded: "Seeber's refusal to condemn the political maneuvering in Ward 1 and defense of having a political partisan for town attorney fall short of the ethical standards town voters should be seeking."[58]

The five editorial board members present voted unanimously to endorse

Strough, saying: "Editorial board members were impressed by Rachel Seeber's professionalism but not by the way she ducked questions about dirty politics in Queensbury and tried to deflect blame elsewhere."[59]

The question was whether anyone was listening. Did the newspaper's editorial page still have the clout of previous years?

On the Wednesday before Election Day, I published a final column on the subject and asked a simple question: Was it right or wrong? I urged local Republicans to take their party back.[60]

"Maybe I am demanding too much with the new political reality where lying is not only overlooked, but condoned," I wrote. "I still believe those values carry weight and give us insight into character and how our leaders will conduct themselves."[61]

The only reason voters knew anything about the back room politics was because of the diligent efforts of the newspaper as it sought answers to important questions.

Going into Election Day, most of us believed Seeber would still be elected supervisor.

Moore, our Queensbury reporter, had done exit polling work in college, so we put it to use on Election Day 2017. She visited several Queensbury polling places in the town and found voters were disgusted by the email scheme and dirty politics of Republicans in the town.

"I think it casts a very poor light on the Republican Party in Queensbury," voter Wayne Woodcock said.[62]

"I thought it was very corrupt," voter Martha Butler said.[63]

Voter turnout was very high for a local election. Nearly 2,000 more votes were cast in the supervisor's race than in the previous contested race in 2009.[64]

Strough defeated Seeber 4,414–3,150.[65]

Voters took their anger out on all the Republicans as incumbents Brian Clements and Tim Brewer, who had replaced Irish after he resigned, both lost. Hal Bain lost, too.

"My grandfather told me nice will always win over nasty, and I guess that old maxim holds true," Strough said after winning.[66]

Seeber never returned Moore's calls on election night.[67]

"It was the accumulated arrogance and hubris of certain members of the Queensbury and Warren

Queensbury Town Supervisor John Strough gets word that he had been reelected on Tuesday, November 7, at the Lawrence Street Tavern. After a long, contentious campaign with Rachel Seeber, Strough was surprisingly reelected when voters rebelled against the dirty tricks by the local Republican Party (*Post-Star* photograph by Kathleen Phalen-Tomaselli).

County Republican leadership," said Queensbury's Democratic Committee Co-Chair Mike Parwana. "They thought they were going to be able to do the same sorts of things that they had apparently done for a really long time, but the public has never known about."[68]

That was a nod to the newspaper reporting and editorials.

Irish did not return a call from the newspaper that night either, nor did county Republican chair Grasso or Seeber's campaign manager Mark Westcott.[69]

Post-Star reporter Michael Goot wrote, "Strough credited his victory to an honest and honorable campaign and his deep roots in the community."[70]

Westcott, who worked with the Seeber campaign, wrote online that *The Post-Star* still has "teeth," which was evidenced in its coverage of the issue. I wasn't sure if it was a compliment or a criticism.

"It's not supposed to happen in small-town Queensbury and yet it did, and it was a real eye-opener to a lot of people," Metivier said the day after the election. "I think it sent a message. They're not going to tolerate it."[71]

There was also this letter to the editor published on Election Day from Brian Farenell of Glens Falls:

> It's interesting to see the extent to which *The Post-Star* has come under attack lately, not for doing its job poorly but for doing it at all.
>
> The main "agenda" I've seen in recent months at *The Post-Star* is against sleaze, cronyism and childish actions by politicians of multiple local governments. My question is, why doesn't everyone have an "agenda" against these things? I'm not an apologist for *The Post-Star*. I've often criticized it in the past, including in its own pages. But those were honest criticisms, based on standards of journalism in the public interest, not because it wasn't adequately tribal on behalf of my preferred politician.
>
> *The Post-Star* is the only outlet for serious oversight journalism in the area. The journalism needs to be better. Most of its critics want the journalism to disappear altogether.[72]

That's why we do the work, because there are citizens like Mr. Farenell who understand its importance.

But Election Day was not the end of the story.

At the Queensbury Town Board's organizational meeting on January 1, 2018—the first with a Democratic majority—the board approved a resolution to rehire its former law firm and make Metivier the deputy supervisor.[73]

Kevin Geraghty, a longtime Republican in the county and a town supervisor in Warrensburg, also predicted the politics in Queensbury would continue.[74]

"This is not one of those things that I think they will let go of," Geraghty said.[75] He knew what he was talking about.

On Monday, March 12, 2018, John Strough and his wife, Christianne, were arrested by state police on charges related to election fraud.[76]

The 66-year-old Strough faced one misdemeanor count of second-degree offering a false instrument for filing, while his 63-year-old wife faced three misdemeanor counts of making a false statement or affidavits on nominating petitions.[77]

The charges related to gathering signatures for a Conservative Party primary in 2017, which Strough lost. Because Strough was not a Conservative Party member, any signatures he secured for his petition had to be witnessed by a party member or a notary. His wife, who is a notary, signed she had witnessed the signatures. A number of the signers said that Strough's wife had waited in the car and had not witnessed the signatures. Strough argued his wife could see him from the car.[78] It appeared Strough was caught in a technicality. It was small-town politics at its worst.

Not surprisingly, the complaint originated with Seeber after a voter told her a notary was not present when he signed Strough's petition. Seeber's campaign paid an investigator to ask signers whether they met a notary when they signed, then brought the case to the Warren County Sheriff's Office where her husband was an investigator—just as she had done with the allegations of newspaper littering.[79] Seeber appeared to be the sheriff's office biggest tipster.

During the supervisor race, Sheriff York had left handwritten notes on many conservative voters' doors, saying he personally endorsed Seeber and urged voters to write in her name on primary day.[80]

"The root cause of all this is the involvement of the local Sheriff's department in politics," Strough's attorney, E. Stewart Jones, said in May when the Stroughs accepted a plea deal. "They initiated it. They didn't look into any other notary in the county. It was a selective and discriminatory prosecution."[81]

After the Stroughs were arrested, Grasso issued a press release to address the charges and said Strough might need to step down until the case was decided.[82]

"I think it is a damn shame and of no benefit to the community," Democratic Town Board member Catherine Atherden wrote in an email to reporter Moore. "Supervisor Strough has lived here his entire life without a blemish to his character—an honest man—and now this. For four years, a small faction of the community has been trying to smear his name. I do not know all the reasons for that, but it is quite obvious this faction will do anything to achieve their goal, and this charge proves it. This 'faction' is not working on behalf or for the community. They are disrupters preventing us from doing what we signed up for. They are only sowing discord and ugliness."[83]

On Tuesday, May 15, John and Chris Strough entered the courtroom at Glens Falls City Hall at 9:04 a.m.[84]

Strough was dressed in a blue blazer, pink shirt, striped tie and khaki pants while his wife sported a purple sweater, white pants and a smart-looking orange scarf.[85]

They were the best-dressed defendants in court and given the courtesy of having their case heard first.

Bonnie and Clyde they were not.

The couple agreed to a plea deal, clearing John Strough of any wrongdoing after six months, with his wife, Chris, pleading guilty to disorderly conduct. Her notary license was revoked for one year, and she was fined $200, including $120 in court costs.[86]

It was over in a matter of minutes.

Unlike many court cases, the accused couple did not dash toward the exits or hide behind their lawyer. They lingered, waiting to talk to reporter Moore and me.

They had something to say.

"If I was a Republican, I wouldn't be here today," Strough said. "If I had a spouse who worked in the Sheriff's Department, I wouldn't be here today."[87]

The message was clear. These charges were politically motivated.

"When I first ran for office, I never thought that I would face this type of pain," Strough said. "I didn't deserve this."[88]

Strough said local Republicans were sending a message to the next Democrat intending to run for public office that they should think twice.[89] There was bitterness in his words.

In April, the newspaper's lawyer asked the Queensbury town justice to dismiss littering charges against its publisher. The lawyer argued that newspapers have delivered in similar fashion around the country for decades.[90]

The Warren County District Attorney's Office did not oppose the motion.[91]

The Post-Star lawyer did point out that "the government is prohibited from sanctioning, effectively censoring home delivery of a free newspaper containing First Amendment protected speech by calling it 'litter' and fining, much less imprisoning its publisher."[92]

In May, Queensbury Town Justice Michael Muller dismissed all charges against publisher Forcey for littering.[93]

It took more than a year, but Warren County Republicans made several changes to their ethics code. Unfortunately, none of the changes addressed the dirty tricks that occurred before the Queensbury election.[94]

The new Republican rules banned all candidates from spying on other candidates or parties, distributing fraudulent writing, misrepresenting the results of pre-election polling and hindering eligible people from registering to vote or voting.[95]

The Queensbury Democrats, who were initially enthusiastic at adopting an ethics policy immediately after the 2017 election, never got around to putting it in writing. No reforms were pushed among the Warren County Democrats either.[96]

"We are on the right track," longtime Republican Geraghty said after the reforms were adopted, but he indicated they needed to go further. "We should get back to it and rehash everything and finish it. We need to figure out if Mike [Grasso] is going to remain chairman."[97]

"This was good news for all voters, whether you belong to a political party or not," we wrote in an editorial. "It was an acknowledgment that dirty politics have no place locally and party leaders here are willing to stand up for standards of integrity."[98]

On August 19, 2020, Grasso announced he was stepping down as chairman of the Warren County Republican Committee so he could take a seat on the Warren-Washington Industrial Development Agency Board. The newspaper earlier objected to him taking the position while he was still GOP chairman.[99]

VanNess, who cast one of the votes to change insurance companies that led to the email controversy, took over as acting chairman of the Republicans.[100] He did not see a conflict with his position as Warren County Board of Elections Republican Commissioner.[101]

Before the 2017 election, Strough said it might be the last time he ran for office. I asked him if anything had changed that day in City Court.

"I'm leaving my options open," Strough said. "If people want me to continue, I will continue."[102]

It sounded like a threat.

Later, Strough was critical of the newspaper's coverage of his arrest and prosecution.

Ironically, Strough continued his criticism of Moore's coverage of the town's business and indicated the newspaper was out to get him. At one point, I reminded Strough in a blog post that the newspaper editorial board had endorsed him in the last election.[103]

After the 2017 election, I received a letter from a Ward 1 Queensbury resident named Tom Jenkin that reminded readers of the newspaper's important work: "In my earlier years as a business executive, I attended numerous management seminars and got some sage advice, 'When plans go wrong, or not as expected, the first thing to do is look in a mirror.' But of course it is easier to blame the press."[104]

At the end of 2018, Strough's arrest was voted one of the ten most significant stories of the year by the newspaper.[105]

In 2019, John Strough won reelection as supervisor in the Town of Queensbury. He was unopposed. Town voters also returned Rachel Seeber to her previous position as a Queensbury county supervisor.[106]

In January 2021, Seeber was selected to be the first woman to chair the Warren County Board of Supervisors.[107] When committee chairs were announced, John Strough—one of the most experienced members on the board—was not appointed chairman of any committees.[108]

It seemed like nothing had changed.

26

The Alzheimer's Chronicles

When Will Doolittle started dating his wife Bella, she was working three jobs, caring for two young kids and commuting between two North Country communities an hour apart.[1]

He marveled at how she didn't seem to need any sleep.[2]

How she seemed to have this unending capacity to push past fatigue.[3]

How her love and energy filled an entire third-floor apartment with warmth and comfort in one of the coldest places in the country.

Will had just returned home for a visit after a year teaching in Japan when he ran into Bella bartending at a local pub.

The plan was to embark on more adventures overseas, but Bella changed that.

Will began staying at her apartment and sharing her life. Once, when Will and his brother were painting the bedroom in the apartment, Bella returned to tell them the color—a lemony yellow—was not right. The brothers laughed, thinking she was joking, and locked her out of the room. There was beer involved.[4]

But it wasn't long before Will was repainting the room a color more to Bella's liking.[5]

"Her will could not be denied for long, at least not by me," Will wrote.[6]

It was Bella who insisted he take the job in Glens Falls that changed their destinies and impacted so many of our readers over the years.[7]

It was Bella who insisted to Will they adopt a black baby in an almost all-white community, and then her niece's daughter not long afterward.[8]

It was Bella who continued to go to school and work in Glens Falls so they could buy that little house over on South Street and raise the girls.

She worked weekends and overnight at a residential facility for people with disabilities while holding down a job at the kitchen at Olive Garden.[9] The walk was only a mile or two. No big deal for someone like Bella.

In her spare time—spare time?—she volunteered at the Domestic Violence Project at Catholic Charities, which eventually led to a full-time job.[10]

She got her bachelor's degree, then started working on the master's and a teaching certificate, too.

It wasn't unusual to find Bella in the kitchen on a Sunday afternoon, whipping up a variety of family meals for the week ahead. With the older children grown, the two girls became the center of both their universes. Zoe was the athlete, Tam the artist.

In 2003, Bella was hired as campus coordinator for the Ticonderoga branch of North Country Community College where she was a counselor, party planner and all-around driving force on campus.[11] It was a tedious hour-long commute over heavily traveled two-lane roads—especially in the winter—but Bella imposed her will there, too.

Will wrote she had helped scores of young people get degrees and find jobs. "She understands North Country kids who have no money and want to work their way into better circumstances, because she was one. Out of eight children in her family, she's the only one who went to college," Will wrote.[12]

She was a force of nature, and no one knew it better than Will.

From time to time, my wife and I had dinner with Will and Bella. Since our kids were the same age, we crossed paths at their house for picnics, Little League games and Halloween parties over on South Street, where it was clear Will was a supporting cast member in a show Bella was running.

While Will wrote extensively in his column about the girls and their lives growing up, there were only occasional glimpses of Bella, and when there were, she insisted he not use her name.[13]

One day in October 2017, Will Doolittle came into my office and said he needed to talk to me.

After 18 years as editor, I

Early in 2017, Will Doolittle's wife Bella was diagnosed with early onset Alzheimer's. She was just 59 years old. By the fall, Will and Bella were doing a podcast called "The Alzheimer's Chronicles" in hopes of helping other families deal with the disease. Over the next three years, the couple chronicled the ups and downs of dealing with the disease as Bella got progressively worse. For three straight years, the podcast was honored by the Associated Press as one of the best in the state, and in 2018, Lee Enterprises honored Will and Bella with its "Spirit Award" (photograph courtesy of Will and Bella Doolittle).

knew the body language when someone didn't want to look me in the eye. I could tell it was bad news.

Will told me Bella, 59, had been diagnosed with early-onset Alzheimer's. He had been living with that news for eight months, but he had not said a word to anyone at work. That's not unusual in newsrooms where our own personal lives take a backseat to the news we put in the newspaper.

Will said they wanted to do a podcast about Alzheimer's. He admitted he didn't know how to do that, but they wanted to do something to make a difference for other couples in the same predicament.

The first column appeared on November 3, 2017, and served as an introduction to a podcast that initially dragged on too long with inferior sound quality. But it got better.

Will explained a year earlier Bella complained of being "mentally fuzzy." They went to see a neurologist who said the test results were "inconclusive." A second specialist said it was "Alzheimer's." Bella was one of those rare people suffering from the disease under the age of 65.[14]

Will wrote these jarring words:

> The doctor who delivered the diagnosis told Bella she had eight years left, based on the average. Other doctors have said the progression is unpredictable and can be much longer. But they all agree Alzheimer's is fatal and there is no cure.[15]

Bella called Will from the parking lot of the doctor's office, crying.

"I didn't have much to say," Will wrote.[16]

The man who had directed the coverage of so many difficult, pressing issues in our community, chronicling people's most painful life experiences was now volunteering to do the same about his own life with Bella by his side.

Will explained the point of the podcast was to talk about Alzheimer's and how it was affecting them as a couple.[17]

"Maybe we'll find some purpose in chronicling what we're going through," Will suggested in the first column. "We don't know."[18]

The Alzheimer's diagnosis definitively changed their lives. By December, Bella retired and money was tighter. Will started going home for lunch each day.

Will wrote this in the second column in November 2017:

> We wonder how long we have, how long before things get worse. But if and when more changes happen, will they be "worse"? Or will we be able to find our connection still, despite the different circumstances? Will there be something deeper in what we share, because we will it, because we have to work for it?
> We hope so. We don't know.[19]

Like a good reporter, Will explained what early-onset Alzheimer's was, how it affected their lives and the reality there was no cure. He said people often confused Alzheimer's with old age. The difference with Bella, he said, was not forgetfulness. It was that Bella's brain was under attack.

It was clear from the beginning that Will and Bella would be brutally honest about what was happening to them. At first it was about what was happening to Bella and the symptoms Will was seeing.

> Bella wants me to tell her when I notice she is being "Alzheimerish," but I struggle with that. Sometimes, I tell her she's repeating herself. But I don't point out the subtle differences in the way she acts just about all the time—that she is more jolly and forgiving; that her affection for her pets, always strong, is now overflowing; that she is more likely to agree with me now, and when she disagrees, is more likely to shrug it off; that the side of her that is nurturing and easygoing has taken over, while the side that was tough and demanding is all but gone.[20]

Between November 2017 and September 2020, the couple produced 26 podcasts with an accompanying column from Will as part of a regular update on how they were coping and how their lives and relationship were changing.

"I think it helps me more than it helps her," Will told me in September 2020. "Bella does it [the podcast], and I think it was true from the beginning, for my sake. I think she would be just as happy not to do it."[21]

The podcast is conversational and often includes the type of verbal good-natured jousting couples of that age are comfortable doing. Bella is honest and forthright and not afraid to push back when she disagrees with Will, but more often than not she digresses into conversations about her love of her dog and pet rabbit.

"I think it probably has a good therapeutic effect," Will said. "The two of us are in this together. It is a joint effort. A big part of living with Alzheimer's is that this is our life together. You have to be honest, or what would be the point of it. My hope for it is that it affects other people who are struggling with this same situation. I think both of us have accepted this as something where we attempt to bare our souls, and that is sort of the whole point, and that is going to make it worthwhile."[22]

In one podcast before Thanksgiving 2019, Will tried to steer the conversation toward what they had to be thankful for that year. The conversation veered into an incident at the supermarket where Bella had trouble paying for the groceries with her credit card. She insisted it was Will's fault because he had changed the PIN number without telling her.[23]

Will firmly corrected her: "No, that was the Alzheimer's."[24]

Bella, once again exerting her renowned life force, refused to accept the blame, telling Will, "You need to get your shit together."[25]

Will started to chuckle as he let it go, and they continued the conversation on another subject.[26]

"It is a very tricky balance," Will said about the podcasts. "I don't want it to always be about poor, poor pitiful me. That wouldn't work. There has to be a lot more there than this is hard. It is hard and I do want people to know that, but I want to have more of the flavor of what life is like. There is a lot more living with Alzheimer's than grief, frustration or struggle. That is one of the great things about doing it [the podcasts] over a long period of time. We communicate about our life that a lot of this is great."[27]

This business of telling people's stories—honestly and factually—often comes back to our own stories, our own lives and who we are, what we believe and what we see happening around us. There is great value to that because our readers can relate.

The best of those journalists bring a brutal honesty to that type of personal reporting. That doesn't sound good, but it is imperative to accurately tell the stories of everyday people.

I do fear, we too often hesitate in some small way when it comes to the truth. We are often afraid to go too far, to upset our readers or face some unintended accusation about bias, so we play it safe to make our lives a little easier professionally.

This was clearly not the case with Will and Bella. The great reporters and writers are not afraid of the truth, and they tell it without reservation. That is what our readers were seeing monthly with Will and Bella. It is even more extraordinary when it is a personal truth.

As each column, each month of experiences piled one on top of another, Will lamented how much their lives had changed in just one year. Bella's online shopping would deliver the same item more than once. Will gradually had to keep track of her medications, and Bella proposed getting a new one-floor home to better take care of her later. She also suggested Will get a girlfriend.

After graduating from the University at Albany, their daughter Zoe returned home to live with her parents. Will believed it was to help with Bella, but the two never said it to each other.[28]

In his December 2018 column, Bella asked Will if her symptoms were getting worse, and a frustrated Will was blunt: "You repeat things more. You lose track of what you're saying. You have a harder time keeping in mind what you're doing or finishing complicated tasks, like preparing a difficult recipe."[29]

Will wrote he believed the exchange was cruel, and that it was his way of venting annoyance at having to reassure Bella repeatedly that something was OK.[30]

"Witnessing the decline of your beloved companion, however, as I and many other caregivers do, is emotional torture administered in a few drops of bitterness each day," Will wrote in January 2019.

The column was often difficult to read, especially for Bella. Will said she often got quiet after reading his latest installment.[31]

"She says she's doing about as well as she was several months ago, and once recently when I said her symptoms have gotten worse, she said she wants me to stop telling her that," Will wrote.

I hoped our readers appreciated that commitment from Will and Bella during a time when "fake news" was a common accusation in the national conversation. Consider the bravery—and maybe the burden—it takes to recount the personal challenges, heartache and frustrations of their everyday life.

It was clear the goal was always to express a brutal honesty so the next couple down the road knows they are not alone.

As the columns continued, it was clear the disease was weighing more and more on Will. He wrote this in March 2018[32]:

> I do not have to work hard to keep her spirits up, but I do to keep my own up.
>
> I notice what she doesn't as the disease progresses. I notice the way the interval of forgetfulness gets shorter, so we will exchange the exact same sentences twice or three times within the same number of minutes.
>
> I notice how confused she can be if she wakes up in the night and how she sees things that aren't there.
>
> I notice the way her concerns are gradually narrowing down to a few familiar things—her family, her pets, her house.
>
> I know she won't be upset by reading in this column that her symptoms are worsening. She'll be upset by reading that this weighs on me—that I worry.[33]

There was a trip to Scotland in the summer of 2018, and Will chronicled his guilt when Bella got lost in the Edinburgh airport when he sent her ahead to the gate.[34]

"The challenge for me is to also enjoy the moment without allowing it to be soured by worries about the future or regrets over the ways I didn't prepare for something like this," Will wrote.[35]

Will could see himself changing, too:

> But I am more interested in saying "yes" these days to whatever gets suggested.
>
> Courage is another word for living in the moment, and Bella has always had a lot of that, while I've always had at least a normal amount of cowardice.
>
> But Alzheimer's is teaching me: Now is the only time, and what we choose to do now is the only choice we have.[36]

In August 2018, I nominated Will and Bella Doolittle for Lee Enterprises' "Spirit Award," recognizing outstanding personal commitment to the company.

"This recognition is for 'Spirit' within the company," I wrote in the nominating letter. "This commitment is far more than that."[37]

Will and Bella Doolittle were honored with a first place award for Best Podcast by the New York State Associated Press Association in June 2019 (photograph by Ken Tingley).

And then quoted directly from Will:

> But the dread of the worst of the decline hangs over you, and it's hard to put out of your mind, because the symptoms, even when they're mild are instant reminders.
>
> Not everyone who has Alzheimer's is able to admit what is happening, or is sensitive as Bella is, to what their spouse is going through.
>
> Looking at myself, I see someone obsessed with his ordeal, and I'm not even the one who has a fatal disease.
>
> Maybe success as an Alzheimer's caregiver comes in accepting failure. Your loved one will not recover. Your life will be changed. You will not handle this well.[38]

I told the leadership at Lee Enterprises, "I think they have handled it perfectly."[39]

While attending Lee's editor conference in Chicago that fall, I asked Lee's CEO Kevin Mowbray if he could include Bella's name on the inscription of the award. He agreed.

Mowbray told me when he announced the honor in a company-wide conference call, he hesitated about whether there should be applause.

"It didn't really seem like the kind of thing to applaud," Mowbray said.

It isn't, but it is, too.

It isn't really "Spirit" that Will and Bella have shown so much as heart, soul and a large dose of bravery that will help the next couple that comes after them.

When Will found out about the honor, he asked if it came with a cash prize. I told him it used to have a $5,000 reward, but not anymore. Another sign of the decline in the newspaper industry.

Not long afterward, Will wrote he believed the project had been a failure. Perhaps, the inspiration he was hoping to show was lost in the regular turmoil of their lives, or maybe it had just been a particularly bad day.

> This column itself is a failure—a failure to find the positive in our experience as I intended to do at first, a failure to affirm that life is good despite the hard things like this disease.
>
> The last time Bella read one of these columns, she stiffened as she reached the part where I get heavy and sad. Tears welled in her eyes.
>
> But she tossed the paper aside, and she waved her hand in front of her face. I could see her put aside the grief with an effort of will.
>
> "That's OK I don't care. That's fine," she said.
>
> She has always been so strong-minded, and she still can be sometimes. She has always been the strong one, and when that is not possible for her, I doubt it will be for me either.[40]

Yeah, it is OK to shed a tear reading the morning newspaper. That's journalism, too.

By the end of the second year, it was clear the disease was wearing on Will, but you couldn't tell by his demeanor at work, and you certainly could not tell by the quality of his writing. His column showed the life of a colleague we never saw.

"Now that two years have passed, I've experienced the way the symptoms accumulate, light as snow at first but piling up until each step forward takes an extra effort and each week is a little more tiring than the last."[41]

For those of us reading the column, we felt a little of that weight, too, just in smaller doses.

In December, after limping around the newsroom for months, Will had his hip replaced. He said he wanted to do it now while Bella was still OK.

Over the next summer, Bella's beloved dog Pepper died, but they adopted a puppy named Ringo.

Bella and Ringo happily went off on daily jaunts into the neighborhood that summer, often getting lost not far from the South Street house. Navigating the internet became impossible for Bella, and she regularly asked Will the same question repeatedly over shorter intervals of time.

In that September column, Will wrote, "This project, too—the Alzheimer's Chronicles—is a collection, gathering moments from our lives that show what is happening to us and how we're reacting to it. But I hope it is also a record of who Bella is, her facets and her edges, so they can be seen and appreciated before the disease wears them away."[42]

Bella's older daughter Ginny regularly listens to the podcast and reads Will's column. Zoe does sometimes, too, but Tam, the artist, told Will it is too hard for her.

"I want to do it [the podcast and column] as long as I feel it has something to offer," Will said. "The thing is, the situation is changing all the time."[43]

For three years in a row, "The Alzheimer's Chronicles" was named the best newspaper podcast by the New York State Associated Press Association. It earned a second place from the National Headliners Awards for journalistic innovation.[44] But most of all, it allowed Will and Bella to talk to each other like the old, committed couple they are, still trying to make a difference in the world and in their own relationship. Each conversation renewed their commitment to each other. That is the true force of nature here, a force maybe even larger than Bella.

And the fact they share their story with an entire community is remarkable.

In April of 2018, Will wrote this:

> We like our routine, because it gives us each time to do things we enjoy and also to spend hours together, not necessarily speaking but sitting with the heightened awareness of each other's presence that people have when they are saying goodbye.[45]

27

"We've got one
coming for you, *Post-Star*"

Elise Stefanik, Harvard-educated and not yet 30, was the fresh-faced kid on the political block in 2014.

She worked in the Bush White House as a policy adviser and helped Rep. Paul Ryan with debate preparation when he ran for vice president in 2012. She had powerful friends in Washington and plenty of money behind her.

During one early editorial board meeting with Will Doolittle and me, we asked her about her position on climate change. She claimed she wasn't a scientist. Earlier in the week, I had heard Rep. John Boehner say the exact same thing. Stefanik was repeating the latest Republican talking point.

"Come on, you went to Harvard," Doolittle said, challenging her.

But she didn't budge.

For Stefanik, like many of our recent representatives in Congress, this seemed like a short stop on the way to somewhere else.

Stefanik was elected to Congress in 2014, the youngest woman ever elected to Congress, then won reelection in 2016 as a moderate Republican who wanted to forge bipartisan legislation.

Her politics would change dramatically over the next two years.

Tedra Cobb, a longtime resident of Canton in the extreme northern end of the district near Canada, won the Democratic Party primary against four other rivals for the right to challenge Stefanik in the 2018 midterms.[1]

The day after the primary, the Stefanik campaign labeled Cobb with the nickname "Taxin Tedra" in a political advertisement. It was the type of juvenile pronouncement perfected by President Trump, and it didn't matter if the moniker had any basis in fact. It was going to be a long slog to Election Day, but I had an idea that might make a difference.

"What if we ask them not to lie?" I suggested to our editorial board members about the congressional candidates.

It was a novelty for modern-day politics.

The July 1, 2018, editorial started:

Congressional politics is the big leagues, where it gets ugly early and evil often.

The professional operatives and consultants craft messages of destruction without regard for morality or accuracy, and we wonder how they sleep at night.

To survive, you need the hide of a dinosaur.

To win, you have to be willing to go for the jugular, because all that matters in the

On his way with his wife to a craft show in downtown Glens Falls in June 2019, *Post-Star* editor Ken Tingley stopped by an anti–Trump protest at Centennial Circle where he encountered a pro–Trump demonstrator, Mike Kibling (left), embroiled in a heated exchange with Sara Carpenter (right). Kibling would be at the center of the contentious downtown protests for the rest of the year (photograph by Ken Tingley).

mud-slinging, tweet-shaming world of professional politics these days is getting one more vote than the other person, and it doesn't matter who you hurt along the way.

If that means ruining their reputation, so be it.

If that means staring straight into the eyes of every man, woman and child in the district and telling an occasional bald-faced lie, that's in the job description.

This is a blood sport, and like it or not, the 21st Congressional District is no different.[2]

It was a simple argument of right vs. wrong that had resonated with voters a year earlier during the email scandal in Queensbury.

We appealed to the humanity of the candidates and the greater good of the voters as we asked the candidates to commit to one overriding principle over the next four months: "We ask them not to lie."

But this was a new era of congressional politics built on a foundation of lies.

Cobb submitted a letter to the editor, saying she would take the pledge.[3] The editorial board never heard from Rep. Stefanik.

Two weeks later, reporter Michael Goot reached out to her campaign to find out whether she vowed not to lie. Her statement was not from her but one of her campaign officials: "Of course Congresswoman Stefanik has overwhelmingly earned the trust of her constituents who re-elect her with a record margin. Congresswoman Stefanik is proud of her record of real results for her district."[4]

There was no pledge to be truthful, only an acknowledgment that her supporters believed what she said. The question remained unanswered.

More shocking to me, when we conducted a totally unscientific poll on our website, 80 percent of the 100 or so readers who responded said they believed the candidates should not lie during the campaign. Did that mean the other 20 percent believed it was OK if they did?[5]

Just after our editorial board asked Stefanik not to lie, a video surfaced on the website "Democrat Tracking" on July 9, showing a recording from a "Teens for Tedra" event at a private residence. Cobb was shown saying she could not come out publicly for banning certain types of assault weapons because it would cost her votes in the conservative district.[6]

It soon appeared in a television ad claiming Cobb was against Second Amendment rights, a death knell in the rural North Country of upstate New York.

Reporter Goot found out the recording was made by a 17-year-old from a nearby Albany suburb who was a senior in high school.[7]

The next day, Goot learned Preston Scagnelli was paid nearly $1,000 by the National Republican Congressional Committee to track candidates. The political disclosure forms from the NRCC disclosed that Scagnelli was paid $970.57 for "research materials consulting." A member at the NRCC said that Scagnelli was recruited.[8]

Our editorial board was disgusted that a professional politician used a teenager to spy on an opponent. The editorial board characterized it as "dirty and unseemly."[9]

During a meeting with the editorial board, Rep. Stefanik confirmed the young man worked as an unpaid intern for her, then said he had done nothing wrong.[10]

"We find that disturbing, and fear our congresswoman has spent too much time in Washington, D.C. and lost any sense of what is right and what is wrong when it comes to the political wars," the editorial said. "Earlier this year, we asked the candidates in the congressional campaign not to lie. It turns out lying is the least of the problems."[11]

After the email scandal in Queensbury in 2017, the Warren County Republicans adopted a policy against individuals misrepresenting themselves to spy on a candidate. They still endorsed Stefanik in 2018 and 2020.[12]

On October 28, 2018, *The Post-Star* editorial board endorsed Cobb by a 4–2 vote, expressing disgust at how Stefanik ran her campaign with misleading ads and spying.[13]

Stefanik won reelection in resounding fashion with 56 percent of the vote. Cobb received 41 percent.[14] It was one of the few bright spots in the midterm elections for Republicans, and it was about to propel Stefanik to greater stardom within Trump's orbit.

My wife wanted to go to the craft show downtown. It was June 2019, and I wanted to see the 20-foot-tall Trump chicken that was promised for the protest. It's not often you see a giant chicken balloon in downtown Glens Falls.

The Lower Adirondack Regional Arts Council holds its annual arts and crafts festival each June downtown. It's one of those throwback small-town events worthy of Bedford Falls. Hundreds of white tents stretch from one end of City Park to the other as artisans from all over the region descend on Glens Falls to sell their hand-made jewelry, artwork and farm-made products. Parts of Bay Road and Maple Street were closed so the Rotary Club and Kiwanis could sell freshly squeezed lemonade and funnel cakes while people browsed between the rows of tents. This is the family face of Glens Falls.

We also reported in the Saturday newspaper a political rally was scheduled at the five-way intersection known as Centennial Circle, just around the corner from the craft festival. It was part of the national "Impeach Trump National Day of Action."[15]

Over the years, there had been small protests—usually fewer than ten people—in the proximity of the local congressperson's office downtown, no matter who was in office. Recently, it was a group of liberal Democrats demonstrating in front of Rep. Stefanik's office. It never caused much of a fuss.

As my wife and I walked down Broad Street past St. Mary's School, we could see a crowd gathered around the five-way intersection with the 20-foot chicken prominently displayed.

It was 12:15 p.m. on June 15, 2019.[16]

The crowd chanted anti–Trump slogans but smiled and seemed to be having fun in the sunshine.

On a small pedestrian island halfway between the part of Glen Street that feeds into the road toward South Glens Falls, there were a half-dozen Trump supporters wearing red MAGA hats and waving Trump banners. They were separated from the other group by about 15 feet with cars regularly passing between them.[17]

I crossed over Broad Street to take photographs. A man held up a sign, "Impeach Trump Now," in front of the big chicken. On the bottom right corner of the sign was pasted our editorial from that morning criticizing Rep. Stefanik for voting against legislation that would have forced the attorney general and White House counsel to testify before Congress. The man smiled as I took his photo.

Another sign was of more concern. It read: "Impeach the motherf*cker."

It was the type of language previously considered unacceptable in most small communities like Glens Falls, even in political discourse.

It is not often you see a giant Trump chicken in downtown Glens Falls. While protesters gathered in support of #Impeach Trump National Day of Action on June 15, 2019, *The Post-Star* had published an editorial that week criticizing local Congresswoman Elise Stefanik for not supporting the rule of law when she voted against a measure that would have required the attorney general and White House counsel to answer a subpoena from Congress. This protester attached the editorial to his sign with the message "Party Politics must end!" (photograph by Ken Tingley).

None of the protesters appeared especially angry as I strolled through the crowd, until I got to the island where the pro–Trump protesters had staked a claim.

I noticed a man and woman screaming at each other.[18]

The woman was older with gray hair and glasses, holding a sign that read "My husband's CHEMO $12,000 a month." Her name was Sara Carpenter, and her husband had cancer.[19]

The man was stocky with a white shirt and jeans and a red MAGA hat turned backward. He waved a large Trump flag. His name was Mike Kibling.

Carpenter poured out a steady stream of invective. At times, she looked menacing.[20] As I shot video, it occurred to me I had seen this scene before on the evening news. But this was Glens Falls. This was Hometown, USA, where a couple of months earlier the community had rallied around the bandstand at City Park to honor Glens Falls' state championship boys basketball team. That's the type of community gatherings we usually had.[21]

This was different.

This could get violent.[22]

When Trump ran for president in 2016, Rep. Stefanik initially distanced herself, saying she would support whoever was the "Republican nominee." When Trump was nominated, she passed up attending the national convention in Cleveland and refrained from saying his name in public.

By 2019, she had emerged as a head-over-heels fanatic for the president. During one House Intelligence Committee hearing the previous fall, she took on Democratic Chairman Adam Schiff in an exchange that went national and got Trump's attention.

Trump hailed her as "a new Republican star."[23] She was named one of the House members of Trump's Impeachment Defense Team during the first Senate impeachment trial,[24] then a co-leader of Trump's reelection campaign in New York. She later had a prime speaking slot at the national convention in 2020.[25]

Our editorial board was dismayed by Stefanik's continued desire to bring Washington politics to all those friendly front porches in Glens Falls. I repeatedly expressed my own concerns about the congresswoman putting party politics before national and local issues.

In a column just before the midterm election in 2018, I wrote that Rep. Stefanik had completed the transformation from idealistic leader of promise to seasoned politician of position.[26]

"The professionals that groomed her have beaten the truth and trust right out of her because those qualities are no longer considered important in the current political landscape," I wrote.[27]

The rally with the Trump chicken was the beginning of six months of unrest in Glens Falls in 2019. Two weeks after the initial protest, the reporter who covered it, Kathleen Phalen-Tomaselli, told me she was concerned about one of the Trump protesters.

Phalen-Tomaselli, now in her 60s, was originally hired from the *Rutland Herald* as a feature writer, left us to write a book, then returned as a news reporter. She was a gifted writer and photographer who still did some of our best feature writing. In another sign of the times, she was also the only reporter who worked Saturdays, often covering two or three stories during a shift.

Kibling, the man waving the Trump flag while arguing with Sara Carpenter about her husband's chemotherapy, criticized Phalen-Tomaselli in a Facebook post shortly after her story ran.[28]

"She is a biased reporter. If the story isn't exciting enough for her or if the story favors a side that she doesn't agree with, she wrote whatever pops into her head that fits her agenda. She would do well working with fake news outlets."[29]

It was the type of comment we usually ignored, but after the *Capital Gazette* shooting a year earlier, it was Kibling's next post that Phalen-Tomaselli found frightening: "I'm so sick of MOTHERFUCKING MEXICANS crossing the border that I want to set up a 50 cal and just start wasting them," Kibling wrote. "There is only 1 alternative. Start wasting them like dogs in the street, men women and children alike. It's a necessary evil. They will get the message very quickly and may decide they have a better chance against thugs and drug dealers than pissed-off Americans."[30]

It was an example of the anger bubbling up at Trump rallies in Glens Falls. This was two years before rioters stormed the Capitol.

As Rep. Stefanik embraced Trumpism, we embraced fact-checks that exposed the half-truths and outright lies in national politics and then local politics. That brought further charges of "bias" against us at the newspaper. My colleagues at other newspapers saw the same thing.

At the next protest, Phalen-Tomaselli sought out the leaders of the pro–Trump group to get their side of the story.[31] Instead, she found herself a target of verbal abuse and accusations the newspaper was biased.

In a blog post later, Phalen-Tomaselli said she felt "uncomfortable."[32] "I have been in lots of dicey situations in my career, but in today's unpredictable and volatile climate, it is disconcerting to be a lone reporter in the mid–60s amidst shouting, angry men, especially when some of the shouting is directed at me," she wrote in her blog.[33]

During a protest on immigration outside Rep. Stefanik's office on August 8, six anti–Stefanik protesters entered the lobby of her office and asked to speak with her. Stefanik was in Washington at the time. The protesters demanded to talk by phone with Stefanik. Instead, they were told the office was immediately closing and that the police had been called.[34]

The six were arrested for trespassing.[35]

In a September 6 editorial, we asked Rep. Stefanik to drop the charges against what we called the "Glens Falls 6" after seeing a photograph of the group.[36]

"We don't want the 'Glens Falls 6' to take offense, but they were a little beyond middle age, and frankly, they didn't look dangerous to us," we wrote in the editorial. In the photo from an earlier court appearance, the six looked more like 1960s hippies than any threat to the safety of anyone in Stefanik's office. We compared what we do at the newspaper when readers walk in the door with a complaint: "We talk to them."[37]

Our political discourse had descended into Rep. Stefanik arresting grandparents.

In September, tensions escalated further.

The two opposing protest groups were regularly invading each other's space downtown. The Trump supporters were using bullhorns to drown out chants from the other side. Four-letter words flew around downtown, people were spit on and some of the outdoor cafe workers told Phalen-Tomaselli "off the record" there had been a reduction in business.[38]

The Albany *Times Union* described one September rally this way: "Two mundane political demonstrations devolved into a tense, profanity-laced powder keg when they literally came face to face Friday outside U.S. Rep. Elise Stefanik's Glens Falls office."[39]

The liberal protesters said they feared for their safety and suggested the flag poles the Trump supporters were waving be banned because they could be used as weapons. Two years later, we saw that at the U.S. Capitol.[40]

After reporting the concerns about safety, this comment was sent to us:

"It's only gonna get worse because the liberals can't handle the truth and the truth is they're losing 2 to 1 and the fake news isn't being honest. Wait until me and my friends start to show up. That's when muscle overcomes nerdy ideas. See you soon Democrats."[41]

I read it as a threat for violence.

In an attempt to avoid further confrontations, the liberal group moved its protests around the corner to City Park. Accompanied by police officers, they walked peaceably the two blocks to Stefanik's office and stayed on the opposite side of the street. The Trump group, mostly middle-aged men, ran up and down the street shouting obscenities at them.

"I thought it was one step from actual violence," Phalen-Tomaselli wrote me in an email.[42]

On Friday, October 4, I received a phone call from Glens Falls Mayor Dan Hall asking if I could come to City Hall.

On Saturday, October 5, 2019, protesters again gathered in downtown Glens Falls to taunt each other with opposing political messages. After taunting and repeatedly insulting *Post-Star* reporter Kathleen Phalen-Tomaselli through a bullhorn, Mike Kibling pointed a toy gun at her and bellowed, "We've got one coming for you, *Post-Star.*" Later that week, Representative Elise Stefanik invited Kibling to her town hall meeting in nearby Kingsbury (*Post-Star* photograph by Kathleen Phalen-Tomaselli).

When I arrived, a group of city officials were holed up in a conference room on the second floor. Included was Mayor Hall, Chief of Police Tony Lydon, the city lawyer, the assistant mayor and councilwoman Jane Reid. They told me police had been monitoring Facebook posts, and one of the pro–Trump groups was asking its members to come to the rally the next day with unloaded weapons as a show of support for the Second Amendment.

The bigger concern for city officials was there was a professional hockey game at the Civic Center that evening. Fans and families would have to walk through Centennial Circle while men with rifles protested.

They wanted my advice on what to do.

I told them bluntly they had to make the information public.

"Thank you," Reid said with a hint of exasperation.

I told them the newspaper would immediately put the information online and get a story in the newspaper the next day.[43]

Phalen-Tomaselli covered the rally the next day. There were only a handful of Trump supporters, and there was only one visible weapon.[44]

Kibling, who once wrote about gunning down Mexicans on the border and argued passionately with Sara Carpenter back on June 15, was carrying a ridiculous-looking orange toy gun.[45]

Phalen-Tomaselli said it may have been a Nerf Blaster that looked like a brightly colored machine gun.[46]

When Kibling saw Phalen-Tomaselli standing across the street taking photographs, he cocked the gun twice, held it up in the air and shouted through a bullhorn, "Here *Post-Star* is my unloaded rifle. Here is my 10-round clip."[47]

He continued to scream profanities with a barrage of "fake news" epithets before he finally turned toward Phalen-Tomaselli, lifted the fake gun and pointed it directly at her face while calling out her name.[48]

"Here, Tomaselli, you are a fake reporter," he screamed. "Tomaselli is a liberal fake reporter."[49]

All the while, the toy gun was pointed at her face while she kept taking photos.[50]

Kibling then screamed into his bullhorn: "We've got one coming for you, *Post-Star.*"[51]

Phalen-Tomaselli posted the photos with her blog, and we ran the photo of Kibling pointing the toy gun on the bottom of the front page, along with the threat from Kibling.[52]

"I hope that shocks you," I wrote in my column afterward. "I hope these events outrage you, because they are happening right here in Glens Falls."[53]

I wrote about the 50 men and women who work at the newspaper and had families. Many had nothing to do with writing or editing the news, and yet they had been threatened, too. I described to our readers what they were feeling:

I believe they are a little nervous today.

They want to know who this man is making threats against the business where they work.

They want to know if they should be worried.

They have husbands, wives and children.

I wonder how many of our readers go to work wondering if someone is going to show up with a weapon like they did at the *Capital Gazette* last year.

That's the world we live in these days, as reporters and editors continue to do an honest day's work serving this community.[54]

Two days later, Kibling, the guy who had made the threats against the newspaper with his toy gun, wrote on Facebook a member of Rep. Stefanik's staff had called on him to pack Stefanik's town hall meeting with supporters that Friday in nearby Kingsbury.[55]

Kibling said that Alex deGrasse, Stefanik's campaign manager, had sent his appreciation on behalf of Elise for holding down her Glens Falls office from the "invasion of socialists and commies."[56]

Kibling posted it all on Facebook.

"She is asking us to all be part of this town hall meeting to show our support for her and our President. This is going to be a media bloodbath with CNN, MSNBC, Fox News and many other media outlets present," Kibling wrote. "She is asking us to show up early to secure all the seating inside the fire station so that the fake news reporters will only capture supporters clapping and cheering as she announces her accomplishments, ideas and future plans."[57]

When I heard the news about Kibling, I immediately sent an email to Rep. Stefanik's director of communications:

> I am shocked that Rep. Stefanik would join forces and give legitimacy to Mike Kibling after his widely reported threats against *The Post-Star* and one of our female reporters this past weekend.
>
> Those threats have made many of the men and women who work at our newspaper— from receptionist to obit clerks to those in our advertising department—nervous about their safety. Considering the times we live in and the *Capital Gazette* shooting from a year ago, we are appalled that the congresswoman has given this bully credibility and support.
>
> I hope she will denounce the actions of her campaign manager and renounce any affiliation with this man.
>
> I would also urge her to make a visit to our newspaper to explain to the regular workers with families why she has put them in danger.
>
> She may not agree with the criticisms we have made about her stands on the issues but this has put people at our newspaper in danger and is not right.
>
> Ken Tingley
> Editor
> *The Post-Star*[58]

Diane Kennedy, president of the New York News Publishers Association, immediately reacted.

"Rep. Stefanik should cut ties with the political activist who threatened a *Post-Star* reporter and the newspaper's staff, and publicly condemn threats against journalists," Kennedy wrote.[59]

I never heard from Rep. Stefanik or anyone on her staff.

The next day, I attended her town hall meeting at the firehouse in Kingsbury where Kibling and his group were holding down several rows of seats near the front.

Stefanik never addressed the specific threats against *The Post-Star* during the meeting.

She never visited any of the men and women who work at our newspaper.

In my column on Friday, the day of her town hall meeting, the headline read "Stefanik backs bullies."[60]

Rep. Stefanik has given him the green light to shout more profanities and take his actions to the next level in the name of a government representative.
This is now Rep. Stefanik's responsibility.
This is on her.
This is not about politics, this is about supporting violence and dividing Hometown, USA further.[61]

Once again it was the readers who came out in our defense with their outrage. At first it was encouraging, then it became inspirational in a series of emails[62]:

- "Thank you for being a strong and courageous voice in our community."
- "I am grateful every day to have *The Post-Star*."
- "I am keeping you all in my prayers for your safety and continued courage in your coverage of the news, despite the very real threats you've endured recently."
- "We are in such a sad time. Thank you for getting the facts out to the community."
- "We appreciate your brave support of the North County and our democracy."

I posted more than a dozen of the emails on the bulletin board in our newsroom.
"The emails, letters and comments have been a consistent stream and have helped to drown out any criticism about our work," I wrote in my column October 19. "Knowing this community, it is not surprising to hear such articulate responses to the difficult times we are going through. That's what makes this community great. We are all in this together."[63]

Three weeks later, the city held a public meeting as it considered guidelines for downtown protests. Most of the regular protesters filled the Common Council chambers, and the pro–Trump group said the newspaper made up the story about the plan to bring unloaded guns to the rally. Neither the mayor nor anyone on the Common Council acknowledged the information came from city police.[64]

When the hearing was over at City Hall and most of the protesters had filed out, Councilwoman Jane Reid thanked the newspaper for its "courageous" reporting on the issue.[65]

It was greatly appreciated. It would have been nicer if it had been said before most of the public left.

After the election in 2020, Rep. Stefanik signed on to a Texas lawsuit that contested the presidential election in multiple states and continued to support President Trump.[66]

On January 4, 2021, Rep. Stefanik told constituents in an open letter she planned to object to certifying Joe Biden's victories in Pennsylvania, Michigan, Georgia and Wisconsin.[67]

On January 6, a mob of Trump supporters stormed the Capitol in an attempt to disrupt the certification of the election by Congress. Many used flag poles to beat the police defending the building.[68]

After reconvening that evening, Rep. Stefanik addressed the chamber and objected to the Pennsylvania election results where she made a false claim about Georgia's voter verification and amplified baseless allegations about illegal ballot-counting in Michigan. She was one of 147 Republicans to vote against certifying Biden's electoral votes in at least one state. But after the violence, Stefanik only objected to Pennsylvania and voted to certify Biden's win in Arizona.[69]

"My constituents support me in that objection," Stefanik told *Fox and Friends* the next morning.[70]

But Aaron Cerbone of the *Adirondack Daily Enterprise* reported not all of her constituents did.[71]

That same morning, a group of activists delivered a letter to Stefanik's Plattsburgh office criticizing her objections to the election. It was signed by more than 1,700 residents of the district.[72]

Later that spring, Rep. Stefanik seized an opportunity when Rep. Liz Cheney continued to criticize Republican lies about election fraud. When Rep. Cheney was ousted from her Republican leadership position, Rep. Stefanik was chosen to replace her as the third-ranking GOP member in the House.

In a fact check by CNN in May 2021, Daniel Dale found she had made false claims about the votes in the Atlanta area, alluded to false claims about Dominion Voting Systems, made false claims about Georgia's voter verification procedures and amplified baseless claims about ballots in Michigan.[73]

On that same day, *The Washington Post* columnist Greg Sargent not only pointed out she was promoting the big lie about election fraud, but something else: "But another crucial credential, one getting less attention, is Stefanik's willingness to deceive her own constituents to justify taking official action to invalidate legitimate election results."[74]

We had been seeing it for years.

28

The Last Year

By December 2018, President Trump's "fake news" mantra had trickled down into the vocabulary of local politicians, while the comments and emails from our readers often accused us of bias and partisanship. Earlier in the year, five newspaper employees were killed at the *Capital Gazette* newspaper in suburban Maryland by a disgruntled reader.

It had been a difficult year for journalists.

I wrote at the time: "It often felt like I was on the front lines of a war where truth was being held hostage."[1]

When our staff talked about the *Capital Gazette* shootings, we recounted instances of our own harassment. Over the years, we had received death threats, been told in emails "they" were coming to "get us," and earlier that year, someone wrapped our newspaper in dog feces and left it on the front step.

What I ultimately realized was the complaints and compliments we received over the years in letters, emails, phone calls and office visits were a daily conversation that questioned our choices on one hand and encouraged our work on the other. Our readers repeatedly told us what they loved and what they hated. It's what made the work so difficult, but also so rewarding.

By the end of 2018, the conversation had changed.

Previously, there had always been a mutual respect. That was gone now. This was something uglier.

The charges of "fake news" were the latest, more insidious incarnation of what had always been there in political subtext. There were many in our community who saw us as the enemy and often accused us of outright lies. The colleagues I talked to at other newspapers were seeing the same thing.

But as was so often the case during the 21 years I was editor of my little community newspaper, it was a reader who lifted me up.

It was the day after Christmas 2018, and our receptionist told me there was a woman who wanted to see me.[2]

I was busy and expected she had a complaint, but as was the case more often than not over the years, when someone demanded to see the editor, I got up to face the music. It was part of the job.

"You've been at the newspaper a long time," the woman began.[3]

"Thirty years," I answered.[4]

She hesitated, her eyes darting left and right as if concerned someone might overhear her in the lobby. She paused again, seemingly struggling to find the words.[5]

"Your articles give me hope," she said staring back at me.[6]

I was at first relieved, then speechless.

It was a reminder why so many of us are in the news business; why we remain committed in the face of adversity, and of course it reminded me of the power of the printed word. We may not be changing the world every day, but giving our readers a little hope is a good place to start.

It reminded me of the dozens and dozens of readers during the course of a year who reach out with a letter to the editor, an encouraging word on the phone or a pat on the back, telling us how much they appreciate the work and the effort.

Sometimes they walk through the front door, too.

I thanked the woman for making my day; heck, I thanked her for making my year. I told her it had buoyed me to face 2019.

Little did I know it would be my last year.

Kathleen Moore was a veteran reporter in her 30s who we hired in July 2015 from *The Daily Gazette* in Schenectady, a larger newspaper about an hour's drive south of Glens Falls.

She was a Joe Friday, "just-the-facts, ma'am" type of reporter who wasn't afraid to stand up for what was right and dig deep into a story. More importantly, she showed little if any ego and was always willing to correct a mistake.

Two years earlier while covering the Town Board in Moreau, board members accused her of making up quotes after the Town Board criticized a youth sports organization.[7]

The town supervisor said she was "fake news."[8]

The only problem was the Town Board tape-recorded all its meetings. Moore went back to the recording, found the quotes to refute the allegations and the editorial board responded with a rare front-page editorial titled "'Fake news' claims have no merit."[9] We were tired of the unwarranted accusations against the media that had become so common in 2019 and responded:

> When we make a mistake, we correct it publicly.
> We now expect the Moreau Town Board members to do the same.
> They have maligned one of our reporters in a public meeting.
> They have attacked the reputation of our newspaper and the dozens of men and women who work here.
> Anyone can make a mistake.
> Anyone can say something stupid in the heat of the moment.
> But the difference between those with character and those without it is their willingness to admit when they are wrong.[10]

The Moreau Town Board never admitted it was wrong. It never apologized to Moore or anyone else at the newspaper.

That same year, Moore was at the Town Board meeting in Queensbury when councilman Doug Irish said the newspaper reporting was "akin to fiction."

She was also on the front lines throughout the ensuing email scandal in Queensbury, but what was to come next would test her more than any previous story.

For at least 20 years, the local nonprofit community hospital had complained about its newspaper coverage. The hospital was a community institution—like the newspaper—and the region's largest employer. It was also a newspaper advertiser.

Hospital officials were often secretive and careful about information they released to the newspaper. They demanded that reporters get permission from hospital officials before visiting a patient for a story so they could be accompanied by a staff member. The policy sometimes reached levels of absurdity, such as when our reporter did the annual story on the first baby born on New Year's Day. The hospital did not trust the newspaper, and although we didn't understand why, we had learned to live with it.

Over the years, the hospital would periodically pull its advertising over some perceived slight. Publisher Rick Emanuel twice called meetings to mend fences with hospital officials. The first meeting with the new CEO Dianne Shugrue devolved into a heated argument in the newspaper's conference room between Shugrue and Will Doolittle about the hospital's secret ways.

After the meeting, Emanuel demanded I fire Doolittle. I argued Doolittle had not done anything wrong and that the argument helped clear the air. Emanuel later met with Doolittle and made it clear his job was at risk.

During the second of the two meetings with the hospital, just before Emanuel left as publisher, I asked one of the hospital vice presidents when the animosity from the newspaper began.

"During the early 1990s," he said. That was 25 years earlier.

I pointed out there were only two newsroom employees still working at the newspaper from the early 1990s. One was our current sports editor, Greg Brownell, and the other was me when I was sports editor. I wondered aloud how we managed to pass on this animosity from one generation of employees to the next.

Shugrue seemed stunned.

Things improved for a while, but the hospital eventually returned to its secret ways.

At the start of 2019, Kathleen Moore had taken on a health care beat that included the hospital. She also had several municipal beats. Because of reduced staffing, she was a busy reporter.

She never had a chance to build a relationship with the hospital. Sometimes, it is not the reporter a source doesn't trust but the newspaper or the entire journalism profession as a whole. That was becoming more and more common by 2019.

The hospital had decades of mistrust baked into management. Moore had been at the paper just three years.

On January 28, 2019, Moore reported Glens Falls Hospital had laid off 25 people and closed two units that provided outpatient services.[11]

Hospital officials would not give a reason for the closures or layoffs and at first didn't even want to say how many people had lost their jobs.[12] This type of secrecy was not new.

A few days later, Glens Falls Hospital's vice president for planning Tracy Mills contacted me about having a meeting between the newspaper's seven-member editorial board and hospital CEO Dianne Shugrue. Mills's one condition was that Moore could not attend. She would not say why.

The meeting on February 12 was productive and newsworthy. Shugrue revealed the hospital had been experiencing financial difficulty, saying it had lost about $12,000,000 in 2017 and a little bit more in 2018.[13] She acknowledged patient volume in the Emergency Department had fallen by 4,000 the previous year, diagnostic X-ray procedures were down 7,000 and surgeries were off 2,000 over the past three years.[14] She said they were planning an invitation-only forum the next month with community leaders to explain the challenges ahead.[15] She said "the hospital's survival cannot be taken for granted."[16]

Near the end of the meeting, Connie Bosse, one of our citizen representatives on the editorial board, asked a question about the hospital's financial losses. She had found information online that Glens Falls Hospital had lost more than $30,000,000 in 2017.[17] Shugrue shrugged it off as a one-time accounting write-off that was not relative.

Back at the office, Will Doolittle did more digging on Bosse's information and reported this about the $30,000,000 loss: "The American Hospital Directory, a website that collects data from public and private sources to compile hospital profiles, reports that in 2017, Glens Falls Hospital recorded a more than $30 million loss on gross revenue of more than $1.1 billion."[18]

The hospital spokesperson told Doolittle the loss was associated with a one-time system conversion but gave no other details. We still did not know the significance of the loss.[19]

In a Sunday editorial, the editorial board expressed concern about the hospital's finances and applauded Shugrue for talking openly about the problem.[20] We were trying to go the extra mile and have a better working relationship.

On Friday, March 1, about 60 community leaders turned out to hear Shugrue's message. In an elaborate PowerPoint presentation, she repeated much of the information she had given the editorial board and added that the hospital had lost $18,000,000 in 2018.[21] In the meeting with the editorial board, she said the hospital had lost "a little bit more" than the $12,000,000 it lost in 2017. The $18,000,000 was a lot more than "a little bit more."

Shugrue told those assembled—a mixture of

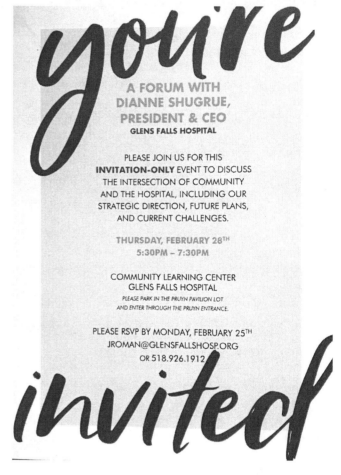

A FORUM WITH DIANNE SHUGRUE, PRESIDENT & CEO
GLENS FALLS HOSPITAL

PLEASE JOIN US FOR THIS **INVITATION-ONLY** EVENT TO DISCUSS THE INTERSECTION OF COMMUNITY AND THE HOSPITAL, INCLUDING OUR STRATEGIC DIRECTION, FUTURE PLANS, AND CURRENT CHALLENGES.

THURSDAY, FEBRUARY 28TH
5:30PM – 7:30PM

COMMUNITY LEARNING CENTER
GLENS FALLS HOSPITAL
PLEASE PARK IN THE PRUYN PAVILION LOT AND ENTER THROUGH THE PRUYN ENTRANCE.

PLEASE RSVP BY MONDAY, FEBRUARY 25TH
JROMAN@GLENSFALLSHOSP.ORG
OR 518.926.1912

After Glens Falls Hospital officials met with *The Post-Star* editorial board to talk about its finances in late January, hospital officials sent out an invitation to community leaders to meet with CEO Dianne Shugrue on Thursday, February 28. At that meeting she described the hospital's finances as "dire" (Glens Falls Hospital Invitation provided by author).

politicians, business owners and hospital staff—the hospital was going to have to cut back on services that brought in less revenue.

"Hospitals close every day," Shugrue said. "Why am I pounding that home? People think the hospital will be here. We gotta figure out how to make ends meet. Hospitals close. We don't want to be one of them."[22]

The message was chilling, yet from my seat in the room, it did not appear the audience members were concerned.

After the presentation, I asked Shugrue if the situation was "dire."

"Yes," she said, "it is dire."[23]

I was startled at her bluntness, so I asked it again.

"You would describe it as dire?"

This time she nodded.[24]

There was a bigger story here. Glens Falls Hospital was not the only medical facility under systemic fiscal duress because of its dependence on Medicare payments instead of the more lucrative commercial insurance, but there was the unexplained $30,000,000 loss Shugrue failed to address in the forum or at the meeting with the editorial board.

A tip from a reader suggested problems with the hospital's billing system caused long delays in bills being processed while some were never processed at all.

After the February meeting with the hospital and the invitation-only forum, Moore asked the hospital for its financial records for the past five years.

They did not respond.[25]

While it is understandable for any business to be skittish about revealing its finances, this was a community hospital, and the entire community had a stake in its success. On her own, Moore found the financial reports for 2014, 2015 and 2016 but had no information on 2017 and 2018.

From the hospital's 2016 IRS filings she found the hospital had made money— $2,900,000 in 2016—and given out $1,150,000 in bonuses. Shugrue received a bonus of $94,531 on top of her salary of $539,266. The spending was curious, considering the enormous losses on the horizon.[26]

Two days later, Moore unloaded a startling piece of news after the hospital provided its audited financials from 2012 through 2017 and its IRS filings for 2014 through 2017:

> GLENS FALLS—A new billing system at Glens Falls Hospital malfunctioned in 2017, costing the hospital $38 million, according to an audit.[27]

It was a staggering number.

While CEO Shugrue previously reported the hospital's biggest long-term problem was its high number of less lucrative Medicare cases, it appeared it was this billing failure that led to the financial disaster in 2017.[28]

The hospital refused to comment to Moore.

According to the audit, the bills for $38,000,000 worth of health care were sent out very late or not at all to programs such as Medicare and then were not paid because of "lack of timeliness."[29] Commercial insurance companies often refuse to pay bills sent three to six months after a procedure, while Medicare allowed longer.

Moore reported the system was installed in November 2016 but continued to malfunction throughout 2017 and wasn't fully functional until June 2018.[30]

Two employees at the hospital, who asked to remain anonymous because they were not authorized to speak to a reporter, told Moore that several months of bills could not be sent out at all because of the problems with the new software. The hospital leaders kept changing their story about the finances and never explained why it took so long to address the problem.[31]

"There has always been times when people won't talk to you," Moore told me in September 2020. "Plenty of times when I find something in a document and someone says, 'Oh yeah,' and it's clear they just forgot about that, but they [hospital officials] were deliberately trying to get me to report the wrong thing. It was really staggering."[32]

This was the newspaper performing community service.

This was a reporter digging into an issue and refusing to be deterred.

Glens Falls Hospital responded, not by calling Moore with an explanation, but by buying a full-page ad in the Sunday newspaper that never mentioned the billing fiasco.

On Monday, Glens Falls Hospital's vice president for planning Tracy Mills notified *The Post-Star*'s circulation manager Tom Salvo that the hospital would no longer distribute free copies of the newspaper at the hospital. "Please stop delivery," she wrote to Salvo.[33] She made sure to copy me on the email.

These were "free" sponsored copies of the newspaper for the benefit of the patients and their families.

In one sense, it was petty payback to our continued reporting that would cost the newspaper a few thousand dollars a month, but Moore wondered if they were trying to make it more difficult for hospital employees to see the coverage.[34]

Further reporting by Moore confirmed the billing problems persisted for more than 20 months. Doctors and workers at the hospital told Moore the system went "live" long before it could handle all the billing needed for the many entities run by the hospital.[35]

Many hospital employees were coming forward to tell the same story about the problem. Many feared for their jobs if their identities were revealed.

"I've had adversarial relationships before, but nothing like this," Moore said. "They had a board member call me and ask to be an unnamed source that Medicaid and Medicare [reimbursements] were the problem. I completely believed that. Why would someone intentionally try to mislead me off the record?[36]

"I read that story [about the February community forum] now and cringe," Moore said. "They changed their story a lot. They were just liars."[37]

Reporters do not make good politicians, and Moore was reporting accurately the hospital administration's behavior.

The most important question was why the problem had festered so long.

When Moore asked that question, Mills said she would take questions by email only, but after Moore sent the questions, Mills did not respond. As is the standard for any news story, the reporter tried to get both sides. If there is no response, the reporter must tell the reader she tried to get a response. It was something I insisted upon. Moore included that information in the fourth paragraph of the story.

Back at the office, Brian Corcoran, the longtime financial guy who had been named interim publisher that month, reviewed the story—which was unusual considering it was not flagged by the editors as being controversial or having any legal issues—and demanded the fourth paragraph be deleted.[38]

The paragraph read:

Hospital Vice President of Planning Tracy Mills said she would review by email any questions for this story, but after questions were emailed to her, she did not respond. Mills did tell *The Post-Star*'s circulation director on Monday that the hospital would no longer distribute free copies of the newspaper throughout its building and asked the newspaper to stop delivery.[39]

The paragraph was a standard acknowledgment that the reporter had asked the hospital to respond and some new information that the hospital appeared to be punishing the newspaper for its reporting.

Corcoran demanded editors Will Doolittle and Bob Condon remove the paragraph.

Three minutes after receiving Corcoran's email, Doolittle shared it with me as I rushed to catch a plane at Miami International Airport while on vacation with my family.[40]

I sent an email to Corcoran objecting to the edit and his involvement in the editing process without first consulting me.

Corcoran demanded the paragraph be taken out anyway, then sent another email that said we had to have a long talk about the hospital when I got back and that unless there was breaking news, we were not to publish any further articles until after we talked. This included an editorial scheduled to run that Sunday.[41]

Since Jim Marshall retired 13 years earlier, we had seen a stream of publishers from outside the community.

With all the changes in the newspaper industry, the role of the newspaper publisher had evolved in recent years. Publishers had always been the conduit between the community, the advertising department and the newsroom. If a major advertiser or community institution was rankled, the publisher's job was to smooth things over, even if it cost the newspaper revenue. Publishers had to walk a fine line between defending the newsroom and not hurting business.

They traditionally served on nonprofit boards and helped out at soup kitchens. They sometimes mediated disputes between the newsroom and the advertising department. What they weren't supposed to do was get involved in newsroom decisions and the content of stories.

But with new ownership by a publicly traded company in 2002, publishers were held to stricter standards for revenue and profit.

Corcoran, 49, was the interim publisher in 2019 and the sixth publisher since 2006. He was an accountant who had worked at the newspaper for 15 years after being hired from a stone quarry.

Up until that point, no publisher had ever asked me for changes to a story without first consulting me.

Corcoran wrote me that the reporting had gotten personal between Moore and the hospital. I disagreed and insisted that reporting the hospital had not responded to questions was an essential component to the story.

The next morning, Doolittle confronted the issue more directly in an email with Corcoran, threatening to resign if the reporting on the hospital was limited.[42]

This was a veteran editor putting his job on the line just months after his wife had retired because she had been diagnosed with early-onset Alzheimer's. Those are the type of people who work in newsrooms. That is the character they display every day.

On March 20, William G. Powers, Jr., the chairman of the Glens Falls Hospital board of governors, posted a lengthy statement on the hospital's Facebook page, saying, "*The Post-Star* has been on an almost daily campaign to discredit Glens Falls Hospital."[43]

It was the most aggressive attack yet on the newspaper's credibility and ethics.

"Many of its stories and blogs appear not intended to inform or illuminate but to incite anger, inflame controversy, and inflict harm. The coverage is misleading to our community and our local leaders and a disservice to our dedicated employees," Powers wrote.[44]

The attack especially stung Kathleen Moore.

"I knew I shouldn't take it personally," Moore said a year and a half later. "But I never had someone, or an organization, bash me and question me about my ethics. I was shocked. At that point, I realized there was no possible way of covering them that would satisfy them. It would be a completely adversarial relationship. There was no way of saving this."[45]

The attack left me disgusted. I took it as a personal affront to my own 20 years of service to the community and the great work the newspaper had done over the years on so many critical community issues.

I wondered if Powers ever talked to David Saffer about our work on underage drinking or Judy Moffitt about how critical our stories were in informing the public about the heroin epidemic.

I wondered if Powers knew how Thom Randall lived in the fleabag Madden Hotel and how his reporting paved the way for a downtown revitalization just around the corner from the hospital.

I wondered if he appreciated the way the newspaper brought domestic violence out of the closet after Mark Mahoney witnessed a husband murdering his wife—both employees of the hospital—at a local convenience store.

I wondered if he read any of Maury Thompson's heartbreaking commentary about his dying wife? Or Mark Mahoney's Pulitzer Prize–winning editorials. Or Will and Bella Doolittle's podcast "The Alzheimer's Chronicles."

In 2019, it was a new world where the press was relentlessly questioned, but it wasn't supposed to be like that locally, and not from a community hospital in Hometown, USA.

"I felt like I was sort of walking around while blind," Moore related. "I had a friend who was blind and I asked her how she did it, and she said you eventually just trust yourself. It was the same thing with reporting, I just had to be rock-solid with my reporting. I would talk with a dozen anonymous sources who confirmed all the same thing. I absolutely knew that everything was true. It didn't matter what they [the hospital] said, it wasn't true because they always said that."[46]

Many of our readers defended our work with letters and emails. But once again, we could count on Brian Farenell—who defended our coverage during the Queensbury email controversy—to have our back.[47]

"I'd like to commend *The Post-Star* on its excellent reporting on the fiasco at Glens Falls Hospital, one of our community's most critical institutions. This illustrates the importance of good local journalism," Farenell wrote in a March 24 letter to the editor. "As such, it is disheartening to see the 'shoot the messenger' approach from the hospital administration and some staff. Since this story broke, the administration's contradictory statements have been, at best, confusing to the public. At worst, the defensiveness and bunker mentality make people wonder if they're trying to hide something [else]."[48]

In late September, Moore reported Dr. Jack Leary, a recently retired and well-respected anesthesiologist at the hospital, was trying to get the hospital to apply for "Sole Community Hospital" designation so it could qualify for more federal aid.[49]

Dr. Leary clearly wanted to make a difference and help the hospital's bottom line. While meeting with Moore, Leary told her the hospital had lost money again in 2018. He also suggested it would be valuable for her to talk to members of the board of governors. He suggested an upcoming fundraiser for the hospital foundation might be the perfect opportunity.[50]

He offered to take her as his guest to a gala complete with master chefs from around the region and fireworks over Lake George afterward. It would give him the opportunity to introduce her to board members. He even volunteered to pay for her $225 ticket.[51]

But when Leary told the hospital the ticket was for a *Post-Star* reporter, hospital officials told Leary the reporter would not be allowed to attend. It was the first time one of our reporters was banned from a fundraiser.[52]

I responded with an editorial to run on the day of the hospital gala that questioned the hospital's secrecy and its attacks on the newspaper after banning the reporter[53]:

> That's a shame because the hospital administration, led by CEO Dianne Shugrue, has been keeping the board in the dark for far too long.
> And the Board of Governors has supported that secrecy. If this is truly a community hospital, the community has to be a partner with the hospital. To do that, the hospital must be willing to be candid about the challenges it faces.
> We believe the public has many questions about what is going on at the hospital.
> Maybe, the answers could be had at the Inn at Erlowest on Thursday night.
> If someone wants to ask the questions, we believe Dr. Jack Leary has an extra ticket.[54]

Corcoran refused to publish the editorial. His defense of the hospital and limitations on our coverage were starting to add up.

These arguments, these conflicts may seem petty to the outsider, but those of us who made a career trying to do the right thing believe our cause is of a higher calling. It is why we fight those battles with such religious fervor. By the end of 2019, there weren't many of us left to fight.

I took the editorial, reworked it, and ran it as an opinion column under my own byline.[55]

By the end of October, I had bigger problems than holding the hospital accountable. Corcoran told me cuts in the newsroom needed to be made the day after Election Day. He ordered me to lay off Will Doolittle and our longtime clerk Nancy Gautier—two of our longest-serving employees—and two other reporters. There was no discussion.

Eliminating Doolittle's job looked to me like payback for Doolittle's support of Moore when I was on vacation the previous March, and a way to short circuit any further criticism of Glens Falls Hospital by eliminating one of our two editorial writers (I was the other).

Doolittle had a long track record of great journalism in our newsroom. He was the guy who got a veteran's benefits restored after he became projects editor, got the state to streamline liquor license procedures for local businesses and drew attention to the Adirondack Park Agency's heavy-handed tactics in the Adirondacks. He was named Journalist of the Year by Suburban Newspapers of America that year. He had repeatedly made a difference with his own stories and countless other stories as an editor. He was the best we had.

A year earlier, Will and his wife Bella were honored with Lee Enterprises' "Spirit Award" for their podcast dealing with Bella's early-onset Alzheimer's.

I had one more card to play. I reached out to John Humenik, Lee's vice president for news, and informed him I was told to lay off one of our best and most versatile journalists, who also was the "Spirit Award" winner the previous year.

On Election Day, Corcoran sent me another email saying the positions of two reporters and Gautier would be eliminated the next day. He never explained why Doolittle was taken off the list.[56]

A week later, Will Doolittle rejected for publication a letter to the editor from Dr. Howard Fritz at Glens Falls Hospital because it included misinformation about *The Post-Star*'s coverage. As is our policy, Doolittle gave Dr. Fritz an opportunity to correct the misinformation so the letter could be published. Fritz wrote to Doolittle that he was disappointed with the decision.[57]

Corcoran, who was copied on the email from Fritz, jumped into the fray and ruled the letter would be published with the misleading information. He even suggested it be run as a guest essay.[58]

"If you establish a policy that any reader can cite us as 'fake news' or our stories are 'misleading' under the guise of opinion, then you are opening an enormous can of worms regarding our credibility," I wrote to Corcoran. "Letters cannot be allowed to have baseless claims. That will lead to lawsuits. I officially and strongly object to allowing the term 'misleading' to appear in the letter."[59]

Corcoran published the letter over my objection.

The Post-Star staff voted the hospital controversy the biggest story of the year in 2019.[60] When Moore asked CEO Shugrue for an interview for the year-end story, she declined.[61]

Nancy Gautier was hired as a newsroom clerk in 1998. But as our newsroom got smaller, Gautier's role grew larger as a "Girl Friday" for whatever needed doing.

She inputted letters to the editor, births, calendar items and watered the plants in my office. Now in her 70s, she was a vigorous worker and a pleasure to be around. She quietly got the job done without complaint and was always looking for more to do.

"I just want to stay busy," Gautier told me repeatedly.

Facing the front door just off the newspaper's lobby, Gautier existed in two worlds. She observed the stream of customers coming through the front door and heard their complaints and compliments, while the editors and reporters behind her crafted the next day's newspaper.

"I loved listening to everyone talking about their stories and what was going on," Gautier said. "I loved being around the people."[62]

It was the energy that filled that room.

On the day after the 2019 election, I called Gautier into my office. I told her I had bad news. The interim publisher, Brian Corcoran, insisted we lay her off, despite my objections. She had worked at the newspaper for 21 years.

Gautier looked stunned and tears welled up in her eyes.

It was a scenario repeated too many times with many dedicated and loyal newsroom professionals over the past ten years. We had seen a vibrant newsroom with nearly 50 people reduced a few reporters at a time. I had become numb to it.

When the Press Club of Atlantic City honored the newsroom for its coverage of the 9/11 attacks, they asked for a group photo for their awards program. Looking back at the photo now, staff members are spilling out of the photo in all directions.

But this one hurt a little more, and it was a stark reminder of all we had lost.

The newsroom that morning was empty after a late night of reporting on Election Day. As Gautier struggled to keep her composure, it was clear it wasn't anger so much as a deep sense of betrayal she was feeling. Corcoran did not sit in on the meeting. It was the first time I remember eliminating someone's job without the publisher being present.

"I never saw it coming," Gautier said ten months later.[63]

As she tried to hold it together, I talked to her about what she meant to the newsroom, and how it would not be the same without her. They were hollow words I don't recall using before. I told her it wouldn't be long before I was gone, too.

We sat there for some time in the quiet. When she had composed herself, I walked around my big wooden desk and gave her a long hug. Gautier walked out of the office and told our longtime reporter Don Lehman she had been let go.

Lehman went out back into the packaging department and found a box so she could pack up her personal belongings. When she was ready, Lehman—never the warm and fuzzy type—carried the box out to her car. Nancy doesn't remember walking to the car.[64]

When I finally called Gautier ten months later to see how she was doing, she called back and left a message.

"One thing I wanted to tell you in case we got talking about things and I forgot," Nancy said hesitantly. "On my last day there, I have to tell you, if you didn't keep me in your office for awhile talking, and then before I had to walk out, wrapped your arms around me, I would not have been able to walk out of your office. That was the best thing you could have ever done for me and I just wanted to thank you. I think about it a lot. You helped me."[65]

It was a reminder of our newsroom's greatest asset—people.

Eliminating Gautier's position put an exclamation point on what was gone and would not return.

That left ten of us.

When I came home that night with a newsroom three people smaller, I told my wife I would never do it again.

It had been the longest and most difficult of years.

By the time of the layoffs in November 2019, the newspaper was under assault on three fronts: the local community hospital, our ambitious congresswoman and a group of Trump supporters who threatened violence.

The most discouraging development was a new publisher who was calling our journalism into question. The gravest threat to the work we did was now internal.

When talking to our two sportswriters after the layoff, I told them I would need them to help out with news coverage. Their jobs depended on it.

"You looked beaten during that meeting," sportswriter Will Springstead later told me. "I told people, I had never seen Ken like that."[66]

A year later, Springstead was also laid off after more than 15 years at the newspaper.

Epilogue

The cutbacks the past November made it clear to me our newspaper could no longer provide the type of in-depth journalism we had done in the past.

When the terms of our two citizen representatives expired on December 31, 2019, I did not replace them, and we reduced the frequency of the editorial page to four times a week.

Over the first three months of 2020, I wrote almost all the editorials and often three columns a week. I knew I was running out of time. It wasn't a matter of "if" I would retire, but when.

I expected more cutbacks and believed if I retired, my position would remain vacant so the newspaper could save money. My retirement could protect the jobs of some of my colleagues.

Each day, I felt a renewed urgency. We published 35 editorials—almost all written by me—through the first three months of the year, but just seven over the next six months. It was another loss for the community.

On March 20, Don Lehman sent me an early-morning email that he was resigning his position at the newspaper after 28 years to take a job with Warren County. It was effective immediately. He posted a farewell blog on our website. Corcoran made me take it down.

Lehman told me later he did not believe there was a future for him at the newspaper.[1]

Glens Falls Hospital hired a new public relations person, Ray Agnew, who had previously worked at the hospital. He suggested a meeting to reintroduce himself.[2]

"I'm sure you are aware that over the past year, the hospital has undertaken a campaign to smear the newspaper, its reporters and editors, while continuing an ongoing campaign of disinformation," I responded. "While I am aware that you were not a party to those actions, I hope that you are aware of what has transpired and it is a sign the hospital will work diligently to repair relations with the newspaper. It is hard to be optimistic considering the number of falsehoods perpetrated by the hospital and its board of governors on social media and in other media."[3]

Agnew suggested that hospital officials felt they had been treated unfairly and that the newspaper's coverage was "inaccurate and misleading." He suggested a "reset."[4]

Kathleen Moore was livid.

"Mistakes made on both sides?" Moore said sarcastically when I asked her about it in September 2020. "What exactly were my mistakes? Other than believing anything they told me. I should have never believed them on anything."[5]

Glens Falls mayor Dan Hall proclaimed Friday, July 17, as "Ken Tingley Day" in the city of Glens Falls. The author retired after 32 years at the newspaper (photograph by Gillian Tingley).

I told Agnew we stood by our previous reporting.

"I can assure you, we will continue to cover the hospital—as we do with every story—with accuracy and fairness," I wrote. "In that regard, there is no need for a 'reset' on our part. We will continue that mission as we have in the past."[6]

There was no meeting with Moore or the editors, but a few days later Agnew did meet with Corcoran.

In late March, the newsroom was closed because of the pandemic, and all editors and reporters worked from home.

On Friday, March 27, in the early days of the pandemic, Moore reported Glens Falls Hospital and Saratoga Hospital were addressing the pandemic in different ways with frontline health care workers.[7]

The story said that Glens Falls nurses were wearing surgical masks instead of the N95 masks that provide greater protection. Nurses who worked at both facilities told Moore they would no longer volunteer for extra shifts at Glens Falls Hospital because they preferred the greater precautions taken at Saratoga Hospital.[8]

On the morning Moore's story ran, we received a tip from a nurse at Glens Falls Hospital.

"The hospital has not been transparent with the nursing staff," it read. "Medical providers are receiving emails about the possible negative future of what is to come in relation to COVID-19. ... As the largest discipline to be employed by the hospital, we will be the ones on the front lines fighting the virus. ... The Hospital seems to only respond to needs when the media is alerted. Please do what you can do to support the nurses of Glens Falls."

On the editorial page the next day, the "Don Coyote" cartoon read, "If Saratoga Hospital can provide needed protection to its doctors and nurses, why can't Glens Falls Hospital?"[9]

The cartoon had been a daily feature on our editorial page for nearly 30 years since first being introduced by former publisher Jim Marshall. The daily comment was intended to be a quip, biting sarcasm or a solitary truth.

On Saturday, March 28, the comment was critical but based on facts from Moore's story and the concerns from a Glens Falls Hospital nurse.

The day before Moore's story was published, Glens Falls Hospital was not using N95 masks. The day after Moore's story, my wife—a cancer patient at the hospital and a nurse—told me that everyone was wearing an N95 mask.[10]

Moore's reporting had again made a difference.[11]

That Saturday evening, Corcoran fired off an email to me as I was sitting down for dinner, demanding I explain the Don Coyote.

After 31 years at the newspaper, it can be the simplest thing that is the last straw.

It started a year earlier with Corcoran deleting important parts of a story on the hospital, continued when he killed an editorial critical of the hospital, then allowed an inaccurate letter to the editor from a hospital doctor to be published over my objections and culminated in his attempt to eliminate the position of our best journalist, Will Doolittle.

I was done with him protecting the hospital. Three minutes after receiving the email, I pecked out an answer on my phone while sitting at the dinner table: "If you want to fire me, go ahead. I'm done with the second guessing!"[12]

Later, I found out the complaint originated with a doctor at the hospital who demanded a public apology and had previously voiced complaints about our coverage to officials at corporate.

In Tuesday's newspaper, Corcoran—who had been promoted to publisher ten days earlier—wrote a publisher's note in the place of the "Don Coyote" feature that read: "The Don Coyote cartoon on Saturday was presented without context. Glens Falls Hospital currently follows WHO and CDC guidelines related to the use and distribution of PPE equipment during this Covid-19 crisis, albeit with limited supplies. *The Post-Star* respects and admires the sacrifices that GFH staff has made during this difficult and scary time. *The Post-Star* is committed to providing the Glens Falls community with the most accurate and thorough coverage you have come to expect from us."[13]

It was as if Kathleen Moore's important reporting holding the hospital responsible for its employees' health had not even happened.

In an email to the editors on March 30, Corcoran ordered the Don Coyote cartoon not be run again without publisher approval.[14]

It was the death of the long-standing opinion page feature. It was not discussed with me or any member of the newsroom. It was clear to me Corcoran no longer had the best interests of the community or the newspaper at heart. I told him I would be taking paid personal time the next week.

The next week, Corcoran informed the editors that "the columns of Will Doolittle and Ken Tingley will no longer run on the front of the local section."[15] They would be relegated to a less prominent inside page.

Earlier in the day, both our columns had been named finalists in the New York State Associated Press Association's annual contest. I had been writing my news column for 21 years, Doolittle for 27. I had been a finalist in the National Society of Newspaper Columnists annual writing contest eight times in the past ten years. Both columns were popular and an asset to the newspaper.

This was personal.

Corcoran did not discuss the decision with either of us. When I protested, he said it was to allow more news to be played on the local front. At the time, we were producing fewer news stories than ever.[16]

I cherished my column and the long relationship I had with readers. I told Corcoran I would immediately begin two more weeks of vacation. Two weeks later, I began ten weeks of paid family leave to care for my wife, who had been battling ovarian cancer since 2011.

Once I went on leave, Corcoran told the editors we would publish a weekly guest essay authored by Glens Falls Hospital in place of the regular Sunday editorial. It was still running more than a year later.

On March 31, Lee Enterprises announced all employees would be furloughed two weeks without pay between April 1 and June 30. Executives had their pay cut 20 percent.[17]

There were no more stories from Kathleen Moore about the hospital's finances as her skills were diverted to cover the health emergency. In May 2021, she took a job with the Albany *Times Union*. "Thank you again for hiring me," she wrote to me. "It was a wonderful six years."

The New York State Associated Press Association announced *The Post-Star* had won 19 awards in its annual journalism contest at the end of May 2020. The 19 awards were more than any newspaper in the state.[18]

The newspaper was also honored with the Newspaper of Distinction—sort of a newspaper of the year honor—for our circulation size.[19] It was the ninth time we were honored with the award—all since I became editor in 1999.

I won first place for column writing.[20]

Will Doolittle won first place for editorial writing.[21]

Kathleen Moore won first place in the Best Public Service category for a 12-story entry on the coverage of Glens Falls Hospital's finances. It was titled "What is Glens Falls Hospital hiding?"[22] Later that summer, the New York News Publishers Association also honored her hospital reporting with its Community Service Award.[23]

At the end of June, I called each of the remaining ten members of the newsroom and told them I would return to work at the beginning of July for two weeks, then retire.

On Tuesday, July 7, I published a note to readers on the front page that I was stepping down as editor.[24]

"I worry a lot about the newspaper industry, and the effect its struggles will have on maintaining a strong watchdog presence, not only in this community, but in small towns all across the country. I urge all of you to continue to support the great journalism that takes place here every day at *The Post-Star*. Few of you will ever realize the dedication that goes into putting out a daily news product. Please, don't take it for granted."[25]

I still found it difficult to let go those final two weeks. On Sunday, July 12, I wrote an editorial that the new Warren County sheriff should not be allowed to hire his son because it violated established nepotism guidelines at the county.[26]

It was my last chance to make a difference.

Four days later, the sheriff rescinded the hiring. I'd like to think the editorial gave county politicians cover to enforce the nepotism policy.[27]

It was the only editorial published since I started family leave three months earlier.

In the two weeks after the retirement announcement I received more than 100 emails, cards and letters—people still write letters in Glens Falls—from readers thanking me for my work while saying they were sad they would not be able to read my column anymore.

On Friday, July 17, Glens Falls Mayor Dan Hall proclaimed it "Ken Tingley Day" in the city of Glens Falls. I joined my colleagues Maury Thompson and Mark Mahoney in receiving that honor.[28]

My wife concocted a silly little sign that read "Ken Tingley Day," and we marched through downtown with me holding my sign aloft while taking photos at various downtown landmarks.

This was my city.

As I walked down Glen Street, one man sitting on a bench asked, "Who the heck is Ken Tingley?"

"That's me," I said.

"What did you do?" he asked.

"I'm not sure," I said.

When I left the newspaper, no successor was named. At the end of September, just days before a new fiscal year was to begin, two more staff members had their jobs eliminated. Will Doolittle, Bob Condon, Greg Brownell, Michael Goot and Kathleen Moore were among the eight still left at the time.

In August, Ben Rogers was named president and director of sales and local marketing of *The Post-Star*.[29] Corcoran was assigned a corporate role in regional finance with responsibility for four newspapers.[30] He remained a member of a *Post-Star* editorial board that no longer met regularly and weighed in on community issues infrequently. The newspaper no longer had a publisher or an editor.

On Sunday, July 19, I published my last column in *The Post-Star*. It ran on the local front, despite Corcoran's ban against commentary by me on the local front.

I reminded readers of the spirit of the dying Mary Joseph,[31] the heart of Maury Thompson, the professionalism of a young photographer named T.J. Hooker at the *Ethan Allen* sinking, Mark Mahoney's devotion to his daughter after witnessing a murder and how Konrad Marshall would always carry the stories of the women of domestic violence with him.[32]

"What a charmed life I have led," I wrote. "How lucky I have been to have the privilege of walking in the shadows of such men and women on a daily basis, to cheer them on, to challenge them, to pick them up when they stumbled, defend them when they were attacked, but more often than not, watching them succeed beyond their wildest dreams."[33]

But here's the thing that is most satisfying of all. It was the readers who shared their own lives, who gave me an audience that made the journey so fulfilling.

I still had this gnawing feeling I had let them down.

"I've tried to be authentic and honest as I address community and personal issues alike," I wrote. "Along the way, I opened my heart to you about my own trials and tribulations in being a son, a husband and a father. And while it was cathartic for me at times, I believed many of you related to these stories about life, death and heartbreak because we all have them."[34]

There would be no one to do that anymore.

That is what the people leading Glens Falls Hospital were trying to kill.

It was what the new publisher was trying to end.

It is the ultimate mission of community newspapers.

To report on life.

To help its readers celebrate it, make sense of it and make it more enjoyable for friends and neighbors alike.

That's what we were losing.

It was happening in similar communities all across the country. There were scores of us leaving the work we loved and the mission we took so seriously every day.

It was the end of an era.

We were the last editors at the last American newspapers.

Chapter Notes

Introduction

1. Ken Tingley, "One Final Request for *The Post-Star*," www.poststar.com, February 17, 2016, https://poststar.com/blogs/the_front_page/one-final-request-for-the-post-star/article_cacf6eac-d42a-11e5-8663-7710e3fda1dd.html.

2. *Granville Sentinel*, November 12, 1875.

3. Ken Tingley, "Newspapers Must Adapt to Changing Times," *The Post-Star*, April 23, 2000, F1.

4. Jim Marshall, "Letter from the Publisher—A Century of Service," *The Post-Star*, January 24, 2004, F2.

5. Sen. Elizabeth Little, Sen. Joseph Bruno, Sen. Hugh Farley, Assemblywoman Teresa Sayward, Assemblyman Roy McDonald, Assemblyman James Tedisco, State of New York, Legislative Resolution, February 3, 2004.

6. Maury Thompson, "State Senate Salutes Post-Star's 100 Years," *The Post-Star*, February 4, 2004, B1.

7. Ken Tingley, "The Post-Star Looks to the Future," *The Post-Star*, January 24, 2004, A1.

8. *Ibid.*

9. *Ibid.*

10. Ken Tingley, "Time to Take Another Look at Our Improved Arts Section," *The Post-Star*, November 2, 2008, E1.

11. Ken Tingley, "There Is Heart Beyond the Newsprint," *The Post-Star*, November 21, 2001, B8.

12. *Ibid.*, B1.

13. Ken Tingley, "Death of Newseum, Free Press Is Mourned," *The Post-Star*, January 2, 2020, B3.

14. Lee Shaker, "Dead Newspapers and Citizens' Civic Engagement, Political Communications," January 30, 2014, https://www.tandfonline.com/doi/full/10.1080/10584609.2012.762817.

15. Pengie Gao, Chang Lee, Dermot Murphy, "Financing Dies in the Darkness? The Impact of Newspaper Closures on Public Finance."-Bookings Institute, September 24, 2018, https://www.brookings.edu/research/financing-dies-in-darkness-the-impact-of-newspaper-closures-on-public-finance/.

16. David Adria, Victoria Smith Ekstrand, Ashley Fox, Evan Ringel, "Addressing the Decline of Local News, Rise of Platforms, and Spread of Mis- and Disinformation Online," Univeristy of North Carolina, December 2020, https://citap.unc.edu/local-news-platforms-mis-disinformation/.

17. Ken Tingley, "Communities Lose a Lot Without a Daily Newspaper," www.poststar.com, January 12, 2020, https://poststar.com/news/local/from-the-editor-communities-lose-a-lot-without-a-daily-newspaper/article_044cbb63-0874-5f60-8678-c30f041941b2.html.

Chapter 1

1. *www.heritage.org,* https://nyheritage.org/collections/glens-falls-hometown-usa.

2. *Bob Condon, Phone interview with author, September 19, 2020.*

3. Will Doolittle, Phone interview with author, September 11, 2020.

4. Will Doolittle, Phone interview with author, September 13, 2020.

5. Patrick Ridgell, "Shooting Stirs Happier Memories," *The Post-Star*, April 21, 1999, A1.

6. *Ibid.*

7. Tucker Cordani, "Suburban Nightmare," *The Post-Star*, April 21, 1999, A1.

8. *Ibid.*

9. *Ibid.*

10. *Ibid.*

11. *Ibid.*

12. Ken Tingley, "Colorado Tragedy Hits Us at Home," *The Post-Star*, April 25, 1999, F2.

13. Mark Mahoney, Phone interview with author, August 29, 2020.

14. Nick Reisman, Phone interview with author, August 20, 2020.

15. Will Doolittle, Phone interview with author, September 13, 2020.

16. *Ibid.*

17. *Ibid.*

18. *Ibid.*

19. *Ibid.*

20. Will Doolittle, Phone interview with author, September 11, 2020

21. *Ibid.*

22. Will Doolittle, Letter to Stephen Bennett, September 1993

Chapter 2

1. Pam Brooks, "Get Up! We Have to Get Out," *The Post-Star*, August 31, 2000, A1.
2. Bob Condon, "She Was Special to the Post-Star," www.facebook.com/bob.condonpoststar/, August 31, 2019, https://www.facebook.com/notes/bob-condon-post-star/she-was-special-to-the-post-star/2380830835343067.
3. Pam Brooks, "Get Up! We Have to Get Out," *The Post-Star*, August 31, 2000, A1.
4. Don Lehman, "Leaking Tanker Cripples Village," *The Post-Star*, August 31, 2000, A1.
5. Pam Brooks, "Get Up! We Have to Get Out," *The Post-Star*, August 31, 2000, A1.
6. *Ibid.*
7. *Ibid.*
8. *Ibid.*
9. *Ibid.*
10. Bob Condon, "She Was Special to the Post-Star," www.facebook.com/bob.condonpoststar/, August 31, 2019, https://www.facebook.com/notes/bob-condon-post-star/she-was-special-to-the-post-star/2380830835343067
11. Don Lehman, Phone interview with author, September 25, 2020.
12. *Ibid.*
13. *Ibid.*
14. *Ibid.*
15. *Ibid.*
16. *Ibid.*
17. *Ibid.*
18. David Blow, Phone interview with author, September 26, 2020.
19. Don Lehman, Phone interview with author, September 25, 2020.
20. *Ibid.*
21. *Ibid.*
22. *Ibid.*
23. *Ibid.*
24. *Ibid.*
25. Bob Condon, Phone interview with author, September 19, 2020.
26. *Ibid.*
27. Don Lehman, Phone interview with author, August 11, 2020.
28. *Ibid.*
29. Don Lehman, "Leaking Tanker Cripples Village," *The Post-Star*, August 31, 2000, A1.
30. *Ibid.*, A6.
31. Thom Randall, "Quiet Village Disrupted for a Day: Hospital Keeps Busy During Emergency," *The Post-Star*, August 31, 2000, B9.
32. *Ibid.*
33. *Ibid.*
34. Don Lehman, "Leaking Tanker Cripples Village," *The Post-Star*, August 31, 2000, A1.
35. Staff Report, "Post-Star Will Be Dropped Off," *The Post-Star*, August 31, 2000, B1.
36. National Headliner Awards, May 5, 2001, https://www.headlinerawards.org/2001-tvradio/.
37. "Pamela Anne (French) Brooks-Gibbs," *The Post-Star*, February 26, 2019, B4.
38. Bob Condon, "She Was Special to the Post-Star," www.facebook.com/bob.condonpoststar/, August 31, 2019, https://www.facebook.com/notes/bob-condon-post-star/she-was-special-to-the-post-star/2380830835343067.

Chapter 3

1. Ken Tingley, "Responding to Tragedy with Purpose," *The Post-Star*, September 16, 2001, F1.
2. David Blow, "Tower Witness Hears Whine, Explosion," *The Post-Star*, September 12, 2001, A1.
3. *Ibid.*
4. *Ibid.*, A7.
5. *Ibid.*
6. Pat Dowd, Phone interview with author, August 13, 2020.
7. Mark Mahoney, Phone interview with author, August 29, 2020.
8. David Blow, "Smoke Filled City Streets, Blocking Out the Sun," *The Post-Star*, September 12, 2001, A7.
9. *Ibid.*
10. *Ibid.*
11. *Ibid.*
12. *Ibid.*
13. Matthew Sturdevant, "Residents Watch in Disbelief and Anguish," *The Post-Star*, September 12, 2001, A3.
14. *Ibid.*
15. *Ibid.*
16. *Ibid.*
17. Martha Petteys, "Transportation Halted in Area," *The Post-Star*, September 12, 2001, A5.
18. *Ibid.*
19. Thom Randall, "Pentagon Attack Shakes Up City Native," *The Post-Star*, September 12, 2001, A1.
20. *Ibid.*, A3.
21. *Ibid.*
22. David Blow, "Smoke Filled City Streets, Blocking Out the Sun," *The Post-Star*, September 12, 2001.
23. Jim Tracy, "Hickins Are Eyewitness to New York Terror," *The Post-Star*, September 12, 2001, C1.
24. *Ibid.*
25. *Ibid.*
26. *Ibid.*
27. Jim Bishop, "The Day Kennedy Was Shot," Funk & Wagnalls, 1968, 149, 164–165.
28. "Attacked, Extra—Special Edition," *The Post-Star*, September 12, 2001, 1–12.
29. Pat Dowd, Phone interview with author, August 13, 2020.
30. Mark Mahoney, Phone interview with author, August 29, 2020.
31. *Ibid.*
32. Pat Dowd, Phone Interview with Author, August 13, 2020.
33. *Ibid.*

34. *Ibid.*

35. Bob Condon, Phone Interview with Author, September 19, 2020.

36. Thom Randall, Phone Interview with Author, August 11, 2020.

37. Ken Tingley, "Responding to Tragedy with Purpose," *The Post-Star*, September 16, 2001, F1.

38. Thom Randall, Phone interview with author, August 11, 2020.

39. Pat Dowd, Phone interview with author, August 13, 2020.

40. *Ibid.*

41. *Ibid.*

42. Thom Randall, "Train Ride to NYC Is Lonely Trip," *The Post-Star*, September 13, 2001, A1.

43. *Ibid.*

44. *Ibid.*, A3.

45. Thom Randall, Phone interview with author, August 11, 2020.

46. *Ibid.*

47. Thom Randall, "Anguish and Confusion Abound at Barricades," *The Post-Star*, September 13, 2001, A1.

48. Thom Randall, Phone interview with author, August 11, 2020.

49. *Ibid.*

50. Mark Mahoney, "Residents Show Generosity," *The Post-Star*, September 13, 2001, A6.

51. Staff Report, "Region Joins Hands in Mourning Losses," *The Post-Star*, September 15, 2001, A1.

52. Ken Tingley, "All Is Wrong with the World," *The Post-Star*, September 21, 2001, B1.

53. John Gereau, "Prayers Answered for Queensbury Family in Tragedy," *The Post-Star*, September 15, 2001, B1.

54. *Ibid.*

55. *Ibid.*

56. Thom Randall, "Luck in the Ruins," *The Post-Star*, September 23, 2001, A3.

57. Ryan O'Halloran, "Kathleen Remembers," *The Post-Star*, December 23, 2001, A1.

58. *Ibid.*

59. *Ibid.*

60. *Ibid.*

61. Mike Mender, "CNA Workers United in Grief," *The Post-Star*, September 15, 2001, A5.

62. The Press Club of Atlantic City, "2002 National Headliner Awards," May 4, 2002. https://www.headlinerawards.org/2002-print photo/.

63. Jim Marshall, "Post-Star Wins National Award for Sept. 11 Coverage," *The Post-Star*, March 2002, B1.

Chapter 4

1. Maury Thompson, Phone interview with author, June 1, 2020.

2. *Ibid.*

3. *Ibid.*

4. *Ibid.*

5. *Ibid.*

6. *Ibid.*

7. *Ibid.*

8. *Ibid.*

9. *Ibid.*

10. *Ibid.*

11. Kathleen Phalen-Tomaselli, "Post-Star Reporter Maury Thompson Steps Away from Beat," www.poststar.com, August 31, 2017, https://poststar.com/news/local/post-star-reporter-maury-thompson-steps-away-from-the-beat/article_5d14fac2-0619-54e9-892c-17f1e834a85d.html.

12. Maury Thompson, Phone interview with author, June 1, 2020.

13. *Ibid.*

14. *Ibid.*

15. *Ibid.*

16. *Ibid.*

17. *Ibid.*

18. Ken Tingley, "You Don't Replace Reporters Like Maury Thompson," *The Post-Star*, September 3, 2017, A6.

19. *Ibid.*

20. *Ibid.*

21. Kathleen Phalen-Tomaselli, "Post-Star Reporter Maury Thompson Steps Away from Beat," www.poststar.com, August 31, 2017, https://poststar.com/news/local/post-star-reporter-maury-thompson-steps-away-from-the-beat/article_5d14fac2-0619-54e9-892c-17f1e834a85d.html.

22. Maury Thompson, Phone interview with author, June 1, 2020.

23. Ken Tingley, "You Don't Replace Reporters Like Maury Thompson," September 3, 2017, A6.

24. Maury Thompson, Phone interview with author, June 1, 2020.

25. *Ibid.*

26. Maury Thompson, "Finding Fellowship as the Husband of a Cancer Patient," *The Post-Star*, June 27, 2002, D1.

27. *Ibid.*

28. *Ibid.*, D3.

29. Maury Thompson, "Few Words Seem Fitting in the Face of Death," *The Post-Star*, July 4, 2002, D1.

30. *Ibid.*

31. Maury Thompson, "Grandmother and Child Find Bond in Death," *The Post-Star*, July 11, 2002, D3.

32. Maury Thompson, Phone interview with author, June 1, 2020.

33. *Ibid.*

34. *Ibid.*

35. *Ibid.*

36. Maury Thompson, "His Stories Live On," www.poststar.com, October 15, 2006, https://poststar.com/news/commentary-his-stories-live-on/article_78692a41-a3df-5584-b55a-d09cef2ebfd2.html.

37. *Ibid.*

38. *Ibid.*

39. Maury Thompson, Phone interview with author, June 1, 2020.

40. Staff Report, "Thompson Honored with Spirit Award," www.poststar.com, November 16, 2007, https://poststar.com/news/local/thompson-honored-with-spirit-award/article_6e1e4ec1-ed09-5174-a7de-dc2c93120abb.html.

41. Maury Thompson, "The 55: After Vietnam Veterans Fought Battles at Home," www.poststar.com, November 12, 2010, https://poststar.com/news/local/after-vietnam-veterans-fought-battles-at-home/article_f381440a-edef-11df-9a6d-001cc4c002e0.html.

42. Maury Thompson, "The Biggest Kid at the Balloon Festival: The Walter Griskot Story," MDT Publishing, 2011.

43. Chad Arnold, "Mountain Lake PBS to Show Charles Evans Hughes Documentary," *The Post-Star*, April 5, 2021, https://poststar.com/news/local/mountain-lake-pbs-to-show-charles-evans-hughes-documentary/article_316718de-cbef-5dbd-83d9-efd2f37691c9.html.

44. Ken Tingley, "You Don't Replace Reporters Like Maury Thompson," *The Post-Star*, September 3, 2017, A6.

Chapter 5

1. Matthew Sturdevant, "Growing Up Gay," *The Post-Star*, July 14, 2002, A1.

2. *Ibid.*

3. Ken Tingley, "Controversial Photo Sends a Message," *The Post-Star*, July 14, 2002, F1.

4. Jim Marshall, Phone interview with author, June 22, 2020.

5. *Ibid.*

6. *Ibid.*

7. *Ibid.*

8. *Ibid.*

9. Ruby A. Hayner, "I Appreciated Your 'Growing Up' Story," *The Post-Star*, July 31, 2002, A5.

10. Ken Tingley, "Controversial Photo Sends a Message," *The Post-Star*, July 14, 2002, F1.

11. Matt Sturdevant, Phone interview with author, June 24, 2020.

12. David Moats, Phone interview with author, July 28, 2020.

13. *Ibid.*

14. *Ibid.*

15. *Ibid.*

16. *Ibid.*

17. David Moats, "Civil Wars: A Battle for Gay Marriage," Harcourt Books, 2004, 242–243.

18. Matt Sturdevant, Phone interview with author, June 24, 2020.

19. *Ibid.*

20. *Ibid.*

21. *Ibid.*

22. *Ibid.*

23. Matthew Sturdevant, "Growing Up Gay," *The Post-Star*, July 14, 2002, A1.

24. Matthew Sturdevant, Phone interview with author, June 24, 2020.

25. Matthew Sturdevant, "Growing Up Gay," *The Post-Star*, July 14, 2002, A1.

26. *Ibid.*

27. *Ibid.*, A4.

28. *Ibid.*

29. *Ibid.*

30. *Ibid.*

31. *Ibid.*, A5.

32. *Ibid.*

33. *Ibid.*

34. *Ibid.*

35. *Ibid.*

36. Matt Sturdevant, Phone interview with author, June 24, 2020.

37. *Ibid.*

38. Ken Tingley, "Hoping for Dialogue and Less Hate," *The Post-Star*, July 28, 2002, F1.

39. Jamie Thew and Barbara Thew, "Paper Should Avoid Offensive Subjects," *The Post-Star*, July 22, 2002, A5.

40. Carl Thomas, "Politically Correct Is Not Morally Correct," *The Post-Star*, July 22, 2002, A5.

41. Robert Lockrow, "Homosexuality Just a Human Weakness," *The Post-Star*, July 23, 2002, A5.

42. David B. Holck, "Picture Offensive, Story Misleading," *The Post-Star*, July 23, 2001, A5.

43. David M. Montgomery, "Story on Homosexuals Inappropriate, Trashy," *The Post-Star*, July 25, 2002, A5.

44. Pamela Zaugg, "Lonely Men, Women Should Turn to God," *The Post-Star*, July 28, 2002, F2.

45. Fred Curtis, "Story Did Not Address Needs of Readers," *The Post-Star*, July 28, 2002, F2.

46. Wade H. Balla, "Gays Should Stay in the Closet," *The Post-Star*, July 29, 2002, A5.

47. Glen A. Buell, "Photo Choice Was Disgusting," *The Post-Star*, July 29, 2002, A5.

48. Pastor Mark Bell, "Media Promotes Liberal Agenda," *The Post-Star*, August 3, 2002, A5.

49. Sylvia Zetterstrom, "'Tender Moment,' Subject Are Sickening," *The Post-Star*, August 4, 2002, F2.

50. Paula Huber, "Front-page Photo Was in Poor Taste," *The Post-Star*, August 10, 2002, A5.

51. Jamie and Barbara Thew, "Paper Should Avoid Offensive Subjects," *The Post-Star*, July 22, 2002, A5.

52. Carl Thomas, "Politically Correct Is Not Morally Correct," *The Post-Star*, July 22, 2002, A5.

53. Robert Lockrow, "Homosexuality Just a Human Weakness," *The Post-Star*, July 23, 2002, A5.

54. Ken Tingley, "Hoping for Dialogue and Less Hate," *The Post-Star*, July 28, 2002, F1.

55. Matt Sturdevant, Phone interview with author, June 24, 2020.

56. Rev. Anthony W. Green, "Running Recent Story Was Act of Courage," *The Post-Star*, July 28, 2002, F2.

57. Mary Hewitt, "Story on Homosexuals Was a Courageous Act," *The Post-Star*, July 27, 2002, A5.

58. Al Laubinger, "Persecution by Arbiters Bigoted," *The Post-Star*, August 7, 2002, A5.

59. Jennifer Leitch, "Fort Ann Resident Appalled by Response," *The Post-Star*, August 7, 2002, A5.

60. Jim Marshall, Phone interview with author, June 22, 2020.

61. Pulitzer.org, https://www.pulitzer.org/prize-winners-by-year/2001

62. David Moats, Phone interview with author, July 28, 2020.

63. *Ibid.*

64. Ken Tingley, "Small Paper's Prize Is Something to Celebrate," April 22, 2001, F1.

65. Ken Tingley, "Hoping for a Dialogue and Less Hate," July 28, 2002, F1.

66. *Ibid.*

67. Matthew Sturdevant, Phone interview with author, June 24, 2020.

68. Henry Epp, Melody Bodette, "Rutland Herald, Times Argus Lay Off Pulitzer Prize-winning Editor," vpr.org, February 28, 2018, https://www.vpr.org/post/rutland-herald-times-argus-lay-pulitzer-prize-winning-editor#stream/0.

69. Bonnie Parker, RN, "Article on Gays Deserves Bravo," *The Post-Star*, July 23, 2002, A5.

70. "Walter Lape Obituary," www.poststar.com, May 6, 2010, https://poststar.com/lifestyles/announcements/obituaries/walter-broc-lape/-article_f7446b5e-597e-11df-ab92-001cc4c002e0.html.

Chapter 6

1. Don Lehman, Darrin Youker, "Fire Kills 4 Children," *The Post-Star*, November 27, 2002, A1.

2. *Ibid.*

3. *Ibid.*

4. Darrin Youker, "Boy Had Chance to Escape Burning Home," www.poststar.com, December 6, 2002, https://poststar.com/news/local/boy-had-chance-to-escape-burning-home/article_376dc7b7-47f8-521f-b78b-06691cf972f2.html.

5. *Ibid.*

6. *Ibid.*

7. Don Lehman, Darrin Youker, "Mother, Neighbors Attempted to Rescue Kids," November 27, 2002, A5.

8. Richard Perez-Pena, "4 Children Die in Fire at House Said to Be Condemned," The New York Times, November 27, 2002, 8.

9. Darrin Youker, "Boy Had Chance to Escape Burning Home," www.poststar.com, December 6, 2002, https://poststar.com/news/local/boy-had-chance-to-escape-burning-home/article_376dc7b7-47f8-521f-b78b-06691cf972f2.html.

10. Don Lehman, Darrin Youker, "Mother, Neighbors Attempted to Rescue Kids," November 27, 2002, A5.

11. Darrin Youker, Phone interview with author, August 4, 2020.

12. *Ibid.*

13. *Ibid.*

14. *Ibid.*

15. Darrin Youker, "House Had Caught Fire Before," *The Post-Star*, November 27, 2002, A6.

16. *Ibid.*

17. Don Lehman, Darrin Youker, "Fire Kills 4 Children," *The Post-Star*, November 27,2002, A1.

18. Darrin Youker, "House Had Caught Fire Before," *The Post-Star*, November 27, 2002, A6.

19. *Ibid.*

20. *Ibid.*

21. *Ibid.*

22. *Ibid.*

23. Darrin Youker, Phone interview with author, August 4, 2020.

24. Don Lehman, Darrin Youker, "Fire Kills 4 Children, November 27, 2002, A1.

25. Darrin Youker, "In Fire's Wake," www.poststar.com, December 29, 2002, https://poststar.com/news/local/in-fires-wake/article_1ae3aeb6-cf44-5071-9997-d25ef9b458bd.html.

26. Darrin Youker, "Boy Had Chance to Escape Burning Home," www.poststar.com, December 6, 2002, https://poststar.com/news/local/boy-had-chance-to-escape-burning-home/article_376dc7b7-47f8-521f-b78b-06691cf972f2.html.

27. *Ibid.*

28. Judy Bernstein and Matthew Sturdevant, "It Is Not a Final Goodbye," *The Post-Star*, December 1, 2002, A1.

29. *Ibid.*

30. *Ibid.*

31. *Ibid.*

32. Ken Tingley, "What Would You Do?" *The Post-Star*, December 13, 2002, B1.

33. *Ibid.*

34. *Ibid.*, B9.

35. Ken Tingley, "Rejecting Rumors Is Part of Our Job," *The Post-Star*, December 15, 2002, F1.

36. *Ibid.*

37. Darrin Youker, Phone interview with author, August 4, 2020.

38. Darrin Youker, "In Fire's Wake," www.poststar.com, December 29, 2002, https://poststar.com/news/local/in-fires-wake/article_1ae3aeb6-cf44-5071-9997-d25ef9b458bd.html.

39. *Ibid.*

40. Darrin Youker, "Children Died of Smoke Inhalation," *The Post-Star*, December 28, 2002, A9.

41. Darrin Youker, "Fatal Fire Traced to Floorboards," *The Post-Star*, December 5, 2002, A1.

42. *Ibid.*

43. *Ibid.*

44. Kathy Knights, "Smoke Detectors Should Be Distributed," *The Post-Star*, December 7, 2002, A7.

45. Mark Mahoney, "Tragedy Has Ways to Be Averted," *The Post-Star*, December 8, 2002, F1.

46. *Ibid.*

47. *Ibid.*

48. *Ibid.*

49. Gretta Nemcek, "Fort Edward Town Board to Crack Down on 'slumlords,'" www.poststar. com, October 17, 2002, https://poststar.com/ news/local/fatal-fire-traced-to-floorboards/-article_32738b47-fcf0-5b64-9622-ca84e3f1ddc2. html.

50. Gretta Nemcek, "Village Might Inspect Rentals," *The Post-Star*, December 12, 2002, A1.

Chapter 7

1. Ken Tingley, "Photo of Mourning Child Put Face on War," *The Post-Star*, September 28, 2003, F1.

2. Abigail Tucker, "A Town's Hero Is Laid to Rest," *The Post-Star*, September 25, 2003, A1.

3. *Ibid.*

4. Will Doolittle, "Where No Comfort Is Found," *The Post-Star*, September 25, 2003, A1.

5. *Ibid.*

6. Ken Tingley, "Photo of Mourning Child Put a Face on War," *The Post-Star*, September 28, 2003, F1.

7. Will Doolittle, "Where No Comfort Is Found," *The Post-Star*, September 25, 2003, A1.

8. Inge Kimmerly, Phone interview with author, "*The Post-Star*, June 22, 2020.

9. Thom Randall, "'We Were Like One Person,'" *The Post-Star*, October 23, 2005, A1.

10. *The Post-Star*, September 25, 2003, A1.

11. *Ibid.*

12. *Ibid.*

13. Ken Tingley, "Photo of Mourning Child Put a Face on War," *The Post-Star*, September 28, 2003, F1.

14. *Ibid.*

15. *Ibid.*

16. *Ibid.*

17. *Ibid.*

18. *Ibid.*

19. Thom Randall, "'We Were Like One Person,'" *The Post-Star*, October 23, 2005, A1.

20. *Ibid.*

21. *Ibid.*

22. *Ibid.*

23. Inge Kimmerly, Phone interview with author, June 22, 2020.

24. *Ibid.*

25. Thom Randall, "'We Were Like One Person,'" *The Post-Star*, October 23, 2005, A1.

26. *Ibid.*

27. Inge Kimmerly, Phone interview with author, June 22, 2020.

28. *Ibid.*

29. *Ibid.*

30. *Ibid.*

Chapter 8

1. Blake Jones, "Madden Hotel Comes Crashing Down," www.poststar.com, July 19, 2011, https://poststar.com/news/local/madden-hotel-comes-crashing-down/article_5c4a4884-b24d-11e0-8028-001cc4c03286.html.

2. Thom Randall, "A Place Nearby, a World Apart," *The Post-Star*, January 11–12, 2004, A1.

3. Maury Thompson, "Madden's Past Obscured by Decline," www.poststar.com, April 9, 2011, https://poststar.com/news/local/-maddens-past-obscured-by-decline/article_f0432018-6326-11e0-a18a-001cc4c002e0.html.

4. *Ibid.*

5. Thom Randall, Interview with author, August 11, 2020.

6. Bob Condon, Interview with author, September 19, 2020.

7. Thom Randall, "Behind Bars," *The Post-Star*, June 15, 2002, A1.

8. *Ibid.*

9. *Ibid.*

10. *Ibid*, A4.

11. *Ibid.*

12. *Ibid.*

13. Post-Star Staff Report, "Post-Star Reporter Earns National Excellence in Journalism Award," *The Post-Star*, April 22, 2005, B1.

14. Thom Randall, Phone interview with author, July 29, 2020.

15. Thom Randall, "Train Ride to NYC Is Lonely Trip," *The Post-Star*, September 13, 2001, A1.

16. Thom Randall, "'We Were Like One Person,'" *The Post-Star*, October 23, 2005, A1.

17. Thom Randall, Email to author, August 11, 2020.

18. *Ibid.*

19. *Ibid.*

20. Thom Randall, "Phone Interview with Author, July 29, 2020.

21. *Ibid.*

22. *Ibid.*

23. *Ibid.*

24. Thom Randall, "Madden 'sticks with You Like Cancer,'" *The Post-Star*, January 12, 2004, A5.

25. *Ibid.*

26. Thom Randall, Phone interview with author, July 29, 2020.

27. *Ibid.*

28. Thom Randall, "Trading Hard Labor for Some Quick Cash," *The Post-Star*, January 12, 2004, A5.

29. Thom Randall, Phone interview with author, July 29, 2011.

30. *Ibid.*

31. Thom Randall, "A Place Nearby, a World Apart," *The Post-Star*, January 11, 2004, A1.

32. Thom Randall, Phone interview with author, July 29, 2011.

33. Will Doolittle, Email to author, July 27, 2020.

34. Thom Randall, Phone interview with author, July 29, 2020.

35. *Ibid.*

36. Thom Randall, "Morning. Noon. Night. An Endless Cycle," *The Post-Star*, January 12, 2004, A1.

37. *Ibid.*

38. Mark Mahoney, "Hearing from You," www.poststar.com, February 15, 2004, https://poststar.com/opinion/commentary/hearing-from-you/article_e06f7c2a-0e16-5658-8fe7-b42f8e65ad24.html.

39. Ken Tingley, "We're Not Perfect, but We Take It Seriously," *The Post-Star*, February 29, 2004, F1.

40. *Ibid.*

41. *Ibid.*

42. *Ibid.*

43. Fran Williams, "Stories on Madden, Gripping, Wonderful," *The Post-Star*, January 14, 2004, A5.

44. Thom Randall, Phone interview with author, July 29, 2020.

45. Mark Mahoney, "Madden Stories Raise Questions," *The Post-Star*, January 18, 2004, F1.

46. Thom Randall, "Madden's Owner: It's a Struggle," *The Post-Star*, February 22, 2004, A1.

47. Maury Thompson, "City Searching for Madden Alternative," *The Post-Star*, August 19, 2004, A1.

48. Maury Thompson, "The Madden File," *The Post-Star*, June 12, 2009, A5.

49. *Ibid.*, A1.

50. Mark Mahoney, "Keep Pressure High on Madden," June 19, 2009, A4.

51. Maury Thompson, "Mayor: Tear Down This Hotel," *The Post-Star*, October 22, 2009, A1.

52. Ken Tingley, "A New Breeze Blows on South Street," July 24, 2011, B1.

53. Maury Thompson, "Glens Falls National Bank to Purchase, Demolish, Madden Hotel," www.poststar.com, July 9, 2010, https://poststar.com/news/local/glens-falls-national-bank-to-purchase-demolish-madden-hotel/article_c0d8ff1c-8b60-11df-b284-001cc4c002e0.html.

54. *Ibid.*

55. *Ibid.*

56. Ken Tingley, "A New Breeze Blows on South Street," July 24, 2011, B1.

57. *Ibid.*

58. Ken Tingley, "Setting South Street in the Right Direction," November 20, 2011, B1.

59. Maury Thompson, "Glens Falls Mayor Wants Earlier Closing Time for City Bars," www.poststar.com, December 26, 2012, https://poststar.com/news/local/glens-falls-mayor-wants-earlier-closing-time-for-city-bars/article_77393e1e-4fab-11e2-b53f-0019bb2963f4.html?mode=comments.

60. Maury Thompson, "State Announces $10 Million to Revitalize South Street in Glens Falls," www.poststar.com, August 18, 2016, https://poststar.com/news/local/state-announces-10-million-to-revitalize-south-street-in-glens-falls/-article_d7b4f053-aa9d-514f-aafc-c69a6e967be7.html.

61. Mark Mahoney, "Madden Stories Raise Questions," *The Post-Star*, January 18, 2004, F1.

62. Thom Randall, "ER," *The Post-Star*, October 24, 2004, A1.

63. *Ibid.*, A7.

64. Thom Randall, "ER," *The Post-Star*, October 24, 2004, A1.

65. Post-Star Staff Report, "Post-Star Reporter Earns National Excellence in Journalism Award," April 22, 2005, B1.

66. Thom Randall, Email to author, August 11, 2020.

67. Thom Randall, Phone interview with author, July 29, 2020.

Chapter 9

1. Ken Tingley, "A Message That Sinks In," *The Post-Star*, May 19, 2010, B1.

2. *Ibid.*

3. *Ibid.*

4. *Ibid.*

5. *Ibid.*

6. *Ibid.*

7. Matthew Sturdevant, "Greenwich Teenagers Killed in Crash," www.poststar.com, April 7, 2002, https://poststar.com/news/local/greenwich-teen-agers-killed-in-crash/article_de05071d-8cc1-5610-8fb2-86733ada6ca0.html.

8. *Ibid.*

9. Darrin Youker, "Students Mourn Loss of Classmates," *The Post-Star*, April 9, 2002, A1.

10. Darrin Youker, "Driver, 16, Is Charged in Crash," *The Post-Star*, April 10, 2002, A1.

11. Gretta Nemcek, Darrin Youker, "Greenwich Teen-agers Laid to Rest," *The Post-Star*, April 11, 2002, A1.

12. *Ibid.*

13. Don Lehman, "Fatal February Crash Leads to Four-count Indictment," *The Post-Star*, Feb. 27, 2002, B1.

14. Darrin Youker, "Charge Prelude to Grand Jury," *The Post-Star*, April 9, 2002, A6.

15. Darrin Youker, "Teen Admits Guilt in Fatal Car Crash," *The Post-Star*, September 5, 2002, A1.

16. *Ibid.*, A6.

17. *Ibid.*

18. *Ibid.*

19. *Ibid.*

20. Ken Tingley, "Let's Learn from This Tragedy," *The Post-Star*, April 9, 2002, B1.

21. *Ibid.*

22. Ken Tingley, "Why Names Matter in Underage Drinking Coverage," www.poststar.com, April 1, 2012, https://poststar.com/news/opinion/columns/ktingley/column-why-names-matter-in-underage-drinking-coverage/article_f539efba-7b9f-11e1-94e2-0019bb2963f4.html.

23. *Ibid.*

24. Don Lehman, "Easy Does It: Officials Argue Laws on Underage Drinking Are Not

Tough Enough to Prevent Tragedies," *The Post-Star*, May 10, 2004, A4.

25. *Ibid.*

26. *Ibid.*

27. *Ibid.*

28. Don Lehman, "Party Host Pleads Guilty," *The Post-Star*, July 26, 2003, B1.

29. Marc Mularz, "It's Time to Open Our Eyes to Teen Drinking," *The Post-Star*, May 24, 2003, A6.

30. *Ibid.*

31. *Ibid.*

32. Darrin Youker, "Things Are Forgotten," *The Post-Star*, May 24, 2004, A1, A4.

33. *Ibid.*

34. Don Lehman, "Easy Does It: Officials Argue Laws on Underage Drinking Are Not Tough Enough to To Prevent Tragedies," *The Post-Star*, May 10, 2004, A4.

35. Kate Perry, "First Curfew, Then Calm," *The Post-Star*, November 21, 2004, B1.

36. Ken Tingley, "Tragic Pages," *The Post-Star*, May 24, 2003, B1.

37. Ken Tingley, "Seeking a Cure to Underage Drinking Epidemic," *The Post-Star*, June 29, 2003, F1.

38. *Ibid.*

39. *Ibid.*

40. *Ibid.*

41. Darrin Youker, "Teen Sentenced to Prison in Fatal Crash," *The Post-Star*, July 15, 2003, B1.

42. *Ibid.*, B8.

43. Ken Tingley, "A Message That Sinks In," www.poststar.com, May 18, 2010, https://post star.com/news/opinion/columns/ktingley/a-message-that-sinks-in/article_328f1fcc-62c3-11df-82ba-001cc4c03286.html.

44. *Ibid.*

45. *Ibid.*

46. *Ibid.*

47. Will Doolittle, Phone interview with author, September 13, 2020.

48. Matt Volke, "Separate Crashes Kill Two Young Area Men," *The Post-Star*, September 14, 2003, A1.

49. Don Lehman, "Police Say Teen Drunk at Time of Fatal Crash," *The Post-Star*, September 26, 2003, A1.

50. Mike Mender, "Just the Kid Next Door," *The Post-Star*, May 10, 2004, A1, A4.

51. Staff Report, "State Newspaper Publishers Association Honors Post-Star," *The Post-Star*, May 8, 2004, B1.

52. *Ibid.*

53. Ken Tingley, "Exploring the Realities of Teenage Drinking," April 25, 2004, F1.

54. *Ibid.*

55. Martha Petteys, "Changing Attitudes, Saving Lives," *The Post-Star*, May 2, 2004, A1.

56. Ken Tingley, "Exploring the Realities of Teenage Drinking," *The Post-Star*, April 25, 2004, F1.

57. Martha Petteys, Phone interview with author, June 1, 2020.

58. *Ibid.*

59. *Ibid.*

60. Martha Petteys, "The Path to Adulthood: Still-Developing Brain Cause of Common Teen Woes," *The Post-Star*, May 16, 2004, A1.

61. Don Lehman, "Hague Teen Dies After Sunday Accident," *The Post-Star*, August 13, 2003, B1.

62. Abigail Tucker, "'This Is Just What We Do': From Forests to Family Rooms, Underage Drinking Rates in This Area Surpass National Averages," *The Post-Star*, May 2, 2003, A1.

63. *Ibid.*

64. Brett Orzechowski, "Playing with Fire: Sports, Drinking Can Often Go Hand in Hand," *The Post-Star*, May 10, 2004, A1, A4.

65. *Ibid.*

66. *Ibid.*

67. Gretta Nemcek Stanclift, "What's a Parent to Do? Navigating the Teen Years Can Be a Challenge for the Adults," *The Post-Star*, May 16, 2004, A5.

68. Martha Petteys, "A Look at a Youth's Life Cut Short by Drinking," *The Post-Star*, May 2, 2004, A1.

69. Martha Petteys, Phone interview with author, June 1, 2020.

70. Martha Petteys, "It Happened to My Family," *The Post-Star*, May 17, 2004, A1.

71. *Ibid.*

72. Martha Petteys, Phone interview with author, June 1, 2020.

73. *Ibid.*

74. *Ibid.*

75. *Ibid.*

76. *Ibid.*

77. *Ibid.*

78. *Ibid.*

79. Martha Petteys, "A Look at a Youth's Life Cut Short by Drinking," *The Post-Star*, May 2, 2004, A1.

80. Darrin Youker, "A Look at a Youth's Life Cut Short by Drinking," *The Post-Star*, May 16, 2004, A8.

81. Don Lehman, "Dealing with a New Life," *The Post-Star*, May 23, 2004, A4.

82. *Ibid.*

83. *Ibid.*

84. Don Lehman, "A Look at a Youth's Life Cut Short by Drinking," *The Post-Star*, May 9, 2004, A1.

85. *Ibid.*

86. *Ibid.*

87. *Ibid.*

88. *Ibid.*, A5.

89. Abigail Tucker, "Drinking Rates Are Sky-High Among Area Teenagers; Reasons Are Varied," *The Post-Star*, May 2, 2004, A6.

90. Abigail Tucker, "'This Is Just What We Do': From Forests to Family Rooms, Underage Drinking Rates in This Area Surpass National Averages," *The Post-Star*, May 2, 2003, A6.

91. Brett Orzechowski, "Playing with Fire: Sports, Drinking Can Often Go Hand in Hand," *The Post-Star*, May 10, 2004, A4.

92. *Ibid.*

93. Mark Mahoney, "Baby Steps Needed to Fight Teen Drinking," *The Post-Star*, May 23, 2004, F1.

94. Ken Tingley, "Plenty of Work Left to Do," *The Post-Star*, June 20, 2004, F1.

95. *Ibid.*

96. *Ibid.*

97. *Ibid.*

Chapter 10

1. Mark Mahoney, Phone interview with author, July 1, 2020.

2. Don Lehman and Thom Randall, "Police Hunt Loose Killer," *The Post-Star*, February 21, 2005, A1.

3. Don Lehman, "Victim Sought Police Minutes Before Death," *The Post-Star*, February 23, 2005, A1.

4. Mark Mahoney, "In Seconds, a Witness to a Homicide," *The Post-Star*, February 21, 2005, A1.

5. *Ibid.*

6. *Ibid.*

7. Mark Mahoney, Phone interview with author, July 1, 2020.

8. *Ibid.*

9. *Ibid.*

10. *Ibid.*

11. Mark Mahoney, "In Seconds, a Witness to a Homicide," *The Post-Star*, February 21, 2005, A6.

12. *Ibid.*

13. *Ibid.*

14. *Ibid.*

15. *Ibid.*

16. *Ibid.*

17. Ken Tingley, "Editor Went Above and Beyond," *The Post-Star*, February 27, 2005, E1.

18. Mark Mahoney, Phone interview with author, July 1, 2020.

19. *Ibid.*

20. *Ibid.*

21. *Ibid.*

22. Mark Mahoney, "In Seconds, a Witness to a Homicide," *The Post-Star*, February 21, 2005, A6.

23. Mark Mahoney, "Shooting Won't Be Forgotten," *The Post-Star*, October 27, 2005, A6.

24. *Ibid.*

25. *Ibid.*

26. Don Lehman, "Suspect's Car Found Abandoned," *The Post-Star*, February 22, 2005, A1.

27. *Ibid.*

28. *Ibid.*

29. Don Lehman, "Brazen Afternoon Shooting Stuns Local Residents," *The Post-Star*, February 22, 2005, A6.

30. *Ibid.*

31. Mark Mahoney, Phone interview with author, July 1, 2020.

32. Mark Mahoney, "Shooting Won't Be Forgotten," *The Post-Star*, October 27, 2005, A6.

33. Don Lehman, "Victim Had Faced Years of Abuse, Sister Says," *The Post-Star*, February 22, 2005, A1.

34. *Ibid.*

35. Don Lehman, "Victim Sought Police Minutes Before Death," *The Post-Star*, February 23, 2005, A1.

36. *Ibid.*

37. *Ibid.*

38. Don Lehman, "Couple's Home Reveals Anger," *The Post-Star*, February 23, 2005, A1.

39. *Ibid.*

40. *Ibid.*

41. *Ibid.*

42. *Ibid.*, A5.

43. *Ibid.*

44. Don Lehman, "Suspect Caught in Syracuse: DiLorenzo Found at Shelter for Homeless," *The Post-Star*, February 24, 2005, A1.

45. Mark Mahoney, Phone interview with author, July 1, 2020.

46. Don Lehman, "DiLorenzo Pleads Guilty," *The Post-Star*, August 13, 2005, A1.

47. *Ibid.*

48. *Ibid.*, A6.

49. *Ibid.*

50. *Ibid.*

51. *Ibid.*

52. Don Lehman, "Christin DeLorenzo to Live with Her Brother," *The Post-Star*, August 13, 2005, A6.

53. *Ibid.*

54. *Ibid.*

55. *Ibid.*

56. Mark Mahoney, Phone interview with author, July 1, 2020.

57. Don Lehman, "DiLorenzo Gets 25 Years to Life," *The Post-Star*, October 27, 2005, A1.

58. *Ibid.*

59. *Ibid.*

60. *Ibid.*

61. *Ibid.*

62. Mark Mahoney, Phone interview with author, July 1, 2020.

63. *Ibid.*

64. Mark Mahoney, "Shooting Won't Be Forgotten," *The Post-Star*, October 27, 2005, A1.

65. *Ibid.*

66. *Ibid.*

67. Mark Mahoney, Phone interview with author, July 1, 2020.

68. *Ibid.*

69. *Ibid.*

70. Mark Mahoney, "Shooting Won't Be Forgotten," *The Post-Star*, October 27, 2005, A1.

71. *Ibid.*

72. Don Lehman and Thom Randall, "Police Hunt Loose Killer," *The Post-Star*, February 21, 2005, A5.

73. Mark Mahoney, "Shooting Won't Be Forgotten," *The Post-Star*, October 27, 2005, A6.

Chapter 11

1. Betsy DeMars, Phone interview with author, July 20, 2020.
2. *Ibid.*
3. *Ibid.*
4. *Ibid.*
5. Konrad Marshall, Phone interview with author, July 3, 2020.
6. *Ibid.*
7. *Ibid.*
8. *Ibid.*
9. *Ibid.*
10. Konrad Marshall, "Abuse Escalates: Victims Speak Out," *The Post-Star*, July 11, 2005, A5.
11. *Ibid.*
12. *Ibid.*
13. Konrad Marshall, Phone interview with author, July 3, 2020.
14. *Ibid.*
15. *Ibid.*
16. Konrad Marshall, "Breaking Their Silence: In Their Own Words," *The Post-Star*, July 10, 2005, A1.
17. Betsy DeMars, Phone interview with author, July 20, 2020.
18. Konrad Marshall, "In Their Own Words," *The Post-Star*, July 10, 2005, A4.
19. Konrad Marshall, "Breaking Their Silence: How It Begins, Victims Speak Out," *The Post-Star*, July 10, 2005, A1.
20. *Ibid.*, A5.
21. Konrad Marshall, Phone interview with author, July 3, 2020.
22. Konrad Marshall, "In Their Own Words," *The Post-Star*, Sunday, July 10, 2005, A4.
23. Konrad Marshall, "Breaking Their Silence: Relationships Start Fine, but Turn Violent," *The Post-Star*, July 10, 2005, A5.
24. *Ibid.*
25. Bonnie Naumann, "On Patrol, Domestic Calls Take Many Forms," *The Post-Star*, July 10, 2005, A1, A4.
26. Konrad Marshall, "Abuse Escalates: Victims Speak Out," *The Post-Star*, July 11, 2005, A1.
27. Bonnie Naumann, "Statistics, Don't Show the Whole Truth," *The Post-Star*, July 10, 2005, A4.
28. *Ibid.*
29. Konrad Marshall, "In Their Own Words," *The Post-Star*, July 11, 2005, A1.
30. Kate Perry, "The Ordinary Face of Abuse: Painting a Picture of a Batterer," *The Post-Star*, July 11, 2005, A5.
31. *Ibid.*
32. Konrad Marshall, "Abuse Escalates: Victims Speak Out," *The Post-Star*, July 11, 2005, A1, A6.
33. Konrad Marshall, "In Their Own Words," *The Post-Star*, July 11, 2005, A1.
34. Konrad Marshall, "Memories of Pain Vivid in Victims' Minds," *The Post-Star*, July 11, 2005, A6

35. *Ibid.*
36. Don Lehman, "Death Threats Were Made Before Murder," *The Post-Star*, July 12, 2005, A6.
37. *Ibid.*
38. Konrad Marshall, "Leaving Is Often Just the Beginning," *The Post-Star*, July 12, 2005, A5.
39. *Ibid.*
40. *Ibid.*
41. *Ibid.*
42. *Ibid.*
43. Betsy DeMars, Phone interview with author, July 20, 2020.
44. Mark Mahoney, "Shining Light on a Dark Problem," *The Post-Star*, July 10, 2005, E1.
45. *Ibid.*
46. *Ibid.*
47. *Ibid.*
48. Ken Tingley, "Paper Belongs to All of You," *The Post-Star*, July 17, 2005, E1, E3.
49. *Ibid.*
50. Staff Report, "Post-Star Named Top Paper," www.poststar.com, September 23, 2006, https://poststar.com/news/local/post-star-honored-as-top-paper/article_45be3894-83b7-5d3f-a6d6-93237c08c062.html.
51. *Ibid.*
52. Konrad Marshall, "Leaving Is Often Just the Beginning," *The Post-Star*, July 12, 2005, A3.
53. *Ibid.*
54. *Ibid.*
55. *Ibid.*

Chapter 12

1. "911 Transcripts," *The Post-Star*, October 5, 2005, A1.
2. Don Lehman, "Boat Recovered from Lake for NTSB Investigation," *The Post-Star*, October 4, 2005, A3.
3. Josh Harkinson, "What Went Wrong: Lake George Disaster," www.popularmechanics.com, October 1, 2009, https://www.popularmechanics.com/science/a953/4199636/.
4. Will Doolittle, "New Regulations Might Have Prevented Sinking," *The Post-Star*, October 4, 2005, A1.
5. Bonnie Naumann, "Life Preservers Weren't Accessible for the Elderly," *The Post-Star*, October 4, 2005, B1.
6. Don Lehman, "Boat Recovered from Lake for NTSB Investigation," *The Post-Star*, October 4, 2005, A3.
7. Don Lehman, "At Least 20 Dead After Tour Boat Capsizes, Sinks in Lake George," *The Post-Star*, October 3, 2005, A1.
8. Don Lehman, "10 Years Later, Survivor, Rescuers Remember Ethan Allen Capsizing," www.poststar.com, September 27, 2015, https://poststar.com/news/local/10-years-later-survivor-rescuers-remember-ethan-allen-capsizing/article_6c4f6358-d5b1-555f-b647-c672c00214d5.html.

9. Amanda Bensen, "'I Don't Know Where My Husband Is,'" *The Post-Star*, October 3, 2005, A5.

10. *Ibid.*, A1.

11. Brendan McGarry, "Survivor: 'I Thanked God for Letting Me Live,'" October 4, 2005, B8.

12. *Ibid.*

13. Amanda Bensen, "'I Don't Know Where My Husband Is,'" *The Post-Star*, October 3, 2005, A5.

14. *Ibid.*

15. Josh Harkinson, "What Went Wrong: Lake George Disaster," www.popularmechanics.com, October 1, 2009, https://www.popularmechanics.com/science/a953/4199636/.

16. Don Lehman, "Boat Capsizes on Lake George; at Least 20 Confirmed Dead," *The Post-Star*, October 3, 2005, A6.

17. Don Lehman, "Rescue Plan Was Followed in Capsizing Incident," *The Post-Star*, October 4, 2005, B7.

18. T.J. Hooker, Phone interview with author, July 7, 2020.

19. *Ibid.*

20. *Ibid.*

21. *Ibid.*

22. *Ibid.*

23. *Ibid.*

24. *Ibid.*

25. Amanda Bensen, "'I Don't Know Where My Husband Is,'" *The Post-Star*, October 3, 2005, A5.

26. *Ibid.*

27. *Ibid.*

28. Don Lehman, "At Least 20 Dead After Tour Boat Capsizes, Sinks in Lake George: Ethan Allen Goes Under During Tour," *The Post-Star*, October 3, 2005, A6.

29. *Ibid.*

30. Don Lehman, "Rescuers, Witnesses Recall Acts of Heroism, Compassion," *The Post-Star*, October 4, 2005, B1, B2.

31. Don Lehman, Phone interview with author, August 11, 2020.

32. Don Lehman, "10 Years Later, Survivor, Rescuers Remember Ethan Allen Capsizing," www.poststar.com, September 27, 2015, https://poststar.com/news/local/10-years-later-survivor-rescuers-remember-ethan-allen-capsizing/article_6c4f6358-d5b1-555f-b647-c672c00214d5.html.

33. Don Lehman, "Rescuers, Witnesses Recall Acts of Heroism, Compassion," *The Post-Star*, October 4, 2005, B1.

34. Scott Donnelly, "Hospital Goes to 'Code Yellow,'" *The Post-Star*, October 3, 2005, B1.

35. T.J. Hooker, Phone interview with author, July 7, 2020.

36. *Ibid.*

37. *Ibid.*

38. *Ibid.*

39. *Ibid.*

40. *Ibid.*

41. *Ibid.*

42. *Ibid.*

43. Amanda Bensen, "'I Don't Know Where My Husband Is,'" *The Post-Star*, October 3, 2005, A1.

44. *Ibid.*

45. *Ibid.*

46. *Ibid.*

47. T.J. Hooker, Phone interview with author, July 7, 2020.

48. Don Lehman, "Rescuers, Witnesses Recall Acts of Heroism, Compassion," *The Post-Star*, October 4, 2005, B2.

49. Don Lehman, Phone interview with author, August 11, 2020.

50. Ken Tingley, "Web Site Adds Immediacy to Paper," *The Post-Star*, October 9, 2005, E1.

51. T.J. Hooker, Phone interview with author, July 7, 2020.

52. *Ibid.*

53. *Ibid.*

54. *Ibid.*

55. *Ibid.*

56. Scott Donnelly, "Hospital Goes to 'Code Yellow,'" *The Post-Star*, October 3, 2005, B1.

57. David Blow, "Ark. Boating Tragedy Spurs Little Worry on Lake George," *The Post-Star*, May 5, 1999, A1.

58. *Ibid.*, A6.

59. *Ibid.*

60. *Ibid.*, A1.

61. Ken Tingley, "Didn't You Ever Hear of Titanic?" *The Post-Star*, May 9, 1999, F2.

62. *Ibid.*

63. Konrad Marshall, Phone interview with author, July 3, 2020.

64. Don Lehman, "Tour Boat Raised from Lake George; Weight Limit, Crew Size Is Questioned," *The Post-Star*, October 4, 2005, A1.

65. Will Doolittle, "New Regulations Might Have Prevented Sinking," *The Post-Star*, October 4, 2005, A1.

66. *Ibid.*

67. Josh Harkinson, "What Went Wrong: Lake George Disaster," www.popularmechanics.com, October 1, 2009, https://www.popularmechanics.com/science/a953/4199636/.

68. *Ibid.*

69. Mark Mahoney, "Limits Should Reflect Reality," *The Post-Star*, October 5, 2005, A4.

70. Don Lehman, "10 Years Later, Survivor, Rescuers Remember Ethan Allen Capsizing," *The Post-Star*, September 27, 2015, A1.

71. *Ibid.*

72. *Ibid.*

73. Don Lehman, "Ethan Allen Pilot Offers Blood and Urine Samples," *The Post-Star*, October 5, 2005, A1.

74. T.J. Hooker, Phone interview with author, July 7, 2020.

75. Ken Tingley, "Web Site Adds Immediacy to Paper," *The Post-Star*, October 9, 2005, E1.

76. Amanda Bensen, "Ethan Allen Rescuers Honored," *The Post-Star*, February 2, 2006, A1.

77. *Ibid.*

78. *Ibid.*

79. Don Lehman, "10 Years Later, Survivor, Rescuers Remember Ethan Allen Capsizing," *The Post-Star*, September 27, 2015, A1.

80. Don Lehman, "Captain, Boat Owner Indicted in Tour Boat Tragedy," *The Post-Star*, February 5, 2007, A1.

81. Don Lehman, "Ethan Allen Guilty Pleas Entered," www.poststar.com, March 27, 2007, https://poststar.com/news/local/ethan-allen-guilty-pleas-entered/article_d50f72e2-8bbc-547a-a497-db69cdcba2aa.html.

82. *Ibid.*

83. *Ibid.*

84. *Ibid.*

85. Don Lehman, "Shoreline Insurance Insufficient," www.poststar.com, February 21, 2006, https://poststar.com/news/local/shoreline-insurance-insufficient/article_d5f093e2-cac0-5eeb-944d-c7fe051d824d.html.

86. Mike Goodwin, "Netflix's 'The Laundromat' Dramatizes Ethan Allen Boat Disaster," www.timesunion.com, October 18, 2019, https://www.timesunion.com/news/article/-Netflix-s-The-Laundromat-dramatizes-Ethan-Allen-14543997.php.

87. Brian Nearing, "Restitution in Ethan Allen Insurance Scam Appears Unlikely," www.timesunion.com, April 24, 2016, https://www.timesunion.com/tuplus-local/article/-Restitution-in-Ethan-Allen-insurance-scam-appears-7306956.php.

88. *Ibid.*

89. *Ibid.*

90. Don Lehman, "Ethan Allen Lawsuit Settled," *The Post-Star*, August 11, 2009, https://poststar.com/news/local/ethan-allen-lawsuit-settled/article_47a3baff-8f9c-5694-8144-00531a7eaa0c.html.

91. Brian Nearing, "Restitution in Ethan Allen Insurance Scam Appears Unlikely," www.timesunion.com, April 24, 2016, https://www.timesunion.com/tuplus-local/article/-Restitution-in-Ethan-Allen-insurance-scam-appears-7306956.php.

92. Don Lehman, "Police: LG Drowning Was Suicide," www.poststar.com, September 14, 2009, https://poststar.com/news/local/police-lg-drowning-was-suicide/article_d2a184bb-3cec-56c3-b020-876bf1cc4181.html.

93. Don Lehman, "Last Lawsuit in Ethan Allen Capsizing Dismissed," www.poststar.com, November 29, 2012, https://poststar.com/news/local/last-lawsuit-in-ethan-allen-capsizing-dismissed/article_33c80116-3a3d-11e2-906f-001a4bcf887a.html.

94. Post-Star Staff report, "Post-Star Honored as Top Paper," www.Post-Star.com, September 23, 2006, https://poststar.com/news/local/post-star-honored-as-top-paper/article_45be3894-83b7-5d3f-a6d6-93237c08c062.html.

95. *Ibid.*

96. T.J. Hooker, Phone interview with author, July 7, 2020.

97. Don Lehman, "10 Years Later, Survivor, Rescuers Remember Ethan Allen Capsizing," www.poststar.com, September 27, 2015, https://poststar.com/news/local/10-years-later-survivor-rescuers-remember-ethan-allen-capsizing/article_6c4f6358-d5b1-555f-b647-c672c00214d5.html.

98. *Ibid.*

99. Don Lehman, "Ethan Allen Captain Dies," www.poststar.com, August 17, 2016, https://poststar.com/blogs/don_lehman/ethan-allen-captain-dies/article_b7eca45a-646f-11e6-b821-7bddc5896855.html.

100. Don Lehman, "10 Years Later, Survivor, Rescuers Remember Ethan Allen Capsizing," www.poststar.com, September 27, 2015, https://poststar.com/news/local/10-years-later-survivor-rescuers-remember-ethan-allen-capsizing/article_6c4f6358-d5b1-555f-b647-c672c00214d5.html.

101. *Ibid.*

102. Don Lehman, "NTSB: Ethan Allen Was Overloaded," www.poststar.com, July 26, 2006, https://poststar.com/news/local/ntsb-ethan-allen-was-overloaded/article_680f7fae-d8db-5bb8-bd8c-8957a1bbee5b.html.

103. Don Lehman, "10 Years Later, Survivor, Rescuers Remember Ethan Allen Capsizing," www.poststar.com, September 27, 2015, https://poststar.com/news/local/10-years-later-survivor-rescuers-remember-ethan-allen-capsizing/-article_6c4f6358-d5b1-555f-b647-c672c00214d5.html.

104. *Ibid.*

105. *Ibid.*

106. T.J. Hooker, Phone interview with author, July 7, 2020.

107. *Ibid.*

108. *Ibid.*

109. Don Lehman, Phone interview with author, August 11, 2020.

110. Madeline Farbman, "An Anniversary of Tears," www.poststar.com, October 2, 2006, https://poststar.com/news/local/an-anniversary-of-tears/article_d59d62c4-95ea-584c-8ea5-0a8c33aaa158.html.

111. *Ibid.*

112. *Ibid.*

Chapter 13

1. Ken Tingley, "From Mailroom to Corner Office," *The Post-Star*, February 23, 2004, B1.

2. Ken Tingley, "Paper Has Seen Changes," *The Post-Star*, February 24, 2004, B5.

3. Mike Mender, "Lee Enterprises Takes Control of Post-Star, www.poststar.com, April 2, 2002, Https://poststar.com/business/local/-lee-enterprises-takes-control-of-post-star/-article_09fcc591-1fd2-5735-89e4-543ae83b50b9.html

4. Jim Marshall, Phone Interview with Author, June 22, 2020.

5. *Ibid.*

6. Erin DeMuth, "Longtime Post-Star Publisher Retiring," *The Post-Star*, March 18, 2006, A1.

7. Jim Marshall, Phone interview with author, June 22, 2020.

8. *Ibid.*

9. Ken Tingley, "Losing an Old Friend, Welcoming a New One," *The Post-Star*, March 26, 2006, E1.

10. *Ibid.*

11. Post-Star Staff Report, "Post-Star Honored as Top Paper," *The Post-Star*, September 23, 2006, B1.

12. Erin DeMuth, "Marshalls to Receive Community Service Award," *The Post-Star*, January 5, 2008, B1.

13. Ken Tingley, "Paper Has Seen Changes," *The Post-Star*, February 24, 2004, B5.

14. *Ibid.*

15. Staff, Wire reports, "Lee Enterprises to Buy Berkshire Hathaway Newspaper Operations," www.poststar.com, January 29, 2020, https://poststar.com/news/local/lee-enterprises-to-buy-berkshire-hathaway-newspaper-operations/article_212110dc-ceb8-58b0-991f-a107b24c1a44.html.

Chapter 14

1. Staff Report, "Sweeney Unhurt in Crash," *The Post-Star*, February 1, 2001, B1.

2. Mark Mahoney, "Sweeney Portrayed on HBO," www.poststar.com, May 29, 2008, https://poststar.com/news/local/sweeney-portrayed-on-hbo/article_88d9e597-0724-50fa-94c6-7a9b024d917b.html.

3. Don Lehman, "Sweeney in Bar Before Crash," *The Post-Star*, February 3, 2001, A1.

4. Don Lehman, "Sweeney Talked to Patron," *The Post-Star*, February 3, 2001, A6.

5. Don Lehman, "Police: No Bias in Crash," *The Post-Star*, February 2, 2001, A6.

6. Will Doolittle, "Sweeney's Crash Raises Questions," *The Post-Star*, February 4, 2001, B1.

7. *Ibid.*

8. Staff Report, "Sweeney Unhurt in Crash," *The Post-Star*, February 1, 2001, B1.

9. Don Lehman, "Police: No Bias in Crash," *The Post-Star*, February 2, 2001, A1.

10. *Ibid.*

11. Don Lehman, "Sweeney in Bar Before Crash," *The Post-Star*, February 3, 2001, A1.

12. Don Lehman, "Police: No Bias in Crash," *The Post-Star*, February 2, 2001, A1.

13. *Ibid.*, A6.

14. *Ibid.*

15. Don Lehman, "Union: Captain Is the Scapegoat in Sweeney Probe," www.Post-Star.com, November 17, 2006, https://poststar.com/news/union-captain-is-the-scapegoat-in-sweeney-probe/article_6e32a5b7-0534-5379-9d7e-d525b0acb239.html.

16. Don Lehman, "Sweeney in Bar Before Crash," *The Post-Star*, February 3, 2001, A1.

17. *Ibid.*

18. Will Doolittle, "Sweeney's Crash Raises Questions," *The Post-Star*, February 4, 2001, B1.

19. *Ibid.*

20. *Ibid.*, B11.

21. Ken Tingley, "The Labeling of Newspapers Is Not Fair," *The Post-Star*, November 5, 2000, F1.

22. House Archives, www.historycms2.house.gov, Pg. 55, https://historycms2.house.gov/Institution/Election-Statistics/1998election/.

23. Election Results, 2020, www.few.gov, https://www.fec.gov/resources/cms-content/documents/federalelections00.pdf.

24. Election Results, 2002, www.historycms2.house.gov, Pg. 33, https://historycms2.house.gov/Institution/Election-Statistics/1998election/.

25. Election Results, 2004, www.historycms2.house.gov, Pg. 40, https://historycms2.house.gov/Institution/Election-Statistics/2004election/.

26. Ken Tingley, "Trying to Figure Out Sweeney," *The Post-Star*, November 20, 2005, C1.

27. Ken Tingley, "Sweeney May Have Competition," *The Post-Star*, February 19, 2006, C1.

28. Jason McCord, "John Sweeney's Son Indicted in '04 Fight," www.poststar.com, April 15, 2005, https://poststar.com/news/local/-john-sweeney-s-son-indicted-in-fight/article_a26f8f38-4943-53c4-b65c-e0f26d2b3296.html.

29. John Warren, "20th CD—The End of Congressman John Sweeney?" November 1, 2006.

30. Brendan Lyons, "Congressman's Wife Called Police," www.timesunion.com, October 31, 2006, https://web.archive.org/web/20061213205513/http://timesunion.com/AspStories/storyprint.asp?StoryID=530664.

31. Politics blog, "A Sweeney Mystery," *New York Daily News*, December 18, 2010, https://www.nydailynews.com/blogs/dailypolitics/-sweeney-mystery-blog-entry-1.1667425.

32. Brendan McGarry, "Young Sweeney Avoids Jail Term," www.poststar.com, December 17, 2005, https://poststar.com/news/local/young-sweeney-avoids-jail-term/article_d8182818-ad2b-5192-8dfb-7aab056aff15.html.

33. *Ibid.*

34. *Ibid.*

35. Maury Thompson, "Sweeney Explains Ski Trip," www.poststar.com, January 19, 2006, https://poststar.com/news/local/sweeney-explains-ski-trip/article_f913bedf-0942-54aa-9c61-8a17d991154c.html.

36. Post-Star Staff, wire reports, "Sweeney Trip Raises Questions," www.poststar.com, October 19, 2006, https://poststar.com/news/sweeney-trip-raises-questions/article_6a0b9507-e158-50d4-a91c-b6305d8bb4eb.html.

37. Zachary Roth, "'Caribbean Caucus' Lawmakers Took Trips on Stanford Jets," TPM, February 17, 2009, https://talkingpointsmemo.com/muckraker/caribbean-caucus-lawmakers-took-trips-on-stanford-jets.

38. Dominic Rushe, "Allen Stanford Sentenced to 110 Years in Jail for $7bn Investment Fraud," www.the guardian.com, June 14, 2012, https://www.theguardian.com/world/2012/jun/14/allen-stanford-110-years-jail.

39. Elizabeth Benjamin, "Sweeney Pays Wife," www.timesunion.com, April 11, 2006, https://blog.timesunion.com/capitol/411-sweeney-pay-wife/.

40. Raymond Hernandez, "Party Photograph Put a Congressman on the Defensive," www.nytimes.com, April 29, 2006, https://www.nytimes.com/2006/04/29/nyregion/-party-photographs-put-a-congressman-on-the-defensive.html?referringSource=articleShare

41. Maury Thompson, "Sweeney Refutes Story," www.poststar.com, April 29, 2006, https://poststar.com/news/local/sweeney-refutes-story/article_e7cb4ab4-aace-5813-83f2-602e2cc550a9.html.

42. Ibid.

43. Will Doolittle, "Saving the Sweeney Campaign," www.poststar.com, May 5, 2006, https://www.timesunion.com/local/article/-Redemption-of-John-Sweeney-a-work-in-progress-12713399.php.

44. Maury Thompson, Phone interview with author, June 1, 2020.

45. Ibid.

46. Craig Burnham, "20 Most Corrupt Members of Congress," www.dailykos,com, September 20, 2006, https://www.dailykos.com/stories/2006/9/20/248172/.

47. Charles Fiegl, "Gillibrand Calls on Sweeney to Release Run-ins with Police," www.poststar.com, October 10, 2006, https://poststar.com/news/local/gillibrand-calls-on-sweeney-to-release-police-records/article_4dd1d0a4-85a1-5b82-830c-4288f062726a.html.

48. Maury Thompson, "Sweeney's Refusal Cancels Local Debate," www.poststar.com, October 23, 2006, https://poststar.com/news/sweeney-s-refusal-cancels-local-debate/article_eb627a9e-b3d1-59b5-a0c7-321322d8ce32.html.

49. Ibid.

50. Mark Mahoney, "Sweeney's Record Overshadows His Shortcomings," www.poststar.com, October 29, 2006, https://poststar.com/opinion/editorials/sweeneys-record-overshadows-his-shortcomings/article_99a513fa-6279-5e41-a297-a4a043ace6e6.html.

51. Ibid.

52. Brendan Lyons, "Congressman's Wife Called Police," www.timesunion.com, October 31, 2006, https://web.archive.org/web/20061213205513/http://timesunion.com/AspStories/storyprint.asp?StoryID=530664.

53. Post-Star Staff Report, "Report: Wife Called 911 on Congressman," www.poststar.com, November 1, 2006, https://poststar.com/news/article_de946e07-5b8a-5adc-8a60-a42409782d22.html.

54. Brendan Lyons, "Congressman Wife Called Police," www.timesunion.com, October 31, 2006, https://web.archive.org/web/20061213205513/http://timesunion.com/AspStories/storyprint.asp?StoryID=530664.

55. Ibid.

56. Ibid.

57. Maury Thompson, "Sweeney Refutes Allegation," www.poststar.com, November 1, 2006, https://poststar.com/news/sweeney-refutes-allegation/article_a6cba495-48e6-588d-9bd1-9d36dfbffe2e.html.

58. Ibid.

59. Ibid.

60. Charles Fiegl, "Sweeney Announces Grant, Avoids Questions of Abuse," www.poststar.com, November 6, 2006, https://poststar.com/news/sweeney-announces-grant-avoids-questions-of-abuse/article_1fa578c6-f23d-5008-8064-ecb5695fb2cf.html.

61. Maury Thompson, "Sweeney's Refutes Allegation," www.poststar.com, November 1, 2006, https://poststar.com/news/sweeney-refutes-allegation/article_a6cba495-48e6-588d-9bd1-9d36dfbffe2e.html.

62. Maury Thompson, "GOP Leaders Stump for Sweeney," www.poststar.com, November 4, 2006, https://poststar.com/news/local/gop-leaders-stump-for-sweeney/article_1bbe0c7c-5cf1-5c52-b951-16785d743a6d.html.

63. Mark Mahoney, "Endorsement Withdrawn: Character Questions Continue to Dog Sweeney," www.poststar.com, November 3, 2006, https://poststar.com/news/editorial-endorsement-withdrawn-character-questions-continue-to-dog-sweeney/article_34b1143e-9f69-5fc2-bca7-7622dac81e71.html.

64. Ibid.

65. Charles Fiegl, "Sweeney Announces Grant, Avoids Questions of Abuse," www.poststar.com, November 6, 2006, https://poststar.com/news/sweeney-announces-grant-avoids-questions-of-abuse/article_1fa578c6-f23d-5008-8064-ecb5695fb2cf.html.

66. Ibid.

67. Konrad Marshall, "Sweeney: `I'm Only Sorry That I Let You Down,'" www.poststar.com, November 8, 2006, https://poststar.com/news/local/sweeney-im-only-sorry-that-i-let-you-down/article_ddac5b7d-8567-5e22-92a3-1aae6cb2b526.html.

68. Ibid.

69. Police Benevolent Association of New York, "Media Probes Wrongful Transfer of PBA Member," www.nystbpa.org, November 17, 2006, https://www.nystpba.org/blog/breaking-news/-media-probes-wrongful-transfer-of-pba-member/.

70. Ibid.

71. Ibid.

72. Don Lehman, "Union: Captain Scapegoat in Sweeney Probe," www.poststar.com, November 17, 2006, https://poststar.com/news/union-captain-is-the-scapegoat-in-

sweeney-probe/article_6e32a5b7-0534-5379-9d7e-d525b0acb239.html.

73. *Ibid.*

74. *Ibid.*

75. *Ibid.*

76. *Ibid.*

77. Patrick O'Connor, "Sweeney's Wife Claims Abuse," www.politico.com, July 23, 2007, https://www.politico.com/blogs/politico-now/2007/07/-sweeneys-wife-claims-abuse-002299.

78. Alyson Martin, "Sweeney Arrest on DWI Charges," www.poststar.com, November 12, 2007, https://poststar.com/news/local/sweeney-arrested-on-dwi-charges/article_9ce44c1a-b943-5a57-b622-da357df428b2.html.

79. Neil Kirby, "Sweeney Charged with Felony DWI," www.poststar.com, April 6, 2009, https://poststar.com/news/local/sweeney-charged-with-felony-dwi/article_e8adc0ec-2f66-5819-a1f4-8fb5208079d8.html.

80. Neil Kirby, "Sweeney Charged with Felony DWI," www.poststar.com, April 6, 2009, https://poststar.com/news/local/sweeney-charged-with-felony-dwi/article_e8adc0ec-2f66-5819-a1f4-8fb5208079d8.html.

81. Paul Grondahl, "Redemption of John Sweeney a Work in Progress," www.timesunion.com, February 27, 2018, https://www.timesunion.com/local/article/Redemption-of-John-Sweeney-a-work-in-progress-12713399.php.

82. Thomas Dimopoulos, "Former Congressman Sweeney Sentenced in Drunken Driving Case," www.poststar.com, April 23, 2010, https://poststar.com/news/local/former-congressman-sweeney-sentenced-in-drunken-driving-case/article_9dc557b6-4efa-11df-8488-001cc4c002e0.html.

83. *Ibid.*

84. Staff Report, "Sweeney Granted Early Release from Jail," www.poststar.com, April 30, 2010, https://poststar.com/news/local/sweeney-granted-early-release-from-jail/article_6536d09a-54b4-11df-95e0-001cc4c002e0.html.

85. Carol DeMare, "Sweeney Talks of Loss, Healing," www.timesunion.com, March 6, 2011, https://www.timesunion.com/local/article/-Sweeney-talks-of-loss-healing-1044313.php.

86. *Ibid.*

87. Paul Grondahl, "Redemption of John Sweeney a Work in Progress," www.timesunion.com, February 27, 2018, https://www.timesunion.com/local/article/Redemption-of-John-Sweeney-a-work-in-progress-12713399.php.

88. Carol DeMare, "Sweeney Talks of Loss, Healing," www.timesunion.com, March 6, 2011, https://www.timesunion.com/local/article/-Sweeney-talks-of-loss-healing-1044313.php.

89. Michael DeMasi, "New Owners Will Keep DiCarlo's Gentleman's Club in Albany Kicking," www.bizjournals.co, October 2, 2014, https://www.bizjournals.com/albany/morning_call/2014/10/new-owners-will-keep-dicarlos-gentlemens-club-in-albany.html.

90. Associated Press and Daily Freeman, "Former Mid-Hudson Rep. John Sweeney Failed to Pay Private Investigator's Bill, Lawsuit Alleges," www.daily freeman.com, August 23, 2018, https://www.dailyfreeman.com/news/former-mid-hudson-rep-john-sweeney-failed-to-pay-private-investigator-s-bill-lawsuit-alleges/article_6c36d357-6536-5327-80e7-c21cf36153fb.html.

91. Kyle Hughes, "Ex-Congressman Sweeney Joins Trump's Team," www.saratogian.com, December 15, 2016, https://www.saratogian.com/news/ex-congressman-sweeney-joins-trump-team/article_e0c7cbde-e537-539e-b308-a7847c6c474b.html.

92. Michael Goot, "Former Rep. Sweeney Lobbying for Kremlin-controlled Bank," wwwpoststar.com, September 16, 2019, https://poststar.com/news/local/govt-and-politics/-former-rep-sweeney-lobbying-for-kremlin-controlled-bank/article_a259b64c-bf9e-5e21-9d28-6d9928fbb3bf.html.

93. Dan Friedman, "Trump Insider as a Lobbyist," www.motherjones.com, September 13, 2019, https://www.motherjones.com/politics/2019/09/-kremlin-controlled-russian-bank-hires-trump-insider-as-a-lobbyist/.

Chapter 15

1. Nick Reisman, Phone interview with author, August 20, 2020.

2. *Ibid.*

3. RPA-PAC, "Saratoga County Gives Post-Star Pistol Permit Holders," www.keepandbearmarks.com, February 27, 2018.

4. "Another Paper in NY State Wants to Publish a List of Concealed Carriers!" www.highroad.com, February 4, 2008, https://www.thehighroad.org/index.php?threads/another-paper-in-ny-state-wants-to-publish-a-list-of-concealed-carriers.336892/.

5. Laurence Hammack, "roanoke.com drops list of gun owners," www.Roanoke.com, March 12, 2007, https://roanoke.com/archive/-roanoke-com-drops-list-of-gun-owners/article_a6e79c93-7d63-5b87-a16c-fed05df29799.html.

6. Megan O'Matz, John Maines, "License to Carry," www.sun-sentinel.com, January 28, 2007, https://www.sun-sentinel.com/news/sfl-guns.-storygallery-storygallery.html.

7. *Ibid.*

8. Ken Tingley, "Post-Star Addresses Pistol Permit Controversy," www.poststar.com, February 4, 2008, https://poststar.com/news/latest/the-post-star-addresses-pistol-permit-controversy/article_1ba7c108-8116-5940-8139-d4ec01e5d55e.html.

9. *Ibid.*

10. "Another Paper in NY State Wants to Publish a List of Concealed Carriers!" www.high road.com, February 4, 2008, https://www.thehighroad.

org/index.php?threads/another-paper-in-ny-state-wants-to-publish-a-list-of-concealed-carriers.336892/.

11. *Ibid.*

12. *Ibid.*

13. Nick Reisman, Phone interview with author, August 20, 2020.

14. Kathleen A. Marchione, Letter to Nick Reisman, From author's personal files, February 21, 2008.

15. Nicholas Confessore, "State Clerks' Group to Oppose License Policy," www.nytimes.com, October 5, 2007, https://www.nytimes.com/2007/10/05/nyregion/05spitzer.html?referringSource=articleShare.

16. Nick Reisman, Phone interview with author, August 20, 2020.

17. *Ibid.*

Chapter 16

1. Don Lehman, "Girl, 16, Dies in Crash," *The Post-Star*, April 21, 2008, A1.

2. Don Lehman, "Speed Cited in Fatal Crash," www.poststar.com, June 6, 2008, https://poststar.com/news/local/speed-cited-in-fatal-crash/-article_f4f74852-ecd7-5a4f-9acd-8e281ffcc62b.html.

3. Don Lehman, "Girl, 16, Dies in Crash," *The Post-Star*, April 21, 2008, A1.

4. *Ibid.*, A6.

5. Don Lehman, "Speed Cited in Fatal Crash," www.poststar.com, June 6, 2008, https://poststar.com/news/local/speed-cited-in-fatal-crash/-article_f4f74852-ecd7-5a4f-9acd-8e281ffcc62b.html.

6. Don Lehman, "Sentencing in Fatal Crash Bring Stories of Sadness," www.poststar.com, October 17, 2008, https://poststar.com/news/local/sentencing-in-fatal-crash-brings-stories-of-sadness/article_94ef3fb0-c372-546f-a5af-983b41bd7c96.html.

7. *Ibid.*

8. *Ibid.*

9. *Ibid.*

10. Anne Kumar, "Fatal Crash Claims Two," *The Post-Star*, February 21, 2005, A1.

11. Ken Tingley, "Keep Talking About Teen Drinking," *The Post-Star*, March 2, 2005, B1.

12. *Ibid.*

13. Ken Tingley, "Just a Sip or Two? Teen Drinking Still a Problem," *The Post-Star*, April 24, 2005, C1.

14. *Ibid.*

15. Don Lehman, "Party Results in 13 Arrests," www.poststar.com, December 14, 2004, https://poststar.com/news/local/party-results-in-13-arrests/article_36b10015-8b40-56de-905c-e55d86d790d6.html.

16. *Ibid.*

17. *Ibid.*

18. *Ibid.*

19. Jason McCord, "Program Fights Underage Drinking," www.poststar.com, April 29, 2005, https://poststar.com/news/local/program-fights-underage-drinking/article_602c843f-866d-56a9-8e47-a5862914a7da.html.

20. Don Lehman, "Parents of Teen in Fatal DWI to Stand Trial, www.poststar.com, November 26, 2008, Https://poststar.com/news/local/parents-of-teen-in-fatal-dwi-to-stand-trial/-article_1225574c-4764-53e8-8623-1411594fce7d.html.

21. Don Lehman, "Driver in Fatal Crash: `I'm Sorry,'" www.poststar.com, October 18, 2008, https://poststar.com/news/local/driver-in-fatal-crash-im-sorry/article_fd3b5b79-331d-56c9-b26e-b980d440a8b3.html.

22. *Ibid.*

23. Don Lehman, "Underage Drinking Trial Delayed," www.poststar.com, December 17, 2008, https://poststar.com/news/local/underage-drinking-trial-delayed/article_3e4dd9e7-3ba0-5bb4-a512-46ec7518bc99.html.

24. Mark Mahoney, "Parents, Take Note of This," *The Post-Star*, February 8, 2009, E1.

25. Don Lehman, "St. Andrewses: We Didn't Know of Drinking at Parties, www.poststar.com, February 11, 2009, https://poststar.com/news/local/updated-st-andrewses-we-didnt-know-of-drinking-at-parties/image_8be61cbf-d3cd-5963-bd60-f88ef38be55b.html?mode=comments.

26. *Ibid.*

27. *Ibid.*

28. *Ibid.*

29. *Ibid.*

30. *Ibid.*

31. Ken Tingley, "Parents Guilty, but So Are Many Others," *The Post-Star*, February 15, 2009, C1.

32. *Ibid.*

33. *Ibid.*

34. *Ibid.*

35. Don Lehman, "Parents of Teen in Fatal DWi to Stand Trial," www.poststar.com, November 26, 2008, https://poststar.com/news/local/parents-of-teen-in-fatal-dwi-to-stand-trial/article_1225574c-4764-53e8-8623-1411594fce7d.html.

36. Ken Tingley, "Parents Guilty, but So Are Many Others," *The Post-Star*, February 15, 2009, C1.

37. Don Lehman, Nick Reisman, "Parents Get Split Verdict," www.poststar.co, February 14, 2009, https://poststar.com/news/local/parents-get-split-verdict/article_1aa93582-d940-5f3c-b28f-bcc95c85bb46.html.

38. *Ibid.*

39. *Ibid.*

40. *Ibid.*

41. *Ibid.*

42. *Ibid.*

43. *Ibid.*

44. Don Lehman, "In Putnam Double Fatal Crash Case, Court Finds Father Does

Not Share in Guilt with Son," www.poststar.com, March 10, 2011, https://poststar.com/news/local/in-putnam-double-fatal-crash-case-court-finds-father-does-not-share-in-guilt-of/article_1fb7c362-4b62-11e0-b917-001cc4c03286.html.

45. Don Lehman, "Sentencing in Fatal Crash Brings Stories of Sadness," www.poststar.com, October 17, 2008, https://poststar.com/news/local/sentencing-in-fatal-crash-brings-stories-of-sadness/article_94ef3fb0-c372-546f-a5af-983b41bd7c96.html.

46. Don Lehman, "Parents Get Split Verdict," www.poststar.com, February 14, 2009, https://poststar.com/news/local/parents-get-split-verdict/article_1aa93582-d940-5f3c-b28f-bcc95c85bb46.html.

47. Ken Tingley, "Getting Through to Kids on Underage Drinking," *The Post-Star*, October 10, 2009, C1.

48. *Ibid.*

49. *Ibid.*

50. *Ibid.*

51. *Ibid.*

52. Cathleen F. Crowley, "Cops: Suspect Targeted Wife," www.timesunion.com, July 18, 2012, https://www.timesunion.com/local/article/-Cops-Suspect-targeted-wife-3713836.php.

53. *Ibid.*

54. *Ibid.*

55. Don Lehman, "Double-fatal Car Crash Convict Jailed Again, www.poststar.com, June 5, 2018, https://poststar.com/news/local/double-fatal-car-crash-convict-jailed-again/article_2a4db890-a31e-5267-a578-d125191893fd.html.

56. *Ibid.*

57. *Ibid.*

58. Don Lehman, "Woman Arrested After Underage Drinking Party," www.poststar.com, November 2, 2009, https://poststar.com/news/local/woman-arrested-after-underage-drinking-party/article_83dd5460-c7d3-11de-b7f7-001cc4c002e0.html.

59. *Ibid.*

60. *Ibid.*

61. *Ibid.*

62. Don Lehman, "LaPoint Cleared of Providing Alcohol to Minors," www.poststar.com, July 2, 2010, https://poststar.com/news/local/lapoint-cleared-of-providing-alcohol-to-minors/article_114d85c4-861d-11df-8b13-001cc4c03286.html.

63. *Ibid.*

64. Ken Tingley, "Saving Even a Single Life Makes Fight Worthwhile," www.poststar.com, October 10, 2010, https://poststar.com/news/opinion/columns/ktingley/saving-even-a-single-life-makes-fight-worthwhile/article_2aaf36d6-d3f0-11df-ad45-001cc4c002e0.html.

65. *Ibid.*

66. Ken Tingley, "Make Sure Your Teen Gets It," *The Post-Star*, June 14, 2009, C1.

67. *Ibid.*

68. Ken Tingley, "Father Did Right Thing," *The Post-Star*, January 24, 2010, C1.

69. *Ibid.*

70. Ken Tingley, "Parents, This Is Your Wake Up Call," *The Post-Star*, April 7, 2010, B1.

71. *Ibid.*

72. *Ibid.*

73. *Ibid.*

74. *Ibid.*

75. *Ibid.*

76. *Ibid.*

77. *Ibid.*

78. *Ibid.*

79. Ken Tingley, "A Message That Sinks In," www.poststar.com, May 18, 2010, https://poststar.com/news/opinion/columns/ktingley/-a-message-that-sinks-in/article_328f1fcc-62c3-11df-82ba-001cc4c03286.html.

80. *Ibid.*

81. *Ibid.*

82. *Ibid.*

83. *Ibid.*

84. *Ibid.*

85. *Ibid.*

86. *Ibid.*

87. *Ibid.*

88. Ken Tingley, "South High Parents Earn `F,'" www.poststar.com, May 17, 2011, https://poststar.com/news/opinion/columns/ktingley/-south-high-parents-earn-f/article_5565b13e-80bb-11e0-a43d-001cc4c03286.html.

89. Ken Tingley, "Scrapbook Puts Us on the Same Page," www.poststar.com, February 16, 2013, https://poststar.com/news/local/flashback-scrapbook-puts-us-on-the-same-page/article_f7696558-31cc-5e29-ab81-8247ad3a0b2b.html.

90. *Ibid.*

91. *Ibid.*

92. *Ibid.*

93. Joseph Tingley, "Scrapbook Teaches a Lesson Not Soon Forgotten," www.poststar.com, March 2, 2013, https://poststar.com/news/opinion/guest-essay-scrapbook-teaches-a-lesson-not-soon-forgotten/article_359096e6-83b4-11e2-a040-001a4bcf887a.html.

94. *Ibid.*

95. *Ibid.*

96. *Ibid.*

97. *Ibid.*

Chapter 17

1. Mark Mahoney, Phone interview with author, August 29, 2020.

2. *Ibid.*

3. Adam Patterson, "Putting the 'Star' in Post-Star," All Points North, November 21, 2017.

4. Mark Mahoney, Interview with author, August 29, 2020.

5. Ken Tingley, "Small Paper's Prize Is Something to Celebrate," *The Post-Star*, April 22, 2001, F1.

6. Mark Mahoney, Phone interview with author, August 29, 2020.

7. *Ibid.*

8. Post-Star Staff Report, "Post-Star Pulitzer: Mahoney Honored for Editorials," *The Post-Star*, April 21, 2009, A1.

9. Ken Tingley, "An Honor for Battle's Worth Fighting," *The Post-Star*, April 22, 2009, A4.

10. *Ibid.*

11. Mark Mahoney, Phone interview with author, August 29, 2020.

12. *Ibid.*

13. Pulitzer.org, https://www.pulitzer.org/winners/mark-mahoney

14. Staff Report, "Post-Star Editor Honored at Pulitzer Prize Event," *The Post-Star*, April 22, 2010, A1.

15. Post-Star Staff Report, "Mark Mahoney, Pulitzer Winner, Leaving Post-Star," www.poststar.com, October 19, 2011, https://poststar.com/news/local/mark-mahoney-pulitzer-winner-leaving-post-star/article_38fc76f2-fa8e-11e0-b38b-001cc4c002e0.html.

16. Mark Mahoney, Phone Interview with Author, August 29, 2020.

17. Ken Tingley, "Things Won't Be the Same Without Mahoney," www.poststar.com, October 22, 2011, https://poststar.com/article_c2e0b02c-fd22-11e0-af37-001cc4c03286.html

18. *Ibid.*

19. Mark Mahoney, Phone interview with author, August 29, 2020.

20. *Ibid.*

21. *Ibid.*

22. *Ibid.*

23. *Ibid.*

24. *Ibid.*

Chapter 18

1. Thomas Dimopoulos, "Friends of the Victims Have Started Raising Funds for Survivors," *The Post-Star*, June 28, 2010, A6.

2. Don Lehman and Thomas Dimopoulos, "Six Children Killed in Blaze: Authorities Are Still Investigating Cause of Fort Edward Fire," *The Post-Star*, June 28, 2010, A1.

3. *Ibid.*, A6.

4. *Ibid.*

5. Lydia Wheeler, "Several People Killed in Fire at Fort Edward Home: Victims Yet to Be Identified," *The Post-Star*, June 27, 2010, A1.

6. Don Lehman, "Investigators: Electrical Outlet Likely Cause of Deadly Blaze," www.poststar.com, June 28, 2010, https://poststar.com/news/local/investigators-electrical-outlet-likely-cause-of-deadly-blaze/article_d3bc70e6-82b9-11df-b21c-001cc4c002e0.html.

7. Thomas Dimopoulos, "Loss Overwhelming for Community," *The Post-Star*, June 28, 2010, A1.

8. Lydia (Wheeler) Davenport, Phone interview with author, August 4, 2020.

9. *Ibid.*

10. *Ibid.*

11. *Ibid.*

12. *Ibid.*

13. Don Lehman," New investigations lead to same conclusion in deadly Fort Edward fire," www.poststar.com, April 10, 2012, https://poststar.com/news/local/new-investigations-lead-to-same-conclusion-in-deadly-fort-edward/-article_9a854352-8352-11e1-9adf-0019bb2963f4.html.

14. Don Lehman, "Incorrect Fuse Played Role in Fort Edward Fatal Fire," www.poststar.com, August 24, 2010, https://poststar.com/news/local/incorrect-fuse-played-role-in-fort-edward-fatal-fire/article_27d63092-afc7-11df-9580-001cc4c002e0.html.

15. Lydia (Wheeler) Davenport, Phone interview with author, August 4, 2020.

16. Don Lehman, "Incorrect Fuse Played Role in Fort Edward Fatal Fire," www.poststar.com, August 24, 2010, https://poststar.com/news/local/incorrect-fuse-played-role-in-fort-edward-fatal-fire/article_27d63092-afc7-11df-9580-001cc4c002e0.html.

17. *Ibid.*, A1.

18. *Ibid.*

19. Ken Tingley, "Fatal Fire Sparks Tough Questions," www.poststar.com, June 29, 2010, https://poststar.com/news/opinion/columns/ktingley/fatal-fire-sparks-tough-questions/-article_55828982-83b7-11df-9125-001cc4c03286.html.

20. Lydia (Wheeler) Davenport, Phone interview with author, August 4, 2020.

21. *Ibid.*

22. Lydia Wheeler, "Hundreds Mourn Fire Victims," www.poststar.com, June 27, 2012, https://poststar.com/news/local/hundreds-mourn-fire-victims-at-funeral/article_64ddf3b2-8b78-11df-af94-001cc4c03286.html.

23. *Ibid.*

24. Ken Tingley, "Community Bids Heartbroken Farewell," www.poststar.com, July 9, 2010, https://poststar.com/news/opinion/columns/ktingley/-community-bids-heartbroken-farewell/article_f9cb67e0-8b8f-11df-a5c3-001cc4c03286.html.

25. Lydia Wheeler, "No. 1 Story of 2010: Six Children Die in Fatal Fort Edward Fire," www.poststar.com, January 1, 2011, https://poststar.com/news/local/no-1-story-of-2010-six-children-die-in-fatal-fort-edward-fire/article_2f655612-12cd-11e0-ad1d-001cc4c03286.html.

26. *Ibid.*

27. *Ibid.*

28. *Ibid.*

29. Don Lehman, "New Investigations Lead to Same Conclusion in Deadly Fort Edward Fire," www.poststar.com, April 10, 2012, https://poststar.com/news/local/new-investigations-lead-to-same-conclusion-in-deadly-fort-edward/-article_9a854352-8352-11e1-9adf-0019bb2963f4.html.

30. Lydia Wheeler, "No. 1 Story of 2010: Six Children Die in Fatal Fort Edward Fire," www.poststar.com, January 1, 2011, https://poststar.com/news/local/no-1-story-of-2010-six-children-die-in-fatal-fort-edward-fire/article_2f655612-12cd-11e0-ad1d-001cc4c03286.html.

31. Lydia Wheeler, "Donations Are Being Accepted," *The Post-Star*, June 27, 2010, A8.

32. Don Lehman, "Woman Charged with Fire Charity Thefts Pleads Not Guilty," www.poststar.com, April 29, 2011, https://poststar.com/news/local/woman-charged-with-fire-charity-thefts-pleads-not-guilty/article_48a7d156-7298-11e0-80f3-001cc4c03286.html.

33. Don Lehman, "Family Eyes Start in New Home," www.poststar.com, August 21, 2010, https://poststar.com/family-eyes-new-start-in-new-home/article_b0e93914-ad98-11df-bcf6-001cc4c002e0.html.

34. Don Lehman, "Woman Charged with Fire Charity Thefts Pleads Not Guilty," www.poststar.com, April 29, 2011, https://poststar.com/news/local/woman-charged-with-fire-charity-thefts-pleads-not-guilty/article_48a7d156-7298-11e0-80f3-001cc4c03286.html.

35. Don Lehman, "Woman Pleads Guilty in Fort Edward Fire Fund Theft Case," www.poststar.com, July 21, 2011, https://poststar.com/news/local/woman-pleads-guilty-in-fort-edward-fire-fund-theft-case/article_ec8b237c-b3d9-11e0-acbc-001cc4c002e0.html.

36. Don Lehman, "Woman Pleads Guilty in Fort Edward Fire Fund Theft Case," www.poststar.com, July 21, 2011, https://poststar.com/news/local/woman-pleads-guilty-in-fort-edward-fire-fund-theft-case/article_ec8b237c-b3d9-11e0-acbc-001cc4c002e0.html.

37. Don Lehman, "Heart Attack Killed Smith, Father of Kids Who Died in Fire," www.poststar.com, July 30, 2012, https://poststar.com/news/local/heart-attack-killed-smith-father-of-kids-who-died-in-fire/article_8b93bfc0-da84-11e1-9f3e-0019bb2963f4.html.

38. *Ibid.*

39. Don Lehman, "Officials: Home Short on Smoke Detectors," www.poststar.com, June 29, 2010, https://poststar.com/news/local/officials-home-short-on-smoke-detectors/article_48bd3f9e-83f8-11df-8786-001cc4c03286.html.

40. Lydia Wheeler, "No. 1 Story of 2010: Six Children Die in Fatal Fort Edward Fire," www.poststar.com, January 1, 2011, https://poststar.com/news/local/no-1-story-of-2010-six-children-die-in-fatal-fort-edward-fire/article_2f655612-12cd-11e0-ad1d-001cc4c03286.html.

41. *Ibid.*

42. *Ibid.*

43. David Taube, "Fort Edward Student's 'Hope' Fire Safety Project Needs More Votes to Get Funding," www.poststar.com, November 17, 2010, https://poststar.com/news/local/fort-edward-student-s-hope-fire-safety-project-needs-more-votes-to-get-funding/-article_46b46b86-f271-11df-aa1c-001cc4c002e0.html.

44. David Taube, "Project Hope Students Win $5,000 in Fire Education Grant Quest," www.poststar.com, February 1, 2011, https://poststar.com/news/local/project-hope-students-win-5-000-in-fire-education-grant-quest/-article_66f3fcb8-2e44-11e0-a92c-001cc4c03286.html.

45. Don Lehman, "Smoke Detectors Credited for Alerting Fort Edward Family to Fire," www.poststar.com, October 2, 2011, https://poststar.com/news/local/smoke-detectors-credited-for-alerting-fort-edward-family-to-fire/-article_935180f4-ece0-11e0-abf4-001cc4c002e0.html.

46. *Ibid.*

47. *Ibid.*

Chapter 19

1. Thomas J. Lueck, "Police Charge New Paltz Mayor for Marrying Same-sex Couples," www.nytimes.com, March 3, 2004, https://www.nytimes.com/2004/03/03/nyregion/police-charge-new-paltz-mayor-for-marrying-same-sex-couples.html?referringSource=articleShare.

2. Amenas Hartocollas, "NY Court Upholds Gay Marriage Ban," www.nytimes.com, July 6, 2006, https://www.nytimes.com/2006/07/06/nyregion/06cnd-marriage.html?referringSource=articleShare.

3. Ken Tingley, "McDonald Set to Charge," wwwpoststar.com, November 2, 2010, https://poststar.com/news/opinion/columns/ktingley/-mcdonald-set-to-charge/article_bb28c932-e6cb-11df-acad-001cc4c03286.html.

4. *Ibid.*

5. *Ibid.*

6. *Ibid.*

7. *Ibid.*

8. Drew Kerr, "Same-sex Marriage Lobbying Intensifies," www.poststar.com, June 12, 2011, https://poststar.com/news/local/same-sex-marriage-lobbying-intensifies/article_9f3abe2e-9535-11e0-868c-001cc4c03286.html.

9. *Ibid.*

10. Mark Mahoney, "Law Would Correct Unfairness," www.poststar.com, May 27, 2011, https://poststar.com/news/opinion/editorial/editorial-law-would-correct-unfairness/-article_09962656-88b5-11e0-b6b4-001cc4c03286.html.

11. *Ibid.*

12. Drew Kerr, "Billboard Urges McDonald to Support 'all Loving Couples,'" www.poststar.com, June 6, 2011, https://poststar.com/blogs/saratoga_snippets/billboard-urges-mcdonald-to-support-all-loving-couples/article_6fd00354-caed-55d0-a5d7-901ad4c28f84.html.

13. Drew Kerr, "Same-sex Marriage Lobbying Intensifies," www.poststar.com, June 12,

2011, https://poststar.com/news/local/same-sex-marriage-lobbying-intensifies/article_9f3abe2e-9535-11e0-868c-001cc4c03286.html.

14. Nicholas Confessore and Michael Barbaro, "New York Allows Same-sex Marriage, Becomes Largest State to Pass Law," www.nytimes.com, June 25, 2011, https://www.nytimes.com/2011/06/25/nyregion/gay-marriage-approved-by-new-york-senate.html?referringSource=article Share.

15. Drew Kerr, "Same-sex Marriage Lobbying Intensifies," wwwpoststar.com, June 12, 2011, https://poststar.com/news/local/same-sex-marriage-lobbying-intensifies/article_9f3abe2e-9535-11e0-868c-001cc4c03286.html.

16. Jimmy Vielkind, "GOP Senator from Saratoga Becomes 31st Vote for Same-sex Marriage," www.timesunion.com, June 15, 2011, https://www.timesunion.com/local/article/-GOP-senator-from-Saratoga-becomes-31st-vote-for-1424481.php.

17. Joseph Spector, "Second Republican Senator Comes Forward to Back Same-sex Marriage," www.democratandchronicle.com, June 14, 2011, https://www.democratandchronicle.com/story/news/politics/blogs/vote-up/2011/06/14/-second-senate-republican-senator-comes-forward-to-back-same-sex-marriage/2177361/.

18. Jimmy Vielkind, "Shove It: A Portrait of a Gay Marriage Republican in Limbo," www.politico.com, September 20, 2012, https://www.politico.com/states/new-york/albany/story/2012/09/shove-it-a-portrait-of-a-gay-marriage-republican-in-limbo-000000.

19. Ibid.

20. Nicholas Confessore and Michael Barbaro, "New York Allows Same-sex Marriage; Becomes Largest State to Pass Law," www.nytimes.com, June 25, 2011, https://www.nytimes.com/2011/06/25/nyregion/gay-marriage-approved-by-new-york-senate.html?referringSource=articleShare.

21. Ken Tingley, "Respecting McDonald's Choices," www.poststar.com, July 26, 2011, https://poststar.com/news/opinion/columns/ktingley/mcdonald-breaks-ranks-and-votes-for-change/article_877bb17a-9a18-11e0-9ea4-001cc4c03286.html.

22. Ibid.

23. Mark Mahoney, "Law Would Correct Unfairness," www.poststar.com, May 27, 2011, https://poststar.com/news/opinion/editorial/editorial-law-would-correct-unfairness/article_09962656-88b5-11e0-b6b4-001cc4c03286.html.

24. Ken Tingley, "Respecting McDonald's Choices," www.poststar.com, July 26, 2011, https://poststar.com/news/opinion/editorial/editorial-law-would-correct-unfairness/article_09962656-88b5-11e0-b6b4-001cc4c03286.html.

25. Maury Thompson, "Advocacy Group Seeks to Oust McDonald Over Same-sex Marriage Vote," www.poststar.com, July 19, 2011, https://poststar.com/news/local/advocacy-group-seeks-to-oust-mcdonald-over-same-sex-marriage-vote/article_dc5f2ebe-b247-11e0-845a-001cc4c002e0.html.

26. Ibid.

27. Jimmy Vielkind, "Shove It: A Portrait of a Gay Marriage Republican in Limbo," www.politico.com, September 20, 2012, https://www.politico.com/states/new-york/albany/story/2012/09/shove-it-a-portrait-of-a-gay-marriage-republican-in-limbo-000000.

28. Thomas Kaplan, "Gay Marriage Vote Rises as Test in Upstate G.O.P. Race," www.nytimes.com, September 11, 2012, https://www.nytimes.com/2012/09/12/nyregion/after-vote-for-gay-marriage-senator-roy-mcdonald-faces-gop-primary-fight.html?referringSource=articleShare.

29. Ibid.

30. Roy McDonald, Interview with author, July 2020.

31. Jimmy Vielkind, "Shove It: A Portrait of a Gay Marriage Republican in Limbo," www.politico.com, September 20, 2012, https://www.nytimes.com/2012/09/27/nyregion/cuomo-endorses-senator-roy-mcdonald-republican-in-possible-third-party-bid.html?referringSource=articleShare.

32. Thomas Kaplan, "Cuomo Backs Republican Who Lost Primary After Vote for Gay Marriage," www.nytimes.com, September 26, 2012, https://www.nytimes.com/2012/09/27/nyregion/-cuomo-endorses-senator-roy-mcdonald-republican-in-possible-third-party-bid.html?ref erringSource=articleShare.

33. Ken Tingley, "By Quitting Race, Roy McDonald Disappoints," www.poststar.com, September 30, 2012, https://poststar.com/news/opinion/columns/ktingley/column-by-quitting-race-roy-mcdonald-disappoints/-article_1da723fa-0ab6-11e2-beae-001a4bcf887a.html.

34. Ibid.

35. Ibid.

36. Ibid.

37. Jamie Baer, "Roy McDonald: Protector of the Party of Lincoln," https://www.jfklibrary.org/learn/education/profile-in-courage-essay-contest/past-winning-essays/2013-winning-essay-by-jamie-baer.

38. Ibid.

39. Drew DeSilver, "How Many Same-sex Marriages in the U.S.? at Least 71,165, Maybe More," www.pewresearch.org, June 26, 2013, https://www.pewresearch.org/fact-tank/2013/06/26/-how-many-same-sex-marriages-in-the-u-s-at-least-71165-probably-more/.

40. Nick Reisman, "Republican Backs Democrat in 43rd District Race," www.spectrumlocalnews.com, October 9, 2018, https://spectrumlocalnews.com/nys/central-ny/politics/2018/10/10/aaron-gladd-roy-mcdonald-endorsement.

41. Ibid.

42. Roy McDonald, Interview with author, July 2020.

43. *Ibid.*

44. Roy McDonald, Interview with author, July 2020.

45. Roy McDonald, Email to author, December 16, 2020.

Chapter 20

1. Thomas Dimopoulos, "Wilton Father, Son Charged in Shooting Death of 12-year-old," www.poststar.com, December 28, 2010, https://poststar.com/news/local/wilton-father-son-charged-in-shooting-death-of-12-year-old/article_86124902-120f-11e0-9517-001cc4c002e0.html.

2. *Ibid.*

3. *Ibid.*

4. Lucian McCarty, "12-year-old Admits Guilt in Shooting Death of Nicholas Naumkin in December as Part of Plea Arrangement; Likely to Receive Probation," www.saratogian.com, August 11, 2011, https://www.saratogian.com/news/12-year-old-admits-guilt-in-the-shooting-death-of-nicholas-naumkin-in-december-as/article_8c4308c6-84be-51ef-a464-b14e1b78114a.html.

5. Post-Star Editorial Board, "Another Tragedy Must Be Prevented," www.poststar.com, January 2, 2011, https://poststar.com/news/opinion/editorial/editorial-another-tragedy-must-be-prevented/article_62ec4f28-1623-11e0-b5f2-001cc4c002e0.html.

6. *Ibid.*

7. Thomas Dimopoulos, "Man Killed Crossing Northway Was Grandfather of 12-year-old Shooting Victim," www.poststar.com, January 5, 2011, https://poststar.com/news/local/man-killed-crossing-northway-was-grandfather-of-12-year-old-shooting-victim/article_44957692-17f1-11e0-80ea-001cc4c002e0.html.

8. *Ibid.*

9. *Ibid.*

10. *Ibid.*

11. *Ibid.*

12. Ken Tingley, "Once Again, We Are Forced to Look at Tragedy," www.poststar.com, December 15, 2012, https://poststar.com/news/opinion/columns/ktingley/once-again-we-are-forced-to-look-at-tragedy/article_35ebd27c-472d-11e2-ac0c-001a4bcf887a.html.

13. Ken Tingley, "Let's Start the Conversation," www.poststar.com, December 22, 2012, https://poststar.com/news/opinion/editorial/editorial-lets-start-the-conversation/article_6e2d4790-4cb1-11e2-a85c-0019bb2963f4.html.

14. *Ibid.*

15. Shushannah Walsh, "New York Passes Nation's Toughest Gun-control Law," www.abcnews.go.com, January 13, 2013, https://abcnews.go.com/Politics/york-state-passes-toughest-gun-control-law-nation/story?id=18224091.

16. Post-Star Editorial Board, "Gov. Andrew Cuomo Misused Power to Get Gun Bill Passed," www.poststar.com, January 16, 2013, https://poststar.com/news/opinion/editorial/editorial-gov-andrew-cuomo-misused-power-to-get-gun-bill-passed/article_bb16972c-6049-11e2-b9f0-0019bb2963f4.html.

17. Ken Tingley, "We Sparked the Conversation We Were Hoping For," www.poststar.com, January 26, 2013, https://poststar.com/news/opinion/columns/editor/from-the-editor-we-sparked-the-conversation-we-were-hoping-for/article_3a6f4a82-682e-11e2-a37d-001a4bcf887a.html.

18. Ken Tingley, "Trust Me, You Don't Want to Read This," www.poststar.com, November 12, 2017, https://poststar.com/opinion/columnists/column-trust-me-you-dont-want-to-read-this/article_1e427375-453e-5dbb-bbcd-669037a8459b.html.

19. *Ibid.*

20. *Ibid.*

21. *Ibid.*

22. *Ibid.*

23. *Ibid.*

24. *Ibid.*

25. Ken Tingley, "Living in the Shadow of Sandy Hook and More School Violence," www.poststar.com, February 25, 2018, https://poststar.com/opinion/columnists/column-living-in-the-shadow-of-sandy-hook-and-more-school-violence/article_18e8ac86-6b19-5cd3-8675-60650a1e71a5.html.

26. *Ibid.*

27. *Ibid.*

28. Ken Tingley, "To the Readers: You Don't Hear About the Harassment," *The Post-Star*, June 30, 2018.

29. Ken Tingley, "Journalists Have Become Targets," www.poststar.com, July 1, 2018, https://poststar.com/opinion/columnists/column-journalists-have-become-targets/article_bfdba753-5854-5749-b535-c2760f9afdda.html.

30. *Ibid.*

31. Nick Reisman, "Cuomo Signs Bills for Safe Storage, Banning 3-D Guns," www.spectrumnews.com, July 30, 2019, https://spectrumlocalnews.com/nys/central-ny/politics/2019/07/30/cuomo-signs-bills-for-safe-storage—banning-3-d-guns.

32. Ken Tingley, "Let's Be Thoughtful When It Comes to Guns," www.poststar.com, March 10, 2019, https://poststar.com/news/local/column-lets-be-thoughtful-when-it-comes-to-guns/article_cb9cb803-746b-5b1f-a896-84d8220b2179.html.

33. *Ibid.*

34. *Ibid.*

35. *Ibid.*

Chapter 21

1. Ken Tingley, "Capturing All Sides of Nursing Home Story," www.poststar.com, May

4, 2013, https://poststar.com/news/opinion/columns/editor/from-the-editor-capturing-all-sides-of-nursing-home-story/article_dbc0156c-b52a-11e2-b98d-0019bb2963f4.html.

2. *Ibid.*

3. *Ibid.*

4. *Ibid.*

5. *Ibid.*

6. Meg Hagerty, "Making the Move: Nursing Homes Can Offer Care and Companionship," www.poststar.com, May 2, 2013.

7. Jon Alexander, "Old Age Is Coming and We're Not Ready," www.poststar.com, May 2, 2013, https://poststar.com/old-age-is-coming-and-we-re-not-ready/article_1522d38c-b367-11e2-bed7-0019bb2963f4.html.

8. *Ibid.*

9. *Ibid.*

10. Post-Star Editorial board, Ready or not, we're all aging," www.poststar.com, May 4, 2013, https://poststar.com/news/opinion/editorial/-editorial-ready-or-not-were-all-aging/article_f7c0a768-b52a-11e2-9c0c-0019bb2963f4.html.

11. *Ibid.*

12. Jamie Munks, "As Workload Grows, Nursing Home Staffing Woes Persist," www.poststar.com, May 11, 2013, https://poststar.com/news/local/as-workload-grows-nursing-home-staffing-woes-persist/article_e86d5664-baaf-11e2-a4a8-001a4bcf887a.html.

13. *Ibid.*

14. Jamie Munks, "Families Find Safety Net Is Full of Holes," www.poststar.com, May 25, 2013, https://poststar.com/news/local/families-find-safety-net-is-full-of-holes/article_d3d42fcc-c5ac-11e2-84e1-0019bb2963f4.html.

15. *Ibid.*

16. *Ibid.*

17. *Ibid.*

18. Post-Star Staff Report, "Post-Star Honored for Elderly Care Series," www.poststar.com, April 19, 2014, https://poststar.com/news/article_c36d5c46-c72f-11e3-99c9-001a4bcf887a.html.

19. *Ibid.*

20. Post-Star Staff Report, "Post-Star's Nursing Home Series Honored by Lee Enterprises," www.poststar.com, November 28, 2013, https://poststar.com/news/local/post-stars-nursing-home-series-honored-by-lee-enterprises/-article_7c69117e-5870-11e3-bfd1-0019bb2963f4.html.

21. Post-Star Staff Report, "Post-Star Lays Off 11 Employees," www.poststar.com, March 24, 2009, https://poststar.com/news/local/post-star-lays-off-11-employees/article_0da8d248-cd28-5da0-bb01-579d14323273.html.

22. *Ibid.*

23. Ken Tingley, "Improve Nursing Home Care," *The Post-Star*, July 16, 2017, A6.

24. *Ibid.*

25. Post-Star Editorial Board, "Nursing Home Company Meets with Post-Star Board," www.poststar.com, August 20, 2017, https:// poststar.com/opinion/editorial/editorial-nursing-home-company-meets-with-post-star-board/article_32c2b979-b570-5095-a4de-5a2850a925d0.html.

26. *Ibid.*

27. *Ibid.*

28. *Ibid.*

29. *Ibid.*

30. *Ibid.*

31. *Ibid.*

32. *Ibid.*

33. Kathleen Moore, Phone interview with author, August 26, 2020.

34. Ken Tingley, "Renewed Concern About Nursing Home Care," www.poststar.com, June 10, 2018, https://poststar.com/opinion/editorial/-editorial-renewed-concern-about-nursing-home-care/article_aee8a0d1-a4fd-565f-b594-6de0099897bf.html.

35. *Ibid.*

36. Don Lehman, "Family Concerns Linger Despite Nursing Home Ratings Boost," www.poststar.com, June 16, 2018, https://poststar.com/news/local/family-concerns-linger-despite-nursing-home-ratings-boost/article_c2cf5ca1-33f8-5dcb-ad9b-6b5b08819c04.html.

37. *Ibid.*

38. Don Lehman, "Former Nursing Home Worker Indicted," www.poststar.com, October 20, 2017, https://poststar.com/news/local/crime-and-courts/former-nursing-home-worker-indicted/article_ad806b06-5dc4-5546-8ad5-ea3d62e62cd4.html.

39. *Ibid.*

40. *Ibid.*

41. *Ibid.*

42. N.Y. State Office of the Comptroller, "State Health Department Should Improve Enforcement of Nursing Home Violations," www.osc.state.ny.us, February 22, 2016, https://www.osc.state.ny.us/press/releases/2016/02/state-health-department-should-improve-enforcement-nursing-home-violations.

43. *Ibid.*

44. Kristen Hare, "Lee Enterprises Announces Pay Cuts and Furloughs," www.Poynter.org, March 31, 2020, https://www.poynter.org/-business-work/2020/lee-enterprises-announces-pay-cuts-and-furloughs/.

Chapter 22

1. Meg Hagerty, "Librarian Suggests Turning the Page on Longtime Reading Club Winner," www.poststar.com, August 15, 2013, https://poststar.com/news/local/librarian-suggests-turning-the-page-on-longtime-reading-club-winner/article_bdbebbc6-0625-11e3-b6f4-0019bb2963f4.html.

2. *Ibid.*

3. Meg Hagerty, "Saying Good Bye," www.poststar.com, December 30, 2014, https://

poststar.com/blogs/meg_hagerty/saying-good-bye/article_36da8392-9030-11e4-9c46-1b194abfb617.html.

4. *Ibid.*

5. Meg Hagerty, "Stefanik Campaign Ramping Up," www.poststar.com, May 6, 2014, https://poststar.com/news/local/stefaniks-campaign-ramping-up/article_d2154512-d3b7-11e3-9a69-0019bb2963f4.html.

6. Meg Hagerty, "Librarian Suggests Turning the Page on Longtime Reading Club Winner," www.poststar.com, August 15, 2013, https://poststar.com/news/local/librarian-suggests-turning-the-page-on-longtime-reading-club-winner/article_bdbebbc6-0625-11e3-b6f4-0019bb2963f4.html.

7. *Ibid.*

8. *Ibid.*

9. Ken Tingley, "Well It Was Supposed to Be a Feel-good Story," www.poststar.com, August 16, 2013, https://poststar.com/blogs/the_front_page/well-it-was-supposed-to-be-a-feel-good-story/article_a48e48d8-068e-11e3-b6c5-001a4bcf887a.html.

10. Neetzan Zimmerman, "Evil Librarian Tells Kid Who Loves Books to Stop Reading So Much," www.gawker.com, August 19, 2013, https://gawker.com/evil-librarian-tells-kid-who-loves-books-to-stop-readin-1167265926.

11. "World's Worst Librarian Wants Nine-Year-Old Kid to Stop Winning Reading Contests," www.yahoo.com, August 20, 2013, https://news.yahoo.com/world-worst-librarian-wants-nine-old-kid-stop-145030798.html.guccounter=1&guce_referrer=aHR0cHM6Ly93d3cuZ29vZ2xlLmNvbS8&guce_referrer_sig=AQAAALNHpjCVcuyaoiH0uhw1O0NUDjwTNRBgTPc4xlNFi4bULj9nmXrLhIIWR575QujDuCdPa1pedcC9fV-8TI6aampyh7Ukm8cUExEIlcMR7uLuKy2UAgPzBkR8y_ynnyp6YJL1RRZgdz1qhkTfm5ifr5B1GO9s0qWBibw8bw2n2Mu6.

12. Meg Hagerty, "Big Reader Story from Hudson Falls Spreads Around the World," www.poststar.com, August 20, 2013, https://poststar.com/news/local/big-reader-story-from-hudson-falls-spreads-around-world/article_86123af2-09d8-11e3-8471-001a4bcf887a.html.

13. Ken Tingley, "It Is Always Uncomfortable Being Part of the Story," www.poststar.com, August 22, 2013, https://poststar.com/blogs/the_front_page/it-is-always-uncomfortable-being-part-of-the-story/article_2033e270-0b50-11e3-8ffe-0019bb2963f4.html.

14. *Ibid.*

15. *Ibid.*

16. Post-Star Staff Report, "Hudson Falls Library President Releases Statement on Reading Program," www.poststar.com, August 22, 2013, https://poststar.com/news/local/hudson-falls-library-president-releases-statement-on-reading-program-controversy/article_85df4dfe-0b36-11e3-bcd9-0019bb2963f4.html.

17. "Meg Hagerty, "Young Reader Interviews on National TV," www.poststar.com, August 21, 2013, https://poststar.com/news/local/young-reader-interviewed-on-national-tv/article_1cc89364-0aa7-11e3-8a66-0019bb2963f4.html.

18. *Ibid.*

19. *Ibid.*

20. Ken Tingley, "Letter to Editor Was Especially Harsh," www.poststar.com, September 17, 2013, https://poststar.com/blogs/the_front_page/letter-to-the-editor-was-especially-harsh/article_b188d324-1fc9-11e3-96b9-0019bb2963f4.html.

21. Meg Hagerty, Phone interview with author, August 23, 2020.

22. Post-Star Staff Report, "Hudson Falls Library President Releases Statement on Reading Program," www.poststar.com, August 22, 2013, https://poststar.com/news/local/hudson-falls-library-president-releases-statement-on-reading-program-controversy/article_85df4dfe-0b36-11e3-bcd9-0019bb2963f4.html.

23. Amanda Mae Metzger, "After Reading Contest Blowups, Librarian Has Left Her Job," www.poststar.com, September 13, 2013, https://poststar.com/news/local/after-reading-contest-blowup-librarian-has-left-her-job/article_eb3c2f9a-1ca8-11e3-ba4d-001a4bcf887a.html.

24. *Ibid.*

25. Bill Toscano, "Petition Asks Hudson Falls Library to Rehire Aide," www.poststar.com, October 7, 2013, https://poststar.com/news/local/petition-asks-hudson-falls-library-to-rehire-aide/article_66c0cc5a-2f93-11e3-82d7-001a4bcf887a.html.

26. Amanda Mae Metzger," After reading contest blowup, librarian has left her job," www.poststar.com, September 13, 2013, https://poststar.com/news/local/after-reading-contest-blowup-librarian-has-left-her-job/article_eb3c2f9a-1ca8-11e3-ba4d-001a4bcf887a.html.

27. *Ibid.*

28. *Ibid.*

29. Bill Toscano, "Second Hudson Falls Library Worker Loses Job in Wake of Reading Program," www.poststar.com, September 17, 2013, https://poststar.com/news/local/-second-hudson-falls-library-worker-loses-job-in-wake-of-reading-program-controversy/-article_473a459c-1fca-11e3-9aee-0019bb2963f4.html.

30. *Ibid.*

31. *Ibid.*

32. *Ibid.*

33. Bill Toscano, "Petition Asks Hudson Falls Library to Rehire Aide," www.poststar.com, October 7, 2013, https://poststar.com/news/local/petition-asks-hudson-falls-library-to-rehire-aide/article_66c0cc5a-2f93-11e3-82d7-001a4bcf887a.html.

34. Ken Tingley, "Hudson Falls Library Board Wrote the Book on What Not to Do,"

www.poststar.com, September 21, 2013, https://poststar.com/news/opinion/hudson-falls-library-board-wrote-the-book-on-what-not-to-do/article_39fe95da-232c-11e3-bd86-0019bb2963f4.html.

35. *Ibid.*

36. *Ibid.*

37. *Ibid.*

38. Bill Toscano, "Petition Asks Hudson Falls Library to Rehire Aide," www.poststar.com. October 7, 2013, https://poststar.com/news/local/petition-asks-hudson-falls-library-to-rehire-aide/article_66c0cc5a-2f93-11e3-82d7-001a4bcf887a.html.

39. *Ibid.*

40. *Ibid.*

41. Post-Star Staff Report, "Post-Star Announces Top Local Stories of 2013," www.poststar.com, December 28, 2013, https://poststar.com/news/local/post-star-announces-top-local-stories-of-2013/article_e68d3146-703c-11e3-bc64-001a4bcf887a.html.

42. Meg Hagerty, Phone interview with author, August 23, 2020.

43. Meg Hagerty, "Saying Good Bye," www.poststar.com, December 30, 2014, https://poststar.com/blogs/meg_hagerty/saying-good-bye/article_36da8392-9030-11e4-9c46-1b194abfb617.html.

44. Meg Hagerty, Phone interview with author, August 23, 2020.

45. "Class of 2021 Honors Graduates," Hudson Falls School district, www.hfcsd.org, https://www.hfcsd.org/class-of-2021-honors-graduates/.

Chapter 23

1. Will Doolittle, "A Forced Relocation: Parents' Drug Addiction Leaves Three Girls No Choice but to Start Over," *The Post-Star*, June 29, 2014, A1.

2. *Ibid.*

3. *Ibid.*

4. *Ibid.*

5. Will Doolittle, Phone interview with author, September 13, 2020.

6. Will Doolittle, "A Forced Relocation: Parents' Drug Addiction Leaves Three Girls No Choice but to Start Over," *The Post-Star*, June 29, 2014, A1.

7. *Ibid.*

8. *Ibid.*

9. *Ibid.*

10. *Ibid.*

11. *Ibid.*

12. *Ibid.*

13. *Ibid.*

14. *Ibid.*, A5.

15. Anne Kumar, "Fatal Crash Claims Two," *The Post-Star*, February 21, 2005, A1.

16. Ken Tingley, "Keep Talking About Teen Drinking," *The Post-Star*, March 2, 2005, B1.

17. *Ibid.*

18. Ken Tingley, "Post-Star Staff Will Tackle Heroin Epidemic in Series," www.poststar.com, June 14, 2014, https://poststar.com/news/opinion/columns/editor/post-star-staff-will-tackle-heroin-epidemic-in-series/article_f04156e8-f3e2-11e3-a401-0019bb2963f4.html.

19. Will Doolittle, Phone interview with author, September 13, 2020.

20. *Ibid.*

21. Will Doolittle, "Caretaker Battles Health Issues, Financial Problems," *The Post-Star*, June 30, 2014, A5.

22. Don Lehman, "An Unwanted Visitor: Heroin Creeps Into Glens Falls," www.poststar.com, June 15, 2014, https://poststar.com/news/local/an-unwanted-visitor-heroin-creeps-into-glens-falls-region/article_64ead8f6-f439-11e3-936b-001a4bcf887a.html.

23. *Ibid.*

24. *Ibid.*

25. Ken Tingley, "Post-Star Staff Will Tackle Heroin Epidemic in Series," www.poststar.com, June 14, 2014, https://poststar.com/news/opinion/columns/editor/post-star-staff-will-tackle-heroin-epidemic-in-series/article_f04156e8-f3e2-11e3-a401-0019bb2963f4.html.

26. Judy Chittenden Moffitt, Phone interview with author, September 14, 2020.

27. *Ibid.*

28. *Ibid.*

29. Meg Hagerty, "Mother Takes Comfort in Son's Survival of Drug Abuse," www.poststar.com, June 21, 2014, https://poststar.com/news/local/mother-takes-comfort-in-son-s-survival-of-drug-abuse/article_aa46759a-f9b6-11e3-8ab9-001a4bcf887a.html.

30. Meg Hagerty, "Long Road to a Dark Place," www.poststar.com, June 22, 2014, https://poststar.com/news/local/long-road-to-a-dark-place/article_174c08fe-fa7e-11e3-b387-001a4bcf887a.html.

31. Meg Hagerty, "Mother Takes Comfort in Son's Survival of Drug Abuse," www.poststar.com, June 21,2014, https://poststar.com/news/local/mother-takes-comfort-in-son-s-survival-of-drug-abuse/article_aa46759a-f9b6-11e3-8ab9-001a4bcf887a.html.

32. *Ibid.*

33. Meg Hagerty, "Long Road to a Dark Place," www.poststar.com, June 22, 2014, https://poststar.com/news/local/long-road-to-a-dark-place/article_174c08fe-fa7e-11e3-b387-001a4bcf887a.html.

34. *Ibid.*

35. *Ibid.*

36. *Ibid.*

37. *Ibid.*

38. *Ibid.*

39. *Ibid.*

40. *Ibid.*

41. *Ibid.*

42. *Ibid.*

43. Judy Chittenden Moffitt, Phone interview with author, September 14, 2020.

44. *Ibid.*

45. Meg Hagerty, "Mother Takes Comfort in Son's Survival of Drug Abuse," www.poststar.com, June 21, 2014, https://poststar.com/news/local/mother-takes-comfort-in-son-s-survival-of-drug-abuse/article_aa46759a-f9b6-11e3-8ab9-001a4bcf887a.html.

46. Judy Chittenden Moffitt, Phone interview with author, September 14, 2020.

47. *Ibid.*

48. *Ibid.*

49. Michael Goot, "Taking Young Lives: Death of Student, 22, Shows Heroin's Reach," *The Post-Star*, June 23, 2014, A1.

50. Legacy.com, April 29, 2014, https://www.legacy.com/us/obituaries/timesunion-albany/name/sean-demerchant-obituary?pid=170840199.

51. *Ibid.*

52. Michael Goot, "Colleges Boost Anti-Heroin Efforts," *The Post-Star*, June 23, 2014, A6.

53. *Ibid.*

54. Bill Toscano, "Struggle to Get Clean," www.poststar.com, July 5, 2014, https://poststar.com/news/local/struggle-to-get-clean/article_c2ae0fb8-04b9-11e4-a81e-0019bb2963f4.html.

55. Post-Star Editorial Board, "Region Needs Recovery Options," www.poststar.com, July 5, 2014, https://poststar.com/news/opinion/editorial/editorial-region-needs-recovery-options/article_e4ab4198-04b5-11e4-8393-0019bb2963f4.html.

56. Ken Tingley, "Forum Puts Drug Problem in Focus," www.poststar.com. July 26, 2014, https://poststar.com/news/opinion/columns/ktingley/forum-puts-drug-problem-in-focus/-article_45092afa-1532-11e4-82c2-0019bb2963f4.html.

57. *Ibid.*

58. *Ibid.*

59. *Ibid.*

60. Will Doolittle, "After Addiction's Upheaval, Sisters Get on with Life," www.poststar.com, May 31, 2015, https://poststar.com/news/local/after-addictions-upheaval-sisters-get-on-with-life/article_beea8d99-a3fd-5c68-b18a-518b8bbbff43.html.

61. Will Doolittle, "Phone Interview with Author, September 13, 2020."

62. *Ibid.*

63. Will Doolittle, "After Addiction's Upheaval, Sisters Get on with Life," www.poststar.com, May 31, 2015, https://poststar.com/news/local/after-addictions-upheaval-sisters-get-on-with-life/article_beea8d99-a3fd-5c68-b18a-518b8bbbff43.html.

64. *Ibid.*

65. Post-Star Staff Report, "Post-Star Honored in National Contest," www.poststar.com, March 18, 2015, https://poststar.com/news/local/post-star-honored-in-national-contest/article_72caa03e-cdb2-11e4-b7da-53381bccca98.html.

66. Post-Star Staff Report, "Post-Star Wins Lee President's Award," www.poststar.com, November 23, 2014, https://poststar.com/news/local/post-star-wins-lee-presidents-award/article_f2e358c8-7340-11e4-96e0-d3bebddb1275.html.

67. Post-Star Staff Report, "Heroin Series Earns 2nd National Honor," www.poststar.com, May 5, 2015, https://poststar.com/news/local/article_f0acc7e4-5114-581f-be93-c8aad4142d01.html.

68. Will Doolittle, Phone interview with author, September 13, 2020.

69. Post-Star Staff Report, "Post-Star's Heroin Series Raises Awareness," www.poststar.com, July 24, 2014, https://poststar.com/news/local/post-stars-heroin-series-raises-awareness/-article_4e6f6aa4-13a8-11e4-8f10-0019bb2963f4.html.

70. *Ibid.*

71. Don Lehman, "No. 4: Heroin Use on Rise," www.poststar.com, December 27, 2014, https://poststar.com/no-4-heroin-use-on-rise/article_8a24b0fa-8e3b-11e4-9a16-c3db7d884096.html.

72. *Ibid.*

73. *Ibid.*

74. Don Lehman, "Group Seeks Heroin 'Recovery Center' in Glens Falls," www.poststar.com, January 6, 2016, https://poststar.com/news/local/group-seeks-heroin-recovery-center-in-glens-falls/article_15e8de85-b259-5f46-80d0-fa4063109e67.html/?&logged_out=1.

75. Bill Toscano, "Local Collaboration Steps Up in Drug Fight," www.poststar.com, March 25, 2017, https://poststar.com/news/local/local-collaboration-steps-up-in-drug-fight/article_79ccec77-45b5-5ae3-a3f6-cfbca150ebe4.html.

76. Don Lehman, "Glens Falls City Court Expanding 'Opioid Diversion Program,'" www.poststar.com, November 12, 2019, https://poststar.com/news/local/glens-falls-city-court-expanding-opioid-diversion-program/article_bf11b20b-9618-5861-8fff-e13ff8cfc73c.html.

77. Judy Chittenden Moffitt, Phone interview with author, September 14, 2020.

78. *Ibid.*

79. *Ibid.*

80. *Ibid.*

81. *Ibid.*

82. *Ibid.*

83. *Ibid.*

84. *Ibid.*

Chapter 24

1. Will Doolittle, Phone interview with author, September 28, 2020.

2. *Ibid.*

3. *Ibid.*

4. *Ibid.*

5. David Blow, Phone interview with author, September 25, 2020.

6. Don Lehman, Phone Interview with Author, September 29, 2020.

7. David Blow, Phone Interview with Author, September 25, 2020.

8. Don Lehman, Phone Interview with Author, September 29, 2020.

9. *Ibid.*

10. David Blow, Phone Interview with Author, September 25, 2020.

11. Don Lehman, "Man Has Spent Decades in the Woods of Queensbury," www.poststar. com, July 17, 2017, Https://poststar.com/news/local/man-has-spent-decades-in-the-woods-of-queensbury/article_2fda3977-7a0b-577b-a315-02c55aacfd7a.html.

12. Don Lehman, "About 'Bottle Bob,'" www. poststar.com, July 16, 2017, https://poststar.com/blogs/don_lehman/about-bottle-bob/article_e8976198-6a69-11e7-9387-3392a668abc3.html.

13. *Ibid.*

14. *Ibid.*

15. *Ibid.*

16. *Ibid.*

17. *Ibid.*

18. Don Lehman, "Man Has Spent Decades in the Woods of Queensbury," www.poststar. com, July 17, 2017, https://poststar.com/news/local/man-has-spent-decades-in-the-woods-of-queensbury/article_2fda3977-7a0b-577b-a315-02c55aacfd7a.html.

19. *Ibid.*

20. *Ibid.*

21. David Blow, Phone interview with author, September 25, 2020.

22. Don Lehman, "Gregg Burdo Gets Ready for Winter," www.poststar.com, November 27, 2017, https://poststar.com/blogs/don_lehman/-blog-gregg-burdo-gets-ready-for-winter/-article_1fa4039e-d360-11e7-b440-d7f2c1c40fe5.html.

23. *Ibid.*

24. Don Lehman, "Our Readers Did Some Good This Year," www.poststar.com, December 24, 2019, https://poststar.com/blogs/don_lehman/blog-our-readers-did-some-good-this-year/article_78d615ec-d757-52c3-b39b-eaf8e0c3aff7.html.

25. *Ibid.*

26. Don Lehman, Email to author, September 25, 2020.

27. Don Lehman, Email to author, September 30, 2020.

Chapter 25

1. Ken Tingley, "Doing the Right Thing Is Rare, but Still Heroic," *The Post-Star*, June 28, 2017, B6.

2. *Ibid.*

3. *Ibid.*

4. *Ibid.*

5. *Ibid.*

6. Ken Tingley, "Political Leaders Becoming Puppets," *The Post-Star*, October 29, 2017, C5.

7. Maury Thompson, "Queensbury Votes 3–2 to Replace Law Firm," www.poststar.com, November 22, 2016, https://poststar.com/news/local/queensbury-votes---to-replace-law-firm/article_03443ca6-9bd5-5205-a26d-4cb33cbadbb1.amp.html.

8. *Ibid.*

9. *Ibid.*

10. *Ibid.*

11. *Ibid.*

12. Ken Tingley, "Doing the Right Thing Is Rare, but Still Heroic," *The Post-Star*, June 28, 2017, B6.

13. Maury Thompson, "Queensbury Votes 3–2 to Replace Law Firm," www.poststarcom, November 22, 2016, https://poststar.com/news/local/queensbury-votes---to-replace-law-firm/article_03443ca6-9bd5-5205-a26d-4cb33cbadbb1.amp.html.

14. Ken Tingley, "Political Leaders Becoming Puppets," *The Post-Star*, C5.

15. Ken Tingley, "Doing the Right Thing Is Rare, but Still Heroic," *The Post-Star*, June 28, 2017, B6.

16. *Ibid.*

17. *Ibid.*

18. Post-Star Editorial board, "Metivier Makes Fiery Indictment of Party Politics in Queensbury," www.poststar.com, October 27, 2017, https://poststar.com/opinion/editorial/-endorsement-metivier-makes-fiery-indictment-of-party-politics-in-queensbury/article_d60d6f9d-6d20-5d70-a702-b33fbefda1d7.html.

19. *Ibid.*

20. Ken Tingley, "Doing the Right Thing Is Rare, but Still Heroic," *The Post-Star*, June 28, 2017, B6.

21. *Ibid.*

22. *Ibid.*

23. Kathleen Moore, "Doug Irish: Post-Star Is 'Akin to Fiction,'" www.poststar.com, June 6, 2017, https://poststar.com/blogs/kathleen_moore/doug-irish-post-star-is-akin-to-fiction/-article_d1d703b2-f711-545c-aadf-68fbe72d8a56.html.

24. *Ibid.*

25. *Ibid.*

26. Post-Star Editorial Board, "The Lying Can't Continue," *The Post-Star*, June 18, 2017, A4.

27. *Ibid.*

28. *Ibid.*

29. Kathleen Moore, "Tony Metivier Wins Ward 1 GOP Line in Primary Election," *The Post-Star*, September 13, 2017, B1.

30. Kathleen Moore, "Complaint Filed with AG Over Email Use," *The Post-Star*, October 11, 2017, A1.

31. *Ibid.*

32. Ken Tingley, "Queensbury Town Attorney Has Ethics Problem," www.poststar.com, October 22, 2017, https://poststar.com/opinion/columnists/column-queensbury-town-attorney-has-ethics-problem/article_6e505191-d4c9-5b24-b94e-2a0ccf73f0d3.html.

33. Post-Star Editorial Board, "Emails Reveal Dirty Politics," *The Post-Star*, October 15, 2017, A6.

34. *Ibid.*

35. Kathleen Moore, "Complaint Filed with AG Over Email Use," *The Post-Star*, October 12, 2017, A6.

36. Kathleen Moore, "Candidate Motives Questioned," *The Post-Star*, October 18, 2017, A1.

37. *Ibid.*

38. *Ibid.*

39. Ken Tingley, "More Board Members in Need of Moral Compass," *The Post-Star*, October 18, 2017, B1.

40. Don Lehman, "Sheriff's Office Cites Post-Star with Littering," *The Post-Star*, October 18, 2017, A1.

41. *Ibid.*

42. *Ibid.*, A3.

43. Don Lehman, "'Littering' Case Was the Height of Hypocrisy," www.poststar.com, May 11, 2018, https://poststar.com/blogs/don_lehman/blog-littering-case-was-the-height-of-hypocrisy/-article_89f98c8d-872b-5008-ab01-baa70de5c81f.html.

44. *Ibid.*

45. *Ibid.*

46. Don Lehman, "Sheriff's Office Cites Post-Star with Littering," *The Post-Star*, October 18, 2017, A3.

47. Ken Tingley, "More Board Members in Need of Moral Compass," *The Post-Star*, October 18, 2017, B1.

48. *Ibid.*

49. Kathleen Moore, "Queensbury Councilman Resigns," *The Post-Star*, October 24, 2017, A1.

50. Ken Tingley, "Bain Says He Won't Serve," *The Post-Star*, October 24, 2017, A1.

51. *Ibid.*

52. *Ibid.*

53. Kathleen Moore, "Lawyer Tied to Scheme Resigns," *The Post-Star*, October 26, 2017, A1.

54. *Ibid.*

55. *Ibid.*

56. *Ibid.*, A2.

57. Post-Star Editorial Board, "Strough Puts Queensbury First," *The Post-Star*, October 29, 2017, C3.

58. *Ibid.*

59. Post-Star Editorial Board, "Inside the Editorial Board," *The Post-Star*, October 29, 2017, C3.

60. Ken Tingley, "Simple Question Left Unanswered," *The Post-Star*, November 1, 2017, C6.

61. *Ibid.*

62. Kathleen Moore, "Strough Is Re-elected: Supervisor Race in Queensbury Draws Big Turnout," *The Post-Star*, November 8, 2017, A5.

63. *Ibid.*

64. *Ibid.*, A1.

65. Election Archives, www.warrencountyny.gov, https://warrencountyny.gov/sites/default/files/boe/election/2017/g_accumulated.pdf.

66. Kathleen Moore, "Strough Is Re-elected: Supervisor Race in Queensbury Draws Big Turnout," *The Post-Star*, November 8, 2017, A1, A4.

67. *Ibid.*, A5.

68. Michael Goot, "Democrats Survey Change: Queensbury Victories Attributed to Contrasts in Party Priorities," *The Post-Star*, November 9, 2017, A1, A4.

69. *Ibid.*

70. *Ibid.*

71. *Ibid.*

72. Brian Farenell, "Post-Star Under Unwarranted Fire," *The Post-Star*, November 7, 2017, C3.

73. Michael Goot, "New Queensbury Board Gets to Work," *The Post-Star*, January 2, 2018, A1.

74. Ken Tingley, "GOP Boss Is Called on to Step Aside," *The Post-Star*, November 26, 2017, C5.

75. *Ibid.*

76. Kathleen Moore, "Queensbury Supervisor, Wife Charged," *The Post-Star*, March 13, 2018, A1.

77. *Ibid.*

78. *Ibid.*, A5.

79. *Ibid.*

80. Kathleen Moore, "Strough Takes Plea Deal: Attorney: Politics Behind Plea Deal," *The Post-Star*, May 16, 2018, A1.

81. *Ibid.*

82. Kathleen Moore, "Queensbury Supervisor, Wife Charged," *The Post-Star*, March 13, 2018, A5.

83. *Ibid.*

84. Ken Tingley, "Strough Refuses to Back Down," *The Post-Star*, May 16, 2018, C1.

85. *Ibid.*

86. *Ibid.*

87. *Ibid.*, C6.

88. *Ibid.*

89. *Ibid.*

90. Don Lehman, "Post-Star Seeks Dismissal of Case: Prosecutor Does Not Oppose the Request," *The Post-Star*, April 19, 2018, C1.

91. *Ibid.*, C5.

92. *Ibid.*

93. Don Lehman, "Post-Star Littering Charges Dismissed," *The Post-Star*, May 9, 2018, C1.

94. Kathleen Moore, "County Republicans Revise Ethics Code," *The Post-Star*, December 2, 2018, C1.

95. *Ibid.*, C6.

96. *Ibid.*

97. Post-Star Editorial Board, "Republicans Upgrade Code of Ethics," *The Post-Star*, December 9, 2018, C3.

98. *Ibid.*

99. Michael Goot, "Warren County GOP Chair Resigns," *The Post-Star*, August 25, 2020, B1.

100. *Ibid.*

101. *Ibid.*, A6.

102. Ken Tingley, "Strough Refuses to Back Down," *The Post-Star*, May 16, 2018, C6.

103. Ken Tingley, "Strough's Arrest Was News Demanding Coverage," www.poststar.com, January 9, 2019, https://poststar.com/blogs/the_front_page/blog-stroughs-arrest-was-news-demanding-coverage/article_edd17c40-142f-11e9-bdc8-bf660c1c9a54.html.

104. Tom Jenkin, "Excuses for Losses Speak of Disrespect," *The Post-Star*, November 14, 2017, C3.

105. Kathleen Moore, "No. 10: Strough Arrested, Take Plea Deal," *The Post-Star*, December 30, 2018, A5.

106. Don Lehman, "Seeber Returns to Warren County Board of Supervisors as GOP Picks Up Two Seats," www.poststar.com, November 6, 2019, https://poststar.com/news/local/seeber-returns-to-warren-county-board-of-supervisors-as-gop-picks-up-two-seats/-article_c2f26ede-5a8b-58c4-81c1-42d1bafd570c.html.

107. Michael Goot, "First Woman to Lead Board," *The Post-Star*, Jan. 9, 2021, A1.

108. Michael Goot, "Seeber Reorganizes Warren County Board Committees," www.poststar.com, January 15, 2021, https://poststar.com/news/local/govt-and-politics/seeber-reorganizes-warren-county-board-committees/-article_15d9ae88-55bb-572e-9a3d-13807646182e.html.

Chapter 26

1. Will Doolittle, "For a Workaholic, Disease Forces Change of Pace," *The Post-Star*, December 8, 2017, C1.

2. *Ibid.*

3. *Ibid.*

4. Will Doolittle, "Uncertainty Defines Where We Are Now," *The Post-Star*, November 17, 2017, C1.

5. *Ibid.*, C7.

6. *Ibid.*

7. Will Doolittle, "Walking Together Into a New World," *The Post-Star*, November 4, 2017, C1.

8. Will Doolittle, Phone interview with author, September 11, 2020.

9. Will Doolittle, "For a Workaholic, Disease Forces Change of Pace," December 8, 2017, C1.

10. Will Doolittle, Email to author, September 15, 2020.

11. Will Doolittle, "For a Workaholic, Disease Forces Change of Pace," *The Post-Star*, December 8, 2017, C1.

12. *Ibid.*, C1, C5.

13. Will Doolittle, "Walking Together Into a New World," *The Post-Star*, November 4, 2017, C5.

14. *Ibid.*, C1.

15. *Ibid.*, C5.

16. Will Doolittle, "Walking Life's Tightrope," *The Post-Star*, February 21, 2019, C1.

17. Will Doolittle, "Walking Together Into a New World," *The Post-Star*, November 4, 2017, C5.

18. *Ibid.*

19. Will Doolittle, "Uncertainty Defines Where We Are Now," *The Post-Star*, November 17, 2017, C7.

20. *Ibid.*

21. Will Doolittle, Phone interview with author, September 13, 2020.

22. *Ibid.*

23. Will and Bella Doolittle, "The Alzheimer's Chronicles, Part 21," November 21, 2019, https://poststar.com/news/local/column-carrying-on-is-the-biggest-challenge/article_e585cd86-df63-523e-a2a6-e89735c94785.html.

24. *Ibid.*

25. *Ibid.*

26. *Ibid.*

27. Will Doolittle, Phone interview with Author, September 13, 2020.

28. Will Doolittle, "Living Through a Year Full of Changes," *The Post-Star*, December 27, 2018, C5.

29. Will Doolittle, "With Alzheimer's, Failure Is the Rule," *The Post-Star*, December 7, 2018, C1.

30. *Ibid.*, C5.

31. *Ibid.*, C1.

32. Will Doolittle, "Our Home Improvement Projects Continue," *The Post-Star*, March 8, 2018, C1.

33. *Ibid.*

34. Will Doolittle, "Mind the Gap: A Journey in Scotland," www.poststar.com, June 30, 2018, Https://poststar.com/news/local/mind-the-gap-a-journey-in-scotland/article_480e8adf-b71b-5d34-951c-d6d34926f67f.html.

35. Will Doolittle, "Our Home Improvement Projects Continue," *The Post-Star*, March 8, 2018, C5.

36. *Ibid.*

37. Ken Tingley, Nomination letter to Lee Enterprises for Spirit Award, From author's files, August 26, 2018.

38. Will Doolittle, "Many Share the Alzheimer's Experience," *The Post-Star*, May 18, 2018, C6.

39. Ken Tingley, Nomination letter to Lee Enterprises for Spirit Award, From author's files, August 26, 2018.

40. Will Doolittle, "With Alzheimer's Failure Is the Rule," *The Post-Star*, December 6, 2018, C1.

41. Will Doolittle, "Walking Life's Tightrope," *The Post-Star*, February 22, 2019, C1.

42. Will Doolittle, "Trying to Save the Memories," *The Post-Star*, September 11, 2020. B2.

43. Will Doolittle, Phone interview with author, September 13, 2020.

44. Post-Star Staff Report, "Much More Than Just a Story," *The Post-Star*, April 26, 2019, A1.

45. Will Doolittle, "Drug Trial Offers Us Something to Do," *The Post-Star*, April 12, 2018, C6.

Chapter 27

1. Michael Goot, Kathleen Moore, "Cobb Wins Democratic Nomination in NY-21 Primary," *The Post-Star*, June 26, 2018, https://poststar.com/news/local/cobb-wins-democratic-nomination-in-ny-21-primary/article_d2ad1204-415e-537a-a84a-20e3e92e3f23.html.

2. Post-Star Editorial Board, "We Ask Cobb, Stefanik Not to Lie," *The Post-Star*, July 1, 2018, C3.

3. Tedra Cobb, "Cobb Vows Honesty, Integrity in Campaign," *The Post-Star*, July 7, 2018, C3.

4. Ken Tingley, "New Policy Seeks Candidate Accountability," *The Post-Star*, July 15, 2018, C3.

5. Ken Tingley, "Changing How We Cover NY21 Candidates," *The Post-Star*, July 8, 2018, C3.

6. Abraham Kenmore, "Cobb's Stand on Guns Under Microscope After Secret Video Surfaces," Watertown Daily Times, July 11, 2018, https://poststar.com/news/local/ny-21-cobbs-stance-on-guns-under-microscope-after-secret-video-surfaces/article_a0b24185-c42a-5409-918c-b715062c7268.html.

7. Michael Goot, "Teen Who Recorded Cobb ID'd," *The Post-Star*, July 31, 2018, A1.

8. Michael Goot, "Report: Teen Was Paid by NRCC," *The Post-Star*, August 1, 2018, A1.

9. Post-Star Editorial Board, "Is There Any Morality Left in Politics," *The Post-Star*, August 3, 2018, C3.

10. *Ibid.*

11. *Ibid.*

12. Kathleen Moore, "County Republicans Revise Ethics Code," *The Post-Star*, December 2, 2018, C1.

13. Post-Star Editorial Board, "Cobb Is Right Choice for Congress," *The Post-Star*, October 28, 2018, C3.

14. Michael Goot, "Rep. Stefanik Re-elected to Third Term," www.poststar.com, November 7, 2018, https://poststar.com/news/local/govt-and-politics/rep-stefanik-re-elected-to-third-term/article_9df65e84-077e-5471-8711-dd7383fdc154.html.

15. Staff Report, "Protest Set for Saturday in Front of Stefanik's Office," www.poststar.com, June 13, 2019, https://poststar.com/news/local/protest-set-for-saturday-in-front-of-stefaniks-office/article_7484a079-5807-521c-8125-c1b4dd11d76a.html.

16. Ken Tingley, "Violence Could Be Ahead Even Here," *The Post-Star*, June 23, 2019, C1.

17. *Ibid.*

18. *Ibid.*

19. *Ibid.*

20. *Ibid.*

21. *Ibid.*, C6.

22. *Ibid.*

23. Ken Tingley, "Stefanik Is No Longer an Independent Thinker," *The Post-Star*, November 20, 2019, https://poststar.com/opinion/columnists/commentary-stefanik-is-no-longer-an-independent-thinker/article_2cd0353d-a277-5f0d-a7a1-c1129d8bec07.html.

24. Post-Star Staff Report, "Stefanik Named to Trump's Impeachment Defense Team," *The Post-Star*, January 20, 2020, https://poststar.com/news/local/govt-and-politics/stefanik-named-to-trumps-impeachment-defense-team/article_47b61c9a-cba8-5a99-95be-0282ebedbe5b.html.

25. Alex Gault, "Rep. Stefanik Takes Stage at RNC, Tackling Impeachment, Biden," Watertown, Daily Star, August 26, 2020, https://poststar.com/news/local/govt-and-politics/rep-stefanik-takes-stage-at-rnc-tackling-impeachment-biden/article_cab7810a-1774-5c0b-9800-73e48f714f5f.html.

26. Ken Tingley, "Truth and Trust Missing from Congressional Debate," *The Post-Star*, October 17, 2018, C1.

27. *Ibid.*

28. Mike Kibling, Facebook.com, Post on June 16, 2019.

29. *Ibid.*

30. Mike Kibling, facebook.com, Post on June 29, 2019.

31. Kathleen Phalen-Tomaselli, "Anger Vs. Love and a Pro-Trump Rally," www.poststar.com, August 24, 2019, https://poststar.com/news/local/blog-anger-vs-love-and-a-pro-trump-rally/-article_7153fb12-95eb-53c5-8cb2-acf46b0eba19.html.

32. *Ibid.*

33. *Ibid.*

34. Michael Goot, "Protesters Arrested at Stefanik Office Plead to Lesser Charge," www.poststar.com, September 26, 2019, https://poststar.com/news/local/govt-and-politics/-protesters-arrested-at-stefaniks-office-plead-to-lesser-charge/article_53560bef-b259-58fe-a5b2-8785b1cc532a.html.

35. *Ibid.*

36. Post-Star Editorial Board, "Charges Should Be Dropped Against Protesters," *The Post-Star*, September 7, 2019, C3.

37. *Ibid.*

38. Kathleen Phalen-Tomaselli, "Police Keep Order as Dueling Political Gatherings Continue in Glens Falls," www.poststar.com, September 21, 2019, https://poststar.com/news/local/police-keep-order-as-dueling-political-gatherings-continue-in-glens-falls/article_bac069c6-8a55-5f03-beed-dbfde530cd5d.html.

39. David Lombardo, "Political Forces Square Off in Glens Falls," www.timesunion.com, September 13, 2019, https://www.timesunion.com/news/article/Political-forces-square-off-in-Glens-Falls-14438868.php.

40. Kathleen Phalen-Tomaselli, "Police Keep

Order as Dueling Political Gatherings Continue in Glens Falls," www.poststar.com, September 21, 2019, https://poststar.com/news/local/police-keep-order-as-dueling-political-gatherings-continue-in-glens-falls/article_bac069c6-8a55-5f03-beed-dbfde530cd5d.html.

41. Ken Tingley, "Should We Worry About Threats?" www.poststar.com, September 20, 2019, https://poststar.com/blogs/the_front_page/blog-should-we-worry-about-threats/-article_ab096030-bdfc-5901-93f3-ad155acd2f07.html.

42. Kathleen Phalen-Tomaselli, Email to author, September 13, 2019.

43. Kathleen Moore, "Rally to Include Displaying Unloaded Rifles," www.poststar.com, October 5, 2019, https://poststar.com/news/local/rally-to-include-displaying-unloaded-rifles/article_25e17395-07c0-517c-bcb3-18bb5765112e.html.

44. Kathleen Phalen-Tomaselli, "Pro-Trump Groups Feel Fractures," *The Post-Star*, October 6, 2019, A1.

45. Kathleen Phalen-Tomaselli, "Threats with Toy Guns Feel Real," www.poststar.com, October 5, 2019, https://poststar.com/blogs/kathleen_phalen-tomaselli/blog-threats-with-toy-guns-feel-real/-article_beeba039-7cad-5049-b49a-a723ffdada82.html.

46. *Ibid.*
47. *Ibid.*
48. *Ibid.*
49. *Ibid.*
50. *Ibid.*
51. *Ibid.*
52. *Ibid.*

53. Ken Tingley, "Threats Should Shock, Outrage," *The Post-Star*, October 8, 2019, B1.

54. *Ibid.*

55. Kathleen Phalen-Tomaselli, "Groups: Stefanik Put Out Call," *The Post-Star*, October 11, 2019, A1.

56. *Ibid.*
57. *Ibid.*

58. Ken Tingley, "Still No Word from Rep. Stefanik," www.poststar.com, October 11, 2019, https://poststar.com/blogs/the_front_page/blog-still-no-word-from-rep-stefanik/article_70518460-1e77-58d3-868a-b3649cbad3c9.html.

59. Kathleen Phalen-Tomaselli, "Groups: Stefanik Put Out Call," *The Post-Star*, October 11, 2019, A5.

60. Ken Tingley, "Stefanik Backs Bullies," *The Post-Star*, October 11, 2019, C1.

61. *Ibid.*, C6.

62. Ken Tingley, "Words of Encouragement," *The Post-Star*, October 19, 2019, C3.

63. *Ibid.*

64. Ken Tingley, "Newspaper Called Out During Meeting, Too," www.poststar.com, October 23, 2019, https://poststar.com/blogs/the_front_page/blog-newspaper-called-out-during-meeting-too/article_38725096-bb3b-57d9-99e5-ba3dc1c4e3f4.html.

65. Ken Tingley, "Newspaper Called Out During Meeting, Too," www.poststar.com, October 23, 2019, https://poststar.com/blogs/the_front_page/blog-newspaper-called-out-during-meeting-too/article_38725096-bb3b-57d9-99e5-ba3dc1c4e3f4.html.

66. Daniel Dale, "Fact Check: Elise Stefanik Tried to Get Election Overturned, Promoted Election Lies," www.cnn.com, May 6, 2021, https://www.cnn.com/2021/05/06/politics/fact-check-stefanik-big-lie-election-trump/index.html.

67. *Ibid.*
68. *Ibid.*
69. *Ibid.*

70. Aaron Cerbone, "Stefanik Objects to Electors After Capitol Riot," www.adirondackdailyenterprise.com, January 8, 2021, https://www.adirondackdailyenterprise.com/news/-local-news/2021/01/stefanik-objected-to-pennsylvania-electors/.

71. *Ibid.*
72. *Ibid.*

73. Daniel Dale, "Face Check: Elise Stefanik Tried to Get Election Overturned, Promoted Election Lies," www.cnn.com, May 6, 2021, https://www.cnn.com/2021/05/06/politics/fact-check-stefanik-big-lie-election-trump/index.html.

74. Greg Sargent, "Elise Stefanik Is a Perfect Leader of Today's GOP. Her Own Statements, Show Why," www.washingtonpost.com, May 6, 2021, https://www.washingtonpost.com/opinions/2021/05/06/elise-stefanik-perfect-gop-leader-trump/.

Chapter 28

1. Ken Tingley, "Buoyed to Face Another Year," *The Post-Star*, December 30, 2018, C6.

2. *Ibid.*
3. *Ibid.*
4. *Ibid.*
5. *Ibid.*
6. *Ibid.*

7. Kathleen Moore, "Moreau Town Officials Blame 'Fake News,'" *The Post-Star*, June 29, 2017, B1.

8. *Ibid.*

9. Post-Star Editorial Board, "'Fake News' Claims Have No Merit," *The Post-Star*, June 30, 2017, A1.

10. *Ibid.*, A6.

11. Kathleen Moore, "Hospital Lays Off 25 Employees," *The Post-Star*, January 29, 2019, A1.

12. *Ibid.*

13. Kathleen Moore, "Hospital Seeks Turnaround," *The Post-Star*, A1.

14. *Ibid.*, A8.

15. *Ibid.*

16. *Ibid.*, A1.

17. Will Doolittle, "Hospital Seeks Turnaround," *The Post-Star*, February 14, 2019, A1.

18. *Ibid.*

19. *Ibid.*

20. Editorial Board, "Concerns Raised Over Hospital Finances," *The Post-Star*, February 17, 2019, C3.

21. Kathleen Moore, "Hospital CEO Says Situation Is 'Dire,'" *The Post-Star*, March 3, 2019, A1.

22. *Ibid.*, A8.

23. Ken Tingley, "Hospital Faces Uncertain Future," *The Post-Star*, March 3, 2019, C5.

24. *Ibid.*

25. Kathleen Moore, "Waiting for Numbers from Glens Falls Hospital," March 4, 2019, https://poststar.com/blogs/kathleen_moore/-blog-waiting-for-numbers-from-glens-falls-hospital/article_7ebb8418-d606-5eb3-bdd0-a4d75e397223.html.

26. Kathleen Moore, "Parsing Highs from Lows: Hospital Finances Get Close Look," *The Post-Star*, March 6, 2019, A1.

27. Kathleen Moore, "Audit: Hospital Lost $38M," *The Post-Star*, March 8, 2019, A1.

28. *Ibid.*

29. *Ibid.*, A6.

30. *Ibid.*

31. *Ibid.*

32. Kathleen Moore, Phone interview with author, September 23, 2020.

33. Tracy Mills, Email to Tom Salvo, March 11, 2019.

34. Kathleen Moore, Phone interview with author, September 23, 2020.

35. Kathleen Moore, "Hospital Faced Billing Issues," *The Post-Star*, March 13, 2019, A1.

36. Kathleen Moore, Phone interview with author, September 23, 2020.

37. *Ibid.*

38. Brian Corcoran, Email to Bob Condon, Will Doolittle, March 12, 2019.

39. Kathleen Moore, "Hospital Faced Billing Issues," *The Post-Star*, March 12, 2019, Original copy of story from author's files.

40. Will Doolittle, Email to Ken Tingley, March 12, 2019,

41. Brian Corcoran, Email to Ken Tingley, March 12, 2019.

42. Will Doolittle, Email to Brian Corcoran, March 13, 2019.

43. William G. Powers, Post on Glens Falls Hospital Facebook page, March 20, 2019.

44. *Ibid.*

45. Kathleen Moore, Phone interview with author, September 23, 2020.

46. *Ibid.*

47. Brian Farenell, "Stories Show Need for Local Journalism," *The Post-Star*, March 23, 2019, C3.

48. *Ibid.*

49. Kathleen Moore, "Retired Doctor Urges Letter-writing Campaign," *The Post-Star*, September 25, 2019, A1.

50. Ken Tingley, Email to Brian Corcoran with first draft of editorial, October 3, 2019.

51. *Ibid.*

52. *Ibid.*

53. *Ibid.*

54. *Ibid.*

55. Ken Tingley, "Hospital Bigwigs Come Up Short," October 10, 2019.

56. Brian Corcoran, Email to Ken Tingley, November 5, 2019.

57. Dr. Howard Fritz, Email to Will Doolittle, Kathleen Moore, Brian Corcoran, Ken Tingley, Chris White, Tracy Mills, November 13, 2019.

58. Brian Corcoran, Email to Bob Condon, Will Doolittle, Ken Tingley, November 15, 2019.

59. Ken Tingley, Email to Brian Corcoran, November 15, 2019.

60. Kathleen Moore, "Coping with Hard Times: Glens Falls Hospital Audits Voted Top Story of Year," *The Post-Star*, December 29, 2019, A1.

61. *Ibid.*

62. Nancy Gautier, Phone interview with author, September 22, 2020.

63. *Ibid.*

64. *Ibid.*

65. *Ibid.*

66. Will Springstead, Phone interview with author, July 2020.

Epilogue

1. Don Lehman, Interview with author, September 25, 2020.

2. Ray Agnew, Email to Ken Tingley, February 14, 2020.

3. Ken Tingley, Email to Ray Agnew, February 17, 2020.

4. Ray Agnew, Email to Ken Tingley, February 18, 2020.

5. Kathleen Moore, Interview with author, September 23, 2020.

6. Ken Tingley, Email to Ray Agnew, February 19, 2020.

7. Kathleen Moore, "Hospitals Differ on Mask Usage: Glens Falls Hospital Holding Back from Using N95 Masks," *The Post-Star*, March 27, 2020, A1.

8. *Ibid.*

9. Don Coyote, *The Post-Star*, March 28, 2020, C3.

10. Gillian Tingley, Interview with author, March 30, 2020.

11. Ken Tingley, Email to Brian Corcoran, March 29, 2020.

12. Ken Tingley, Email to Brian Corcoran, March 28, 2020.

13. Brian Corcoran, "Publishers Note," *The Post-Star*, March 31, 2020, A4.

14. Brian Corcoran, Email to Adam Colver, Bob Condon, Will Doolittle, Ken Tingley, March 30, 2020.

15. Brian Corcoran, Email to Will Doolittle, Ken Tingley, Adam Colver, Bob Condon, April 3, 2020.

16. Brian Corcoran, Email to Ken Tingley, April 6, 2020.

17. Kristen Hare, "Lee Enterprises Announces Pay Cuts and Furloughs," www.Poynter.org, March 31, 2020, https://www.poynter.org/-business-work/2020/lee-enterprises-announces-pay-cuts-and-furloughs/.

18. Post-Star Staff Report, "The Post-Star Wins Top State Award," *The Post-Star*, June 4, 2020, B1.

19. *Ibid.*

20. *Ibid.*, A5.

21. *Ibid.*

22. *Ibid.*

23. Post-Star Staff Report, Post-Star honored with 11 awards by NYNPA," *The Post-Star*, September 24, 2020, B1.

24. Ken Tingley, "To the Readers," *The Post-Star*, July 7, 2020, A1.

25. *Ibid.*, A5.

26. Ken Tingley, "When the Sheriff Hires His Son, It's Nepotism," *The Post-Star*, July 12, 2020, C3.

27. Michael Goot, "Sheriff Rescinds Son's Hiring," *The Post-Star*, July 18, 2020, A1.

28. Post-Star Staff Report, "City Honors Ken Tingley with Proclamation," *The Post-Star*, July 17, 2020, B1.

29. Post-Star Staff Report, "Ben Rogers to Lead the Post-Star," *The Post-Star*, August 21, 2020, A1.

30. *Ibid.*, A6.

31. *Ibid.*

32. *Ibid.*, C4.

33. *Ibid.*

34. *Ibid.*

Bibliography

Adria, David, Victoria Smith Ekstrand, Ashley Fox, and Evan Ringel. "Addressing the decline of local news, rise of platforms, and spread of mis- and disinformation online," University of North Carolina, December 2020, *https://citap.unc.edu/local-news-platforms-mis-disinformation/.*

Alexander, Jon. "Old Age Is Coming and We're Not Ready," www.poststar.com, May 2, 2013, https://poststar.com/old-age-is-coming-and-we-re-not-ready/article_1522d38c-b367-11e2-bed7-0019bb2963f4.html.

Arnold, Chad. "Mountain Lake PBS to Show Charles Evans Hughes Documentary," www.poststar.com, April 5, 2021, https://poststar.com/news/local/mountain-lake-pbs-to-show-charles-evans-hughes-documentary/-article_316718de-cbef-5dbd-83d9-efd2f37691c9.html.

Baer, Jamie. "Roy McDonald: Protector of the Party of Lincoln," www.jfklibrary.org, 2013, https://www.jfklibrary.org/learn/education/profile-in-courage-essay-contest/-past-winning-essays/2013-winning-essay-by-jamie-baer.

Balla, Wade H. "Gays Should Stay in the Closet," *Post-Star*, July 29, 2002, A5.

Bell, Pastor Mark. "Media Promotes Liberal Agenda," *Post-Star*, August 3, 2002, A5.

Benjamin, Elizabeth. "Sweeney Pays Wife," www.timesunion.com, April 11, 2006, *https://blog.timesunion.com/capitol/411-sweeney-pay-wife/.*

Bensen, Amanda. "Ethan Allen Rescuers Honored," *Post-Star*, February 2, 2006, A1.

Bensen, Amanda. "'I Don't Know Where My Husband Is,'" *Post-Star*, October 3, 2005, A5.

Bernstein, Judy, and Matthew Sturdevant. "'It Is Not a Final Goodbye,'" *Post-Star*, December 1, 2002, A1.

Bishop, Jim. "The Day Kennedy Was Shot," Funk & Wagnalls, 1968 149, 164–165.

Blow, David. "Ark. Boating Tragedy Spurs Little Worry on Lake George," *Post-Star*, May 5, 1999, A1.

Blow, David. "Tower Witness Hears Whine, Explosion," *Post-Star*, September 12, 2001, A1.

Brooks, Pam. "'Get Up! We Have to Get Out,'" *Post-Star*, August 31, 2000, A1.

Brooks, Pamela. "Pamela Anne (French) Brooks-Gibbs, obituary," *Post-Star*, February 26, 2019, B4.

Buell, Glen A. "Photo Choice Was Disgusting," *Post-Star*, July 29, 2002, A5.

Citiizens for Responsibiliity and Ethics in Washington. "The 20 Most Corrupt Members of Congress (and Five to Watch)," October 2, 2006, *https://web.archive.org/web/20061002040702/http://www.beyonddelay.org/summaries/sweeney.php.*

Cobb, Tedra. "Cobb Vows Honesty, Integrity in Campaign," *Post-Star*, July 7, 2018, C3.

Condon, Bob. "She Was 'Special to the Post-Star,'" *Post-Star* Facebook page, August 31, 2019.

Corcoran, Brian. "Publishers Note," *Post-Star*, March 31, 2020, A4.

Confessore, Nicholas. "State Clerks' Group to Oppose License Policy," www.nytimes.com, October 5, 2007, *https://www.nytimes.com/2007/10/05/nyregion/05spitzer.html?referringSource=articleShare.*

Confessore, Nicholas, and Michael Barbaro, "New York Allows Same-sex Marriage, Becomes Largest State to Pass Law," www.nytimes.com, June 25, 2011, https://www.nytimes.com/2011/06/25/nyregion/gay-marriage-approved-by-new-york-senate.html?referringSource=articleShare.

Cordani, Tucker. "Suburban Nightmare," *Post-Star*, April 21, 1999, A1.

Coyote, Don. *Post-Star*, March 28, 2020, C3.

Crowley, Cathleen F. "Cops: Suspect Targeted Wife," www.timesunion.com, July 18, 2012, https://www.timesunion.com/local/article/-Cops-Suspect-targeted-wife-3713836.php.

Curtis, Fred. "Story Did Not Address Needs of Readers," *Post-Star*, July 28, 2002, F2.

Daily Freeman and Associated Press. "Former Mid-Hudson Rep. John Sweeney Failed to Pay Private Investigator's Bill, Lawsuit Alleges," www.dailyfreeman.com, August 23, 2018, *https://www.dailyfreeman.com/news/former-mid-hudson-rep-john-sweeney-failed-to-pay-private-investigator-s-bill-lawsuit-alleges/article_6c36d357-6536-5327-80e7-c21cf36153fb.html.*

DeMare, Carol. "Sweeney Talks of Loss, Healing," www.timesunion.com, March 6, 2011, https://www.timesunion.com/local/article/-Sweeney-talks-of-loss-healing-1044313.php.

DeMasi, Michael. "New Owners Will Keep DiCarlo's Gentleman's Club in Albany Kicking," www.bizjournals.com, October 2, 2014, https://www.bizjournals.com/albany/morning_call/2014/10/new-owners-will-keep-dicarlos-gentlemens-club-in.html.

DeMerchant, Sean. "Sean DeMerchant Obituary," *Legacy.com*, April 29, 2014, https://www.legacy.com/us/obituaries/-timesunion-albany/name/sean-demerchant-obituary?pid=170840199.

DeMuth, Erin. "Longtime Post-Star Publisher Retiring," *Post-Star*, March 18, 2006, A1.

DeMuth, Erin. "Marshalls to Receive Community Service Award," *Post-Star*, January 5, 2008, B1.

DeSilver, Drew. "How Many Same-sex Marriages in the U.S.? at Least 71,165, Maybe More," www.pewresearch.org, June 26, 2013, https://www.pewresearch.org/fact-tank/2013/06/26/-how-many-same-sex-marriages-in-the-u-s-at-least-71165-probably-more/.

Dimopoulos, Thomas. "Friends of the Victims Have Started Raising Funds for Survivors," *Post-Star*, June 28, 2010, A6.

Dimopoulos, Thomas. "Former Congressman Sweeney Sentenced in Drunken Driving Case," www.poststar.com, April 23, 2010, *https://poststar.com/news/local/former-congressman-sweeney-sentenced-in-drunken-driving-case/article_9dc557b6-4efa-11df-8488-001cc4c002e0.html.*

Dimopoulos, Thomas. "Loss Overwhelming for Community," *Post-Star*, June 28, 2010, A1.

Dimopoulos, Thomas. "Man Killed Crossing Northway Was Grandfather of 12-year-old Shooting Victim," www.poststar.com, January 5, 2011, https://poststar.com/news/local/man-killed-crossing-northway-was-grandfather-of-12-year-old-shooting-victim/article_44957692-17f1-11e0-80ea-001cc4c002e0.html.

Dimopoulos, Thomas. "Wilton Father, Son Charged in Shooting Death of 12-year-old," www.poststar.com, December 28, 2010, *https://poststar.com/news/local/wilton-father-son-charged-in-shooting-death-of-12-year-old/article_86124902-120f-11e0-9517-001cc4c002e0.html.*

Donnelly, Scott. "Hospital Goes to 'code Yellow,'" *Post-Star*, October 3, 2005, B1.

Doolittle, Will. "After Addiction's Upheaval, Sisters Get on with Life," www.poststar.com, May 31, 2015, *https://poststar.com/news/local/after-addictions-upheaval-sisters-get-on-with-life/article_beea8d99-a3fd-5c68-b18a-518b8bbbff43.html.*

Doolittle, Will. "Caretaker Battles Health Issues, Financial Problems," *Post-Star*, June 30, 2014, A5.

Doolittle, Will. "Drug Trial Offers Us Something to Do," *Post-Star*, April 12, 2018, C6.

Doolittle, Will. "For a Workaholic, Disease Forces Change of Pace," *Post-Star*, December 8, 2017, C1.

Doolittle, Will. "A Forced Relocation: Parents' Drug Addiction Leaves Three Girls No Choice but to Start Over," *Post-Star*, June 29, 2014, A1.

Doolittle, Will. "Hospital Seeks Turnaround," *Post-Star*, February 14, 2019, A1.

Doolittle, Will. "Living Through a Year Full of Changes, *Post-Star*, December 27, 2018, C5.

Doolittle, Will. "Many Share the Alzheimer's Experience," *Post-Star*, May 18, 2018, C6.

Doolittle, Will. "Mind the Gap: A Journey in Scotland, www.poststar.com, June 30, 2018, Https://poststar.com/news/local/mind-the-gap-a-journey-in-scotland/article_480e8adf-b71b-5d34-951c-d6d34926f67f.html.

Doolittle, Will. "New Regulations Might Have Prevented Sinking," *Post-Star*, October 4, 2005, A1.

Doolittle, Will. "Our Home Improvement Projects Continue," *Post-Star*, March 8, 2018, C1.

Doolittle, Will. "Saving the Sweeney Campaign," www.poststar.com, May 5, 2006, *https://www.timesunion.com/local/article/Redemption-of-John-Sweeney-a-work-in-progress-12713399.php.*

Doolittle, Will. "Sweeney's Crash Raises Questions," *Post-Star*, February 4, 2001, B1.

Doolittle, Will. "Trying to Save the Memories," *Post-Star*, September 11, 2020, B2.

Doolittle, Will. "Uncertainty Defines Where We Are Now," *Post-Star*, November 17, 2017, C1.

Doolittle, Will. "Walking Life's Tightrope," *Post-Star*, February 21, 2019, C1.

Doolittle, Will. "Walking Together into a New World," *Post-Star*, November 4, 2017, C1.

Doolittle, Will. "Where No Comfort Is Found," *Post-Star*, September 25, 2003, A1.

Doolittle, Will. "With Alzheimer's, Failure Is the Rule," *Post-Star*, December 7, 2018, C1.

Doolittle, Will, and Bella Doolittle. "The Alzheimer's Chronicles, Part 21, www.poststar.com, November 21, 2019, Https://poststar.com/news/local/column-carrying-on-is-the-biggest-challenge/article_e585cd86-df63-523e-a2a6-e89735c94785.html.

Election Results, 2000, www.few.gov, *https://www.fec.gov/resources/cms-content/documents/federalelections00.pdf.*

Election Results, 2002, www.historycms2.house.gov, p. 33, https://historycms2.house.gov/Institution/Election-Statistics/1998election/.

Election Results, 2004, www.historycms2.house.gov, p. 40, https://historycms2.house.gov/Institution/Election-Statistics/2004election/.

Epp, Henry, and Melody Bodette. "Rutland Herald, Times Argus Lay Off Pulitzer Prize-winning Editor," vpr.org, February 28, 2018, https://www.vpr.org/post/rutland-herald-times-argus-lay-pulitzer-prize-winning-editor#stream/0.

Farbman, Madeline. "An Anniversary of Tears,"

www.poststar.com, *https://poststar.com/news/local/an-anniversary-of-tears/article_d59d62c4-95ea-584c-8ea5-0a8c33aaa158.html*.

Farenell, Brian. "Post-Star Under Unwarranted Fire," *Post-Star*, November 7, 2017, C3.

Farenell, Brian. "Stories Show Need for Local Journalism," *Post-Star*, March 23, 2019, C3.

Fiegl, Charles. "Gillibrand Calls on Sweeney to Release Run-ins with Police," www.poststar.com, October 10, 2006, https://poststar.com/news/local/gillibrand-calls-on-sweeney-to-release-police-records/article_4dd1d0a4-85a1-5b82-830c-4288f062726a.html.

Fiegl, Charles. "Sweeney Announces Grant, Avoids Questions of Abuse," www.poststar.com, November 6, 2006, *https://poststar.com/news/sweeney-announces-grant-avoids-questions-of-abuse/article_1fa578c6-f23d-5008-8064-ecb5695fb2cf.html*.

Friedman, Dan. "Trump Insider as a Lobbyist," www.motherjones.com, September 13, 2019, https://www.motherjones.com/politics/2019/09/kremlin-controlled-russian-bank-hires-trump-insider-as-a-lobbyist/.

Fritz, Howard. Email to Will Doolitttle, Kathleen Moore, Brian Corcoran, Ken Tingley, Chris White, Tracy Mills, November 13, 2019.

Gault, Alex. "Rep. Stefanik Takes Stage at RNC, Tackling Impeachment, Biden," *Watertown Daily Star*, August 26, 2020, *https://poststar.com/news/local/govt-and-politics/rep-stefanik-takes-stage-at-rnc-tackling-impeachment-biden/article_cab7810a-1774-5c0b-9800-73e48f714f5f.html*.

Gereau, John. "Prayers Answered for Queensbury Family in Tragedy," *Post-Star*, September 15, 2001, B1.

Granville Sentinel, November 12, 1875.

Gao, Pengjie, Chang Lee, and Dermot Murphy. "Financing Dies in the Darkness: The Impact of Newspaper Closures on Public Finance." www.brookings.edu, September 24, 2018, *https://www.brookings.edu/research/financing-dies-in-darkness-the-impact-of-newspaper-closures-on-public-finance/*.

Grondahl, Paul. "Redemption of John Sweeney a Work in Progress," www.timesunion.com, February 27, 2018, https://www.timesunion.com/local/article/Redemption-of-John-Sweeney-a-work-in-progress-12713399.php.

Goodwin, Mike. "Netflix's 'The Laundromat' Dramatizes Ethan Allen Boat Disaster," www.timesunion.com, *https://www.timesunion.com/news/article/Netflix-s-The-Laundromat-dramatizes-Ethan-Allen-14543997.php*.

Goot, Michael. "Democrats Survey Change: Queensbury Victories Attributed to Contrasts in Party Priorities," *Post-Star*, November 9, 2017, A1, A4.

Goot, Michael. "First Woman to Lead Board," *Post-Star*, Jan. 9, 2021, A1.

Goot, Michael. "Former Rep. Sweeney Lobbying for Kremlin-controlled Bank," www.poststar.com, September 16, 2019, https://poststar.com/news/local/govt-and-politics/former-rep-sweeney-lobbying-for-kremlin-controlled-bank/article_a259b64c-bf9e-5e21-9d28-6d9928fbb3bf.html.

Goot, Michael. "New Queensbury Board Gets to Work," *Post-Star*, January 2, 2018, A1.

Goot, Michael. "Protesters Arrested at Stefanik Office Plead to Lesser Charge," www.poststar.com, September 26, 2019, *https://poststar.com/news/local/govt-and-politics/protesters-arrested-at-stefaniks-office-plead-to-lesser-charge/article_53560bef-b259-58fe-a5b2-8785b1cc532a.html*.

Goot, Michael. "Rep. Stefanik Re-elected to Third Term," www.poststar.com, November 7, 2018, *https://poststar.com/news/local/govt-and-politics/rep-stefanik-re-elected-to-third-term/article_9df65e84-077e-5471-8711-dd7383fdc154.html*.

Goot, Michael. "Report: Teen Was Paid by NRCC," *Post-Star*, August 1, 2018, A1.

Goot, Michael. "Seeber Reorganizes Warren County Board Committees," www.poststar.com, January 15, 2021, https://poststar.com/news/local/govt-and-politics/-seeber-reorganizes-warren-county-board-committees/article_15d9ae88-55bb-572e-9a3d-13807646182e.html.

Goot, Michael. "Sheriff Rescinds Son's Hiring," *Post-Star*, July 18, 2020, A1.

Goot, Michael. "Taking. Young Lives: Death of Student, 22, Shows Heroin's Reach," *Post-Star*, June 23, 2014, A1.

Goot, Michael. "Teen Who Recorded Cobb ID'd," *Post-Star*, July 31, 2018, A1.

Goot, Michael. "Warren County GOP Chair Resigns," *Post-Star*, August 25, 2020, B1.

Goot, Michael, and Kathleen Moore, "Cobb Wins Democratic Nomination in NY-21 Primary," www.poststar.com, June 26, 2018, https://poststar.com/news/local/cobb-wins-democratic-nomination-in-ny-21-primary/article_d2ad1204-415e-537a-a84a-20e3e92e3f23.html.

Green, Rev. Anthony W. "Running Recent Story Was Act of Courage," *Post-Star*, July 28, 2002, F2.

Hagerty, Meg. "Making the Move: Nursing Homes Can Offer Care and Companionship," www.poststar.com, May 2, 2013,

Hagerty, Meg. "Librarian Suggests Turning the Page on Longtime Reading Club Winner," www.poststar.com, August 15, 2013, https://poststar.com/news/local/librarian-suggests-turning-the-page-on-longtime-reading-club-winner/article_bdbebbc6-0625-11e3-b6f4-0019bb2963f4.html.

Hagerty, Meg. "Big Reader Story from Hudson Falls Spreads Around the World," www.poststar.com, August 20, 2013, https://poststar.com/news/local/big-reader-story-from-hudson-falls-spreads-around-world/article_86123af2-09d8-11e3-8471-001a4bcf887a.html.

Hagerty, Meg. "Young Reader Interviews on National TV," www.poststar.com, August 21, 2013, https://poststar.com/news/local/young-reader-interviewed-on-national-tv/article_1cc89364-0aa7-11e3-8a66-0019bb2963f4.html.

Hagerty, Meg. "Stefanik Campaign Ramping Up," www.poststar.com, May 6, 2014, *https://poststar.com/news/local/stefaniks-campaign-ramping-up/article_d2154512-d3b7-11e3-9a69-0019bb2963f4.html.*

Hagerty, Meg. "Mother Takes Comfort in Son's Survival of Drug Abuse," www.poststar.com, June 21, 2014, https://poststar.com/news/local/mother-takes-comfort-in-son-s-survival-of-drug-abuse/article_aa46759a-f9b6-11e3-8ab9-001a4bcf887a.html.

Hagerty, Meg. "Long Road to a Dark Place," www.poststar.com, June 22, 2014, https://poststar.com/news/local/long-road-to-a-dark-place/article_174c08fe-fa7e-11e3-b387-001a4bcf887a.html.

Hagerty, Meg. "Saying Good Bye," www.poststar.com, December 30, 2014, https://poststar.com/blogs/meg_hagerty/saying-good-bye/article_36da8392-9030-11e4-9c46-1b194abfb617.html.

Hammack, Laurence. "Roanoke.com Drops List of Gun Owners," www.roanoke.com, March 12, 2007, *https://roanoke.com/archive/roanoke-com-drops-list-of-gun-owners/article_a6e79c93-7d63-5b87-a16c-fed05df29799.html.*

Hare, Kristen. "Lee Enterprises Announces Pay Cuts and Furloughs," www.poynter.org, March 31, 2020, *https://www.poynter.org/business-work/2020/lee-enterprises-announces-pay-cuts-and-furloughs/*

Harkinson, Josh. "What Went Wrong: Lake George Disaster," www.popularmechanics.com, *https://www.popularmechanics.com/science/a953/4199636/.*

Hartocollas, Armenia. "NY court upholds gay marriage ban," www.nytimes.com, July 6, 2006, https://www.nytimes.com/2006/07/06/nyregion/06cnd-marriage.html?referringSource=articleShare.

Hernandez, Raymond. "Party Photograph Put a Congressman on the Defensive," www.nytimes.com, April 29, 2006, https://www.nytimes.com/2006/04/29/nyregion/party-photographs-put-a-congressman-on-the-defensive.html?referringSource=articleShare.

Hewitt, Mary. "Story on Homosexuals Was a Courageous Act," *Post-Star*, July 27, 2002, A5.

Hayner, Ruby A. "I appreciated your `Growing Up' story," *Post-Star*, July 31, 2002, A5. www.heritage.org, https://nyheritage.org/collections/glens-falls-hometown-usa.

highroad.com Forum, "Another Paper in NY State Wants to Publish a List of Concealed Carriers!" www.highroad.com, February 4, 2008, https://www.thehighroad.org/index.php?threads/-another-paper-in-ny-state-wants-to-publish-a-list-of-concealed-carriers.336892/.

Holck, David B. "Picture Offensive, Story Misleading," *Post-Star*, July 23, 2002, A5.

House Archives, www.historycms2.house.gov, Pg. 55, https://historycms2.house.gov/Institution/Election-Statistics/1998election/.

Huber, Paula. "Front-page Photo Was in Poor Taste," *Post-Star*, August 10, 2002, A5.

Hughes, Kyle. "Ex-Congressman Sweeney Joins Trump's Team," www.saratogian.com, December 15, 2016, https://www.saratogian.com/news/ex-congressman-sweeney-joins-trump-team/article_e0c7cbde-e537-539e-b308-a7847c6c474b.html.

Jenkin, Tom. "Excuses for Losses Speak of Disrespect," *Post-Star*, November 14, 2017, C3.

Jones, Blake. "Madden Hotel Comes Crashing Down," www.poststar.com, July 19, 2011, https://poststar.com/news/local/madden-hotel-comes-crashing-down/article_5c4a4884-b24d-11e0-8028-001cc4c03286.html.

Kaplan, Thomas. "Cuomo Backs Republican Who Lost Primary After Vote for Gay Marriage," www.nytimes.com, September 26, 2012, https://www.nytimes.com/2012/09/27/nyregion/cuomo-endorses-senator-roy-mcdonald-republican-in-possible-third-party-bid.html?referringSource=articleShare.

Kaplan, Thomas. "Gay Marriage Vote Rises as Test in Upstate G.O.P. Race," www.nytimes.com, September 11, 2012, https://www.nytimes.com/2012/09/12/nyregion/after-vote-for-gay-marriage-senator-roy-mcdonald-faces-gop-primary-fight.html?referringSource=articleShare.

Kenmore, Abraham. "Cobb's Stand on Guns Under Microscope After Secret Video Surfaces," *www.poststar.com* (reprinted from *Watertown Daily Times*), July 11, 2018, https://poststar.com/news/local/ny-21-cobbs-stance-on-guns-under-microscope-after-secret-video-surfaces/article_a0b24185-c42a-5409-918c-b715062c7268.html.

Kerr, Drew. "Billboard Urges McDonald to Support `all Loving Couples,'" www.poststar.com, June 6, 2011, *https://poststar.com/blogs/saratoga_snippets/billboard-urges-mcdonald-to-support-all-loving-couples/-article_6fd00354-caed-55d0-a5d7-901ad4c28f84.html.*

Kerr, Drew. "Same-sex Marriage Lobbying Intensifies," www.poststar.com, June 12, 2011, https://poststar.com/news/local/same-sex-marriage-lobbying-intensifies/article_9f3abe2e-9535-11e0-868c-001cc4c03286.html.

Kibling, Mike. 2019. "I'm so sick of MOTHER-FUCKING MEXICANS crossing the border that I want to set up a 50 cal and just start wasting them." Facebook, June 29, 2019. https://www.facebook.com/michael.kibling.

Kibling, Mike. "She is a biased reporter. If the story isn't exciting enough for her or if the story favors a side that she doesn't agree with, she wrote whatever pops into her head that fits her agenda." Facebook post, June 16, 2019. https://www.facebook.com/michael.kibling.

Kirby, Neil. "Sweeney Charged with Felony DWI," www.poststar.com, April 6, 2009, *https://poststar.com/news/local/sweeney-charged-with-felony-dwi/article_e8adc0ec-2f66-5819-a1f4-8fb5208079d8.html.*

Knights, Kathy. "Smoke Detectors Should Be Distributed," *Post-Star*, December 7, 2002, A7.

Kumar, Anne. "Fatal Crash Claims Two," *Post-Star*, February 21, 2005, A1.

Lape, Walter. "Walter Lape Obituary," www.poststar.com, May 6, 2010, https://poststar.com/lifestyles/announcements/obituaries/-walter-broc-lape/article_f7446b5e-597e-11df-ab92-001cc4c002e0.html.

Laubinger, Al. "Persecution by Arbiters Bigoted," *Post-Star*, August 7, 2002, A5.

Lehman, Don. "About 'Bottle Bob,'" www.poststar.com, July 16, 2017, *https://poststar.com/blogs/don_lehman/about-bottle-bob/article_e8976198-6a69-11e7-9387-3392a668abc3.html.*

Lehman, Don. "At Least 20 Dead After Tour Boat Capsizes, Sinks in Lake George," *Post-Star*, October 3, 2005, A1.

Lehman, Don. "Boat Recovered from Lake for NTSB Investigation," *Post-Star*, October 4, 2005, A3.

Lehman, Don. "Brazen Afternoon Shooting Stuns Local Residents," *Post-Star*, February 22, 2005,

Lehman, Don. "Captain, Boat Owner Indicted in Tour Boat Tragedy," *Post-Star*, February 5, 2007, A1.

Lehman, Don. "Christin DeLorenzo to Live with Her Brother," *Post-Star*, August 13, 2005, A6.

Lehman, Don. "Couple's Home Reveals Anger," *Post-Star*, February 23, 2005, A1.

Lehman, Don. "Dealing with a New Life," *Post-Star*, May 23, 2004, A4.

Lehman, Don. "Death Threats Were Made Before Murder," *Post-Star*, July 12, 2005, A6.

Lehman, Don. "DiLorenzo Gets 25 Years to Life," *Post-Star*, October 27, 2005, A1.

Lehman, Don. "DiLorenzo Pleads Guilty," *Post-Star*, August 13, 2005, A1.

Lehman, Don. "Double Fatal Car Crash Convicted Jailed Again," www.poststar.com, June 5, 2018, https://poststar.com/news/local/double-fatal-car-crash-convict-jailed-again/article_2a4db890-a31e-5267-a578-d125191893fd.html.

Lehman, Don. "Driver in Fatal Crash: 'I'm Sorry,'"

www.poststar.com, October 18, 2008, https://poststar.com/news/local/driver-in-fatal-crash-im-sorry/article_fd3b5b79-331d-56c9-b26e-b980d440a8b3.html.

Lehman, Don. "Easy Does It: Officials Argue Laws on Underage Drinking Are Not Tough Enough to Prevent Tragedies," *Post-Star*, May 10, 2004, A4.

Lehman, Don. "Ethan Allen Captain Dies," www.poststar.com, August 17, 2016, *https://poststar.com/blogs/don_lehman/ethan-allen-captain-dies/article_b7eca45a-646f-11e6-b821-7bddc5896855.html.*

Lehman, Don. "Ethan Allen Guilty Pleas Entered," www.poststar.com, March 27, 2007, https://poststar.com/news/local/ethan-allen-guilty-pleas-entered/article_d50f72e2-8bbc-547a-a497-db69cdcba2aa.html.

Lehman, Don. "Ethan Allen Lawsuit Settled," www.poststar.com, August 11, 2009, https://poststar.com/news/local/ethan-allen-lawsuit-settled/article_47a3baff-8f9c-5694-8144-00531a7eaa0c.html.

Lehman, Don. "Ethan Allen Pilot Offers Blood and Urine Samples," *Post-Star*, October 5, 2005, A1.

Lehman, Don. "Family Concerns Linger Despite Nursing Home Ratings Boost," www.poststar.com, June 16, 2018, https://poststar.com/news/local/family-concerns-linger-despite-nursing-home-ratings-boost/article_c2cf5ca1-33f8-5dcb-ad9b-6b5b08819c04.html.

Lehman, Don. "Family Eyes Start in New Home," www.poststar.com, August 21, 2010, *https://poststar.com/family-eyes-new-start-in-new-home/article_b0e93914-ad98-11df-bcf6-001cc4c002e0.html.*

Lehman, Don. "Fatal February Crash Leads to Four-count Indictment," *Post-Star*, Feb. 27, 2002, B1.

Lehman, Don. "Former Nursing Home Worker Indicted," www.poststar.com, October 20, 2017, https://poststar.com/news/local/crime-and-courts/former-nursing-home-worker-indicted/article_ad806b06-5dc4-5546-8ad5-ea3d62e62cd4.html.

Lehman, Don. "Girl, 16, Dies in Crash," *Post-Star*, April 21, 2008, A1.

Lehman, Don. "Glens Falls City Court Expanding 'Opioid Diversion Program,'" www.poststar.com, November 12, 2019, https://poststar.com/news/local/glens-falls-city-court-expanding-opioid-diversion-program/article_bf11b20b-9618-5861-8fff-e13ff8cfc73c.html.

Lehman, Don. "Gregg Burdo Gets Ready for Winter," www.poststar.com, November 27, 2017, https://poststar.com/blogs/don_lehman/blog-gregg-burdo-gets-ready-for-winter/article_1fa4039e-d360-11e7-b440-d7f2c1c40fe5.html.

Lehman, Don. "Group Seeks Heroin 'recovery Center' in Glens Falls," www.poststar.com, January 6, 2016, https://poststar.com/news/

local/group-seeks-heroin-recovery-center-in-glens-falls/article_15e8de85-b259-5f46-80d0-fa4063109e67.html/?&logged_out=1.

Lehman, Don. "Hague Teen Dies After Sunday Accident," *Post-Star*, August 13, 2003, B1.

Lehman, Don. "Heart Attack Killed Smith, Father of Kids Who Died in Fire," www.poststar.com, July 30, 2012, *https://poststar.com/news/local/heart-attack-killed-smith-father-of-kids-who-died-in-fire/article_8b93bfc0-da84-11e1-9f3e-0019bb2963f4.html*.

Lehman, Don. "In Putnam Double Fatal Crash Case, Court Finds Father Does Not Share in Guilt with Son," www.poststar.com, March 10, 2011, https://poststar.com/news/local/in-putnam-double-fatal-crash-case-court-finds-father-does-not-share-in-guilt/article_1fb7c362-4b62-11e0-b917-001cc4c03286.html.

Lehman, Don. "Incorrect Fuse Played Role in Fort Edward Fatal Fire," www.poststar.com, August 24, 2010, https://poststar.com/news/local/incorrect-fuse-played-role-in-fort-edward-fatal-fire/article_27d63092-afc7-11df-9580-001cc4c002e0.html.

Lehman, Don. "Investigators: Electrical Outlet Likely Cause of Deadly Blaze," www.poststar.com, June 28, 2010, https://poststar.com/news/local/investigators-electrical-outlet-likely-cause-of-deadly-blaze/article_d3bc70e6-82b9-11df-b21c-001cc4c002e0.html.

Lehman, Don. "LaPoint Cleared of Providing Alcohol to Minors," www.poststar.com, July 2, 2010, https://poststar.com/news/local/lapoint-cleared-of-providing-alcohol-to-minors/article_114d85c4-861d-11df-8b13-001cc4c03286.html.

Lehman, Don. "Last Lawsuit in Ethan Allen Capsizing Dismissed," www.poststar.com, November 29, 2012, https://poststar.com/news/local/last-lawsuit-in-ethan-allen-capsizing-dismissed/article_33c80116-3a3d-11e2-906f-001a4bcf887a.html.

Lehman, Don. "Leaking Tanker Cripples Village," *Post-Star*, August 31, 2000, A1.

Lehman, Don. "'Littering' Case Was the Height of Hypocrisy," www.poststar.com, May 11, 2018, https://poststar.com/blogs/don_lehman/blog-littering-case-was-the-height-of-hypocrisy/article_89f98c8d-872b-5008-ab01-baa70de5c81f.html.

Lehman, Don. "A Look at a Youth's Life Cut Short by Drinking," *Post-Star*, May 9, 2004, A1.

Lehman, Don. "Man Has Spent Decades in the Woods of Queensbury," www.poststar.com, July 17, 2017, https://poststar.com/news/local/man-has-spent-decades-in-the-woods-of-queensbury/article_2fda3977-7a0b-577b-a315-02c55aacfd7a.html.

Lehman, Don. "New Investigations Lead to Same Conclusion in Deadly Fort Edward Fire," www.poststar.com, April 10, 2012, https://poststar.com/news/local/new-investigations-lead-to-same-conclusion-in-deadly-fort-edward/article_9a854352-8352-11e1-9adf-0019bb2963f4.html.

Lehman, Don. "No. 4: Heroin Use on Rise," www.poststar.com, December 27, 2014, https://poststar.com/no-4-heroin-use-on-rise/article_8a24b0fa-8e3b-11e4-9a16-c3db7d884096.html.

Lehman, Don. "NTSB: Ethan Allen Was Overloaded," www.poststar.com, July 26, 2006, https://poststar.com/news/local/ntsb-ethan-allen-was-overloaded/article_680f7fae-d8db-5bb8-bd8c-8957a1bbee5b.html.

Lehman, Don. "Officials: Home Short on Smoke Detectors," www.poststar.com, June 29, 2010, https://poststar.com/news/local/officials-home-short-on-smoke-detectors/article_48bd3f9e-83f8-11df-8786-001cc4c03286.html.

Lehman, Don. "Our Readers Did Some Good This Year," www.poststar.com, December 24, 2019, https://poststar.com/blogs/don_lehman/blog-our-readers-did-some-good-this-year/article_78d615ec-d757-52c3-b39b-eaf8e0c3aff7.html.

Lehman, Don. "Parents of Teen in Fatal DWI to Stand Trial," www.poststar.com, November 26, 2008, https://poststar.com/news/local/parents-of-teen-in-fatal-dwi-to-stand-trial/article_1225574c-4764-53e8-8623-1411594fce7d.html.

Lehman, Don. "Party Host Pleads Guilty," *Post-Star*, July 26, 2003, B1.

Lehman, Don. "Party Results in 13 Arrests," www.poststar.com, December 14, 2004, https://poststar.com/news/local/party-results-in-13-arrests/article_36b10015-8b40-56de-905c-e55d86d790d6.html.

Lehman, Don. "Police Say Teen Drunk at Time of Fatal Crash," *Post-Star*, September 26, 2003, A1.

Lehman, Don. "Police: LG Drowning Was Suicide," www.poststar.com, September 14, 2009, *https://poststar.com/news/local/police-lg-drowning-was-suicide/article_d2a184bb-3cec-56c3-b020-876bf1cc4181.html*.

Lehman, Don. "Police: No Bias in Crash," *Post-Star*, February 2, 2001, A6.

Lehman, Don. "Post-Star Littering Charges Dismissed," *Post-Star*, May 9, 2018, C1.

Lehman, Don. "Post-Star Seeks Dismissal of Case: Prosecutor Does Not Oppose the Request," *Post-Star*, April 19, 2018, C1.

Lehman, Don. "Rescue Plan Was Followed in Capsizing Incident," *Post-Star*, October 4, 2005, B7.

Lehman, Don. "Seeber Returns to Warren County Board of Supervisors as GOP Picks Up Two Seats," www.poststar.com, November 6, 2019, https://poststar.com/news/local/seeber-returns-to-warren-county-board-of-supervisors-as-gop-picks-up-two-seats/article_c2f26ede-5a8b-58c4-81c1-42d1bafd570c.html.

Lehman, Don. "Sentencing in Fatal Crash Bring Stories of Sadness," www.poststar.com, October 17, 2008, https://poststar.com/news/local/sentencing-in-fatal-crash-brings-stories-of-sadness/article_94ef3fb0-c372-546f-a5af-983b41bd7c96.html.

Lehman, Don. "Sheriff's Office Cites Post-Star with Littering," *Post-Star*, October 18, 2017, A1.

Lehman, Don. "Shoreline Insurance Insufficient," www.poststar.com, February 21, 2006, *https://poststar.com/news/local/shoreline-insurance-insufficient/article_d5f093e2-cac0-5eeb-944d-c7fe051d824d.html.*

Lehman, Don. "Smoke Detectors Credited for Alerting Fort Edward Family to Fire," www.poststar.com, October 2, 2011, https://poststar.com/news/local/smoke-detectors-credited-for-alerting-fort-edward-family-to-fire/article_935180f4-ece0-11e0-abf4-001cc4c002e0.html.

Lehman, Don. "Speed Cited in Fatal Crash," www.poststar.com, June 6, 2008, *https://poststar.com/news/local/speed-cited-in-fatal-crash/article_f4f74852-ecd7-5a4f-9acd-8e281ffcc62b.html.*

Lehman, Don. "St. Andrewses: We Didn't Know of Drinking at Parties," www.poststar.com, February 11, 2009, https://poststar.com/news/local/updated-st-andrewses-we-didnt-know-of-drinking-at-parties/image_8be61cbf-d3cd-5963-bd60-f88ef38be55b.html?mode=comments.

Lehman, Don. "Suspect Caught in Syracuse: DiLorenzo Found at Shelter for Homeless," *Post-Star*, February 24, 2005, A1.

Lehman, Don. "Suspect's Car Found Abandoned," *Post-Star*, February 22, 2005, A1.

Lehman, Don. "Sweeney in Bar Before Crash," *Post-Star*, February 3, 2001, A1.

Lehman, Don. "10 Years Later, Survivor, Rescuers Remember Ethan Allen Capsizing," www.poststar.com, September 27, 2015, https://poststar.com/news/local/10-years-later-survivor-rescuers-remember-ethan-allen-capsizing/article_6c4f6358-d5b1-555f-b647-c672c00214d5.html.

Lehman, Don. "Tour Boat Raised from Lake George; Weight Limit, Crew Size Is Questioned," *Post-Star*, October 4, 2005, A1.

Lehman, Don. "Underage Drinking Trial Delayed," www.poststar.com, December 17, 2008, *https://poststar.com/news/local/underage-drinking-trial-delayed/article_3e4dd9e7-3ba0-5bb4-a512-46ec7518bc99.html.*

Lehman, Don. "Union: Captain Is the Scapegoat in Sweeney Probe," www.poststar.com, November 17, 2006, https://poststar.com/news/union-captain-is-the-scapegoat-in-sweeney-probe/article_6e32a5b7-0534-5379-9d7e-d525b0acb239.html.

Lehman, Don. "An Unwanted Visitor; Heroin Creeps Into Glens Falls," www.poststar.com, June 15, 2014, https://poststar.com/news/local/an-unwanted-visitor-heroin-creeps-into-glens-falls-region/article_64ead8f6-f439-11e3-936b-001a4bcf887a.html.

Lehman, Don. "Victim Had Faced Years of Abuse, Sister Says," *Post-Star*, February 22, 2005, A1.

Lehman, Don. "Victim Sought Police Minutes Before Death," *Post-Star*, February 23, 2005, A1.

Lehman, Don. "Woman Arrested After Underage Drinking Party," www.poststar.com, November 2, 2009, *https://poststar.com/news/local/woman-arrested-after-underage-drinking-party/article_83dd5460-c7d3-11de-b7f7-001cc4c002e0.html.*

Lehman, Don. "Woman Charged with Fire Charity Thefts Pleads Not Guilty," www.poststar.com, April 29, 2011, https://poststar.com/news/local/woman-charged-with-fire-charity-thefts-pleads-not-guilty/article_48a7d156-7298-11e0-80f3-001cc4c03286.html.

Lehman, Don. "Woman Pleads Guilty in Fort Edward Fire Fund Theft Case," www.poststar.com, July 21, 2011, https://poststar.com/news/local/woman-pleads-guilty-in-fort-edward-fire-fund-theft-case/article_ec8b237c-b3d9-11e0-acbc-001cc4c002e0.html.

Lehman, Don, and Darrin Youker. "Fire Kills 4 Children," *Post-Star*, November 27, 2002, A1.

Lehman, Don, and Nick Reisman, "Parents Get Split Verdict," www.poststar.com, February 14, 2009, *https://poststar.com/news/local/parents-get-split-verdict/article_1aa93582-d940-5f3c-b28f-bcc95c85bb46.html.*

Lehman, Don, and Thomas Dimopoulos. "Six Children Killed in Blaze: Authorities Are Still Investigating Cause of Fort Edward Fire," *Post-Star*, June 28, 2010, A1.

Lehman, Don, and Thom Randall, "Police Hunt Loose Killer," *Post-Star*, February 21, 2005, A1.

Leitch, Jennifer. "Fort Ann Resident Appalled by Response," *Post-Star*, August 7, 2002, A5.

Lockrow, Robert. "Homosexuality Just a Human Weakness," *Post-Star*, July 23, 2002, A5.

Lombardo, David. "Political Forces Square Off in Glens Falls," www.timesunion.com, September 13, 2019, https://www.timesunion.com/news/article/Political-forces-square-off-in-Glens-Falls-14438868.php.

Lueck, Thomas J. "Police Charge New Paltz Mayor for Marrying Same-sex Couples," www.nytimes.com, March 3, 2004, *https://nytimes.com/2004/03/03/nyregion/police-charge-new-paltz-mayor-for-marrying-same-sex-couples.html?referringSource=articleShare.*

Lyons, Brendan. "Congressman's Wife Called Police," www.timesunion.com, October 31, 2006, *https://web.archive.org/web/20061213205513/http://timesunion.com/AspStories/storyprint.asp?StoryID=530664.*

Mahoney, Mark. "Baby Steps Needed to Fight Teen Drinking," *Post-Star*, May 23, 2004, F1.

Mahoney, Mark. "Endorsement Withdrawn: Character Questions Continue to Dog Sweeney," www.poststar.com, November 3, 2006, https://poststar.com/news/editorial-endorsement-withdrawn-character-questions-continue-to-dog-sweeney/article_34b1143e-9f69-5fc2-bca7-7622dac81e71.html.

Mahoney, Mark. "Hearing from You," www.poststar.com, February 15, 2004, https://poststar.com/opinion/commentary/hearing-from-you/article_e06f7c2a-0e16-5658-8fe7-b42f8e65ad24.html.

Mahoney, Mark. "In Seconds, a Witness to a Homicide," *Post-Star*, February 21, 2005, A1.

Mahoney, Mark. "Keep Pressure High on Madden," *Post-Star*, June 19, 2009, A4.

Mahoney, Mark. "Law Would Correct Unfairness," www.poststar.com, May 27, 2011, https://poststar.com/news/opinion/editorial/editorial-law-would-correct-unfairness/article_09962656-88b5-11e0-b6b4-001cc4c03286.html.

Mahoney, Mark. "Limits Should Reflect Reality," *Post-Star*, October 5, 2005, A4.

Mahoney, Mark. "Madden Stories Raise Questions," *Post-Star*, January 18, 2004, F1.

Mahoney, Mark. "Parents, Take Note of This," *Post-Star*, February 8, 2009, E1.

Mahoney, Mark. "Region Joins Hands in Mourning Losses," *Post-Star*, September 15, 2001, A1.

Mahoney, Mark. "Residents Show Generosity," *Post-Star*, September 13, 2001, A6.

Mahoney, Mark. "Shining Light on a Dark Problem," *Post-Star*, July 10, 2005, E1.

Mahoney, Mark. "Shooting Won't Be Forgotten," *Post-Star*, October 27, 2005, A6.

Mahoney, Mark. "Sweeney Portrayed on HBO," www.poststar.com, May 29, 2008, https://poststar.com/news/local/sweeney-portrayed-on-hbo/article_88d9e597-0724-50fa-94c6-7a9b024d917b.html.

Mahoney, Mark. "Sweeney's Record Overshadows His Shortcomings," www.poststar.com, October 29, 2006, https://poststar.com/opinion/editorials/sweeneys-record-overshadows-his-shortcomings/article_99a513fa-6279-5e41-a297-a4a043ace6e6.html.

Mahoney, Mark. "Tragedy Has Ways to Be Averted," *Post-Star*, December 8, 2002, F1.

Marshall, Jim. "Letter from the Publisher—A Century of Service," *Post-Star*, January 24, 2004, F2.

Marshall, Jim. "Post-Star Wins National Award for Sept. 11 Coverage," *Post-Star*, March 2002, B1.

Marshall, Konrad. "Abuse Escalates: Victims Speak Out," *Post-Star*, July 11, 2005, A5.

Marshall, Konrad. "Breaking Their Silence: How It Begins, Victims Speak Out," *Post-Star*, July 10, 2005, A1.

Marshall, Konrad. "Breaking Their Silence: In Their Own Words," *Post-Star*, July 10, 2005, A1.

Marshall, Konrad. "In Their Own Words," *Post-Star*, July 11, 2005, A1.

Marshall, Konrad. "Leaving Is Often Just the Beginning," *Post-Star*, July 12, 2005, A5.

Marshall, Konrad. "Sweeney: 'I'm Only Sorry That I Let You Down,'" www.poststar.com, November 8, 2006, https://poststar.com/news/local/sweeney-im-only-sorry-that-i-let-you-down/article_ddac5b7d-8567-5e22-92a3-1aae6cb2b526.html.

Martin, Alyson. "Sweeney Arrest on DWI Charges," www.poststar.com, November 12, 2007, https://poststar.com/news/local/sweeney-arrested-on-dwi-charges/-article_9ce44c1a-b943-5a57-b622-da357df428b2.html.

McCarty, Lucian. "12-year-old Admits Guilt in Shooting Death of Nicholas Naumkin in December as Part of Plea Arrangement; Likely to Receive Probation," www.saratogian.com, August 11, 2011, https://www.saratogian.com/news/12-year-old-admits-guilt-in-the-shooting-death-of-nicholas-naumkin-in-december-as/article_8c4308c6-84be-51ef-a464-b14e1b78114a.html.

McCord, Jason. "John Sweeney's Son Indicted in '04 Fight," www.poststar.com, April 15, 2005, https://poststar.com/news/local/john-sweeney-s-son-indicted-in-fight/article_a26f8f38-4943-53c4-b65c-e0f26d2b3296.html.

McCord, Jason. "Program Fights Underage Drinking," www.poststar.com, April 29, 2005, https://poststar.com/news/local/program-fights-underage-drinking/article_602c843f-866d-56a9-8e47-a5862914a7da.html.

McGarry, Brendan. "Survivor: 'I Thanked God for Letting Me Live," *Post-Star*, October 4, 2005, B8.

McGarry, Brendan. "Young Sweeney Avoids Jail Term," www.poststar.com, December 17, 2005, https://poststar.com/news/local/young-sweeney-avoids-jail-term/article_d8182818-ad2b-5192-8dfb-7aab056aff15.html.

Mender, Mike. "CNA Workers United in Grief," *Post-Star*, September 15, 2001, A5.

Mender, Mike. "Just the Kid Next Door," *Post-Star*, May 10, 2004, A1, A4.

Mender, Mike. "Lee Enterprises Takes Control of Post-Star," www.poststar.com, April 2, 2002, *https://poststar.com/business/local/lee-enterprises-takes-control-of-post-star/article_09fcc591-1fd2-5735-89e4-543ae83b50b9.html.*

Metzger, Amanda Mae. "After Reading Contest Blowups, Librarian Has Left Her Job," www.poststar.com, September 13, 2013, https://poststar.com/news/local/after-reading-contest-blowup-librarian-has-left-her-job/article_eb3c2f9a-1ca8-11e3-ba4d-001a4bcf887a.html.

Moats, David. "Civil Wars: A Battle for Gay Marriage," *Harcourt Books*, 2004, 242–243.

Montgomery, David M. "Story on Homosexuals Inappropriate, Trashy," *Post-Star*, July 25, 2002, A5.

Moore, Kathleen. "Audit: Hospital Lost $38M," *Post-Star*, March 8, 2019, A1.

Moore, Kathleen. "Candidate Motives Questioned," *Post-Star*, October 18, 2017, A1.

Moore, Kathleen. "Complaint Filed with AG Over Email Use," *Post-Star*, October 11, 2017, A1.

Moore, Kathleen. "Coping with Hard Times: Glens Falls Hospital Audits Voted Top Story of Year," *Post-Star*, December 29, 2019, A1.

Moore, Kathleen. "County Republicans Revise Ethics Code," *Post-Star*, December 2, 2018, C1.

Moore, Kathleen. "Dems Agree to Set Code of Ethics," *Post-Star*, November 16, 2017, C1.

Moore, Kathleen. "Doug Irish: Post-Star Is `akin to Fiction,'" www.poststar.com, June 6, 2017, https://poststar.com/blogs/kathleen_moore/doug-irish-post-star-is-akin-to-fiction/article_d1d703b2-f711-545c-aadf-68fbe72d8a56.html.

Moore, Kathleen. "Hospital CEO Says Situation Is `dire,'" *Post-Star*, March 3, 2019, A1.

Moore, Kathleen. "Hospital Faced Billing Issues," *Post-Star*, March 13, 2019, A1.

Moore, Kathleen. "Hospital Lays Off 25 Employees," *Post-Star*, January 29, 2019, A1.

Moore, Kathleen. "Hospital Seeks Turnaround," *Post-Star*, February 13, 2019, A1.

Moore, Kathleen. "Hospitals Differ on Mask Usage: Glens Falls Hospital Holding Back from Using N95 Masks," *Post-Star*, March 27, 2020, A1.

Moore, Kathleen. "Lawyer Tied to Scheme Resigns," *Post-Star*, October 26, 2017, A1.

Moore, Kathleen. "Moreau Town Officials Blame `fake News,'" *Post-Star*, June 29, 2017, B1.

Moore, Kathleen. "No. 10: Strough Arrested, Take Plea Deal," The *Post-Star*, December 30, 2018, A5.

Moore, Kathleen. "Parsing Highs from Lows: Hospital Finances Get Close Look," *Post-Star*, March 6, 2019, A1.

Moore, Kathleen. "Queensbury Councilman Resigns," *Post-Star*, October 24, 2017, A1.

Moore, Kathleen. "Queensbury Supervisor, Wife Charged," *Post-Star*, March 13, 2018, A1.

Moore, Kathleen. "Rally to Include Displaying Unloaded Rifles," www.poststar.com, October 5, 2019, *https://poststar.com/news/local/rally-to-include-displaying-unloaded-rifles/article_25e17395-07c0-517c-bcb3-18bb5765112e.html.*

Moore, Kathleen. "Retired Doctor Urges Letter-writing Campaign," *Post-Star*, September 25, 2019, A1.

Moore, Kathleen. "Strough Is Re-elected: Supervisor Race in Queensbury Draws Big Turnout," *Post-Star*, November 8, 2017, A5.

Moore, Kathleen. "Strough Takes Plea Deal: Attorney: Politics Behind Plea Deal," *Post-Star*, May 16, 2018, A1.

Moore, Kathleen. "Supervisor Candidates Face Ethical Questions," *Post-Star*, October 31, 2017, A6.

Moore, Kathleen. "Tony Metivier Wins Ward 1 GOP Line in Primary Election," *Post-Star*, September 13, 2017, B1.

Moore, Kathleen. "Waiting for Numbers from Glens Falls Hospital," www.poststar.com, March 4, 2019, https://poststar.com/blogs/kathleen_moore/blog-waiting-for-numbers-from-glens-falls-hospital/article_7ebb8418-d606-5eb3-bdd0-a4d75e397223.html.

Mularz, Marc. "It's Time to Open Our Eyes to Teen Drinking," *Post-Star*, May 24, 2003, A6.

Munks, Jamie. "As Workload Grows, Nursing Home Staffing Woes Persist," www.poststar.com, May 11, 2013, https://poststar.com/news/local/as-workload-grows-nursing-home-staffing-woes-persist/article_e86d5664-baaf-11e2-a4a8-001a4bcf887a.html.

Munks, Jamie. "Families Find Safety Net Is Full of Holes," www.poststar.com, May 25, 2013, *https://poststar.com/news/local/families-find-safety-net-is-full-of-holes/article_d3d42fcc-c5ac-11e2-84e1-0019bb2963f4.html.*

Naumann, Bonnie. "Life Preservers Weren't Accessible for the Elderly," *Post-Star*, October 4, 2005, B1.

Naumann, Bonnie. "On Patrol, Domestic Calls Take Many Forms," *Post-Star*, July 10, 2005, A1, A4.

Naumann, Bonnie. "Statistics, Don't Show the Whole Truth," *Post-Star*, July 10, 2005, A4.

National Headliner Awards, May 5, 2001, *https://www.headlinerawards.org/2001-tvradio/.*

Nearing, Brian. "Restitution in Ethan Allen Insurance Scam Appears Unlikely," www.timesunion.com, April 24, 2016, https://www.timesunion.com/tuplus-local/article/-Restitution-in-Ethan-Allen-insurance-scam-appears-7306956.php.

Nemcek, Gretta. "Fort Edward Town Board to Crack Down on `slumlords,'" www.poststar.com, October 17, 2002, https://poststar.com/news/local/fatal-fire-traced-to-floorboards/-article_32738b47-fcf0-5b64-9622-ca84e3f1ddc2.html.

Nemcek, Gretta. "Village Might Inspect Rentals," *Post-Star*, December 12, 2002, A1.

Nemcek, Gretta, and Darrin Youker, "Greenwich Teen-agers Laid to Rest," *Post-Star*, April 11, 2002, A1.

Nemcek Stanclift, Gretta. "What's a Parent to Do? Navigating the Teen Years Can Be a Challenge for the Adults," *Post-Star*, May 16, 2004, A5.

New York Daily News Politics Blog, "A Sweeney Mystery," www.nydailynews.com, December 18, 2010, *https://www.nydailynews.com/blogs/dailypolitics/sweeney-mystery-blog-entry-1.1667425.*

New York State Legislative Resolution, Sen. Elizabeth Little, Sen. Joseph Bruno, Sen. Hugh Farley, Assemblywoman Teresa Sayward, Assembyman Roy McDonald, Assemblyman James Tedisco, February 3, 2004 (Copy in author's files).

New York State Office of the Comptroller, "State Health Department Should Improve Enforcement of Nursing Home Violations," www.osc.state.ny.us, February 22, 2016, *https://www.osc.state.ny.us/press/releases/2016/02/-state-health-department-should-improve-enforcement-nursing-home-violations.*

"911 Transcripts," *Post-Star*, October 5, 2005, A1.

O'Connor, Patrick. "Sweeney's Wife Claims Abuse," www.politico.com, July 23, 2007, https://www.politico.com/blogs/politico-now/2007/07/sweeneys-wife-claims-abuse-002299.

O'Halloran, Ryan. "Kathleen Remembers," *Post-Star*, December 23, 2001. A1.

O'Matz, Megan, and John Maines. "License to Carry," www.sun-sentinel.com, January 28, 2007, https://www.sun-sentinel.com/news/sfl-guns.storygallery-storygallery.html.

Orzechowski, Brett. "Playing with Fire: Sports, Drinking Can Often Go Hand in Hand," *Post-Star*, May 10, 2004, A1.

Parker, Bonnie. "Article on Gays Deserves Bravo," *Post-Star*, July 23, 2002, A5.

Patterson, Adam. "Putting the 'Star' in Post-Star," *All Points North*, November 21, 2017.

Perez-Pena, Richard. "4 Children Die in Fire at House Said to Be Condemned," *New York Times*, November 27, 2002, 8.

Perry, Kate. "First Curfew, Then Calm," *Post-Star*, November 21, 2004, B1.

Perry, Kate. "The Ordinary Face of Abuse: Painting a Picture of a Batterer," *Post-Star*, July 11, 2005, A5.

Petteys, Martha. "Changing Attitudes, Saving Lives," *Post-Star*, May 2, 2004, A1.

Petteys, Martha. "It Happened to My Family," *Post-Star*, May 17, 2004, A1.

Petteys, Martha. "A Look at a Youth's Life Cut Short by Drinking," *Post-Star*, May 2, 2004, A1.

Petteys, Martha. "The Path to Adulthood: Still-developing Brain Cause of Common Teen Woes," *Post-Star*, May 16, 2004, A1.

Petteys, Martha. "Transportation Halted in Area," *Post-Star*, September 12, 2001, A5.

Phalen-Tomaselli, Kathleen. "Anger Vs. Love and a Pro–Trump Rally," www.poststar.com, August 24, 2019, https://poststar.com/news/local/blog-anger-vs-love-and-a-pro-trump-rally/article_7153fb12-95eb-53c5-8cb2-acf46b0eba19.html.

Phalen-Tomaselli, Kathleen. "Groups: Stefanik Put Out Call," *Post-Star*, October 11, 2019, A5.

Phalen-Tomaselli, Kathleen. "Police Keep Order as Dueling Political Gatherings Continue in Glens Falls," www.poststar.com, September 21, 2019, https://poststar.com/news/local/police-keep-order-as-dueling-political-gatherings-continue-in-glens-falls/article_bac069c6-8a55-5f03-beed-dbfde530cd5d.html.

Phalen-Tomaselli, Kathleen. "Post-Star Reporter Maury Thompson Steps Away from Beat," www.poststar.com, August 31, 2017, *https://poststar.com/news/local/post-star-reporter-maury-thompson-steps-away-from-the-beat/article_5d14fac2-0619-54e9-892c-17f1e834a85d.html.*

Phalen-Tomaselli, Kathleen. "Pro-Trump Groups Feel Fractures," *Post-Star*, October 6, 2019, A1.

Phalen-Tomaselli, Kathleen. "Threats with Toy Guns Feel Real," www.poststar.com, October 5, 2019, https://poststar.com/blogs/kathleen_phalen-tomaselli/blog-threats-with-toy-guns-feel-real/article_beeba039-7cad-5049-b49a-a723ffdada82.html.

Police Benevolent Association of New York, "Media Probes Wrongful Transfer of PBA Member," www.nystbpa.org, November 17, 2006, https://www.nystpba.org/blog/-breaking-news/media-probes-wrongful-transfer-of-pba-member/.

Post-Star. "Attacked, Extra-Special Edition." September 12, 2001, 1–12.

Post-Star Editorial Board. "Another Tragedy Must Be Prevented," www.poststar.com, January 2, 2011, *https://poststar.com/news/opinion/editorial/editorial-another-tragedy-must-be-prevented/article_62ec4f28-1623-11e0-b5f2-001cc4c002e0.html.*

Post-Star Editorial Board. "Atherden Is Good Fit for Queensbury Board," *Post-Star*, October 27, 2017, C3.

Post-Star Editorial Board. "Charges Should Be Dropped Against Protesters," *Post-Star*, September 7, 2019, C3.

Post-Star Editorial Board. "Cobb Is Right Choice for Congress," *Post-Star*, October 28, 2018, C3.

Post-Star Editorial Board. "Concerns Raised Over Hospital Finances," *Post-Star*, February 17, 2019, C3.

Post-Star Editorial Board. "Emails Reveal Dirty Politics," *Post-Star*, October 15, 2017, A6.

Post-Star Editorial Board. "'Fake News' Claims Have No Merit," *Post-Star*, June 30, 2017, A1.

Post-Star Editorial Board. "Gov. Andrew Cuomo Misused Power to Get Gun Bill Passed," www.poststar,com, January 16, 2013, *https://poststar.com/news/opinion/editorial/editorial-gov-andrew-cuomo-misused-power-to-get-gun-bill-passed/article_bb16972c-6049-11e2-b9f0-0019bb2963f4.html.*

Post-Star Editorial Board. "Inside the Editorial Board," *Post-Star*, October 29, 2017, C3.

Post-Star Editorial Board. "Is There Any Morality Left in Politics," *Post-Star*, August 3, 2018, C3.

Post-Star Editorial Board. "Metivier Makes Fiery Indictment of Party Politics in Queensbury," www.poststar.com, October 27, 2017, https://poststar.com/opinion/editorial/endorsement-metivier-makes-fiery-indictment-of-party-politics-in-queensbury/article_d60d6f9d-6d20-5d70-a702-b33fbefda1d7.html.

Post-Star Editorial Board. "Ready or Not, We're All Aging," www.poststar.com, May 4, 2013, *https://poststar.com/news/opinion/editorial-ready-or-not-were-all-aging/article_f7c0a768-b52a-11e2-9c0c-0019bb2963f4.html.*

Post-Star Editorial Board. "Region Needs Recovery Options," www.poststar.com, July 5, 2014, *https://poststar.com/news/opinion/editorial/editorial-region-needs-recovery-options/article_e4ab4198-04b5-11e4-8393-0019bb2963f4.html.*

Post-Star Editorial Board. "Republicans Upgrade Code of Ethics," *Post-Star*, December 9, 2018, C3.

Post-Star Editorial Board. "Strough Puts Queensbury First," *Post-Star*, October 29, 2017, C3.

Post-Star Editorial Board. "The Lying Can't Continue," *Post-Star*, June 18, 2017, A4.

Post-Star Editorial Board. "We Ask Cobb, Stefanik Not to Lie," *Post-Star*, July 1, 2018, C3.

Post-Star front page. September 25, 2003, A1.

Post-Star Staff Report. "Ben Rogers to Lead *Post-Star*," *Post-Star*, August 21, 2020, A1.

Post-Star Staff Report. "City Honors Ken Tingley with Proclamation," *Post-Star*, July 17, 2020, B1.

Post-Star Staff Report. "Heroin Series Earns 2nd National Honor," www.poststar.com, May 5, 2015, *https://poststar.com/news/local/article_f0acc7e4-5114-581f-be93-c8aad4142d01.html.*

Post-Star Staff Report. "Hudson Falls Library President Releases Statement on Reading Program," www.poststar.com, August 22, 2013, *https://poststar.com/news/local/hudson-falls-library-president-releases-statement-on-reading-program-controversy/article_85df4dfe-0b36-11e3-bcd9-0019bb2963f4.html*

Post-Star Staff Report. "Mark Mahoney, Pulitzer Winner, Leaving Post-Star." www.poststar.com, October 19, 2011, *https://poststar.com/news/local/mark-mahoney-pulitzer-winner-leaving-post-star/article_38fc76f2-fa8e-11e0-b38b-001cc4c002e0.html.*

Post-Star Staff Report. "Much More Than Just a Story," *Post-Star*, April 26, 2019, A1.

Post-Star Staff Report. "Post-Star Announces Top Local Stories of 2013," www.poststar.com, December 28, 2013, https://poststar.com/news/local/post-star-announces-top-local-stories-of-2013/article_e68d3146-703c-11e3-bc64-001a4bcf887a.html.

Post-Star Staff Report. "Post-Star Editor Honored at Pulitzer Prize Event," *Post-Star*, May 29, 2009, A1.

Post-Star Staff Report. "Post-Star Honored for Elderly Care Series," www.poststar.com, April 19, 2014, https://poststar.com/news/article_c36d5c46-c72f-11e3-99c9-001a4bcf887a.html.

Post-Star Staff Report. "Post-Star Honored in National Contest," www.poststar.com, March 18, 2015, *https://poststar.com/news/local/post-star-honored-in-national-contest/article_72caa03e-cdb2-11e4-b7da-53381bccca98.html.*

Post-Star Staff Report. "Post-Star Honored With 11 Awards By NYNPA," *Post-Star*, September 24, 2020, B1.

Post-Star Staff Report. "Post-Star Named Top Paper," www.poststar.com, September 23, 2006, https://poststar.com/news/local/post-star-honored-as-top-paper/article_45be3894-83b7-5d3f-a6d6-93237c08c062.html.

Post-Star Staff Report. "Post-Star Pulitzer: Mahoney Honored for Editorials," *Post-Star*, April 21, 2009, A1.

Post-Star Staff Report. "Post-Star Reporter Earns National Excellence in Journalism Award," *Post-Star*, April 22, 2005, B1.

Post-Star Staff Report. "Post-Star Will Be Dropped Off," *Post-Star*, August 31, 2000, B1.

Post-Star Staff Report. "Post-Star Wins Lee President's Award," www.poststar.com, November 23, 2014, *https://poststar.com/news/local/post-star-wins-lee-presidents-award/article_f2e358c8-7340-11e4-96e0-d3bebddb1275.html.*

Post-Star Staff Report. "Post-Star's Heroin Series Raises Awareness," www.poststar.com, July 24, 2014, https://poststar.com/news/local/post-stars-heroin-series-raises-awareness/article_4e6f6aa4-13a8-11e4-8f10-0019bb2963f4.html.

Post-Star Staff Report. "Post-Star's Nursing Home Series Honored by Lee Enterprises," www.poststar.com, November 28, 2013, https://poststar.com/news/local/post-stars-nursing-home-series-honored-by-lee-enterprises/-article_7c69117e-5870-11e3-bfd1-0019bb2963f4.html.

Post-Star Staff Report. "Protest Set for Saturday in Front of Stefanik's Office," www.poststar.com, June 13, 2019, *https://poststar.com/news/local/protest-set-for-saturday-in-front-of-stefaniks-office/article_7484a079-5807-521c-8125-c1b4dd11d76a.html.*

Post-Star Staff Report. "Report: Wife Called 911 on Congressman," www.poststar.com, November 1, 2006, https://poststar.com/news/article_de946e07-5b8a-5adc-8a60-a42409782d22.html.

Post-Star Staff Report. "State Newspaper Publishers Association Honors Post-Star," *Post-Star*, May 8, 2004, B1.

Post-Star Staff Report. "Stefanik Named to Trump's Impeachment Defense Team," www.poststar.com, January 20, 2020, *https://poststar.com/news/local/govt-and-politics/stefanik-named-to-trumps-impeachment-defense-team/article_47b61c9a-cba8-5a99-95be-0282ebedbe5b.html.*

Post-Star Staff Report. "Sweeney Granted

Early Release from Jail," www.poststar.com, April 30, 2010, *https://poststar.com/news/local/sweeney-granted-early-release-from-jail/article_6536d09a-54b4-11df-95e0-001cc4c002e0.html.*

Post-Star Staff Report. "Sweeney Unhurt in Crash," *Post-Star*, February 1, 2001, B1.

Post-Star Staff Report. "The Post-Star Wins Top State Award," *Post-Star*, June 4, 2020, B1.

Post-Star Staff Report. "Thompson Honored with Spirit Award," www.poststar.com, November 16, 2007, *https://poststar.com/news/local/thompson-honored-with-spirit-award/article_6e1e4ec1-ed09-5174-a7de-dc2c93120abb.html.*

Post-Star Staff, Wire Reports. "Lee Enterprises to Buy Berkshire Hathaway Newspaper Operations," www.poststar.com, January 29, 2020, https://poststar.com/news/local/-lee-enterprises-to-buy-berkshire-hathaway-newspaper-operations/article_212110dc-ceb8-58b0-991f-a107b24c1a44.html.

Post-Star Staff, Wire Reports. "Sweeney Trip Raises Questions," www.poststar.com, October 19, 2006, https://poststar.com/news/sweeney-trip-raises-questions/article_6a0b9507-e158-50d4-a91c-b6305d8bb4eb.html.

Powers, William G. 2019. "The Post-Star Has Been on an Almost Daily Campaign to Discredit Glens Falls Hospital." March 20, 2019. https://www.facebook.com/GlensFallsHospital/.

Press Club of Atlantic City, "2002 National Headliner Awards," www.headlinerawards.org, May 4, 2002. https://www.headlinerawards.org/2002-printphoto/.

Pulitzer Prizes, Pulitzer.org, *https://www.pulitzer.org/prize-winners-by-year/2001.*

"Pulitzer Winners: Mark Mahoney," Pulitzer.org, https://www.pulitzer.org/winners/mark-mahoney.

Randall, Thom. "Anguish and Confusion Abound at Barricades," *Post-Star*, September 13, 2001, A1.

Randall, Thom. "Behind Bars," *Post-Star*, June 15, 2002, A1.

Randall, Thom. "ER," *Post-Star*, October 24, 2004, A1.

Randall, Thom. "Luck in the Ruins," *Post-Star*, September 23, 2001, A3.

Randall, Thom. "Madden `sticks with You Like Cancer,'" *Post-Star*, January 12, 2004, A5.

Randall, Thom. "Madden's Owner: It's a Struggle," *Post-Star*, February 22, 2004, A1.

Randall, Thom. "Morning. Noon. Night. an Endless Cycle," *Post-Star*, January 12, 2004, A1.

Randall, Thom. "Pentagon Attack Shakes Up City Native," *Post-Star*, September 12, 2001, A1.

Randall, Thom. "A Place Nearby, a World Apart," *Post-Star*, January 11–12, 2004, A1.

Randall, Thom. "Quiet Village Disrupted for a Day: Hospital Keeps Busy During Emergency," *Post-Star*, August 31, 2000, B9.

Randall, Thom. "Trading Hard Labor for Some Quick Cash," *Post-Star*, January 12, 2004, A5.

Randall, Thom. "Train Ride to NYC Is Lonely Trip," *Post-Star*, September 13, 2001, A1.

Randall, Thom. "'We Were Like One Person,'" *Post-Star*, October 23, 2005, A1.

Reisman, Nick. "Cuomo Signs Bills for Safe Storage, Banning 3-D Guns," www.spectrumnews.com, July 30, 2019, https://spectrumlocalnews.com/nys/central-ny/politics/2019/07/30/-cuomo-signs-bills-for-safe-storage—banning-3-d-guns.

Reisman, Nick. "Republican Backs Democrat in 43rd District Race," www.spectrumlocalnews.com, October 9, 2018, https://spectrumlocalnews.com/nys/central-ny/politics/2018/10/10/aaron-gladd-roy-mcdonald-endorsement.

Ridgell, Patrick. "Shooting Stirs Happier Memories," *Post-Star*, April 21, 1999, A1.

Roth, Zachary. "`Caribbean Caucus' Lawmakers Took Trips on Stanford Jets," *TPM.com*, February 17, 2009, *https://talkingpointsmemo.com/muckraker/caribbean-caucus-lawmakers-took-trips-on-stanford-jets.*

RPA-PAC (user name), "Saratoga County Gives Post-Star Pistol Permit Holders," www.keepandbeararms.com, February 27, 2018.

Rushe, Dominic. "Allen Stanford Sentenced to 110 Years in Jail for $7bn Investment Fraud," www.theguardian.com, June 14, 2012, https://www.theguardian.com/world/2012/jun/14/allen-stanford-110-years-jail.

Shaker, Lee. "Dead Newspapers and Citizens' Civic Engagement," Volume 31, Issue 1, www.tandfonline.com, January 30, 2014, https://www.tandfonline.com/doi/full/10.1080/10584609.2012.762817.

Spector, Joseph. "Second Republican Senator Comes Forward to Back Same-sex Marriage," www.democratandchronicle.com, June 14, 2011, https://www.democratandchronicle.com/story/news/politics/blogs/vote-up/2011/06/14/second-senate-republican-senator-comes-forward-to-back-same-sex-marriage/2177361/.

Sturdevant, Matt. "Greenwich Teen-agers Killed in Crash," www.poststar.com, April 7, 2002, https://poststar.com/news/local/greenwich-teen-agers-killed-in-crash/article_de05071d-8cc1-5610-8fb2-86733ada6ca0.html.

Sturdevant, Matt. "Growing Up Gay," *Post-Star*, July 14, 2002, A1.

Sturdevant, Matt. "Residents Watch in Disbelief and Anguish," *Post-Star*, September 12, 2001, A3.

Taube, David. "Fort Edward Student's `Hope' Fire Safety Project Needs More Votes to Get Funding," www.poststar.com, November 17, 2010, https://poststar.com/news/local/fort-edward-student-s-hope-fire-safety-project-needs-more-votes-to-get-funding/article_46b46b86-f271-11df-aa1c-001cc4c002e0.html.

Taube, David. "Project Hope Students Win $5,000 in Fire Education Grant Quest," www.poststar.com, February 1, 2011, *https://poststar.com/news/local/project-hope-students-win-5-000-in-fire-education-grant-quest/article_66f3fcb8-2e44-11e0-a92c-001cc4c03286.html.*

Thew, Barbara, and Jamie Thew. "Paper Should Avoid Offensive Subjects," *Post-Star*, July 22, 2002, A5.

Thomas, Carl. "Politically Correct Is Not Morally Correct," *Post-Star*, July 22, 2002, A5.

Thompson, Maury. "Advocacy Group Seeks to Oust McDonald Over Same-sex Marriage Vote," www.poststar.com, July 19, 2011, https://poststar.com/news/local/advocacy-group-seeks-to-oust-mcdonald-over-same-sex-marriage-vote/article_dc5f2ebe-b247-11e0-845a-001cc4c002e0.html.

Thompson, Maury. "The Biggest Kid at the Balloon Festival: The Walter Griskot Story," *MDT Publishing*, 2011.

Thompson, Maury. "City Searching for Madden Alternative," *Post-Star*, August 19, 2004, A1.

Thompson, Maury. "Few Words Seem Fitting in the Face of Death," *Post-Star*, July 4, 2002, D1.

Thompson, Maury. "The 55: After Vietnam Veterans Fought Battles at Home," www.poststar.com, November 12, 2010, https://poststar.com/news/local/after-vietnam-veterans-fought-battles-at-home/article_f381440a-edef-11df-9a6d-001cc4c002e0.html.

Thompson, Maury. "Finding Fellowship as the Husband of a Cancer Patient," *Post-Star*, June 27, 2002, D1.

Thompson, Maury. "Glens Falls Mayor Wants Earlier Closing Time for City Bars," www.poststar.com, December 26, 2012, https://poststar.com/news/local/glens-falls-mayor-wants-earlier-closing-time-for-city-bars/article_77393e1e-4fab-11e2-b53f-0019bb2963f4.html?mode=comments.

Thompson, Maury. "Glens Falls National Bank to Purchase, Demolish, Madden Hotel," www.poststar.com, July 9, 2010, https://poststar.com/news/local/glens-falls-national-bank-to-purchase-demolish-madden-hotel/article_c0d8ff1c-8b60-11df-b284-001cc4c002e0.html.

Thompson, Maury. "GOP Leaders Stump for Sweeney," www.poststar.com, November 4, 2006, https://poststar.com/news/local/gop-leaders-stump-for-sweeney/article_1bbe0c7c-5cf1-5c52-b951-16785d743a6d.html.

Thompson, Maury. "Grandmother and Child Find Bond in Death," *Post-Star*, July 11, 2002, D3.

Thompson, Maury. "His Stories Live On," www.poststar.com, October 15, 2006, *https://poststar.com/news/commentary-his-stories-live-on/article_78692a41-a3df-5584-b55a-d09cef2ebfd2.html.*

Thompson, Maury. "The Madden File," *Post-Star*, June 12, 2009, A5.

Thompson, Maury. "Madden's Past Obscured by Decline," www.poststar.com, April 9, 2011, https://poststar.com/news/local/-maddens-past-obscured-by-decline/article_f0432018-6326-11e0-a18a-001cc4c002e0.html.

Thompson, Maury. "Mayor: Tear Down This Hotel," *Post-Star*, October 22, 2009, A1.

Thompson, Maury. "Queensbury Votes 3–2 to Replace Law Firm," www.poststar.com, November 22, 2016, https://poststar.com/news/local/queensbury-votes---to-replace-law-firm/article_03443ca6-9bd5-5205-a26d-4cb33cbadbb1.amp.html.

Thompson, Maury. "State Announces $10 Million to Revitalize South Street in Glens Falls," www.poststar.com, August 18, 2016, https://poststar.com/news/local/state-announces-10-million-to-revitalize-south-street-in-glens-falls/article_d7b4f053-aa9d-514f-aafc-c69a6e967be7.html.

Thompson, Maury. "State Senate Salutes Post-Star's 100 Years," *Post-Star*, February 4, 2004, B1.

Thompson, Maury. "Sweeney Explains Ski Trip," www.poststar.com, January 19, 2006, https://poststar.com/news/local/sweeney-explains-ski-trip/article_f913bedf-0942-54aa-9c61-8a17d991154c.html.

Thompson, Maury. "Sweeney Refutes Allegation," www.poststar.com, November 1, 2006, https://poststar.com/news/sweeney-refutes-allegation/article_a6cba495-48e6-588d-9bd1-9d36dfbffe2e.html.

Thompson, Maury. "Sweeney Refutes Story," www.poststar.com, April 29, 2006, https://poststar.com/news/local/sweeney-refutes-story/article_e7cb4ab4-aace-5813-83f2-602e2cc550a9.html.

Thompson, Maury. "Sweeney's Refusal Cancels Local Debate," www.poststar.com, October 23, 2006, https://poststar.com/news/sweeney-s-refusal-cancels-local-debate/article_eb627a9e-b3d1-59b5-a0c7-321322d8ce32.html.

Tingley, Joseph. "Scrapbook Teaches a Lesson Not Soon Forgotten," www.poststar.com, March 2, 2013, https://poststar.com/news/opinion/guest-essay-scrapbook-teaches-a-lesson-not-soon-forgotten/article_359096e6-83b4-11e2-a040-001a4bcf887a.html.

Tingley, Ken. "All Is Wrong with the World," *Post-Star*, September 21, 2001, B1.

Tingley, Ken. "An Honor for Battle's Worth Fighting," *Post-Star*, April 22, 2009, A4.

Tingley, Ken. "Bain Says He Won't Serve," *Post-Star*, October 24, 2017, A1.

Tingley, Ken. "Buoyed to Face Another Year," *Post-Star*, December 30, 2018, C6.

Tingley, Ken. "By Quitting Race, Roy McDonald Disappoints," www.poststar.com, September 30, 2012, https://poststar.com/news/opinion/columns/ktingley/column-by-quitting-race-roy-mcdonald-disappoints/article_1da723fa-0ab6-11e2-beae-001a4bcf887a.html.

Tingley, Ken. "Capturing All Sides of Nursing Home Story," www.poststar.com, May 4, 2013, https://poststar.com/news/opinion/columns/editor/from-the-editor-capturing-all-sides-of-nursing-home-story/article_dbc0156c-b52a-11e2-b98d-0019bb2963f4.html.

Tingley, Ken. "Changing How We Cover NY21 Candidates," *Post-Star*, July 8, 2018, C3.

Tingley, Ken. "Colorado Tragedy Hits Us at Home," *Post-Star*, April 25, 1999, F2.

Tingley, Ken. "Communities Lose a Lot Without a Daily Newspaper," www.poststar.com, January 12, 2020, *https://poststar.com/news/local/from-the-editor-communities-lose-a-lot-without-a-daily-newspaper/article_044cbb63-0874-5f60-8678-c30f041941b2.html.*

Tingley, Ken. "Community Bids Heartbroken Farewell," www.poststar.com, July 9, 2010, *https://poststar.com/news/opinion/columns/ktingley/community-bids-heartbroken-farewell/article_f9cb67e0-8b8f-11df-a5c3-001cc4c03286.html.*

Tingley, Ken. "Controversial Photo Sends a Message," *Post-Star*, July 14, 2002, F1.

Tingley, Ken. "Death of Newseum, Free Press Is Mourned," *Post-Star*, January 2, 2020, B3.

Tingley, Ken. "Didn't You Ever Hear of Titanic?" *Post-Star*, May 9, 1999, F2.

Tingley, Ken. "Doing the Right Thing Is Rare, but Still Heroic," *Post-Star*, June 28, 2017, B6.

Tingley, Ken. "Editor Went Above and Beyond," *Post-Star*, February 27, 2005, E1.

Tingley, Ken. "Exploring the Realities of Teenage Drinking," *Post-Star*, April 25, 2004, F1.

Tingley, Ken. "Fatal Fire Sparks Tough Questions," www.poststar.com, June 29, 2010, https://poststar.com/news/opinion/columns/ktingley/fatal-fire-sparks-tough-questions/article_55828982-83b7-11df-9125-001cc4c03286.html.

Tingley, Ken. "Father Did Right Thing," *Post-Star*, January 24, 2010, C1.

Tingley, Ken. "Forum Puts Drug Problem in Focus," www.poststar.com. July 26, 2014, *https://poststar.com/news/opinion/columns/ktingley/forum-puts-drug-problem-in-focus/article_45092afa-1532-11e4-82c2-0019bb2963f4.html.*

Tingley, Ken. "From Mailroom to Corner Office," *Post-Star*, February 23, 2004, B1.

Tingley, Ken. "Geraghty Hopeful About Changes in County GOP," www.poststar.com, December 27, 2017, *https://poststar.com/blogs/the_front_page/blog-geraghty-hopeful-about-changes-in-county-gop/article_3256c89e-eb18-11e7-94c0-a70a437b8ef5.html.*

Tingley, Ken. "Getting Through to Kids on Underage Drinking," *Post-Star*, October 10, 2009, C1.

Tingley, Ken. "GOP Boss Is Called on to Step Aside," *Post-Star*, November 26, 2017, C1.

Tingley, Ken. "Hoping for Dialogue and Less Hate," *Post-Star*, July 28, 2002, F1.

Tingley, Ken. "Hospital Bigwigs Come Up Short," *Post-Star*, October 10, 2019.

Tingley, Ken. "Hospital Faces Uncertain Future," *Post-Star*, March 3, 2019, C5.

Tingley, Ken. "Hudson Falls Library Board Wrote the Book on What Not to Do," www.poststar.com, September 21, 2013, *https://poststar.com/news/opinion/hudson-falls-library-board-wrote-the-book-on-what-not-to-do/article_39fe95da-232c-11e3-bd86-0019bb2963f4.html.*

Tingley, Ken. "Improve Nursing Home Care," *Post-Star*, July 16, 2017, A6.

Tingley, Ken. "It Is Always Uncomfortable Being Part of the Story," www.poststar.com, August 22, 2013, https://poststar.com/blogs/the_front_page/it-is-always-uncomfortable-being-part-of-the-story/article_2033e270-0b50-11e3-8ffe-0019bb2963f4.html.

Tingley, Ken. "Journalists Have Become Targets," www.poststar.com, July 1, 2018, https://poststar.com/opinion/columnists/column-journalists-have-become-targets/article_bfdba753-5854-5749-b535-c2760f9afdda.html.

Tingley, Ken. "Just a Sip or Two? Teen Drinking Still a Problem," *Post-Star*, April 24, 2005, C1.

Tingley, Ken. "Keep Talking About Teen Drinking," *Post-Star*, March 2, 2005, B1.

Tingley, Ken. "The Labeling of Newspapers Is Not Fair," *Post-Star*, November 5, 2000, F1.

Tingley, Ken. "Let's Be Thoughtful When It Comes to Guns," www.poststar.com, March 10, 2019, https://poststar.com/news/local/column-lets-be-thoughtful-when-it-comes-to-guns/article_cb9cb803-746b-5b1f-a896-84d8220b2179.html.

Tingley, Ken. "Let's Learn from This Tragedy," *Post-Star*, April 9, 2002, B1.

Tingley, Ken. "Let's Start the Conversation," www.poststar.com, December 22, 2012, https://poststar.com/news/opinion/editorial/editorial-lets-start-the-conversation/article_6e2d4790-4cb1-11e2-a85c-0019bb2963f4.html.

Tingley, Ken. "Letter to Editor Was Especially Harsh," www.poststar.com, September 17, 2013, https://poststar.com/blogs/the_front_page/letter-to-the-editor-was-especially-harsh/article_b188d324-1fc9-11e3-96b9-0019bb2963f4.html.

Tingley, Ken. "Living in the Shadow of Sandy Hook and More School Violence," www.poststar.com, February 25, 2018, *https://poststar.com/opinion/columnists/column-living-in-the-shadow-of-sandy-hook-and-more-school-violence/article_18e8ac86-6b19-5cd3-8675-60650a1e71a5.html.*

Tingley, Ken. "Losing an Old Friend, Welcoming a New One," *Post-Star*, March 26, 2006, E1.

Tingley, Ken. "Make Sure Your Teen Gets It," *Post-Star*, June 14, 2009, C1.

Tingley, Ken. "McDonald Set to Charge," www. poststar.com, November 2, 2010, https:// poststar.com/news/opinion/columns/ ktingley/mcdonald-set-to-charge/article_ bb28c932-e6cb-11df-acad-001cc4c03286. html.

Tingley, Ken. "A Message That Sinks In," www. poststar.com, May 18, 2010, *https://poststar. com/news/opinion/columns/ktingley/a- message-that-sinks-in/article_328f1fcc-62c3- 11df-82ba-001cc4c03286.html.*

Tingley, Ken. "More Board Members in Need of Moral Compass," *Post-Star*, October 18, 2017, B1.

Tingley, Ken. "A New Breeze Blows on South Street," *Post-Star*, July 24, 2011, B1.

Tingley, Ken. "New Policy Seeks Candidate Accountability," *Post-Star*, July 15, 2018, C3.

Tingley, Ken. "Newspaper Called Out During Meeting, Too," www.poststar.com, October 23, 2019, *https://poststar.com/blogs/ the_front_page/blog-newspaper-called-out- during-meeting-too/article_38725096-bb3b- 57d9-99e5-ba3dc1c4e3f4.html.*

Tingley, Ken. "Newspapers Must Adapt to Changing Times," *Post-Star*, April 23, 2000.

Tingley, Ken. "Nomination letter to Lee Enterprises for Spirit Award," *Post-Star*, August 26, 2018.

Tingley, Ken. "Nursing Home Company Meets with Post-Star Board," www.poststar.com, August 20, 2017, https://poststar.com/opinion/ editorial/editorial-nursing-home-company- meets-with-post-star-board/article_32c2b979- b570-5095-a4de-5a2850a925d0.html.

Tingley, Ken. "Once Again, We Are Forced to Look at Tragedy," www.poststar.com, December 15, 2012, https://poststar.com/news/ opinion/columns/ktingley/once-again-we-are- forced-to-look-at-tragedy/article_35ebd27c- 472d-11e2-ac0c-001a4bcf887a.html.

Tingley, Ken. "One Final Request for the Post-Star," www.poststar.com, February 17, 2016, *https://poststar.com/blogs/ the_front_page/one-final-request-for-the- post-star/article_cacf6eac-d42a-11e5-8663- 7710e3fda1dd.html.*

Tingley, Ken. "Paper Belongs to All of You," *Post-Star*, July 17, 2005, E1, E3.

Tingley, Ken. "Paper Has Seen Changes," *Post-Star*, February 24, 2004, B5.

Tingley, Ken. "Parents Guilty, but So Are Many Others," *Post-Star*, February 15, 2009, C1.

Tingley, Ken. "Parents, This Is Your Wake Up Call," *Post-Star*, April 7, 2010, B1.

Tingley, Ken. "Photo of Mourning Child Put Face on War," *Post-Star*, September 28, 2003, F1.

Tingley, Ken. "Plenty of Work Left to Do," *Post-Star*, June 20, 2004, F1.

Tingley, Ken. "Political Leaders Becoming Puppets," *Post-Star*, October 29, 2017, C5.

Tingley, Ken. "Post-Star Addresses Pistol Permit Controversy," www.poststar.com, February 4, 2008, https://poststar.com/news/ latest/the-post-star-addresses-pistol-permit- controversy/article_1ba7c108-8116-5940- 8139-d4ec01e5d55e.html.

Tingley, Ken. "The Post-Star Looks to the Future," *Post-Star*, January 24, 2004, A1.

Tingley, Ken. "Post-Star Staff Will Tackle Heroin Epidemic in Series," www.poststar.com, June 14, 2014, *https://poststar.com/news/opinion/ columns/editor/post-star-staff-will-tackle- heroin-epidemic-in-series/article_f04156e8- f3e2-11e3-a401-0019bb2963f4.html.*

Tingley, Ken. "Queensbury Town Attorney Has Ethics Problem," www.poststar.com, October 22, 2017, https://poststar.com/opinion/ columnists/column-queensbury-town- attorney-has-ethics-problem/article_6e505191- d4c9-5b24-b94e-2a0ccf73f0d3.html.

Tingley, Ken. "Rejecting Rumors Is Part of Our Job," *Post-Star*, December 15, 2002, F1.

Tingley, Ken. "Renewed Concern About Nursing Home Care," www.poststar.com, June 10, 2018, https://poststar.com/opinion/ editorial/editorial-renewed-concern-about- nursing-home-care/article_aee8a0d1-a4fd- 565f-b594-6de0099897bf.html.

Tingley, Ken. "Respecting McDonald's Choices," www.poststar.com, July 26, 2011, https:// poststar.com/news/opinion/columns/ ktingley/mcdonald-breaks-ranks-and-votes- for-change/article_877bb17a-9a18-11e0-9ea4- 001cc4c03286.html.

Tingley, Ken. "Responding to Tragedy with Purpose," *Post-Star*, September 12, 2001, F1.

Tingley, Ken. "Scrapbook Puts Us on the Same Page," www.poststar.com, February 16, 2013, https://poststar.com/news/local/flashback- scrapbook-puts-us-on-the-same-page/article_ f7696558-31cc-5e29-ab81-8247ad3a0b2b. html.

Tingley, Ken. "Seeking a Cure to Underage Drinking Epidemic," *Post-Star*, June 29, 2003, F1.

Tingley, Ken. "Setting South Street in the Right Direction," *Post-Star*, November 20, 2011, B1.

Tingley, Ken. "Should We Worry About Threats?" www.poststar.com, September 20, 2019, https://poststar.com/blogs/ the_front_page/blog-should-we-worry- about-threats/article_ab096030-bdfc-5901- 93f3-ad155acd2f07.html.

Tingley, Ken. "Simple Question Is Left Unanswered," *Post-Star*, November 1, 2017, C1.

Tingley, Ken. "Small Paper's Prize Is Something to Celebrate," *Post-Star*, April 22, 2001, F1.

Tingley, Ken. "Some Just Don't Want to Set High Standards," *Post-Star*, November 19, 2017, C1.

Tingley, Ken. "South High Parents Earn 'F,'" www. poststar.com, May 17, 2011, https://poststar. com/news/opinion/columns/ktingley/south- high-parents-earn-f/article_5565b13e-80bb- 11e0-a43d-001cc4c03286.html.

Tingley, Ken. "Stefanik Backs Bullies," *Post-Star*, October 11, 2019, C1.

Tingley, Ken. "Stefanik Is No Longer and Independent Thinker," *Post-Star*, November 20, 2019, *https://poststar.com/opinion/columnists/commentary-stefanik-is-no-longer-an-independent-thinker/article_2cd0353d-a277-5f0d-a7a1-c1129d8bec07.html*.

Tingley, Ken. "Still No Word from Rep. Stefanik," www.poststar.com, October 11, 2019, *https://poststar.com/blogs/the_front_page/blog-still-no-word-from-rep-stefanik/article_70518460-1e77-58d3-868a-b3649cbad3c9.html*.

Tingley, Ken. "Strough Refuses to Back Down," *Post-Star*, May 16, 2018, C1.

Tingley, Ken. "Strough's Arrest Was News Demanding Coverage," www.poststar.com, January 9, 2019, https://poststar.com/blogs/the_front_page/blog-stroughs-arrest-was-news-demanding-coverage/article_edd17c40-142f-11e9-bdc8-bf660c1c9a54.html.

Tingley, Ken. "Sweeney May Have Competition," *Post-Star*, February 19, 2006, C1.

Tingley, Ken. "There Is Heart Beyond the Newsprint," *Post-Star*, November 21, 2001, B8.

Tingley, Ken. "Things Won't Be the Same Without Mahoney," www.poststar.com, October 22, 2011, https://poststar.com/article_c2e0b02c-fd22-11e0-af37-001cc4c03286.html.

Tingley, Ken. "Threats Should Shock, Outrage," *Post-Star*, October 8, 2019, B1.

Tingley, Ken. "Time to Take Another Look at Our Improved Arts Section," *Post-Star*, November 2, 2008, E1.

Tingley, Ken. "To the Readers," *Post-Star*, July 7, 2020, A1.

Tingley, Ken. "To the Readers: You Don't Hear About the Harassment," *Post-Star*, June 30, 2018, A1.

Tingley, Ken. "Tragic Pages," *Post-Star*, May 24, 2003, B1.

Tingley, Ken. "Trust Me, You Don't Want to Read This," www.poststar.com, November 12, 2017, https://poststar.com/opinion/columnists/column-trust-me-you-dont-want-to-read-this/article_1e427375-453e-5dbb-bbcd-669037a8459b.html.

Tingley, Ken. "Truth and Trust Missing from Congressional Debate," *Post-Star*, October 17, 2018, C1.

Tingley, Ken. "Trying to Figure Out Sweeney," *Post-Star*, November 20, 2005, C1.

Tingley, Ken. "Violence Could Be Ahead Even Here," *Post-Star*, June 23, 2019, C1.

Tingley, Ken. "We Are Sick and Tired of Political Parties," *Post-Star*, November 15, 2017, C1.

Tingley, Ken. "We Sparked the Conversation We Were Hoping For," www.poststar.com, January 26, 2013, https://poststar.com/news/opinion/columns/editor/from-the-editor-we-sparked-the-conversation-we-were-hoping-for/article_3a6f4a82-682e-11e2-a37d-001a4bcf887a.html.

Tingley, Ken. "We're Not Perfect, but We Take It Seriously," *Post-Star*, February 29, 2004, F1.

Tingley, Ken. "Web Site Adds Immediacy to Paper," *Post-Star*, October 9, 2005, E1.

Tingley, Ken. "Well It Was Supposed to Be a Feel-Good Story," www.poststar.com, August 16, 2013, https://poststar.com/blogs/the_front_page/well-it-was-supposed-to-be-a-feel-good-story/article_a48e48d8-068e-11e3-b6c5-001a4bcf887a.html.

Tingley, Ken. "What Would You Do?" *Post-Star*, December 13, 2002, B1.

Tingley, Ken. "When the Sheriff Hires His Son, It's Nepotism," *Post-Star*, July 12, 2020, C3.

Tingley, Ken. "Why Names Matter in Underage Drinking Coverage," www.poststar.com, April 1, 2012, *https://poststar.com/news/opinion/columns/ktingley/column-why-names-matter-in-underage-drinking-coverage/article_f539efba-7b9f-11e1-94e2-0019bb2963f4.html*.

Tingley, Ken. "Words of Encouragement," *Post-Star*, October 19, 2019, C3.

Tingley, Ken. "You Don't Replace Reporters Like Maury Thompson," *Post-Star*, September 3, 2017, A6.

Toscano, Bill. "Local Collaboration Steps Up in Drug Fight," www.poststar.com, March 25, 2017, https://poststar.com/news/local/local-collaboration-steps-up-in-drug-fight/article_79ccec77-45b5-5ae3-a3f6-cfbca150ebe4.html.

Toscano, Bill. "Petition Asks Hudson Falls Library to Rehire Aide," www.poststar.com, October 7, 2013, https://poststar.com/news/local/petition-asks-hudson-falls-library-to-rehire-aide/article_66c0cc5a-2f93-11e3-82d7-001a4bcf887a.html.

Toscano, Bill. "Second Hudson Falls Library Worker Loses Job in Wake of Reading Program," www.poststar.com, September 17, 2013, https://poststar.com/news/local/second-hudson-falls-library-worker-loses-job-in-wake-of-reading-program-controversy/article_473a459c-1fca-11e3-9aee-0019bb2963f4.html.

Toscano, Bill. "Struggle to Get Clean," www.poststar.com, July 5, 2014, https://poststar.com/news/local/struggle-to-get-clean/article_c2ae0fb8-04b9-11e4-a81e-0019bb2963f4.html.

Tracy, Jim. "Hickins Are Eyewitness to New York Terror," *Post-Star*, September 12, 2001, C1.

Tucker, Abigail. "Drinking Rates Are Sky-High Among Area Teenagers; Reasons Are Varied," *Post-Star*, May 2, 2004, A6.

Tucker, Abigail. "'This Is Just What We Do': From Forests to Family Rooms, Underage Drinking Rates in This Area Surpass National Averages," *Post-Star*, May 2, 2003, A1.

Tucker, Abigail. "A Town's Hero Is Laid to Rest," *Post-Star*, September 25, 2003, A1.

Vielkind, Jimmy. "GOP Senator from Saratoga Becomes 31st Vote for Same-sex Marriage," www.timesunion.com, June 15, 2011, https://

www.timesunion.com/local/article/GOP-senator-from-Saratoga-becomes-31st-vote-for-1424481.php.

Vielkind, Jimmy. "Shove It: A Portrait of a Gay Marriage Republican in Limbo," www.politico.com, September 20, 2012, https://www.politico.com/states/new-york/albany/story/2012/09/shove-it-a-portrait-of-a-gay-marriage-republican-in-limbo-000000.

Volke, Matt. "Living Proof: He Started Drinking as a Teen, Then He Got Hooked, Now the Smell of Beer Makes Him Sick," *Post-Star*, May 2, 2004, A6.

Volke, Matt. "Separate Crashes Kill Two Young Area Men," *Post-Star*, September 14, 2003, A1.

Walsh, Shushannah. "New York Passes Nation's Toughest Gun-control Law," www.abcnews.go.com, January 13, 2013, https://abcnews.go.com/politics/york-state-passes-toughest-gun-control-law-nation/story?id=18224091.

Warrren County Election Archives. www.warrencountyny.gov, https://warrencountyny.gov/sites/default/files/boe/election/2017/g_accumulated.pdf.

Warren, John. "20th CD - the End of Congressman John Sweeney?" November 1, 2006.

Westcott, Mark. "The Post-Star Vendetta," October 30, 2017.

Wheeler, Lydia. "Hundreds Mourn Fire Victims," www.poststar.com, July 9, 2010, https://poststar.com/news/local/hundreds-mourn-fire-victims-at-funeral/article_64ddf3b2-8b78-11df-af94-001cc4c03286.html.

Wheeler, Lydia. "Several People Killed in Fire at Fort Edward Home: Victims Yet to Be Identified," *Post-Star*, June 27, 2010, A1.

Wheeler, Lydia. "No. 1 Story of 2010: Six Children Die in Fatal Fort Edward Fire," www.poststar.com, January 1, 2011, https://poststar.com/news/local/no-1-story-of-2010-six-children-die-in-fatal-fort-edward-fire/article_2f655612-12cd-11e0-ad1d-001cc4c03286.html.

Williams, Fran. "Stories on Madden, Gripping, Wonderful," *Post-Star*, January 14, 2004, A5.

Yahoo Staff Report, "World's Worst Librarian Wants Nine-Year-Old Kid to Stop Winning Reading Contests," www.yahoo.com, August 20, 2013, https://news.yahoo.com/world-worst-librarian-wants-nine-old-kid-stop-145030798.htmlguccounter=1&guce_referr=aHR0cHM6Ly93d3cuZ29vZ2xlLmNvbS8&guce_referrer_sig=AQAAALNHpjCVcuyaoiH0uhw1O0NUDjwTNRBgTPc4xlNFi4bULj9nmXrLhIIWR575QujDuCdPa1pedcC9fV-8TI6aampyh7Ukm8cUExEIlcMR7uLuKy2UAgPzBkR8y_ynnyp6YJL1RRZgdz1qhkTfm5ifr5B1GO9s0qWBibw8bw2n2Mu6.

Youker, Darrin. "Boy Had Chance to Escape Burning Home," www.poststar.com, December 6, 2002, https://poststar.com/news/local/boy-had-chance-to-escape-burning-home/article_376dc7b7-47f8-521f-b78b-06691cf972f2.html.

Youker, Darrin. "Charge Prelude to Grand Jury," *Post-Star*, April 9, 2002, A6.

Youker, Darrin. "Children Died of Smoke Inhalation," *Post-Star*, December 28, 2002, A9.

Youker, Darrin. "Driver, 16, Is Charged in Crash," *Post-Star*, April 10, 2002, A1.

Youker, Darrin. "Fatal Fire Traced to Floorboards," *Post-Star*, December 5, 2002, A1.

Youker, Darrin. "House Had Caught Fire Before," *Post-Star*, November 27, 2002, A6.

Youker, Darrin. "In Fire's Wake," www.poststar.com, December 29, 2002, https://poststar.com/news/local/in-fires-wake/article_1ae3aeb6-cf44-5071-9997-d25ef9b458bd.html.

Youker, Darrin. "Students Mourn Loss of Classmates," *Post-Star*, April 9, 2002, A1.

Youker, Darrin. "Teen Admits Guilt in Fatal Car Crash," *Post-Star*, September 5, 2002, A1.

Youker, Darrin. "Teen Sentenced to Prison in Fatal Crash," *Post-Star*, July 15, 2003, B1.

Youker, Darrin. "Things Are Forgotten," *Post-Star*, May 24, 2004, A1, A4.

Youker, Darrin. "Warrensburg Teen-ager Killed in ATV Crash," *Post-Star*, July 29, 2002, A1.

Zaugg, Pamela. "Lonely Men, Women Should Turn to God," *Post-Star*, July 28, 2002, F2.

Zetterstrom, Sylvia. "'Tender Moment,' Subject Are Sickening," *Post-Star*, August 4, 2002, F2.

Zimmerman, Neetzan. "Evil Librarian Tells Kid Who Loves Books to Stop Reading So Much," www.gawker.com, August 19, 2013, https://gawker.com/evil-librarian-tells-kid-who-loves-books-to-stop-readin-1167265926.

Interviews

Blow, David. Phone interview with author, September 25, 2020, September 26, 2020.

Condon, Bob. Phone interview with author, September 19, 2020.

Davenport (Wheeler), Lydia. Phone interview with author, August 4, 2020.

DeMars, Betsy. Phone interview with author, July 20, 2020.

Doolittle, Will. Phone interview with author, September 11, 2020; September 13, 2020; September 28, 2020.

Dowd, Pat. Phone interview with author, August 13, 2020.

Gautier, Nancy. Phone interview with author, September 22, 2020.

Hagerty, Meg. Phone interview with author, August 23, 2020.

Hooker, T.J. Phone interview with author, July 7, 2020.

Kimmerly, Inge. Phone interview with author, June 22, 2020.

Lehman, Don. Phone interview with author, August 11, 2020; September 25, 2020; September 29, 2020.

Mahoney, Mark. Phone interview with author, July 1, 2020, August 29, 2020.

Marshall, Jim. Phone interview with author, June 22, 2020.

Marshall, Konrad. Phone interview with author, July 3, 2020.

McDonald, Roy. Interview with author in Saratoga Springs, N.Y., July 2020.

Moats, David. Phone interview with author, July 28, 2020.

Moore, Kathleen. Phone interview with author, August 26, 2020; September 23, 2020.

Moffitt, Judy. Phone interview with author, September 14, 2020.

Petteys, Martha. Phone interview with author, June 1, 2020.

Randall, Thom. Phone interview with author, July 29, 2020; August 11, 2020.

Reisman, Nick. Phone interview with author, August 20, 2020.

Springstead, Will. Phone interview with author, July 20, 2020.

Sturdevant, Matt. Phone interview with author, June 24, 2020.

Thompson, Maury. Phone interview with author, June 1, 2020.

Youker, Darrin. Phone interview with author, August 4, 2020.

Index

Numbers in **bold italics** indicate pages with illustrations